RATINGS ANALYSIS

This fourth edition of *Ratings Analysis* describes and explains the current audience information system that supports economic exchange in both traditional and evolving electronic media markets. Responding to the major changes in electronic media distribution and audience research in recent years, *Ratings Analysis* provides a thoroughly updated presentation of the ratings industry and analysis processes. It serves as a practical guide for conducting audience research, offering readers the tools for becoming informed and discriminating consumers of audience information.

In its fourth edition, this essential volume covers:

- International markets, reflecting the growth in audience research businesses with the expansion of advertising into new markets such as China;
- Emerging technologies, reflecting the ever increasing ways to deliver advertising electronically and through new channels (social media, Hulu)
- Applications of audience research in advertising, programming, financial analysis, and social policy;
- Audience research data and the history of audience measurement, the research methods most often used, and the kinds of ratings research products currently available; and
- The analysis of audience data by offering a framework within which to understand mass media audiences and by focusing specifically to the analysis of ratings data.

Appropriate for all readers needing an in-depth understanding of audience research, including those working in advertising, electronic media, and related industries, *Ratings Analysis* also has much to offer academics and policy makers as well as students of mass media.

James G. Webster is professor of broadcasting at Northwestern University.

Patricia F. Phalen is associate professor of media at George Washington University.

Lawrence W. Lichty is professor emeritus of media at Northwestern University.

RATINGS ANALYSIS: AUDIENCE MEASUREMENT AND ANALYTICS

FOURTH EDITION

James G. Webster, Patricia F. Phalen,
and Lawrence W. Lichty

Routledge
Taylor & Francis Group

NEW YORK AND LONDON

This edition first published 2014
by Routledge
711 Third Avenue, New York, NY 10017

Published in the UK
by Routledge
2 Park Square, Milton Park, Abingdon, Oxon OX14 4RN

Routledge is an imprint of the Taylor & Francis Group, an informa business

© 2014 Taylor & Francis

The right of James G. Webster, Patricia F. Phalen, and Lawrence W. Lichty to be identified as the authors of the editorial material, and of the authors for their individual chapters, has been asserted in accordance with sections 77 and 78 of the Copyright, Designs and Patents Act 1988.

First edition published by Lawrence Erlbaum Associates, Inc., 1991

Second edition published by Lawrence Erlbaum Associates, Inc., 2001

Third edition published by Lawrence Erlbaum Associates, Inc., 2006

Library of Congress Cataloging-in-Publication Data

Webster, James G.
  Ratings analysis : audience measurement and analytics / by James Webster, Patricia F. Phalen, Lawrence W Lichty. — 4th edition.
      pages cm
  1. Television programs—Rating—Methodology.   2. Television viewers.
3. Radio programs—Rating—Methodology.   4. Radio audiences.   I. Phalen,
Patricia F.   II. Lichty, Lawrence Wilson.   III. Title.
  HE8700.65.W42   2013
  384.54'4—dc23
  2013006689

ISBN: 978-0-415-52651-7 (hbk)
ISBN: 978-0-415-52652-4 (pbk)
ISBN: 978-0-203-11235-9 (ebk)

Typeset in Dante MT Std
by Apex CoVantage, LLC

Printed and bound in the United States of America by Sheridan Books, Inc. (a Sheridan Group Company).

This book is dedicated to our families

Table of Contents in Brief

Table of Contents

PART III: APPLICATIONS

Preface

We wrote the first edition of *Ratings Analysis* over 20 years ago. Much about audience measurement has changed since then, but our overall purpose has not. As we noted in the preface to the first edition, this book was written with two groups of people in mind. First, it is intended for anyone who needs more than a superficial understanding of audience research. This would certainly include many people who work in advertising, the media, and related industries. For them, audience data are a fact of life. Whether they have been specifically trained to deal with research or not, their jobs typically require them to make use of "the numbers" when they buy and sell audiences, or make marketing, programming, and investment decisions. The second group includes those who are not compelled to use audience data, but who nevertheless should know something about it. In this group we would include academics, critics, policy-makers, students of digital media, and even interested members of the general public. For both groups of readers, we have tried to make the book as plainspoken as our subject matter allows.

None of that has changed in the fourth edition. But the world of audience measurement and analytics has changed since the last edition of this volume was published. Global demand for audience measurement has increased as more and more media systems are being driven by advertising revenues. For better or worse, audience ratings are now commonplace around the world. The new edition reflects the global scope of our subject. The ways in which media find an audience have also changed. Much of the world now depends on digital networks to deliver not only television but also a wide range of services over the Internet. Portable devices like tablets and smartphones offer the prospect of anywhere, anytime media consumption. Almost all of these technologies depend on computers to manage the flow of digital media, and these servers can track what is being sent. They represent a new approach to audience measurement, which was only in its infancy when we wrote the previous edition. The new edition now includes an extensive discussion of "server-centric" measurement.

The fourth edition has also been reorganized. As before, the book begins with an overview of audience research in its different forms, from academic studies to commercial audience measurement. Beyond that, the book is divided into three major sections. The first is about audience data and where they come from. It describes the history of audience measurement in the United States and around the world. It then discusses how new media and contemporary business practices shape audience measurement. It concludes with a detailed review of the many methods now being used to create audience data, noting the strengths and weaknesses of each approach. The second section focuses on the analysis of these data. It begins with a theoretical framework for understanding audience behavior and ends with a review of gross and cumulative measures of the audience. These now include the use of various web metrics. The third section illustrates the major applications of audience research in advertising, programming, financial analysis, and social policy.

ACKNOWLEDGMENTS

Many people helped make this book a reality. They include the individuals we acknowledged in earlier editions. Their contributions live on in the new work. In the fourth edition, we are particularly indebted to the following people for their support, guidance, and insights: Brad Bedford, Ed Bowman, Chris Brimer, Ed Cohen, Paul Donato, Kathleen Fox, Brian Fuhrer, Patti Ganguzza, Garry Hart, Jon Marks, Wayne Neiman, Stacey Lynn Schulman, Jamie Sterling, Radha Subramanyam, Bruce Rosenblum, Tom Thai, Robert Verbanac, Michael Vinson, Jack Wakshlag, Henry Webster, and Richard Zackon. We are thankful to countless others at different media and measurement companies for providing data and examples of how research is used. These include Arbitron, comScore Media Metrix, LUC Media, Inc., Nielsen Media Research, Nielsen//NetRatings, Rentrak, GfK Telecontrol, TiVo, Turner Broadcasting, Veronis Suhler Stevenson, and the several major trade associations. We're also appreciative of the anonymous reviewers who suggested many useful changes to the book and of Linda Bathgate and her staff at Routledge. Much of what is good about this book is a result of these many contributions. Anything that is bad, we managed to introduce despite their help. Finally, we want to thank our families; parents, spouses, siblings, and children. All of them have in their own ways, large and small, made it possible for us to do our work.

Ratings Analysis: Audience Measurement and Analytics

You have probably heard the phrase, "What is measured is known." It can be attributed to William Thomson, who is also known as Lord Kelvin. More recently, a management consultant and one of the most influential business thinkers in the last century, Peter Drucker, took the thought further. He observed that *"what's measured is managed."*

Through measurement and analysis, we are able to evaluate relative opportunities, progress, performance, and more. Measurement and information are used to value assets and drive strategic decision making. In many ways, measurement and information define our world.

Measurement is all around us—in clocks, calendars, thermometers, even the stock market. Measurement is inescapable. That's for good reason. Imagine a world without measurement and everything you know quickly unravels. Today, there is more measurement in our grasp than ever. That's thanks to technological advances—just in our lifetime—that relate to obtaining, recording, computing, storing, and analyzing data. These advances are remaking the world.

Today, measurement is driving and transforming entire industries.

Another oft-spoken phrase, that every company and human being is in fact a "media company," appears equally true. The same forces driving measurement allow us to reach audiences like never before. For the media industry—those who by definition seek audiences—the stakes are growing even higher. Media companies require innovation for better-informed decisions. These companies are driving a need to be smarter and more perceptive in understanding the "who, what, where, why, and how" of people's interactions with media.

Global advertising expenditures are predicted to reach $522 billion by 2013. Key to commercializing that ad spend is audience measurement and the ratings that are produced as an output of that effort. Companies selling advertising space use ratings to maximize the value of their inventory, and those buying ads use ratings and audience analytics to identify and reach consumers efficiently and effectively.

Players that rely on accurate measurement to drive business outcomes range from those who have been in business more than a 100 years to others, who may be less than 100 days old. As media consumption choices expand exponentially, and consumer preferences and attitudes evolve in parallel, measurement is the constant. It is the constant that informs what happened in the past, is happening now, and what is to come.

Wherever your career takes you across media and marketing, understanding the theory and practice of audience measurement, insight and analytics will remain vital and omnipresent—and serve as your guide in an ever-changing world.

David Calhoun
Chief Executive Officer
Nielsen Media Research

CHAPTER 1

An Introduction to Audience Research

Audiences are the source of the media's wealth and power. They pay directly for goods and services. And even when audiences choose "free" media, their attention is sold to advertisers for billions of dollars, euros, and yen. Beyond establishing the value of media products, audiences confer social significance on the media through their choices. The programs and websites that succeed in attracting large numbers of followers help set public agendas and shape the cultures in which we live.

However, audiences are elusive. They are dispersed over vast geographical areas, sometimes on a global scale. They are tucked away in homes and businesses, where they move fluidly from one "platform" to the next. For media providers to make sense of their audiences, let alone profit from them, they must be able to see them.

It is audience research that makes them visible. Without it, institutions cannot hope to manage public attention for good or ill. And without an understanding of audience research, media professionals are ill equipped to do their jobs. This research, especially ratings research, is the central focus of this book. In the following pages, we explore audience measurement systems across various countries and what we can learn from these data.

TYPES OF AUDIENCE RESEARCH

To put audience measurement in context, we begin by considering several broad categories of research. These categories are not unique to the study of audiences, nor will we deal with all of them in subsequent chapters. We review them here to provide an overview of research practices, to help readers identify the various motivations and methods of researchers, and to build a vocabulary for talking about the field.

Applied Versus Theoretical

Applied research, sometimes called *action research,* provides practical information that can guide decision making by describing some phenomenon of interest or by illuminating the consequences of a particular course of action. Applied research is typically concerned with an immediate problem or need, and rarely is there any pretense of offering generalizable explanations about how the world works. Nevertheless, this research can produce useful insights and sometimes forms the basis for more enduring theories about audience behavior.

In media industries, applied research dominates audience analysis. Examples from television include surveys that measure which advertisements are well remembered, which celebrities are well liked, and whether the social media "buzz" about a program suggests high levels of viewer engagement. These insights can affect production and programming decisions. Examples from the Internet include web-based experiments that test the effectiveness of various appeals or offers in getting visitors to click through to a purchase. That can affect the sales of books or DVDs. Of course, both television and the websites depend on ratings data to describe the size, composition, and behaviors of their audiences. These become the metrics used to place and evaluate advertising and, as such, are the essence of applied research.

A special type of applied research, sometimes treated as a separate category, is *methodological research.* This is, basically, research on research. As we explain in the chapters that follow, many audience research companies, like Nielsen or Arbitron, rose to prominence by developing new research methods. They are, after all, in the business of selling research products. Like any self-interested company, they engage in product testing and development to provide their clients with the data they need in a fast-changing media environment. Methodological audience research might include questions like, "How can we measure television viewing more accurately?" or "How should we recruit people into our panels?" or "How can we track users across media platforms?" Many of the answers to these methodological questions are discussed in our chapters on audience data.

Theoretical research tests more generalized explanations about how the world operates. If those explanations, or theories, are broad and well supported by evidence, they can be useful in many different settings. As Kurt Lewin, a well-known communication researcher, said, "Nothing is as practical as a good theory" (Rogers, 1994, p. 321). Although theoretical research is sometimes conducted in industry, it is more common in academic settings. Examples include experiments designed to identify the effects of watching violence on television or the factors that determine which songs people download from websites. These studies typically go beyond the specific problems of individual organizations.

Neither applied nor theoretical research is reliably defined by the type of method used by the investigator. Surveys, experiments, in-depth interviews, content analyses, and other methods can all serve applied or theoretical purposes. To make matters even more complicated, a specific research project could conceivably serve either purpose depending on who is reading the study and the lessons they learn. This flexibility is probably a good thing, but it does mean that the boundary between applied and theoretical research is sometimes difficult to determine.

Quantitative Versus Qualitative

Industry researchers and academics alike often make a distinction between quantitative and qualitative research. A good deal of ambiguity surrounds the use of these terms. Strictly speaking, *quantitative research* reduces the object of study to numbers. This allows researchers to analyze of large groups of people and to use statistics to manage the data. *Qualitative research* produces non-numeric summaries such as field notes or comments transcribed from an interview. While qualitative methods allow an investigator to dig deeply into a given topic, it is often hard to generalize the findings to larger populations. Ideally, the two approaches are used in tandem. Qualitative studies provide rich details and unexpected insights, and quantitative studies provide generalizability.

Unlike the differences between theoretical and applied research, qualitative and quantitative categories tend to be associated with particular research methods. Quantitative studies rely heavily on surveys, experiments, and content analyses. These methods identify variables of interest and assign numbers to people, or other units of analysis, based on those attributes. For example, a survey researcher might record people's ages and keep track of their gender by assigning a "1" to males and a "2" to females. An experimenter might quantify physiological responses like heart rates or eye movements to identify response patterns. Similarly, someone studying political communication might record the number of times each politician is quoted in news reports during a presidential campaign, to identify reporting biases.

Qualitative methods such as group interviews or participant observation usually produce non-numeric results like transcripts or field notes. However, to make sense of these records, a bit of quantification can enter the picture. Investigators sometimes categorize and count (i.e., quantify) their observations. For example, an investigator might want to track the prevalence of ideas or phrases. Thus, the richness of open-ended comments and idiosyncratic behaviors are reduced and summarized in a way that looks like quantitative research.

The distinction between qualitative and quantitative becomes even murkier as the terms are used in industry. Many media professionals equate the term "quantitative research" with "audience ratings." As we will see in the chapters that follow, ratings act as a kind of "currency " that drives media industry revenues. Any research that does not provide the hard numbers used to value audiences is rather casually referred to as qualitative research, which includes studies that address less routine audience characteristics such as lifestyles, values, opinions, and product preferences. While these data usually do not replace ratings as the currency used to buy and sell media, they are technically "quantitative" because they reduce the characteristics of interest to statistical summaries.

That said, there are many examples of true qualitative work in industry. *Focus groups,* which involve gathering a small group of people to talk about some topic of interest, are widely used. Krueger and Casey (2000) define this type of study as "a carefully planned discussion designed to obtain perceptions on a defined area of interest in a permissive, non-threatening environment" (p. 5). Focus groups are a popular way to assess radio station formats, news personalities, and program concepts. For example, Warner Bros. routinely tests television pilots using this technique. A skilled moderator probes to determine how prospective audience members react to the various program elements—what works and what does not. These insights can be used to inform decisions about character development, plot lines, and programming.

In the past three decades, another family of qualitative approaches, broadly termed audience *ethnography,* has gained in popularity. Some ethnographies are very much like focus groups. Some involve nonstructured, one-on-one interviews with media users. Others involve studying what people, like fans, are saying on social media sites. Still other ethnographies introduce observers into places of interest like households or fan conventions. In 2008, the Council for Research Excellence (CRE) funded a study that had trained observers to follow people throughout an entire day to better understand how they used different media platforms like televisions, computers, and mobile devices. At the extreme end of the spectrum, ethnographers might immerse themselves in the site of study for months or even years. The best ethnographies can produce a depth of understanding that is hard to match with quantitative methods.

Micro Versus Macro

Audience research can operate at different "levels of analysis." Social scientists often draw a distinction between micro- or macro-level research. *Micro-level* studies, like ethnographies, look at audiences from the inside out, by adopting the perspective of an individual audience member. *Macro-level* studies look at audiences from the outside in, to understand how they behave as large, complex systems. Like the other distinctions we have reviewed, telling the difference can be tricky because macro-level systems, like markets or social networks, are assembled by aggregating individual media users. Knowing when you have moved from one level to the next is not always obvious. Still, it is an important distinction to keep in mind.

Micro-level studies focus on individuals—their traits, predispositions, and media-related behaviors. They frame research questions on an intuitively appealing, human scale. It is natural for us to think about audiences in this way, because we all have experience as media users and, through introspection, can imagine what might explain someone else's actions. Micro-level research often operates on the assumption that if we could only figure out what makes individual media users tick, then we will understand audience behavior. After all, audiences are just collections of people.

Focusing on individuals, though, causes researchers to turn a blind eye to factors that are not person specific. We have known for a long time that program-scheduling practices can affect program choices, sometimes overriding individual program preferences. And now, with the growth of social media, we see patterns of media consumption, like "herding," that are not easily explained by individual traits. As Duncan Watts, a noted sociologist and researcher at Microsoft, observed, "You could know everything about individuals in a given population—their likes, dislikes, experiences, attitudes, beliefs, hopes, and dreams—and still not be able to predict much about their collective behavior" (2011, p. 79).

But most audience research, especially ratings research, is about collective behavior. Audience analysts usually want to make statements about what large numbers of people have done or will do. They generally do not care if Bob Smith in Cleveland sees a newscast, but they do care how many men aged 35 to 64 are watching. This interest in mass behavior, which is typical of macro-level research, turns out to be a blessing. Trying to explain or predict how any one person behaves, on a moment-to-moment, day-to-day basis, can be an exercise in frustration. But when you aggregate individual activities, the behavior of the mass is often quite predictable—and the business of selling audiences to advertisers is built on predictions.

This science of studying large populations has been called *statistical thinking*. It was developed in eighteenth-century Europe by, among others, insurance underwriters. Consider, for example, the problem of life insurance. Predicting when any one person will die is almost impossible, but if you aggregate large numbers, you can estimate how many people are likely to expire in the coming year. You need not predict the outcome of each individual case to predict an outcome across the entire population. In the same sense, we do not need to know what Bob Smith will do on a given evening to predict how many men his age will be watching television.

When we focus on macro-level phenomena, media use becomes much more tractable. We can identify stable patterns of audience size and flow. We can develop mathematical equations, or models, that allow us to predict media use. Some have even gone so far as to posit "laws" of audience behavior. These laws, of course, do not bind each person to a code of conduct. Rather, they are statements that mass behavior is so predictable that it exhibits law-like tendencies. This kind of reasoning is typical of most commercial audience research, and it underlies many of the analytical techniques we discuss in later chapters.

There is no one right way to study audiences. Like qualitative and quantitative methods, each level of analysis has its virtues and limitations. And, as was true with our discussion of methods, using both micro- and macro-level approaches generally leads to a deeper understanding of media use.

Syndicated Versus Custom

The final distinction we will draw is between syndicated and custom research. Syndicated research offers a standardized product that is sold to multiple subscribers. Audience ratings reports, for instance, serve many users in a given market. Custom research is tailored to meet the needs of a single sponsor.

Syndicated research is common anywhere audiences are sold to advertisers, which, these days, is just about everywhere. Table 1.1 lists major suppliers of syndicated audience research around the world, as well as the kinds of products they sell. This list is representative rather than comprehensive. You will note it includes many large international companies that operate in dozens of countries. Many use sophisticated, sometimes expensive, techniques to electronically monitor digital media use. These data are bought by media industries and usually are not available to the general public in much detail. Several companies also provide comparative media reports that track advertising placement and how much it costs to reach listeners or viewers in various markets. A growing number of large media operators, like Google and Facebook, provide data about their own users. All in all, media industries are awash in numbers. And, as the digital media environment becomes more pervasive and complex, the ability to manage and interpret those numbers becomes increasingly important.

Syndicated research has several advantages relative to other kinds of research. Because the cost of a syndicated study is shared by many subscribers, each user pays just a portion of the total. The methods that syndicators use to collect data are generally well understood and sometimes subject to independent audits. They are further motivated to be objective because their reports often serve clients with competing interests. The semi-public nature of the documents makes it harder for any one entity to misrepresent the research, while the standardization of report formats facilitates routine uses of the data. Although they are imperfect, syndicated data, like audience ratings, often become the official numbers used to transact business.

Custom research is designed to meet the needs of a particular sponsor and might not be shared outside the sponsoring organization. These studies could be commissioned from specialists, like news and programming consultants, or conducted by an in-house research department. Many major market radio stations, for example, track public tastes in music through telephone surveys. Researchers call a sample of potential audience members and ask them to listen to the "hook," or most memorable phrase, of several popular songs. Stations use this *call-out research* to adjust their "playlists."

TABLE 1.1
Major Suppliers of Syndicated Audience Measurement Worldwide

Arbitron www.arbitron.com	Best known as the supplier of radio ratings in the United States, Arbitron is an international marketing research firm measuring radio, TV, cable, and out-of-home media. Its "portable people meters" are used for audience measurement in North American, Europe, and Asia.
Audit Bureau of Circulations http://www.accessabc.com/index.html	ABC verifies the circulation claims of print and interactive media. It audits website traffic and, in conjunction with Scarborough, offers reports on newspapers' print and online readership.
comScore http://www.comscore.com	This is an international research firm operating across 170 countries. It is well known for Media Metrix reports, which measures Internet use by combining data from a 2-million-person global panel along with website-based data.
CSM Media Research http://www.csm.com.cn/	A joint venture between CTR Market Research and Kantar Media, CSM provides television and radio ratings in China and Hong Kong. It operates a large audience panel estimating the behavior of over 1 billion people.
GfK Group http://www.gfk.com/group/index.en.html	A large marketing research company that provides media measurement in over 20 countries, it owns Telecontrol, which offers electronic TV audience measurement in several countries including Germany, France, and India. It also owns Mediamark Research (MRI), which publishes a national survey of U.S. consumers including product use, demographics, and general measures of print and electronic media use. MRI sells a service that "fuses" their data with Nielsen's national television panel.
Hitwise http://www.hitwise.com/us	Hitwise aggregates data from Internet service providers (ISPs) to provide a range of standard metrics about websites including page requests, visits, average visit length, search terms, and behavior. This approach yields large samples including 25 million people worldwide and 10 million in the United States. It is a part of Experian Marketing Services.

TABLE 1.1 *continued*

Major Suppliers of Syndicated Audience Measurement Worldwide

IBOPE http://www.ibope.com.br	This Brazilian multinational marketing and opinion research firm operates IBOPE Media, which provides television audience measurement in 13 Latin American countries and Internet measurement in conjunction with Nielsen Online.
Ipsos http://www.ipsos.com	Ipsos is a global marketing research firm that measures audience size and composition across media platforms. Among other things, they measure audiences for print media in 59 countries and radio in 24 countries.
Kantar Media http://www.kantarmedia.com	Kantar Media includes what was once known as TNS media. It offers a range of TV, radio, and Internet audience measurement services in more than 50 countries.
Knowledge Networks, Inc. www.knowledgenetworks.com	Knowledge Networks conducts both custom and syndicated reports, including MultiMedia Mentor, which surveys media use across eight different platforms and is based on a panel of over 50,000 people in the United States.
Marketing Evaluations Inc. www.qscores.com	Best known for "Q Scores" that measure the public's familiarity with and liking of TV programs, brands, and celebrities alive and dead, Marketing Evaluations also have a Social TV Monitor that measures viewer involvement with prime-time TV programs.
Mediametrie http://www.mediametrie.com	A French audience measurement firm owned by the media and advertisers, it tracks radio, Internet, and cinema audiences and produces television ratings using peoplemeters.
Nielsen http://nielsen.com/us/en.html	The largest marketing research firm in the world, Nielsen is best known as the provider of U.S. TV audience ratings in both national and local markets. Nielsen operates in some 100 countries, providing audience measures for television, radio, music, movies, books, DVDs, video games, mobile devices, and online activities including website visits and the "buzz" on social media platforms.
Rentrak http://www.rentrak.com	An audience measurement and research company, Rentrak tracks movie box office numbers in over 25 countries, mobile media use, and television viewing using "set-top box" data.

Roy Morgan Research
http://www.roymorgan.com/
company/index.cfm

An Australian market research and opinion polling firm, Roy Morgan Research surveys consumers in Australian and New Zealand about their lifestyles, product purchases, and media consumption habits.

Scarborough Research
www.scarborough.com

Scarborough Research provides local market reports in over 75 U.S. cities and measures demographics, shopping, lifestyle, and use of electronic, print, and out-of-home media. It is owned by Arbitron and Nielsen.

Simmons
http://www.experian.com

Simmons publishes a national survey of over 25,000 U.S. respondents with demographics, product use, and general measures of print and electronic media use. Data can be fused with Nielsen's national TV ratings. It is a part of Experian Marketing Services.

Synovate
http://www.synovate.com

A large marketing research firm based in the Netherlands, Synovate publishes the European Media & Marketing Survey (EMS), which measures TV, print, and website use across 20 European countries and is useful in pan-European media campaigns. It also publishes PAX, which similarly surveys Asia Pacific and Latin American. Synovate is now part of Ipsos.

The Media Audit
http://www.themediaaudit.com

The Media Audit issues a variety of reports in over 80 U.S. markets. It conducts telephone surveys measuring audience levels and audience characteristics for radio stations, local TV news programs, cable TV viewing, daily newspapers, weekly and monthly publications, the Internet, local media websites, and outdoor media.

Another way to test the audience appeal of new programs is to use a *program analyzer,* a device that CBS developed in the late 1930s. Researchers bring respondents into an auditorium and ask them to listen to programs and then vote at regular intervals on what they like and dislike. This tradition of audience research lives on in a large CBS facility in Las Vegas called "Television City." In addition to program analyzer studies, Television City conducts focus groups and gauges viewers' reactions to programs by measuring eye movements and brain wave activity. Other large media corporations, like Time Warner, operate research labs that engage in similar kinds of activities.

Custom research can be very valuable to its sponsors, but often it goes no further. Those who conduct call-out or program-analyzer research would be loath to share the results with anyone outside their organizations. And if they did, the information might be regarded with some suspicion. Outsiders could have a hard time verifying the methods and might well assume that the sponsor has a self-serving motive for promoting the results.

Although most of research conducted in colleges and universities is customized, it is generally referred to as *original* or *primary research.* When the results of academic studies are published in scholarly journals, they are reviewed by other experts in the field. This process provides some assurance that the authors used defensible research procedures. Occasionally, academic or university research centers are commissioned by industry to perform customized studies. A university affiliation may contribute to greater public credibility.

The attributes of both syndicated and customized research are sometimes combined in *hybrid studies.* Research syndicators will often produce standardized reports, but they still have vast stores of raw data that could be analyzed in ways that are of particular interest to a single client. It is common, these days, for syndicators to provide paying customers with online access to their databases so they can produce "customized" reports. Because they are based on existing data, these studies are called *secondary analyses.*

For example, many companies around the world measure television audiences using "peoplemeters." These devices record who is watching television and what they are watching on a minute-by-minute basis. These are the data used to estimate program ratings. But a client might want to know how their audience moves from one program or channel to the next. With access to the peoplemeter database, it is not hard to conduct studies of "audience flow" that could provide that information. As we will see in chapter 8, this information can be useful to programmers when they make scheduling decisions. Similarly, companies that measure website audiences not only report the number or unique visitors to various sites; they often have online tools their clients can use to identify where those visitors come from and where they go when they leave the site.

Hybrid studies have a number of advantages. They are certainly in the syndicator's interest since they can generate additional revenues while requiring very little additional expenditure. Clients may also find that they are less expensive than trying to conduct original custom research to answer the same questions. Moreover, because the results are based on syndicated data, they have the air of official, objective numbers.

For all these reasons, secondary analyses of existing data can be enormously valuable. But they must also be performed with caution and an understanding of what is sound research practice. Quite often, when data are sliced up in ways that were not intended at the time of collection, the slices become too small to be statistically reliable. We will have much more to say about the problems of sampling and sample sizes in chapter 3.

RATINGS RESEARCH

The type of audience research that is at the heart of this book is ratings research. As such, it is worth saying a few words about what ratings research is and why it is so important.

What Is It?

Historically, the term *ratings* has been used as a kind of shorthand for a body of data on people's exposure to electronic media. Strictly speaking, a rating is a percentage of the entire population who sees or hears something, and it is just one of many audience summaries that can be derived from that data. In the United States, the practice of reporting program ratings goes back to the 1930s, when radio needed to authenticate its audience to advertisers.

Ratings research can be described using the categories we have just reviewed. It is always done for some applied purpose, like selling audiences to advertisers or making programming decisions. However, as we noted, the data that are generated for an applied purpose can also be used to test various theories of media use. Ratings research is always quantitative because its primary purpose is to describe what large populations are doing. For that same reason, it is almost always pitched at the macro level of analysis. When the data are disaggregated, though, it is possible to track individual users to learn things such as what media "repertoires" they use on a day-to-day basis. And ratings research is generally provided by an independent, "third party" syndicator, although that practice is beginning to loosen.

The rapid growth in digital media that are "served" over networks has affected the historic nature of ratings research in two ways. First, it has expanded the list of firms that collect and report audience information. Second, it has changed the kinds of data that are being collected.

Often, the companies that are gathering these novel sorts of data are not traditional research syndicators. For example, Facebook is a media outlet that makes money by selling advertising. At this writing, Facebook has in excess of 800 million users worldwide. Users interact with friends and discuss things, and in the process they divulge a lot of information about themselves. Facebook uses that data to sell highly targeted advertisements. Similarly, Google collects enormous amounts of information and sells advertising. These companies make some of their data publicly available with services like "Facebook Page Insights" and "Google Analytics." Occasionally, they cooperate with traditional syndicators like Nielsen. Still other firms harvest what is available on the web and provide a variety of specialized audience measures. But to the extent that these data come from the media themselves, they are not attributable to the "objective" third parties that have traditionally produced audience ratings.

With these new sources of data, the very notion of what might constitute a rating could change. Since the early twentieth century, ratings research has measured exposure to media: first radio, then television, and now Internet. Of course, whether people see a program or visit a website is not the only thing an advertiser or programmer might want to know. For a long time, ratings users have also wondered whether audiences were "engaged" with what they saw. To address that question, social media like Facebook and Twitter are now monitored to track the amount and type of discussion about programs, products, and personalities. Indeed, the enormous amounts of data being collected by the servers that power digital networks raise the possibility that a whole new array of media ratings might be upon us. This has caused one commentator to predict a "post-exposure audience marketplace" that would offer ratings users a "basket of currencies" (Napoli, 2011, p. 149).

Unfortunately, the wealth of possibilities presents a problem. For any measure to work as a currency, people need to agree that it will be the coin-of-exchange. The new postexposure marketplace offers so many alternatives that agreement is often hard to find. For example, many believe *engagement* could be as valuable a metric as exposure. To build consensus about what exactly it means, the Advertising Research Foundation gathered industry experts and produced a white paper on the subject. After careful deliberations, they identified no fewer than 25 different definitions of "engagement" (Napoli, 2011)—and those definitions do not exhaust the possibilities. Without a shared understanding of what is to be measured and how those metrics are to be used, it is difficult for newer types of ratings to gain traction. While they can undoubtedly enrich our understanding of media use and inform marketing and programming decisions, we suspect they will complement, rather than replace, measures of exposure.

What, then, is the proper scope of a book on "ratings analysis"? Our approach continues to emphasize measures of exposure. We do this for three reasons. First, there are more data on exposure than ever before. Changing the channel on a digital set-top box, clicking on a web page, downloading a song, or streaming a video can all be construed as measures of exposure. While these are not simple, uniform behaviors, they are relatively straightforward compared with concepts like "engagement." Because they are easy for people to understand, they form the basis of useful metrics. Second, inventive analyses of exposure, like noting how much time people spent on a web page or tracking their media choices over time, can often reveal their loyalties or levels of engagement. Third, measures of exposure are still the currency media industries use to transact business. For any media product or service to be successful, it must first attract an audience. Once you know who is out there, you can try to do something more with them, like sell them an idea or a product. But the process generally begins with documenting and understanding patterns of exposure. That is the central focus of ratings research.

Why Is It Important?

It should be apparent by now that ratings research is important to many people in the media industries. In the United States, ratings guide the allocation of some $150 billion in television advertising alone. Worldwide, that number is predicted to exceed $500 billion by 2015. Ratings research is also valuable to people who program stations and television networks, develop websites, assess the value of media properties, and craft public policy. In the chapters that follow, we will discuss how audience ratings are used to support all of these activities. But a simple list of the people who depend on audience data to do their jobs understates the larger social significance of ratings research. To understand why, we need to appreciate the world's growing dependence on electronic media and how audience measurement shapes those systems.

We noted that ratings research began in the 1930s. Listening to radio broadcasts quickly became a popular pastime. In the United States, advertising provided the money needed to operate the industry. However, both broadcasters and advertisers needed ratings data to make that system work. European broadcasting began at about this time, although, initially, most European countries relied on government funding for radio and then television. The rest of the world has followed suit. Today, China has the world's largest television audience, with well over 1 billion viewers. It is also the world's third largest advertising market. India has gone from having five television channels in 1991 to more than 500 active channels (FICCI, 2011, p. 18). And with the introduction of new media platforms like Internet and smartphones, everyone is consuming more digital media. The average American spends almost 5 hours a day watching television and another hour on the Internet. And half of Americans now watch at least some video online (Nielsen, 2011). Although a few media outlets are still state supported, most media are funded by some combination of advertising and direct consumer payments. But regardless of the source of funding, they all depend on market information to operate.

Academicians sometimes call the systems that produce these data "market information regimes." According to sociologists Anand and Peterson, "Market information is the prime source by which producers in competitive fields make sense of their actions and those of consumers, rivals, and suppliers" (2000, p. 217). Ratings data are a prime example of such market information. They allow media institutions, public or commercial, to make sense of their audiences and act accordingly. Without it, they are blind. But like all market information regimes, ratings research is never neutral. Although the best ratings suppliers conform to well-established research practices, they all make decisions about exactly what to measure and how data are to be gathered and reported. Those decisions have consequences, and they almost always operate to the advantage of some and the disadvantage of others. For example, in chapter 2, we will describe the controversy that erupted when Nielsen began replacing diaries with peoplemeters in local U.S. markets. Broadcasters were generally unhappy with the change and argued that it would make minority programming less viable.

That argument proved to be more a rhetorical strategy to delay the implementation of peoplemeters than a real problem with the research. But it illustrates that these arcane audience statistics can have consequences beyond their seemingly narrow purpose. Any change in how you produce audience ratings can have ripple effects throughout the system. *The New York Times* explained it this way:

> Change the way you count, for instance, and you change where the advertising dollars go, which in turn determines what shows are made and what shows then are renewed. Change the way you count, and potentially you change the comparative value of entire genres (news versus sports, dramas versus comedies) as well as entire demographic segments (young versus old, men versus women, Hispanic versus black). Change the way you count, and you might revalue the worth of sitcom stars, news anchors and—when a single ratings point can mean millions of dollars—the revenue of local affiliates and networks alike. Counting differently can even alter the economics of entire industries, should advertisers . . . discover that radio or the Web is a better way to get people to know their brand or buy their products or even vote for their political candidates. Change the way you measure America's cultural consumption, in other words, and you change America's culture business. And maybe even the culture itself. (Gertner, 2005, p. 36)

America is not unique in this regard. As more and more countries use ratings research to understand and manage their own media systems, the ripple effects of audience measurement will be felt around the world.

Audience ratings loom large for virtually everyone with a stake in the operation of electronic media. They are the tools used by advertisers and broadcasters to buy and sell audiences. They are the report cards that lead programmers to cancel some shows and clone others. Ratings are road maps to our patterns of media consumption and, as such, might be of interest to anyone from an investment banker to a social scientist. They are the object of considerable fear and loathing, and they are certainly the subject of much confusion. We hope this book can end some of that confusion and lead to an improved understanding of audience research and the ways in which it can be used.

The rest of the book is divided into three parts. The first considers the audience data itself by reviewing who collects it and the methods that they use. The second provides a way to understand and analyze audience data, including a general framework for explaining audience behavior and a review of useful analytical techniques. And the final part examines the many applications of audience research and how different users, like advertisers and programmers, tend to look at the data.

RELATED READINGS

Balnaves, M., O'Regan, T., & Goldsmith, B. (2011). *Rating the audience: The business of media*. London, UK: Bloomsbury

Beville, H. (1988). *Audience ratings: Radio, television, cable* (Rev. ed.). Hillsdale, NJ: Lawrence Erlbaum Associates.

Easley, D., & Kleinberg, J. (2010). *Networks, crowds, and markets: Reasoning about a highly connected world*. Cambridge, UK: Cambridge University Press.

Ettema, J., & Whitney, C. (Eds.). (1994). *Audiencemaking: How the media create the audience*. Thousand Oaks, CA: Sage.

Gunter, B. (2000). *Media research methods: Measuring audiences, reactions and impact*. London, UK: Sage.

Krueger, R. A., & Casey, M. A. (2000). *Focus groups: A practical guide for applied research* (3rd ed.). Thousand Oaks, CA: Sage.

Lindlof, T. R., & Taylor, B. C. (2011). *Qualitative communication research methods* (3rd ed.). Thousand Oaks, CA: Sage.

Napoli, P. M. (2011). *Audience evolution: New technologies and the transformation of media audiences*. New York: Columbia University Press.

Webster, J., & Phalen, P. (1997). *The mass audience: Rediscovering the dominant model*. Mahwah, NJ: Lawrence Erlbaum Associates.

Wimmer, R., & Dominick, J. (2010). *Mass media research: An introduction* (9th ed.). Belmont, CA: Wadsworth.

Part I

Audience Measurement

CHAPTER 2

The Audience Measurement Business

Ratings data are used in advertising, programming, financial analysis, and policy making. These activities have enormous economic and social consequences. But where do the data come from? Who decides what to measure and report? What determines the quality and availability of that information? One answer has to do with the research methods that are used to produce the data, a topic we discuss at length in the next chapter. But there are other considerations as well. Audience measurement is a business. Sometimes it is done as a nonprofit activity, but often the firms involved are intent on making money. Either way, they must be responsive to their clients, while operating within a budget. They are also subject to public scrutiny and regulatory oversight. Ultimately, economic and political considerations can affect the data as much as research methods. In this chapter, we trace the evolution of the audience measurement business. Doing so will help readers better understand current measurement practices and anticipate how they might change.

THE BEGINNING

Even the first "broadcaster" wanted to know who was listening. After more than 5 years of research and experimentation, an electrical engineer named Reginald A. Fessenden broadcast the sound of human voices on Christmas Eve in 1906. He played the violin, sang, recited poetry, and played a phonograph record. Fessenden promised anyone listening that he would be back on the air again for New Year's Eve, and he asked that they write him a letter—an early attempt at "audience research." Apparently, he got a number of responses from radio operators, many of them on ships at sea. They were astonished to hear more than Morse code on their headphones. Other early station operators asked for letters from listeners as well. Frank Conrad, who in 1920 launched the first U.S. radio station (KDKA), even played records requested by his listeners.

A need to know the audience soon became more than just a question of satisfying the operator's curiosity. AT&T, the American telephone monopoly, hoped
to develop radio as a business. By the early 1920s, it demonstrated that charging
clients a toll to make announcements over its station could be an effective way
to fund the medium. "Toll broadcasting," as it was called, soon led to the practice of selling commercial time to advertisers.

By 1928, U.S. broadcasting was sufficiently advanced to provide listeners with
consistent, good-quality reception. Many people had developed the habit of listening to radio, and broadcasters in cooperation with advertisers were developing program formats "suitable for sponsorship" (Spaulding, 1963). Although
there was some public controversy over whether radio should be used for advertising, the Great Depression, which began in 1929, encouraged radio station
owners to turn to advertisers for support. But for such a system to work, broadcasters had to be able to authenticate the size and composition of their audiences. Without that information, it was hard for broadcasters and advertisers to
negotiate the value of commercial minutes.

Unfortunately, that kind of information was hard to come by. Unlike newspapers, which could document their circulation with audits, radio listening
left very few traces. The first radio stations used primitive techniques to estimate the size of their audience. Some counted fan mail; others simply reported the population or number of receivers sold in their market. Each of
these methods was unreliable and invited exaggeration. The networks were
somewhat more deliberate about audience measurement. In 1927, NBC commissioned a study to determine not only the size of its audience but also the
hours and days of listening. The company also sought information on the
economic status of listeners, foreshadowing the use of "demographics" that
is now so much a part of audience research. In 1930, CBS conducted an on-
the-air mail survey, offering a free map to all listeners who would write to their
local stations. CBS compared the response with the population of each county
and developed its first coverage maps. But none of these efforts offered the
kind of regular, independent measurement of the audience that radio would
need to sustain itself.

Advertiser support was, more than any other factor, responsible for the
emergence of the audience measurement practices that we have today. It is
not surprising, therefore, that many of the methods for gathering ratings data
were developed and institutionalized in countries that relied on commercial
broadcasting. Initially, the United States, Australia, and Canada were more
dependent on this method of funding than were the European countries.
It was only as commercial broadcasting became more prevalent in Europe
that more precise systems of audience measurement were put in place. In
the United Kingdom, this happened in the 1950s. Other European countries

followed a decade later. As Barrie Gunter, a well-known British audience researcher, noted:

> Even in those countries which did not acquire commercial channels until fairly recently, a television audience measurement system nevertheless emerged modeled on those in countries with commercial channels. (2000, p. 122)

Many audience measurement systems were developed in the United States and later adapted for use around the world. So that is where we begin.

THE EVOLUTION OF AUDIENCE MEASUREMENT

The history of audience measurement is a story of individual researchers and entrepreneurs, of struggles for industry acceptance, as well as an account of the media industries themselves. It is also a story of research methods. Most major audience measurement companies rose to prominence by perfecting and promoting their own brand of research. And most major changes in the structure and services of the industry have also been tied to research methods. For this reason, we trace the evolution of audience measurement by organizing it around data-gathering techniques, all of which are still in use today.

Telephone Interviews

From 1930 to 1935, the revenues and profits of U.S. radio networks nearly doubled, all at a time when the country and most other businesses were in a deep economic depression. Because many American families did not have money to spend on other diversions—and because radio was indeed entertaining—the audience grew rapidly. An important stimulant to that growth was the emergence of a system for providing audience estimates that advertisers could believe. The first such system depended on another technological marvel—the telephone.

Then, as now, advertisers were the driving force behind ratings research. They helped create the first ratings company to conduct regular surveys. In 1927, a baking powder company hired the Crossley Business Research Company to survey the effectiveness of its radio advertising. Two years later, Crossley conducted a similar survey for Eastman Kodak, using telephone interviews to ask people if they had heard a specific program. At the time, the telephone was an unconventional tool for conducting survey research, but it seemed well suited for measuring something as far-flung and rapidly changing as the radio audience.

Archibald Crossley, the company president, was a well-known public opinion pollster. He suggested to the Association of National Advertisers (ANA) that a new industry association might use the telephone to measure radio listening.

His report, entitled *The Advertiser Looks at Radio*, was widely distributed, and ANA members quickly agreed to pay a monthly fee to support regular and continuous surveys of radio listening. The American Association of Advertising Agencies (AAAA) also agreed on the need for regular radio audience measurements.

This new service, officially called the Cooperative Analysis of Broadcasting, or CAB, began in March 1930. CAB reports were generally referred to in the trade press simply as "the Crossley ratings." Even the popular press began to note the rise or fall of specific programs or personalities in the ratings. Initially, only advertisers paid CAB for its service but, before long, advertising agencies began to subscribe. The networks had access to the reports as well, using them to sell time and to make programming decisions, but their use was "unofficial." Not until 1937 were NBC and CBS allowed to become subscribers, thus sharing the cost and the data.

In the early years, Crossley revised his methods and expanded the amount of information he provided a number of times. By the 1935–1936 season, surveys were conducted in the 33 cities that had stations carrying CBS and the two NBC networks. Calls were placed four different times during the day and respondents were asked to "recall" the radio listening during the last 3 to 6 hours. Hence, Crossley's method of measurement was known as *telephone recall*. Monthly and, later, biweekly reports were published that gave audience estimates for all national network programs. Further, three times a year, more-detailed summaries provided information about station audiences hour by hour, with breakdowns for geographic and financial categories.

But CAB's methods had serious limitations. Telephone recall surveys could not reach radio listeners who did not have telephones. That limitation was less serious in the early years of the service, because the first families to purchase radios were from higher-income households that were likely to have telephones. By the end of the 1930s, when the growth of homes with radios began to outpace those with telephones, CAB had to alter its sampling procedures to include more low-income households to compensate.

The most serious limitation to the CAB method, however, was that it required listeners to remember what they had heard. Relying on memory was a source of error. As a result, a new method, called a *telephone coincidental*, gained favor among researchers. Coincidentals asked people what they were listening to at the time of the call. George Gallup, another soon-to-be famous pollster, was one of the first to conduct a nationwide telephone coincidental for the advertising agency Young and Rubicam.

Research comparing telephone recall and coincidental methods was done in the early 1930s and reported the following:

> The results showed that some programs, which were listened to by many listeners, were reported the next day by only a few. In general, dramatic programs were better remembered than musical programs. However, the rank

correlation between the percentage of listeners hearing 25 (half-hour) programs and the percentage reporting having heard them was about .78. This is a measure of the adequacy of the Crossley survey as compared with the simultaneous telephone survey. (Lumley, 1934, pp. 29–30)

The telephone coincidental provided a methodological advantage that opened the door for CAB's first ratings competitor. This happened when Claude Hooper and Montgomery Clark quit the market research organization of Daniel Starch in 1934 to start Clark-Hooper. George Gallup assisted them in arranging for their first survey. Hooper later wrote, "Even the coincidental method which we have developed into radio's basic source of audience size measurement was originally presented to us by Dr. George Gallup" (Chappell & Hooper, 1944, p. vii). In the fall of that year, Clark-Hooper launched a syndicated ratings service in 16 cities.

Ironically, Clark-Hooper was first supported by a group of magazine publishers who were unhappy with the fact that radio was claiming an ever-increasing share of advertiser dollars. They believed that Crossley's recall technique overstated the audience for radio. Although it could be expected that coincidental ratings would capture certain unremembered listening, the publishers hoped that Clark-Hooper would show that many people were either not home or doing something else besides listening to the radio. In fact, the first Clark-Hooper results did show lower listening levels than those of CAB.

In 1938, Clark and Hooper split, with the former taking the company's print research business. With great faith in the future of radio, Hooper went into business for himself. His research method was simple. Those answering the telephone were asked:

- Were you listening to the radio just now?
- To what program were you listening?
- Over what station is that program coming?
- What advertiser puts on that program?

Respondents were then asked to report the number of men, women, and children who were listening when the telephone rang.

Hooperatings, as his audience estimates came to be called, were lower than CAB's for some programs but higher for others. As Hooper would argue later, people were better able to remember programs that were longer and more popular and had been on the air for a longer period of time. Respondents were also much more likely to recall variety programs; they were most likely to forget listening to the news (Chappell & Hooper, 1944, pp. 140–150). Over time, the industry began to regard C. E. Hooper's coincidentals as more accurate than CAB's recall techniques.

But methodological superiority was not enough. As the "creature" of the ANA and AAAA, CAB was well entrenched with the advertising industry. Recognizing that CAB served the buyers of radio time, Hooper decided to pursue the broadcast media, and he established a service to supply both the buyer and the seller. CAB might see fit to ignore networks and stations, but Hooper would seek them out as clients and provide them with the kinds of audience research they needed. This strategy was perceptive, for today the media account for the overwhelming majority of ratings service revenues.

Hooper also worked hard for the popular acceptance of Hooperatings. To achieve as much press coverage as possible, each month he released information about the highest rated evening programs. This went not only to the trade press but to popular columnists as well. In this way, C. E. Hooper, Inc. became the most visible and talked about supplier of audience information for the industry. Radio comedians even began to joke about their, or the competition's, Hooperatings.

In addition to promoting popular consciousness of program ratings, Hooper was also responsible for establishing many of the traditions and practices of contemporary audience research. He instituted the "pocketpiece" format for ratings reports, which became the hallmark of Nielsen's national U.S. ratings, as well as concepts like the "available audience" and "sets in use." He also began to report audience shares, which he called "percent of listeners," and the composition of the audience in terms of age and gender. Thus, by the end of the 1930s, the basic pattern of commercial audience research for broadcasting was set.

Hooper and his company were efficient and aggressive. He regularly conducted research to try to make his methods more accurate or to add new services, especially to help the networks and stations. He was also relentlessly critical of the CAB method that still depended on recall. As a part of this battle, in 1941, Hooper hired Columbia University psychology professor Matthew Chappell to study recall and memory. Two years later, they wrote a book trumpeting the advantage of telephone coincidentals.

Hooper's aggressiveness paid off. Just after World War II, he bought out CAB, which was on the verge of collapse. For a brief time, C. E. Hooper was the unquestioned leader in U.S. ratings research. But even as Hooper reached his zenith, the broadcast industry was changing. The new medium of television was about to alter the way people used their leisure time. A new methodology and company were ascendant as well. Although he continued to offer local measurement of radio and television, in 1950, Hooper sold his national ratings service to A. C. Nielsen. As Hugh Beville, sometimes called the "dean of broadcast audience research," noted:

> Unfortunately, Hooper never saw that television was the big future of broadcasting. Had he retained network television when he sold the radio service to Nielsen in early 1950, he could have prospered. Instead, the day after the

deal was announced Hooper held a press conference in which he said that "to make the deal attractive [we] threw in national television ratings." Hooper had almost scornfully thrown away the ticket to the future of his company. (1988, p. 63)

Of course, with the wisdom of hindsight, we now know that television, not radio, was the "future of broadcasting." But in 1950, that was not at all clear. Hooper expected very little of television. Nielsen was prescient enough to take a risk and position his company to become one of the dominant suppliers of television audience measurement (TAM) around the world.

Today, telephone interviews are a common data-gathering technique for marketing researchers and public opinion pollsters. Most ratings companies also use telephones in one capacity or another to identify respondents or secure their cooperation. Many still consider telephone coincidentals the "gold standard" for measuring broadcast audiences, although they are too limiting and expensive to be used on an ongoing basis. In fact, since the late 1990s, telephones have fallen out of favor as the principal means to measure day-to-day media usage.

Personal Interviews

Face-to-face, personal interviews were often used in early radio surveys. Beginning in spring 1928, market researcher Daniel Starch used personal interviews in studies commissioned by NBC. And even after the first ratings services had come into existence, CBS commissioned Starch to provide a series of reports in the 1930s. CBS argued that this provided more accurate information because Hooper's "telephone calls obviously miss all non-telephone homes—which becomes an increasing distortion as one gets into the smaller communities." Because CBS had fewer, often less-powerful affiliated stations than NBC, the network thought it could only benefit from this sort of audience research (CBS, 1937).

In the late 1930s, while Crossley and Hooper argued over different methods of telephone data collection and Nielsen worked to perfect his metering device, the personal interview was still the most accepted method of collecting sociopsychological behavioral information. One man in particular, Dr. Sydney Roslow, who had a doctorate in psychology, became intrigued with the technique while interviewing visitors at the New York World's Fair in 1939. With the encouragement of Paul Lazarsfeld, a pioneer in early audience studies, he started to adapt these techniques to the measurement of radio listening.

In the fall of 1941, he began providing audience estimates, called "The Pulse of New York," based on a personal interview *roster recall* method that he developed. When respondents were contacted, they were given a roster of programs to aid in recalling what they had listened to in the past few hours. Because Hooper, and later Nielsen, concentrated on network ratings, Roslow's local service expanded rapidly—especially with the tremendous expansion of stations after World War II. By the early 1960s, Pulse was publishing reports in 250 radio markets around the country and was the dominant source for local radio measurement.

In Australia, which had advertiser-supported radio as early as the 1930s, personal interviews were also an important means of data collection. The method was particularly appealing because, at the time, so few Australian households had telephones. In the 1940s, two competing ratings companies, the McNair Survey and the Anderson Analysis of Broadcasting, both adopted aided-recall interviews, similar to Pulse, although within a couple of years, Anderson moved to a diary technique. These competing services produced somewhat different audience ratings and appealed to different constituents. In the absence of any formal mechanism to audit their procedures, they also served as a check on one another's results. In 1973, the firms merged and settled on diaries as the method of data collection.

Still, personal interviews had some advantages over the alternatives, particularly telephones. They could include out-of-home listening (e.g., automobile and work) and measure radio use during hours not covered by the telephone coincidental—Hooper was limited to calls from 8 a.m. to 10:30 p.m. Further, they provided demographic details and information on many minority and foreign-language stations popular with those less likely to have telephones.

Because ratings based on personal interviews reported audiences that were hard to see with other methods, they helped reshape U.S. radio. Pulse's emphasis on measuring audiences in the metro area, versus Nielsen's nationwide measurement of network programs, contributed to the rise of "Top 40" and popular music format stations. These became popular with many local advertisers who were only interested in the number of listeners in their marketing area. Thus, Pulse's method was a boon to the growth of rock formats, just as more and more local stations were coming on the air, and more and more network programs and personalities were transferred to television or oblivion.

As was the case in Australia, though, by the 1970s another method took control of local radio ratings. The American Research Bureau (ARB), which we describe in the sections that follow, used its success with television diary techniques to move into radio. As a subsidiary of a large computer company, ARB had superior computing power that aided in the timely production of market reports. It also appears that the rock and ethnic stations favored by the interview method were not as aggressive in selling to advertising agencies, so agencies came increasingly to accept the diary technique being promoted by news and "easy listening" stations. In 1978, Pulse went out of business.

Today, personal interviews are no longer a mainstay of the audience measurement business, although a few operations still use interviewers to gather information or personally place diaries with respondents. Bona fide personal interviews are expensive, and traditional questionnaires based on recall have a hard time tracking media use in a highly fragmented digital media environment. Nonetheless, they can be an important way to study audiences. For example, Mediamark Research (MRI) conducts a survey of 26,000 American consumers. In the first wave of data collection, personal interviewers visit people's homes to gather a range of demographic and media usage data. By doing so, they are able to present respondents with various cards depicting media outlets to aid in the data collection process. While these data do not function like an audience ratings currency, they are wed to extensive information about product purchases, and so help guide the allocation of advertising expenditures.

Diaries

In the 1920s, many radio set builders and listeners were not interested in programs at all. Instead, they were trying to hear as many different and distant stations as possible. To keep track of those stations, they kept elaborate logs of the signals they heard and when they heard them. They noted information such as station call letters, city of origin, slogans, and program titles. Despite this early form of diary keeping, and the occasional use of diaries by radio ratings firms, the diary method did not become an important tool of commercial audience research until the rise of television.

The first systematic research on diaries was done by Garnet Garrison. In 1937, he began to "experiment developing a radio research technique for measurement of listening habits which would be inexpensive and yet fairly reliable" (Garrison, 1939, p. 204). Garrison, for many years a professor at the University of Michigan, noted that at the time the other methods were the telephone survey, either coincidental or unaided recall, personal interviews, mail analysis or surveys, and "the youngster automatic recording." His method, which he called a "listening table," borrowed something from each because it could be sent and retrieved by mail, included a program roster, and was thought to be objective. His form provided a grid from 6 A.M. to midnight divided into 15-minute segments and asked respondents to list station, programs, and the number of listeners. He concluded that:

> With careful attention to correct sampling, distribution of listening tables, and tabulation of the raw data, the technique of "listening tables" should assist materially in obtaining at small cost quite detailed information about radio listening. (Garrison, 1939, p. 205)

CBS experimented with diaries in the 1940s but apparently thought of the data as applicable only to programming and not to sales. Diaries were used to track such things as audience composition, listening to lead-in or lead-out programs, and charting audience flow and turnover. In the late 1940s, Hooper also added diaries to his telephone sample in areas "which cannot be reached practically by telephone." This mixture of diary and coincidental was never completely satisfactory. Indeed, one of the reasons for the slippage of Hooper against Nielsen was that the telephone method was, for the most part, confined to large metropolitan areas where television first began to erode the radio audience. Hence, Hooper tended to understate radio listenership.

It was not until the late 1940s that diaries were introduced as the principal method of a syndicated research service. As director of research for the NBC-owned station in Washington, DC, James Seiler had proposed using diaries to measure radio for several years. The station finally agreed to try a survey for its new television station. NBC helped pay for several tests, but Seiler set up his own company to begin a regular ratings service.

He called the company American Research Bureau (ARB), and in Washington, just after the war, its name sounded very official, even patriotic. ARB issued its first local market report in 1949. Based on a week-long diary, which covered May 11–18, it showed Ed Sullivan's *Toast of the Town* Sunday variety program with an astonishing rating of 66.4. By fall, the company also was measuring local television in Baltimore, Philadelphia, and New York. Chicago and Cleveland were added the next year. The company grew slowly at first—as both television and the diary research methodology gained acceptance. In 1951, it merged with another research company, called Tele-Que, that had begun diary-based ratings on the West Coast, thus adding reports for Los Angeles, San Diego, and San Francisco.

Through the 1950s, ARB emerged as the prime contender to Nielsen's local television audience measurement, especially after 1955, when it took over the local Hooper television ratings business. ARB expanded, and by 1961 it was measuring virtually every television market twice a year, and larger markets more often. The networks and stations responded by putting on especially attractive programming during these "sweeps" periods when diaries were in the field. In 1973, ARB changed its name to Arbitron. Its head-to-head competition with Nielsen would last for another two decades but ultimately fall victim to television industry economics. As television stations' budgets tightened in the more competitive media environments of the late 1980s and early 1990s, stations could no longer afford to buy two ratings services. The balance tipped in Nielsen's favor, and it became the de facto currency in local television. In November 1993, Arbitron ended its television measurement business.

Radio was a different story. For reasons we discuss in the following section, Nielsen ended its radio measurement operations in the early 1960s, at which point Arbitron began using diaries to provide local radio reports. These, as we have seen, eventually put Pulse out of business. Another company, Statistical Research Inc. (SRI), eventually filled the void left by Nielsen's national radio service. SRI was formed in 1969 by Gerald Glasser, a statistics professor at New York University, and Gale Metzger, former director of research for the Nielsen Media division.

Three years later, the company took over operation of a collaborative industry research effort called Radio's All Dimension Audience Research (RADAR), which continued to produce reports on radio network audiences. Harkening back to the days of CAB, SRI used recall telephone techniques to collect their data.

For many years, Arbitron was the undisputed provider of local radio ratings. For a time, a company called Birch/Scarborough Research, which also used a telephone recall technique, posed a challenge. But, once again, the industry was unwilling to adequately fund a second, competitive service. In 1992, Tom Birch stopped producing ratings and sold the more "qualitative" Scarborough service to Arbitron. In 2001, Arbitron acquired the RADAR brand from SRI, establishing it as the dominant supplier of radio ratings in the United States, a position it enjoys to this day.

Despite their limitations, which we discuss in the following chapter, diaries remain an important tool for audience measurement around the world. In the United States, Australia, Russia, Asia, and many European countries, they are still used to measure radio listening, although in some larger markets, more expensive "portable" meters have supplanted them. Even in television, where meters are widely accepted as a more accurate means of measurement, diaries are still in use. For smaller markets, which cannot justify the expense of metering systems, diaries remain the best option for measuring audiences. In fact, at this writing, Nielsen uses diaries to produce television ratings in the majority of local U.S. markets. While that may change, diaries are likely to be in use for some time to come.

Meters

From the earliest days of commercial radio, broadcasters and advertisers recognized the potential advantages of making a simultaneous, permanent, and continuous record of what people actually listened to on the radio. Technical problems involved in developing such a system were solved in the 1930s, and they were in common use by the late 1940s. When these meters finally arrived, however, they had a profound and lasting impact on the ratings business.

While a student at Columbia University in 1929, Claude Robinson—later a partner with George Gallup in public opinion research—patented a device to "provide for scientifically measuring the broadcast listener response by making a comparative record of . . . receiving sets . . . tuned over a selected period of time" (Beville, 1988, p. 17). The patent was sold to RCA, the parent company of NBC, but nothing more is known of the device. Despite the advantages of a meter, none had been perfected, leading Lumley (1934) to report:

> Although the possibilities of measurement using a mechanical or electrical recording device would be unlimited, little development has taken place as yet in this field. Reports have been circulated concerning devices to record the

times at which the set is tuned in together with a station identification mark. None of these devices has been used more than experimentally. Stanton, however, has perfected an instrument which will record each time at which a radio set is turned on. (pp. 179–180)

The reference was to Frank N. Stanton, then Lumley's student, who would later become the president of CBS. For his dissertation, Stanton built and tested 10 devices "designed to record set operation for [a] period as long as six weeks" (Lumley, 1934, p. 180). On wax-coated tape, one stylus marked 15-minute intervals while another marked when the set was turned on. The device did not record station tuning but was used to check against listening as recorded on questionnaires. Stanton, by the way, found that respondents tended to underestimate the time they spent with the set on.

In 1930 and 1931, Robert Elder of the Massachusetts Institute of Technology conducted radio advertising effectiveness studies that were published by CBS. In 1933–1934, he and Louis F. Woodruff, an electrical engineer, designed and tested a device to record radio tuning. The device scratched a record on paper by causing a stylus to move back and forth as the radio tuner was moved across the dial. Elder called his device an audimeter and sought a patent. Discovering the previous Robinson—now RCA—patent, he received permission from RCA to proceed. The first field test used about 100 of the recorders in the Boston area. In 1936, Arthur C. Nielsen heard a speech by Elder describing the device and apparently began negotiating to buy the rights to the technique immediately.

Trained as an electrical engineer, Nielsen had opened a business in 1923 to test the efficiency of industrial equipment. The business survived but did not prosper. Ten years later, a pharmaceutical client suggested to a Nielsen employee that what they really needed was information on the distribution and turnover of their products. In response, Nielsen developed a consumer survey based on a panel of stores to check inventory in stock. The business grew rapidly, a food index was added, and the company thrived. The A. C. Nielsen Company was on its way to becoming the largest marketing research firm in the world. But it was the acquisition of the Elder–Woodruff audimeter that would ultimately make Nielsen's name synonymous with audience measurement.

With his engineering background, and the profits from his successful indices, Nielsen redesigned the device. There were field tests in 1938 in Chicago and North Carolina to compare urban and rural listening. By 1942, the company launched the Nielsen Radio Index (NRI), based on some 800 homes equipped with his device. Nielsen technicians had to visit each home periodically to change the paper tape in the device (Figure 2.1), which slowed data collection. However, the company also provided information about product purchases, based on an inventory of each household's "pantry." Having already established

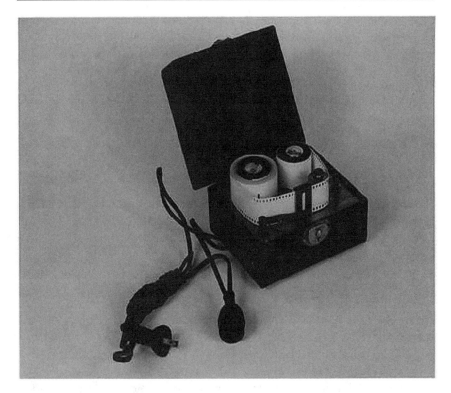

FIGURE 2.1. The First Audimeter (1936)
Source: Nielsen Company. Reprinted by permission.

a good reputation with advertisers, Nielsen began to make progress in overtaking the dominant ratings supplier, C. E. Hooper.

During the 1950s, Nielsen continued to expand his ratings business and to perfect the technology of audience measurement. As we noted, in 1950 he acquired Hooper's national ratings service. In the same year he initiated the Nielsen Television Index (NTI), the company's first attempt to measure that fledgling medium. By the middle of the decade, he launched the Nielsen Station Index (NSI) to provide local ratings in both radio and television. His engineers perfected a new version of the audimeter that recorded tuner activity on a 16-mm film cartridge. More importantly, the cartridge could be mailed directly to Nielsen sample households and then mailed back to Nielsen headquarters, thereby speeding the rate at which data could be collected. Nielsen had also begun to use diaries for gathering audience demographics. To improve their accuracy, he introduced a special device called a "recordimeter," which monitored hours of set usage, and flashed a light to remind people to fill in their diaries.

The 1960s were a tumultuous decade for America and audience measurement companies. In an atmosphere charged by quiz show scandals on television, reports of corruption and "payola" in the music industry, as well as growing social unrest, the U.S. Congress launched a far-reaching investigation of the ratings business. Recognizing the tremendous impact that ratings had on broadcasters and concerned about reports of shoddy research, Oren Harris, chairman of the House Committee on Interstate and Foreign Commerce, orchestrated a lengthy study of industry practices. In 1966, the Harris Committee issued its report. Although it stopped short of recommending legislation to regulate audience measurement, the investigation had a sobering effect on the ratings business—effects that are still evident today in the scrupulous detail with which methods and the reliability of ratings are reported and the existence of what is now called the Media Rating Council (until 1982, the Broadcast Rating Council; from 1982 to 1998, the Electronic Media Rating Council).

As the premier ratings company, Nielsen was particularly visible in the congressional hearings, especially its radio index. In response, Mr. Nielsen personally developed a new radio index that would be above criticism. Unfortunately, potential customers resisted the change because of the increased costs associated with data collection. Angered by this situation, in 1964 Nielsen withdrew from national radio measurement altogether. In fact, a year earlier, Nielsen had discontinued local radio measurement, leaving Pulse unchallenged.

As we noted in the previous section, for the better part of four decades, Nielsen and Arbitron were in direct competition to provide local television ratings. In large markets that could bear the expense, Nielsen used household meters supplemented with diaries. Elsewhere, both companies depended on diaries. What was then the ARB, however, made limited use of meters as well. They even tried to one-up Nielsen by developing a meter whose contents could be retrieved over a telephone. In 1957, ARB placed meters in 300 New York City households and began to provide "instantaneous" day-after ratings. Generally speaking, this move met with the approval of advertisers and the media because it meant Nielsen might face more effective competition. Unfortunately for ARB, Arthur Nielsen and his engineers had patented almost every conceivable way of metering a set. ARB's new owner, a firm named CEIR, was forced to pay Nielsen a fee for the rights to the device. Nevertheless, this spurred Nielsen to quickly wire a New York sample with meters and, later, in 1973, to introduce a storage instantaneous audimeter (SIA) as the data-collection device for its full national sample. By doing so, Nielsen was able to retrieve data over telephone lines and produce household ratings that were referred to as "overnights."

The most important shortcoming of a conventional household meter like Nielsen's was that it provided ratings users with no information about who was watching. As advertisers became more sophisticated about targeting their messages to particular types of viewers, household information seemed less and less useful. Diaries were used to fill that void, but they were slow and error prone and had to be reconciled with the metered data. A better solution would be to collect "people" information in direct conjunction with metered measurement.

By the 1980s, commercial broadcasting was beginning to make headway in Europe. With it, came an increased interest in newer, more accurate audience measurement systems to replace the "hotchpotch of incompatible meter systems, and conventional diary and recall operations" (Gane, 1994, p. 22). In the early 1980s, Audits of Great Britain (AGB) installed "peoplemeters" in a sample of Italian households. These devices not only monitored television set activity; they also allowed people to indicate who was watching. By 1984, AGB was operating a panel of peoplemeters in the United Kingdom as well. At about the same time, Telecontrol, a Swiss company, installed peoplemeters in Switzerland and the former West Germany. By the end of the decade, most of Western Europe was using peoplemeters to measure television viewing. The United States, too, would follow suit.

Since the 1950s, Nielsen has been the sole supplier of national television network ratings in the United States. These data were produced by combining household meters with diaries. AGB hoped its peoplemeter might allow it to compete with Nielsen for the U.S. market. The company secured funding from the industry, including advertisers and the media, and within a couple of years it had sufficient support to install peoplemeters in Boston and begin a field test of the system. Nielsen, which was by then a major international marketing firm, had been monitoring the competition and developing its own peoplemeter. It announced plans to test and implement a national peoplemeter service and in 1987 began basing its national "NTI" services on a sample of households equipped with peoplemeters. AGB held on for a time, but with equivocal support from the industry, especially the broadcast networks, its position became untenable. In 1988, it ended its U.S. operations.

In the 1990s, with $40 million in funding primarily from broadcast networks, the industry considered yet another alternative to Nielsen as the provider of national television ratings (Terranova, 1998). It was called "Systems for Measuring and Reporting Television," or SMART. The SMART project was run by SRI, the company that, at the time, provided national radio network ratings. It used a peoplemeter-like box to measure viewing but offered certain technical differences from Nielsen's system, including the ability to detect a bit of electronic code that identified the source being viewed. It also had a more inclusive definition of who should be counted in the audience, which appealed to the networks. The SMART project began testing by wiring 500 households in Philadelphia. To go national, though, SRI needed another $60 million in funding from the industry. Advertisers, who saw SMART as the creature of the networks, declined to support the effort. At that point, the networks stopped funding the project and it, too, ended its operations.

Peoplemeters are today the preferred method of television audience measurement around the world. In addition to North America and Europe, they are in widespread use in Asia and Latin America. Sometimes they are operated by large international corporations that have a presence in many countries like Nielsen, which now partners with AGB, or the GfK Group, which owns Telecontrol. Sometimes firms operate in a single country, like CSM, which measures China in collaboration with Kantar Media, or Mediametrie, which is a free-standing French ratings company. But if our history of audience measurement teaches us anything, it is that nothing stays the same for very long.

Peoplemeters are, themselves, subject to continuing modifications and improvements. There are now portable peoplemeters (PPMs), which panel members carry with them throughout the day. The fact that many households now receive television via cable or satellite service has encouraged some to use data from digital set-top boxes (STBs) to monitor viewing. In effect, this turns those boxes into household meters. During the 1990s, as Internet use grew, companies like comScore and NetRatings, now owned by Nielsen, started recruiting panels that used people's own computers to monitor and report their site visits. In effect, this turned their machines into a kind of peoplemeter. In fact, the Internet has augured even more radical changes in audience measurement. Because more and more media are served to people via computers, it is possible to track everyone who visits a site or downloads media. This has opened the door to a very different strategy for measuring audiences, which we will describe in the section that follows.

THE AUDIENCE MEASUREMENT BUSINESS TODAY

Understanding how ratings research has evolved over the years can give us a better understanding of today's business arrangements, the kinds of data that are available, and what we might expect in the future. Our abbreviated history of worldwide audience research is not an end in itself but rather a way to learn lessons we might apply going forward. We have seen that audience measurement can be a competitive business. While the accuracy of research methods is important, so are the desires and willingness to pay of the clients. We have also seen that measurement systems can affect the operation of the media themselves. As a result, they can be the subject of industry negotiations and politics. All of this is still true today.

In this section, we will begin by noting the challenges posed by the new media environment, then briefly review the measurement strategies that are being used to address those challenges, and, finally, comment on a number of institutional factors that shape the nature of syndicated audience data.

Challenges of the New Media Environment

The media environment has always affected the business of audience measurement. As radio stations proliferated and people began listening in cars, ratings research was forced to adapt. In the twenty-first century, newer media systems and the demands of advertisers have presented audience measurement companies with serious challenges. Three changes have been particularly troublesome. First, the ever-increasing number of media outlets has fragmented audiences into smaller groups. Second, "nonlinear" systems, like video on demand (VOD), have given users greater control over when media are delivered. Third, new platforms like smartphones have also given people greater control over where they use media. These developments and the difficulties they pose set the stage for any discussion of the merits of contemporary audience measurement systems.

The first problem results from the sheer proliferation of media. People now have hundreds of television channels and millions of websites from which to choose. Each of these options claims a bit of public attention that was once concentrated on just a few outlets. Nowhere have long-term trends in fragmentation been more evident than in the declining viewership of broadcast television. Figure 2.2 depicts the steady erosion of broadcast audiences

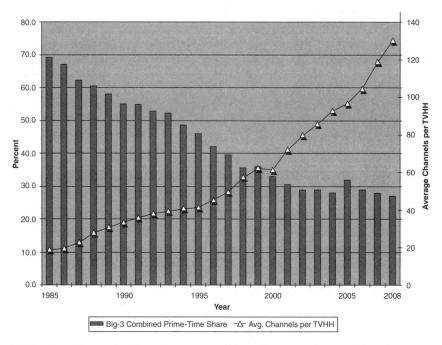

FIGURE 2.2. History of Audience Fragmentation: Network Shares and Average Channels per TVHH by year

Source: Data from Nielsen Media Research. Adapted from Webster (2005).

in the United States. The dark bars show the combined primetime share of ABC, CBS, and NBC beginning with the 1985–1986 television season. In that year, the "Big-3" accounted for almost 70 percent of all the time American households spent watching television. By the 2008–2009 season, their combined market share had dropped below 30 percent—a "+7" number that included live and delayed viewing. Over the same span of years, the number of television channels available to the average household, as indicated by the ascending line, increased sevenfold. As of 2008, the last year for which Nielsen reported numbers, the average U.S. household could watch 130 channels. This change is not unique to the United States. As we noted in chapter 1, in just 10 years, India went from having 5 active television channels to 500. Filling up those channels are new broadcast networks and an avalanche of cable and satellite networks, each one claiming a piece of the audience.

The result is that established outlets have seen their audiences shrink. In the early 1980s, primetime shows with ratings of less than 15 were routinely cancelled (Atkin & Litman, 1986). That is, unless you captured 15 percent of U.S. households, you could expect to be taken off the air. Today, while "media events" like World Cup Soccer or the Superbowl still attract large audiences, successful primetime television programs typically have audience ratings in the low single digits. Cable network ratings are often just a fraction of a ratings point. And most website audiences are smaller still.

Shrinking audiences present a problem for audience measurement, especially when you take into account the advertisers' desire to reach even more narrowly defined segments of the audience. What would seem like very large samples are quickly pushed to their limit. For example, if you had a national panel of 20,000 television households, a program rating of 1 would mean 200 homes were watching that show. If the market the advertiser is after (e.g., young men) is present in only 10 percent of those homes, your program rating for that demographic could be based on just 20 individuals. Unless sample sizes keep pace with fragmentation, estimates of such tiny audiences can be swamped by sampling error, a topic we discuss in the following chapter.

The second problem developed more recently. Historically, radio and television have been "linear" delivery systems, with broadcasters controlling the schedule. Ratings companies could figure out what you were exposed to by keeping track of the station you used and when you used it. Now, "nonlinear" media like VOD, DVRs, and the World Wide Web allow people to watch what they want, when they want it. This presents still more challenges. To begin with, it exacerbates the problem of fragmentation. It is difficult enough to measure audiences when viewing is spread across 500 linear channels; now people have thousands of additional choices at their fingertips. Without fixed schedules to rely on, measurement companies have to find different ways to know exactly what programs and/or commercials are actually being watched. Moreover, time-shifting programs—and avoiding commercials in the process—complicates what used to be a straightforward metric. If measures of exposure are the currency used to transact business, what kind of exposure should it be? In 2007, the national currency in U.S. television shifted from program ratings to what are called "C3" ratings. The latter combines exposure to commercial minutes plus 3 days of delayed viewing.

The third problem is that media content moves across different technological platforms. Increasingly, people control not only when but also where media use occurs. Television can be seen on living room sets, monitors in public places, tablet computers, smartphones, or various websites (with or without ads). People can read news the old fashioned way or on any number of electronic devices. All of these points of contact might be occasions for marketers to reach potential customers and so are of increasing importance to advertisers. It would make sense to track each person's exposure to a program or commercial across platforms. Unfortunately, most audience measurement operations have specialized in a single medium. One company would do radio but not television; another would measure Internet use but not print. And even when one company measured different media, their data collection was typically segregated into separate samples (e.g., one for television and one for the Internet). True "single source" panels that would measure all these activities precisely have often proved unduly burdensome on respondents or prohibitively expensive. Nonetheless, finding a way to track people across platforms remains an important challenge for audience measurement.

Measurement Strategies

In the face of all these challenges, how can any measurement operation hope to produce accurate, useful estimates of people's media use? The first thing to note is that no system of audience measurement is perfect. Beginning with the earliest attempts to audit newspaper circulation, we have about 100 years of experience measuring audiences. In that period of time, no system of measurement has been without its flaws. The same will undoubtedly be true 100 years from now. Each approach has certain strengths and weaknesses. Our history of audience measurement highlighted at least some of those tradeoffs. With that in mind, we will briefly comment on the two basic measurement strategies currently in use. The first is old; the second is new. Each has distinct advantages and drawbacks.

Every audience measurement operation we described in this chapter depended on drawing a sample of people or households, securing their cooperation, and using that data to make inferences about the larger population. This is a *user-centric* measurement strategy. Information is collected from users who agreed to answer questions, fill out diaries, or accept meters. The big advantage of this strategy is that people willingly provide you with information about themselves. You can learn a lot about their individual characteristics. As a result, estimates of media use can be associated with demographics or whatever traits you have measured. But to provide accurate estimates, you have to construct an adequate sample.

There are two ways in which the sample can be problematic. The best samples are usually drawn at random. Unfortunately, not everyone you would like to study will cooperate. If the people who decline to participate are systematically different from those who do participate, you can produce biased estimates. The second problem, as we noted earlier, is that the sample just is not big enough to compensate for audience fragmentation. Of course, the ratings company could always increase the size of the sample. But that comes at a cost, one that ratings users will have to pay. Eventually, you reach a point of diminishing returns that make larger samples unrealistic.

The newer strategy avoids the problem of sample size. Much of the digital media we use is served to us through computers. These machines, or "servers," can easily track what web pages are requested, what videos are streamed, and what ads are being served. They do not see just a sample, they see every such action. If you aggregate those actions, you have another way to measure the audience. This is a *server-centric* measurement strategy. And it has the potential to create a census of the population in real time. Having data on millions of users solves the problem of sample size.

But this approach has drawbacks as well. First, having lots of data does not mean you have a genuine census. For example, millions of homes have digital STBs, which are now being used to measure television audiences. But millions of other homes do not have STBs. As is the case with sample information, our concern is that those with boxes could be systematically different from those without, which would bias the estimates. More importantly, server-centric information often cannot tell you much about who is being served. Was the person visiting that web page a man or a woman? Was the person watching that video young or old? Server-centric information might not be able to tell you much about the characteristics for the audience. While there are ways to estimate those traits, user-centric approaches typically gather more precise information about individual users.

In practice, both strategies are now extensively used. Researchers have developed ways to compensate for the weaknesses of each, which we will describe in the next chapter. Increasingly, measurement companies are trying to "fuse" data from different sources to have the best of both worlds (see, for example, Nielsen, 2009, 2011).

But current audience measurement practices are not just about research methods. Often they are the combined result of what the methods make possible, what the clients want, and what they are willing to pay for. For example, reliable C3 ratings can only be produced if you measure audiences with meters.

But peoplemeters were in place long before the United States made C3 the new "currency." The change was ultimately a matter of ratings users reaching a new consensus. Internet measurement presents even greater challenges in consensus building. Servers collect so much information, they make many audience metrics possible (e.g., clicks, page views, unique visitors, impressions, etc.). While each has potential value, settling in on an agreed currency for transacting business can be difficult. Next, we consider some of the broader institutional factors that shape the audience measurement business.

Institutional Factors

While quality of audience ratings is important, that alone does not determine whether a measurement system will be adopted by the affected industries. As we have shown, there are many ways to measure audiences. Different methods can produce different results. Those differences often operate to the advantage of some ratings users and the disadvantage of others. These considerations, as well as the cost of implementing different methods, all affect the kinds of research services that are available in a given market. Here, we describe the blend of economic and institutional factors that affect the market for audience measurement. We then describe the ways in which different countries organize audience research.

Syndicated audience ratings reports are, like many forms of information, characterized by high "first copy" costs. The machinery needed for state-of-the-art measurement is expensive. Metering technology must be designed, tested, and manufactured. Systems for acquiring and processing the data must be in place. Investors and prospective clients have to be ready to make financial commitments. Whatever the costs, they must be incurred before the first report is produced. Further, the data provided by an incumbent ratings company are often deeply engrained in the institutional practices of advertisers and the media, making users resistant to change. These "facts of life" make it difficult for competitors to enter the market. As the World Federation of Advertisers (WFA) noted:

> The money required for two adequate television panels would fund one good panel. It is also wasteful in terms of agency resources in that multiple data sets have to be purchased and reconciled. (2008, p. 5)

This means that audience ratings are often provided by one dominant firm and, once it is in place, it is not easily changed. Yet, as we have seen, change does occur. But how? It depends, in part, on the actions of the ratings companies themselves. But it also depends on the laws and institutional arrangements in different countries.

The most common way to manage change is through a "joint industry committee" (JIC). In such an arrangement, the principle ratings users (e.g., media, advertisers, and agencies) create a committee that specifies what audience measurement services are required. They put a contract, or tender, out for bids. Typically, established ratings companies like Nielsen, GfK Telecontrol, or Kantar Media will respond to the tender. In this system, differences of opinion about the merits of one method versus another are typically worked out "behind closed doors." The JIC then selects the service it considers to be the best and agrees to fund the measurement operation for however many years the contract is in force. This basic model, in which users not only pay for but control measurement, varies from country to country. In the United Kingdom, for example, the BBC, ITV, and others created a nonprofit entity called the Broadcasters' Audience Research Board (BARB). It commissions specialists, like Kantar Media, to provide television audience measurement services. OzTAM in Australia is similarly structured but uses Nielsen to run its peoplemeter panel. In 1985, the French created a company called Mediametrie, which is owned by French broadcasters and ad agencies. Rather than commissioning outsiders, it has developed its own measurement services. In any of these JIC arrangements, though, the result is a single firm providing a single currency. In fact, that is one of the reasons they exist (WFA, 2008).

In the United States, antitrust laws make JICs of questionable legality. While ratings services can seek accreditation from an industry board called the Media Rating Council, independently owned ratings companies have always been free to challenge one another for contracts with ratings users. Often they will do so by touting the superiority of some new research method. That was true when Hooper finally prevailed over CAB and it is true today. But neither change nor innovation comes easily.

As we have seen, dislodging an incumbent ratings company is a time-consuming, expensive, and risky proposition. Experience at providing ratings in another market, using arguably superior methods, and even attracting widespread encouragement from prospective clients does not guarantee success. That was true of AGB's failed attempt to enter the U.S. market and SMART's unsuccessful effort to challenge Nielsen. Philip Napoli, a business professor at Fordham, summarized the "reality" of the situation:

> Early indications of support for an upstart do not always represent a genuine interest in competition or even a desire to have the new measurement firm supplant the incumbent as the agreed-upon standard. Rather, the apparent show of support for a new measurement firm actually is an effort to compel the incumbent to improve or alter its measurement techniques or technologies. Typically, the incumbent responds to this threat, and the advertiser or media firm stops underwriting the new firm. (2003, pp. 27–28)

While it may be hard for a newcomer to introduce innovations, it can be a challenge for even a well-established incumbent. As the pioneer in metered measurement, Nielsen is constantly devising new ways to collect data. But even making what might seem like uncontroversial improvements can meet powerful resistance. The best example of this is Nielsen's efforts to introduce peoplemeters into local U.S. markets.

As we noted earlier, since the late 1980s peoplemeters have been the preferred method of television audience measurement around the world. Any reputable audience researcher would acknowledge that peoplemeters are more accurate than diaries, especially in the current digital media environment. Yet, when Nielsen wanted to replace a diary/meter method with peoplemeters in local markets, some Nielsen clients objected. A similar change happened nationally in 1987, and local broadcasters feared the new system might benefit cable. While advertisers and the cable industry were typically supportive, broadcasters were generally unhappy with the change. In Boston, the first test market, broadcasters initially refused to subscribe to the service. As Nielsen began rolling out local peoplemeters (LPMs) in other large markets, broadcast industry resistance escalated.

LPM technology was accused of undercounting minority viewers. If that were true, so the argument went, minority oriented programming would lose advertiser support and eventually be canceled. The most vocal and visible of the public interest groups making this case was called Don't Count Us Out (DCUO), a collection of advocacy groups formed as the rollout began. Nielsen was surprised by the ferocity of the resistance. While it did have slightly higher "fault rates" in minority households, that problem was a relatively minor problem and easily fixed.

Less easy to fix was Nielsen's public relations problem. It turned out that one of Nielsen's own corporate clients was secretly behind the protests. News Corporation, the owner of Fox television stations, believed that LPMs would generate lower ratings for its stations. To slow or stop the introduction of LPMs, News Corporation organized DCUO, spent nearly $2 million orchestrating news conferences, running inflammatory ads, and operating telephone banks (Hernandez & Elliot, 2004). The supposed threat to minority interests attracted the attention of then-Senator Hillary Clinton and other national figures and organizations. This, in turn, prompted the U.S. Congress to hold hearings. Legislation was proposed but never passed into law.

Nielsen now has LPMs in more than two dozen of the largest U.S. markets, with plans for more. But the introduction of LPMs should serve as a cautionary tale to any incumbent ratings provider. Even if that firm is the sole supplier of a ratings currency, especially if it operates under a JIC contract, its ability to introduce changes in its methods for gathering and reporting data are limited. It functions within a complex web of competing industry interests and political agendas that are not always apparent. These can have a powerful effect on how the audience measurement business operates.

RELATED READINGS

Balnaves, M., O'Regan, T., & Goldsmith, B. (2011). *Rating the audience: The business of media*. London: Bloomsbury.

Bermejo, F. (2007). *The internet audience: Constitution and measurement*. New York: Lang.

Beville, H. M. (1988). *Audience ratings: Radio, television, cable* (Rev. ed.). Hillsdale, NJ: Lawrence Erlbaum Associates.

Buzzard, K. S. (2012). *Tracking the audience: The ratings industry from analog to digital*. New York: Routledge.

Chappell, M. N., & Hooper, C. E. (1944). *Radio audience measurement*. New York: Stephen Daye.

Gunter, B. (2000). *Media research methods: Measuring audiences, reactions and impact*. London: Sage.

Kent, R. (ed.). (1994). *Measuring media audiences*. London: Routledge.

Lumley, F. H. (1934). *Measurement in radio*. Columbus, OH: The Ohio State University Press.

Napoli, P.M. (2003). *Audience economics: Media institutions and the audience marketplace*. New York: Columbia University Press.

Napoli, P.M. (2011). *Audience evolution: New technologies and the transformation of media audiences*. New York: Columbia University Press.

Turow, J. (2011). *The daily you: How the new advertising industry is defining your identity and your worth*. New Haven: Yale University Press.

CHAPTER 3

Audience Measurement Methods

Audience researchers use a variety of methods to study people's media use. We have mentioned many of these in the preceding pages. In this chapter, we go more deeply into issues of sampling, measurement, and how audience estimates are actually produced. These concerns go directly to the quality of the data. Do different methods have different biases and limitations? How accurate are the estimates available to ratings users? A savvy consumer of audience ratings should know how the data are created.

As we noted in the last chapter, there are two basic strategies for gathering audience data: user-centric approaches and server-centric approaches. Either way, researchers are typically working on one of three major activities. The first is identifying who is to be studied. Historically, this has involved defining the relevant population and then drawing a sample for study. The second is figuring out exactly what you want to measure and how you are going to measure it. The third is gathering the data and processing them into a product that your clients want. So sampling, measurement, and production are activities that cut across the basic strategies for gathering data.

It also bears repeating that no method for measuring audiences is perfect. Researchers often identify and categorize their imperfections into different *sources of error*. In this context, the word "error" has a special meaning. "Error" is the extent to which a method produces a result that is different from reality. Sometimes the source of error is just what you would expect, a mistake. But often, error is a foreseeable consequence of the method being used. Being able to discern possible sources of error will make you better able to judge the quality of research products.

There are four major sources of error in audience measurement. Each tends to crop up at different points in the research process. The first is *sampling error*. Even if you do everything right, this is an inevitable consequence of using samples to estimate populations. In theory, server-centric methods can avoid sampling error. In practice, sampling and its pitfalls can inform our thinking about server-centric data. The second source is *nonresponse error*.

This occurs when the nonresponders are different from those who provide data. Sampling and nonresponse error affect the quality of the sample, so we discuss them at length in the section on sampling. The third is *response error*. Among those who do provide data, are there errors or biases in their responses? As you will see in the section on measurement, different techniques are associated with different types of response error. Finally, there is *production error*. Data must be collected, aggregated, and processed, often using mathematical adjustments. Sometimes mistakes are made. Sometimes the math introduces distortions.

SAMPLING

If you manage to study every member of a population, you are conducting a *census*. If the population you are interested in is too big, or your resources too limited, you can study a subset of the population, called a *sample*, and use it to make inferences about the population. The methods for designing and drawing proper samples were developed in the early twentieth century. When, in the 1930s, it became necessary to describe radio audiences, sampling was used for the job, and it is still an indispensible tool for most ratings services. In fact, sampling is standard operating procedure in all kinds of surveys, ranging from public opinion polling to marketing research.

In any survey research, the quality of the sample has a tremendous impact on the accuracy with which you can describe the population. All samples can be divided into one of two classes: probability and nonprobability samples. They differ in the way researchers identify who they are studying. *Probability samples*, sometimes called *random samples,* use a process of random selection in which every member of the population has an equal, or known, chance of being drawn into the sample. This approach minimizes the odds of drawing an unrepresentative subset of the population. Probability samples can be expensive and time-consuming to construct. But researchers generally have more confidence in them than in *nonprobability* samples, which depend on happenstance or convenience to determine participation.

Most ratings companies try to achieve, or at least to approximate, the benefits of probability sampling. Their technical documents are laced with the language of probability samples. To develop the needed working vocabulary, therefore, one must be familiar with the principles of probability sampling. The following discussion is designed to provide that familiarity, in a way that does not assume a background in quantitative methods on the part of the reader. Those already familiar with sampling may wish to skip to the section on measurement.

Sampling begins with a definition of the population that the researcher wants to study. This requires a decision about what kind of things will be studied;

researchers call these things *elements* or *units of analysis*. In ratings research, the units of analysis are typically people or households. Because the use of radio is individualistic, radio ratings have long used people as the unit of analysis. We still speak of television households as units of analysis, although the buying and selling of advertising time are usually done on the basis of populations of people who are defined by demographics (e.g., women 18–34 years old) or other individual traits that are of interest to advertisers.

Researchers must have a precise definition of the population (or *universe*) they want to study. This lets everyone know which elements are members of the population and, so, qualify for study. For example, if we were attempting to create national television ratings, all households in the United States with one or more sets might be appropriate. Local markets within countries can be more problematic, because households might receive signals from two or more cities. In the United States, Nielsen calls local markets *Designated Market Areas (DMAs)* and defines them by assigning every county to one and only one such market. Assignments are based on which television stations are watched by the people in a particular county.

Once the population is defined, the researcher could try to obtain a complete list of all elements in a population. From this list, called a *sampling frame*, specific elements are chosen for the sample. For example, if we have a sampling frame of 1 million television households in Amsterdam, and randomly pick one home, we would know that it had a one-in-a-million chance of selection—just like every other home in the population. Hence, we would have met the basic requirement of probability sampling. All we would have to do, then, is repeat the process until we have a sample of the desired size.

The procedure we have just described produces a *simple random sample*. Despite its conceptual elegance, this sort of sampling technique is seldom used in audience measurement because the real world is less cooperative than this approach to sampling assumes. It is virtually impossible to compile a list of each and every television home in an entire country. Researchers use more efficient and powerful sampling designs. The most common sampling techniques of the ratings companies are described here.

Sample Designs

Systematic Random Sampling. One probability sampling technique that involves only a minor variation on simple random sampling is called *systematic random sampling*. Like a simple random sample, this approach requires the use of a sampling frame. Usually, audience measurement firms buy sampling frames from companies whose business it is to maintain and sell such lists. Historically, these frames were lists of telephone households. Homes with unlisted numbers were included through the use of randomly generated numbers. Today, some households—especially younger or lower-income households—have dropped land line phones in favor of cell phones. That could bias audience estimates, so some companies have begun using a sampling frames of addresses rather than phone numbers.

Once an appropriate frame is available, systematic sampling is straightforward. Because you have a list of the entire population, you know how large it is. You also know how large a sample you want from that population. Dividing population size by sample size lets you know how often you have to pull out a name or number as you go down the list. For example, suppose you had a population of 10,000 individuals and you wanted to have a sample of 1,000. If you started at the beginning of the list and selected every 10th name, you would end up with a sample of the desired size. That "nth" interval is called the *sampling interval*. The only further stipulation for systematic sampling—an important one—is that you pick your starting point at random. In that way, everyone has had an equal chance of being selected, again meeting the requirement imposed by probability sampling.

Multistage Cluster Sampling. Fortunately, not all probability samples require a complete list of every single element in the population. One sampling procedure that avoids that problem is called *multistage cluster sampling*. Cluster sampling repeats two processes: listing the elements and sampling. Each two-step cycle constitutes a stage. Systematic random sampling is a one-stage process. Multistage cluster sampling, as the name implies, goes through several stages.

A ratings company might well use multistage sampling to identify a national sample. After all, coming up with a list of every single household in the nation would be quite a chore. However, it would be possible to list larger areas in which individual households reside. In the United States, a research company could list all counties then draw a random sample of counties. In fact, this is essentially what Nielsen does to create a national sample of television households. After that, block groups within those selected counties could be listed and randomly sampled. Third, specific city blocks within selected block groups could be listed and randomly sampled. Finally, with a manageable number of city blocks identified, researchers might be placed in the field, with specific instructions, to find individual households for participation in the sample.

Because the clusters that are listed and sampled at each stage are geographic areas, this type of sampling is sometimes called a *multistage area probability sample*. Despite the laborious nature of such sampling techniques, compared with the alternatives, they offer important advantages. Specifically, no sampling frame listing every household is required, and researchers in the field can contact households even if they do not have a telephone.

However, a multistage sample is more likely to be biased than is a single-stage sample. This is because, through each round of sampling, a certain amount of error accompanies the selection process—the more stages, the higher is the possibility of error. For example, suppose that during the sampling of counties described earlier, areas from the Northwestern United States were overrepresented. That could happen just by chance, and it would be a problem carried through subsequent stages. Now suppose that bias is compounded in the next stage by the selection of block groups from a disproportionate number of affluent areas. Again, that is within the realm of chance. Even if random selection is strictly observed, a certain amount of sampling error creeps in. We discuss this more fully later in this chapter when we cover sources of error.

Stratified Sampling. Using a third kind of sampling procedure, called stratified sampling, can minimize some kinds of error. This is one of the most powerful sampling techniques available to survey researchers. Stratified sampling requires the researcher to group the population being studied into relatively homogeneous subsets, called *strata*. Suppose we have a sampling frame that indicates the gender of everyone in the population. We could then group the population into males and females and randomly sample the appropriate number from each strata. By combining these subsamples into one large group, we would have created a probability sample that has exactly the right proportions of men and women. Without stratification, that factor would have been left to chance. Hence, we have improved the representativeness of the sample. That added precision could be important if we are studying behaviors that might correlate with gender, such as watching sports on television, or making certain product purchases like cosmetics and tires.

Stratified sampling obviously requires that the researcher have some relevant information about the elements in a sampling frame (e.g., the gender of everyone in the population). In single-stage sampling, that is sometimes not possible. In multistage sampling, there is often an abundance of information because we tend to know more about the large clusters we begin with. Consider, again, the process that began by sampling counties. Not only could we list all U.S. counties, but we could group them by the state or region of the country they are in, the size of their populations, and so forth. If we drew a systematic sample from that stratified list, we would have minimized error on those stratification variables. Other sorts of groupings, such as the concentration of people with certain demographic characteristics, could be used at subsequent stages in the process. By combining stratification with multistage cluster sampling, therefore, we could increase the representativeness of the final sample. That is what many ratings services do.

Cross-Sectional Surveys. All of the sample design issues we have discussed thus far have dealt with how the elements in the sample are identified. Another aspect of sample design deals with how long the researcher actually studies the population or sample. *Cross-sectional* surveys occur at a single point in time. In effect, these studies take a snapshot of the population. Much of what is reported in a single ratings report could be labeled cross-sectional. Such studies may use any of the sampling techniques just described. They are alike insofar as they tell you what the population looks like now but not how it has changed over time. Information about those changes can be quite important. For instance, suppose the ratings book indicates that your station has an average rating of 5. Is that cause for celebration or dismay?

The answer depends on whether that represents an increase or a decrease in the size of your audience, and true cross-sectional studies will not tell you that.

Longitudinal Studies. These studies are designed to provide you with information about changes over time. Instead of a snapshot, they're more like a movie. In ratings research, there are two kinds of longitudinal designs in common use: *trend studies* and *panel studies*. A trend study is one in which a series of cross-sectional surveys, based on independent samples, is conducted on a population over some period of time. The definition of the population remains the same throughout the study, but individuals may move in and out of the population. In the context of ratings research, trend studies can be created simply by considering a number of market reports done in succession. For example, tracing a station's performance across a year's worth of ratings books constitutes a trend study. People may have moved to or from the market in that time, but the definition of the market (i.e., the counties assigned to it) has not changed. Most market reports, in fact, provide some trend information from past reports. Panel studies draw a single sample from a population and continue to study that sample over time. The best example of a panel study in ratings research involves the metering of people's homes. This way of gathering ratings information, which we describe later in the chapter, may keep a household in the sample for years.

Error in Sampling

Sampling error is an abstract statistical concept that is common to all survey research that uses probability samples. Basically, it is a way to recognize that as long as we try to estimate what is true for a population by studying something less than the entire population, there is a chance that we will miss the mark. Even if we use very large, perfectly drawn random samples, it is possible that they will fail to accurately represent the populations from which they were drawn. This is inherent in the process of sampling. Fortunately, if we use random samples, we can, at least, use the laws of probability to make statements about the amount of sampling error we are likely to encounter. In other words, the laws of probability will tell us how likely we are to get accurate results.

The best way to explain sampling error, and a host of terms that accompany the concept, is to work our way through a hypothetical study. Suppose that the Super Bowl was played yesterday and we wanted to estimate what percentage of households actually watched the game (i.e., the game's rating). Let us also suppose that the "truth" of the matter is that exactly 50 percent of U.S. homes watched the game. Of course, ordinarily we would not know that, but we need to assume this knowledge to make our point. The true population value is represented in the top of Figure 3.1.

To estimate the game's rating, we decide to draw a random sample of 100 households from a list of all the television households in the country. Because

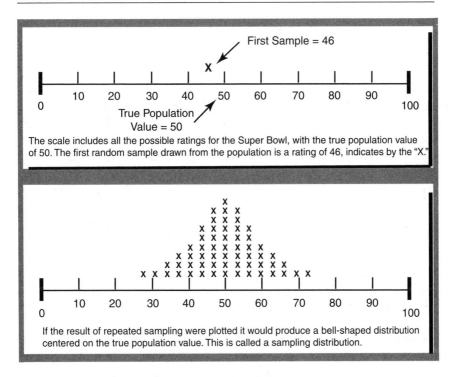

FIGURE 3.1. A Sampling Distribution

we have a complete sampling frame (unlikely, but convenient!), every home has had an equal chance to be selected. Next, we call each home and ask if they watched the game. Because they all have phones, perfect memories, and are completely truthful (again, convenient), we can assume we have accurately recorded what happened in these sample homes. After a few quick calculations, we discover that only 46 percent of those we interviewed saw the game. This result is also plotted in the top of Figure 3.1.

Clearly, we have a problem. Our single best guess of how many homes saw the game is 4 percentage points lower than what was, in fact, true. In the world of media buying, 4 ratings points can mean a lot of money. It should, nevertheless, be intuitively obvious that even with our convenient assumptions and strict adherence to sampling procedures, such a disparity is entirely possible. It would have been surprising to hit the nail on the head the first time out. That difference of 4 ratings points does not mean we did anything wrong; it is just sampling error.

Because we have the luxury of a hypothetical case here, let's assume that we repeat the sampling process. This time, 52 percent of the sample say they watched the game. This is better, but still in error, and still a plausible kind of occurrence. Finally, suppose that we draw 1,000 samples, just like for the first two. Each time, we plot the result of that sample. If we did this, the result would look something like the bottom of Figure 3.1.

The shape of this figure reveals a lot and is worth considering for a moment. It is a special kind of frequency distribution that statisticians call a *sampling distribution*. In our case, it forms a symmetrical, bell-shaped curve indicating that, when all was said and done, more of our sample estimates hit the true population value (i.e., 50 percent) than any other single value. It also indicates that although most of the sample estimates clustered close to 50 percent, a few were outliers. In essence, this means that, if you use probability sampling, reality has a way of anchoring your estimates and keeping most of them fairly close to what is true. It also means that sooner or later, you are bound to hit one that is way off the mark.

What is equally important about this sampling distribution is that it will assume a known size and shape. The most frequently used measure of that size and shape is called the *standard error* (SE). In essence, this is the average "wrong guess" we are likely to make in predicting the ratings. For those familiar with introductory statistics, this is essentially a standard deviation. It is best conceptualized as a unit along the baseline of the distribution. Figure 3.2 gives the simplest formula for calculating the SE with ratings data.

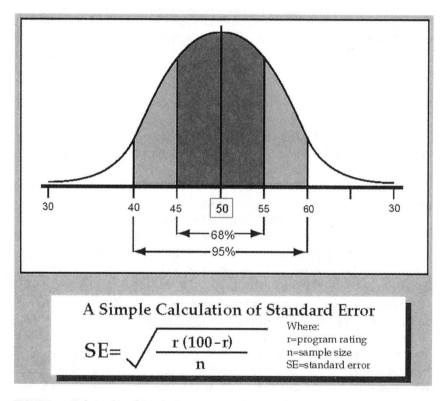

FIGURE 3.2. Relationship of Standard Error to Sampling Distribution

What is remarkable about the SE, and what you will have to accept on faith unless you want to delve much more deeply into calculus, is that when it is laid out against its parent sampling distribution, it will bracket a precise number of samples. Specifically, ±1 SE will always encompass 68 percent of the samples in the distribution; ±2 SEs (technically, that should be 1.96) encompasses 95 percent of all samples. In our example, the SE works out to be approximately 5 ratings points, which means that 68 percent of the hypothetical samples will have produced results between 45 percent and 55 percent (i.e., 50 percent ±5 percentage points). That relationship between SE and the sampling distribution is depicted in Figure 3.2.

None of this would be of interest to anyone other than a mathematician were it not for the fact that such reasoning provides us with a way to make statements about the accuracy of audience data. Remember that in our first sample, we found 46 percent watching the Super Bowl. Ordinarily, that would be our single best guess about what was true for the population. We would recognize, however, that there is a possibility of sampling error, and we would want to know the odds of the true population value being something different than our estimate. We could state those odds by using our estimated rating (i.e., 46) to calculate SE and placing a bracket around our estimate, just like the one in Figure 3.2. Because we know that 95 percent of all sample means would fall between ±2 SEs, we know that 95 percent of all sample means will fall between ±10 points in this example. The resulting statement would sound like this, "We estimate that the Super Bowl had a rating of 46, and we are 95 percent confident that the true rating falls between 36 and 56."

The range of values given in that statement (i.e., 36–56) is called the *confidence interval*. Confidence intervals are often set at ±2 SEs and will therefore have a high probability of encompassing the true population value. When you hear someone qualify the results of a survey by saying something like, "These results are subject to a sampling error of plus or minus 3 percent," they are giving you a confidence interval. What is equally important, but less often heard, is how much confidence should be placed in that range of values. To say we are "95 percent confident," is to express a *confidence level*. At the 95 percent level, we know that in 95 of 100 times, the range we report will include the population value. Of course, that means that 5 percent of the time we will be wrong, because it is always possible our sample was one of those that was way off the mark. But at least we can state the odds and satisfy ourselves that an erroneous estimate is a remote possibility.

Such esoteric concepts take on practical significance, because they go to the heart of ratings accuracy. For example, reporting that a program has a rating of 15, ±10, leaves a lot of room for error. Even fairly small margins of error (e.g., SE +/−1) can be important if the estimates they surround are themselves small (e.g., a rating of 3). That is one reason why ratings services will routinely report *relative standard error* (i.e., SE as a percentage of the estimate) rather than the absolute level of error. In any event, it becomes critically important to reduce sampling error to an acceptable level. Three factors affect the size of that error: complexity of the population, sample size, and sample design. One is beyond the control of researchers; two are not.

The source of sampling error that we cannot control has to do with the population itself. Some populations are just more complicated than others. A researcher refers to these complexities as *variability* or *heterogeneity* in the population. To take an extreme case, if everyone in the population were exactly alike (i.e., perfect homogeneity), then a sample of one person would suffice. Unfortunately, media audiences are not homogeneous, and to make matters worse, they are getting more heterogeneous all the time. Think about how television has changed over the years. It used to be that people could watch the three or four networks and that was it. Today, most homes have cable or satellite, not to mention DVRs and video on demand (VOD). Now think about the complexities that the Internet introduces with services like YouTube. All other things being equal, that makes it more difficult to estimate who is watching what.

The two factors that researchers can control are related to the sample itself. *Sample size* is the most obvious and important of these. Larger samples reduce the magnitude of sampling error. It is just common sense that we should have more confidence in results from a sample of 1,000 than 100. What is counterintuitive is that sample size and error do not have a one-to-one relationship. That means doubling the size of the sample does not cut the SE in half. Instead, you must quadruple the sample size to reduce the SE by half. You can satisfy yourself of this by looking back at the calculation of SE in Figure 3.2. To reduce the SE from 5 to 2.5, you must increase the sample size from 100 to 400. You should also note that the size of the population you are studying has no direct impact on the error calculations. All other things being equal, small populations require samples just as big as large populations.

These aspects of sampling theory are more than just curiosities; they have a substantial impact on the conduct and economics of the ratings business. Although it is always possible to improve the accuracy of the ratings by increasing the size of the samples on which they are based, you very quickly reach a point of diminishing returns. This was nicely demonstrated in research conducted by CONTAM, an industry group formed in response to the U.S. congressional hearing of the 1960s. That study collected viewing records from over 50,000 households around the country. From that pool, eight sets of 100 samples were drawn. Samples in the first set had 25 households each. Sample sizes for the following sets were 50, 100, 250, 500, 1,000, 1,500, and 2,500. The results are shown in Figure 3.3.

At the smallest sample sizes, individual estimates of the cartoon show the *Flintstones* audience varied widely around the actual rating of 26. Increasing sample sizes from these low levels produced dramatic improvements in the consistency and accuracy of sample estimates, as evidenced in tighter clustering. For example, going from 100 to 1,000 markedly reduced sampling error and

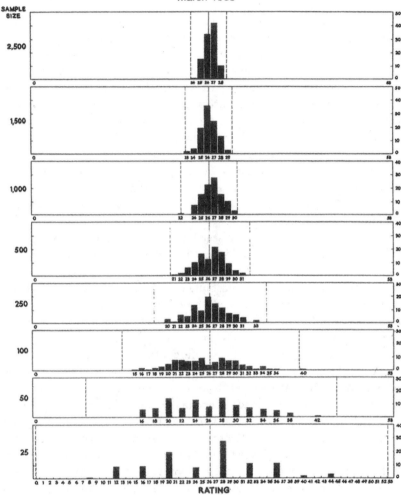

THE FLINTSTONES
U.S. Total Population
March 1963

| True population rating
: Point outside of which 2.6 out of 1,000 sample results should fall according to theory (3σ).
— Represents one sample yielding indicated rating estimate.
Distribution of Sample Ratings Results Based on 100 Diary Samples Each of 8 Different Sizes: 25 to 2500.
Source: CONTAM Study No. 1.

FIGURE 3.3. Effect of Sample Size on Sampling Error

only required adding 900 households. Conversely, going from 1,000 to 2,500 resulted in a modest improvement, yet it required an increase of 1,500 households. Such relationships mean the suppliers of syndicated research and their clients have to strike a balance between the cost and accuracy of audience data.

In practice, several other factors determine the sample sizes used by a research provider. As we suggested earlier, more-complex populations will require larger samples to achieve a certain level of sampling error. This is how the problem of audience fragmentation, which we described in the preceding chapter, comes back to haunt us. As media users spread their attention across more and more outlets, or as we want to measure smaller segments of the audience (e.g., men 18–21 years old), we need larger samples just to keep pace. This can sometimes be done if we are studying large national populations, even though larger populations do not, theoretically, require bigger samples. It happens because larger populations typically have a larger volume of media dollars available, and so justify the investment. In smaller markets, which could be just as complex, it might not be feasible.

The only other factor that the researcher can use to reduce sampling error is to improve the *sample design*. For reasons that we have already discussed, certain kinds of probability samples, like stratified samples, are more accurate than others. This strategy is commonly used, but there is a limit to what can be achieved. We should also note that when these more complex sample designs are used, the calculation of SE becomes a bit more involved than Figure 3.3 indicates. We address those revised computations later.

Nonresponse error is the second major source of error we encounter in the context of sampling. It occurs because not everyone we might wish to study will cooperate or respond. Remember that our entire discussion of sampling error assumed everyone we wanted to include in the sample gave us the information we desired. In the real world, that just does not happen. To the extent that those who do not respond are different from those who do, there is a possibility that the samples we actually have to work with may be biased. Many of the procedures that the ratings services use represent attempts to correct nonresponse error.

The magnitude of nonresponse error varies from one ratings report to the next. The best way to get a sense of it is to look at the response rates reported by the ratings service. Every ratings company will identify an original sample of people or households that it wishes to use in the preparation of its ratings estimates. This ideal sample is usually called the *initially designated sample*. Some members of the designated sample, however, will refuse to cooperate. Others will agree to be in the sample but will for one reason or another fail to provide information. In other words, many will not respond. Obviously, only those who do respond can be used to tabulate the data. The latter group constitutes what is called the *in-tab sample*. The *response rate* is simply the percentage of people from the initially designated sample who actually gave the ratings company useful information. Various techniques for gathering ratings data are associated with different response rates. Telephone surveys, for example, have tended to have relatively high response rates, although these have declined in recent years. The most common measurement techniques, like placing diaries, often produce response rates in the neighborhood of 20 percent. Furthermore, different measurement techniques work better with some kinds of people than others. The nonresponse errors associated with measurement are discussed in the next section.

Because nonresponse error has the potential to bias the ratings, research companies use one of two general strategies to minimize or control it. First, you can take action before the fact to improve the representativeness of the in-tab sample. Second, you can make adjustments in the sample after data have been collected. Often, both strategies are used. Either way, you need to know what the population looks like in order to judge the representativeness of your in-tab sample and to gauge the adjustments that are to be made.

Population or universe estimates, therefore, are essential in correcting for nonresponse error. Determining what the population looks like (i.e., age and gender breakdowns, etc.) often begins with U.S. Census information from the government, although these data are not always up to date. Ratings companies often buy more current universe estimates from other research companies. Occasionally, certain attributes of the population that have not been measured by others, like cable penetration, must be estimated. To do this, it may be necessary to conduct a special study, called either an *enumeration* or *establishment* survey, that determines universe estimates.

Once you known what targets to shoot for, corrections for nonresponse error can be made. Before-the-fact remedies include the use of special recruitment techniques and buffer samples. The most desirable solution is to get as many of those in the originally designated sample as possible to cooperate. Doing so requires a deeper understanding of the reasons for nonresponse and combating those with counteractive measures. For example, ratings services will often provide sample members with some monetary incentive. Perhaps different types of incentives will work better or worse with different types of people. Following up on initial contacts or making sure that interviewers and research materials are in a respondent's primary language will also improve response rates. The major ratings companies are aware of these alternatives and, on the basis of experience, know where they are likely to encounter nonresponse problems. They sometimes use special recruitment techniques to improve, for example, minority representation in the sample.

If improved recruitment fails to work, additional sampling can increase underrepresented groups. *Buffer samples* are simply lists of additional households that have been randomly generated and held in reserve. If, as sampling progresses, it becomes apparent that responses in one county are lagging behind expectations, the appropriate buffer sample can be enlisted to increase the size of the sample drawn from that area. Field workers might use a similar procedure if they encounter a *noncooperating household*. In such an event, they would probably have instructions to sample a second household in the same neighborhood, perhaps even matching the noncooperator on key household attributes.

Once the data are collected, another technique can be used to adjust for nonresponders. *Sample weighting,* sometimes called *sample balancing,* is a statistical procedure that gives the responses of certain kinds of people more influence over the ratings estimates than their numbers in the sample would suggest. Basically, the ratings companies compare the in-tab sample and the universe estimates (usually on geographic, ethnic, age, and gender breakdowns) and determine where they have too many of one kind of person and not enough of another. Suppose, for example, that 18- to 24-year-old men accounted for 8 percent of the population but only 4 percent of the in-tab sample. One remedy for this would be to let the responses of each young man in the in-tab count twice. Conversely, the responses of overrepresented groups would count less than once. The way to determine the appropriate weight for any particular group is to divide their proportion in the population by their proportion in the sample (e.g., 8 percent/4 percent = 2).

For years, Nielsen used an *unweighted sample* to project its national ratings in the United States. But when it introduced the same measurement technology in local markets (i.e., LPMs) that it used nationally, it could greatly increase the size of its national sample, hence reducing sampling error, by folding in LPMs. To do that, however, it had to apply weights so the local data did not swamp the national estimates.

If you think the use of buffer samples or weighting samples is not a completely adequate solution to problems of nonresponse, you are right. Although these procedures may make in-tab samples look like the universe, they do not eliminate nonresponse error. The people in buffer samples who do cooperate or those whose responses count more than once might still be systematically different from those who did not cooperate. That is why some people question the use of these techniques. The problem is that failing to make these adjustments also distorts results. For example, if you programmed a radio station that catered to 18- to 24-year-old men, you would be unhappy that they tend to be underrepresented in most in-tab samples and probably welcome the kind of weighting just described, flaws and all. Today, the accepted industry practice is to weight samples. We return to this topic when we discuss the process of producing the ratings.

The existence of nonresponse error, and certain techniques used to correct for such error, means that samples the ratings services actually use are not perfect probability samples. That fact, in combination with the use of relatively complex sample designs, means that calculations of SE are a bit more involved than our earlier discussion indicated. Without going into detail, error is affected by the weights in the sample, whether you are dealing with households or persons and whether you are estimating the audience at a single point in time or the average audience over a number of time periods. Further, actual in-tab sample sizes are not used in calculating error. Rather, the ratings services derive what they call *effective sample sizes* for purposes of calculating SE. These take into account the fact that their samples are not simple random samples. Effective sample sizes may be smaller than, equal to, or larger than actual sample sizes. No matter the method for calculating SE, however, the use and interpretation of that number are as described earlier.

Sample or Census

Using servers to collect data is often touted as providing a census of media use. That is, it promises to measure every member of the population. If that were true, it would eliminate all of the sampling issues we have just spent several pages describing. Servers can, indeed, "see" the actions of all people who use the server, and by doing so they collect information on enormous numbers of people. But it is not necessarily a census. Google, for example, can see what millions of people around the world are searching for. If the population you wanted to describe were Google users, that data would be a census. But people use other search engines, so if the population you really wanted to describe were everyone conducting searches on the World Wide Web, Google would just have a very big sample. In this case, you would have to ask, "Are Google users systematically different from people who use other services like Bing or the Chinese search engine Badiu?" If so, the problems of sampling and their remedies reemerge.

This has been an important issue in efforts to use digital set-top boxes (STBs) to measure television audiences. A great many households now receive television via cable or satellite services. In the United States, roughly 90 percent of homes are now in that category. Often the signal being served to the television set is managed by an STB, which assembles digital input into programs. If the STB is running the right software, it can detect and report the channels being viewed on a continuous basis. That information, potentially from millions of homes, can be collected by the service provider and aggregated to estimate the size of television audiences.

Proponents of STB measurement sometimes describe this as a census of the television audience. It is not. Remember, ratings companies want to describe the viewing of all homes with television. The first problem is STBs are not in all households. And those with STBs are different from those without. They are often more affluent, and they certainly have more viewing options. Further, even in homes with STBs, some sets are not connected. For example, the main set in the living room might use an STB, while the set in the kitchen or bedroom just gets over-the-air (OTA) signals. In other words, STBs capture some, but not all, television viewing. Add to this the fact that cable and satellite providers who could collect the data might not want to share it. The end result is that STB measurement is typically based on very large samples and these are almost certainly systematically different from the total population you want to describe.

That said, STB data offer an important way to solve the problem of measurement in a world of audience fragmentation. Because STBs collect data from so many homes, they can record very small audiences. But to describe the total audience, the data have to be adjusted, in just the way you would address problems of nonresponse in an ordinary sample. For example, Rentrak is a company that sells STB-derived audience estimates in the United States. It collects data from different platforms or "strata" (e.g., cable, satellites, telephone companies, and OTA), but it rarely has data from all the households in a particular category. It assigns various mathematical weights to these datasets to project total audience size. Hence, even when you have the luxury of "census-like" data, you often have to treat it like a big sample and proceed accordingly.

MEASUREMENT

Sampling has an important bearing on the quality of audience measurement, but methods of measurement are just as important. It is one thing to create a sample that identifies whom you want to study; it is quite another to measure audience activity by recording what they see on television, hear on radio, or use on the Internet. While the sampling procedures used by audience measurement companies are common to all survey research operations, their measurement techniques are often highly specialized.

Technically, *measurement* is defined as a process of assigning numbers to objects, according to some rule of assignment. The "objects" that the audience research companies are usually measuring are people, although, as we have seen, households can also be the unit of analysis. The "numbers" simply quantify the characteristics or behaviors that we wish to study. This kind of quantification makes it easier to manage the relevant information and to summarize the various attributes of the sample. For example, if a person saw a particular football game last night, we might assign him or her a "1." Those who did not see the game might be assigned a "0." By reporting the percentage of 1s we have, we could produce a rating for the game. The numbering scheme that the ratings services actually use is a bit more complicated than that, but in essence, that is what happens.

Researchers who specialize in measurement are very much concerned with the accuracy of the numbering scheme they use. After all, anyone can assign numbers to things, but capturing something meaningful with those numbers is more difficult. Researchers express their concerns about the accuracy of a measurement technique with two concepts: reliability and validity. *Reliability* is the extent to which a measurement procedure will produce consistent results in repeated applications. If what you are trying to measure does not change, an accurate measuring device should end up assigning it the same number time after time. If that is the case, the measure is said to be reliable. Just because a measurement procedure is reliable, however, does not mean that it is completely accurate; it must also be valid. *Validity* is the extent to which a measure actually quantifies the characteristic it is supposed to quantify. For instance, if we wanted to measure a person's program preferences, we might try to do so by recording which shows he or she watches most frequently. This approach might produce a very consistent, or reliable, pattern of results. However, it does not necessarily follow that the program a person sees most often is their favorite. Scheduling, rather than preference, might produce such results. Therefore, measuring preferences by using a person's program choices might be reliable but not particularly valid.

What Is Being Measured?

One of the first questions that must be addressed in any assessment of measurement techniques is, "What are you trying to measure?" Confusion on this point has led to a good many misunderstandings about audience measurement. At first glance, the answer seems simple enough. As we noted in the first chapter, historically ratings have measured exposure to electronic media. But even that definition leaves much unsaid. To think this through, two factors need to be more fully considered: (a) What do we mean by "media"? (b) What constitutes exposure?

Defining the media side of the equation raises a number of possibilities. It might be, for example, that we have no interest in the audience for specific content. Some effects researchers are only concerned with the how much television people watch overall. Although knowing the amount of exposure to a medium might be useful in some applications, it is not terribly useful to advertisers. Radio station audiences and, to a certain extent, cable network audiences have been reported this way. Here, the medium may be no more precisely defined than use of an outlet during a broad time period or an average quarter hour.

In television ratings, exposure is usually tied to a specific program. Here, too, however, questions concerning definition can be raised. How much of a program must people see before they are included in that program's audience? If a few minutes are enough, then the total audience for the show will probably be larger than the audience at any one point in time. Some of the measurement techniques we discuss in the following section are too insensitive to make such minute-to-minute determinations, but for other approaches, this consideration is very important.

Advertisers are, of course, most interested in who sees their commercials. So, a case can be made that the most relevant way to define the media for them is not program content but rather commercial content. We noted in the last chapter that in the United States, commercial ratings, called C3 ratings, were now the currency in the national television marketplace. These report the average rating for all commercials in a program, plus 3 days of replay. Some companies now report the ratings for specific commercials, not just the program average. Internet advertisers have a similar concern. One common way to measure the audience for a display ad on a website is to count "served impressions." That is a server-centric measure of the number of times the ad was served to users. But advertisers know that not all ads that are inserted in web pages are actually viewed. Some fail to load before the user goes to another page, or they are placed on the page such that the user never sees them. Hence, regular served impressions tend to overstate the audiences of Internet ads. Because of that, many advertisers would prefer a new commercial rating called "viewable impressions."

Sometimes the medium we want to measure, like a television program or an ad, can be seen across multiple platforms. So another puzzle in describing the audience for such media is whether to aggregate viewers across all those platforms to produce a single "extended screen" rating. To do that accurately, it would be best to measure the same people across platforms (e.g., television, Internet, smartphones, tablets, etc.). Some measurement services are moving in that direction. Whether the industry wants that kind of aggregated estimate is another question.

The second question we raised had to do with determining what is meant by *exposure*. Since the very first radio surveys in 1930, measuring exposure has been the principal objective of ratings research. Balnaves et al. (2011) noted that Archibald Crossley

> decided to measure 'exposure' in his radio ratings analysis—who listens, for how long and with what regularity. . . . This did not mean that audience researchers did not collect data on whether people did or did not like the radio programmes. But for the purpose of buying and selling radio airtime, or programmes, a metric that showed the fact of tuning in to a programme and the amount of time listening to a programme had a simplicity that was essential for bargaining in highly competitive environments. All competitors, though, had to agree on the measure being used. (p. 22)

Simple as it might seem, even defining *exposure* raises a number of possibilities. *Exposure* is often assumed when a user chooses a particular station, program, or website. Under this definition, *exposure* means that the user was present in the room or car when the computer or radio was in use. At best, this represents a vaguely defined opportunity to see or hear something. Once it has been determined that audience members have tuned to a particular station, further questions about the quality of exposure are left unanswered.

It is well documented, however, that much of our media use is accompanied by other activities. People may talk, eat, play games, or do the dishes while the set is in use. Increasingly, they engage in "concurrent media use," like having the television on while they look at a laptop or tablet. Whatever the case, it is clear that during a large portion of the time that people are "in the audience," they are not paying much attention. This has led some researchers to argue that defining exposure as a matter of choice greatly overstates people's real exposure to the media. An alternative, of course, would be to stipulate that exposure must mean that a person is paying attention to the media, or perhaps even understanding what is seen or heard. Interactive technologies that require someone to "click" on a message or icon offer some evidence that they are paying attention, but for most media, measuring a person's level of awareness or perception is extremely difficult to do in an efficient, valid way.

Obviously, these questions of definition help determine what the data really measure and how they are to be interpreted. If different ratings companies used vastly different definitions of exposure to media, their cost structures and research products might be quite different as well. The significance of these issues has not been lost on the affected industries. In 1954, the Advertising Research Foundation (ARF) released a set of recommendations that took up many of these concerns. In addition to advocating the use of probability samples, ARF recommended that "tuning behavior" be the accepted definition of *exposure*. That standard has been the most widely accepted and has effectively guided the development of most of the measurement techniques we use today.

Another shortcoming that critics of ratings research have raised for some time is that operational definitions of *exposure* tell us nothing about the quality of the experience in a more affective sense. For example, do people like what they see? Do they find it enlightening or engaging? These types of measures are sometimes called *qualitative ratings,* not because they are devoid of numbers but because they attempt to quantify "softer" variables like emotions and cognitions. Many European countries, with strong traditions of noncommercial public broadcasting, have produced such ratings. In the United States, they have been produced on an irregular basis, not so much as a substitute for existing services but rather as a supplement. In the early 1980s, the Corporation for Public Broadcasting, in collaboration with Arbitron, conducted field tests of such a system. Another effort was initiated by an independent Boston-based company named Television Audience Assessment, which tried selling qualitative ratings information. These efforts failed because there simply was not enough demand in the United States to justify the expense of a parallel qualitative ratings service.

Today, that disinterest in the qualitative dimensions of audience measurement is changing. This is happening for two reasons. First, in an abundant and fragmented media environment, where media users are free to indulge wants and loyalties, simple measures of the size and demographic composition of audiences seem impoverished. Certainly outlets or programs with small audiences would like to demonstrate to advertisers that their users have an unusual level of engagement that makes them attractive prospects. Second, the growth of social media like Facebook and Twitter now offers a low-cost way to capture data on what people talk about and share with their friends. Some established measurement companies, like Nielsen, and a great many smaller start-up companies are harvesting such data to produce measures of engagement or "buzz." These are already being used to supplement media buying once done exclusively with

measures of exposure. It may be that these new sources of data eventually produce a "basket of currencies" (Napoli, 2011, p. 149). But the wealth of possibilities also makes it hard to forge any industry consensus on what the new metrics
actually measure and how they are to be used (Napoli, 2012). For now, it appears
that measures of exposure, or measures derived from those data, will continue
to be the principal focus of audience analysis.

Measurement Techniques

There are several techniques that the ratings services use to measure people's exposure to electronic media, and each has certain advantages and disadvantages.
The biases of these techniques contribute to the third kind of error we mentioned
earlier. Response error includes inaccuracies contained in the responses generated
by the measurement procedure. To illustrate these biases, we discuss each major
approach to audience measurement in general terms. To avoid getting too bogged
down in details, we may gloss over differences in how each ratings company op-
erationalizes a particular scheme of measurement. The reader wishing more information should see each company's description of methodology.

Questionnaires. Asking questions is one of the oldest ways to collect data on audiences or, for that matter, any one of countless social phenomena. There are many
books on questionnaire design, so we will not elaborate on their strengths and weaknesses here. We will, however, comment briefly on how question-asking techniques
have been used in audience measurement. As we noted in chapter 2, telephone surveys were the mainstay of the ratings industry at its inception. While telephone
interviews are no longer the workhorse of audience measurement, it is important to
understand the potential and limitations of recall and coincidental surveys.

Telephone recall, as the name implies, requires a respondent to remember
what he or she has seen or heard over some period of time. Generally speaking,
two things affect the quality of recalled information. One is how far back a person is required to remember. Obviously, the further removed something is from
the present, the more it is subject to "memory error." Second is the salience of
the behavior in question. Important or regular occurrences are better remembered than trivial or sporadic events. Because most people's radio listening tends
to be regular and involves only a few stations, the medium is more amenable
than some to measurement with telephone recall techniques.

Like all other methods of data collection, however, telephone recall has certain limitations. First, the entire method is no better than a respondent's memory. Even though people are only expected to recall yesterday's media use, there
is no guarantee that they can accurately do so. There is, for example, good evidence that people overestimate their use of news (Prior, 2009). As more people
screen their calls or rely on primarily on cell phones, they may be less willing to
talk to an interviewer. Finally, the use of human interviewers, while sometimes
a virtue, can also introduce error. Although interviewers are usually trained and

monitored in centralized telephone centers, they can make inappropriate comments or other errors that bias results.

Telephone coincidental can offer a way to overcome problems of memory. These surveys work very much like phone recall techniques, except that they ask respondents to report what they are seeing or listening to at the moment of the call. Because respondents can verify exactly who is using what media at the time, errors of memory and reporting fatigue are eliminated. For these reasons, telephone coincidentals were, for some time, regarded as the "gold standard" against which other methods of measurement should be evaluated.

Despite these acknowledged virtues, no major ratings company routinely conducts telephone coincidental research. There are two problems with coincidentals that militate against their regular use. First, a coincidental interview only captures a glimpse of a person's media use. In effect, it sacrifices quantity of information for quality. As a result, to describe audiences hour to hour, day to day, and week to week, huge numbers of people would have to be called around the clock. That becomes a very expensive proposition. Second, as with all telephone interviews, there are practical limitations on where and when calls can be made. Much radio listening occurs in cars, much television viewing occurs late at night, and much media use is moving to portable devices like tablets. These behaviors are difficult to capture with traditional coincidental techniques.

Just as telephone technology ushered in new methods of data collection in the early twentieth century, the Internet has opened the door for new methods of question asking in the early twenty-first century. A number of firms routinely gather information about media use by presenting questions to web users. Of course, these samples are limited to those with access to the Internet. In fact, many could be considered "opt-in" samples, so generalizing results to larger populations should be done with caution. Still web-based surveys allow for innovation in question asking. For example, respondents needing supplementary material or clarification might have the benefit of drop-down windows. Certain kinds of responses might automatically trigger different kinds of follow-up questions (Walejko, 2010). Even more radical approaches, like building surveys on the model of a wiki, are being developed (Salganik & Levy, 2012). Web-based surveys can take advantage of large samples and offer very quick turnaround times. But, to the extent that these techniques deviate from the well-understood methods of traditional questionnaire design, they might best be thought of as works in progress.

Diaries. Since their introduction in the 1940s, diaries have been widely used to measure media use. Today, they are still the mainstay of radio and television audience measurement in many markets around the world. As we mentioned in the previous chapter, the weeks when diaries are being collected are referred to as "sweeps." During one 4-week sweep, Nielsen alone will gather diaries from over 100,000 respondents to produce audience estimates in local U.S. television markets.

A diary is a small paper booklet in which the diary keeper records his or her media use, generally for 1 week. To produce television ratings, one diary is kept for each television set in the household. The exact format of diaries varies from company to company. Figure 3.4 is an instruction page from a Nielsen television diary. The viewing day begins at 5 A.M., and thereafter it is divided into quarter-hour segments (ending at 4:59 A.M.). Each day of the week is similarly divided. During each quarter hour that the set is in use, the diary keeper is supposed to

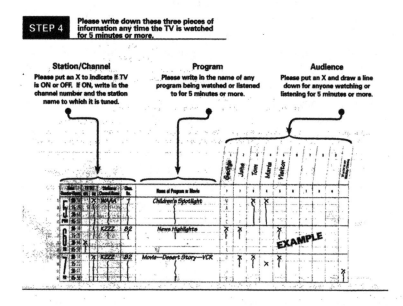

STEP 4   Please write down these three pieces of information any time the TV is watched for 5 minutes or more.

Station/Channel
Please put an X to indicate if TV is ON or OFF. If ON, write in the channel number and the station name to which it is tuned.

Program
Please write in the name of any program being watched or listened to for 5 minutes or more.

Audience
Please put an X and draw a line down for anyone watching or listening for 5 minutes or more.

Please draw lines down to show how long the TV is on, the length of time the program is watched, and how long each person watches or listens.

Note: If the TV is but no one is watching or listening, please put an X and draw a line down in the audience column to the far right of the page.

VCR or DVD

• If watching a program while recording it on your VCR or digital video disc (DVD) recorder, please write it on the daily diary page as shown above and write VCR or DVD next to the program name.

• If recording a program but not watching it, please see back of diary for further instructions.

Please turn the page to begin keeping the diary.

FIGURE 3.4. Sample Page from Nielsen Television Diary
Reprinted by permission of Nielsen Media Research.

note what is being watched, as well as which family members and/or visitors are watching. The diary also includes a few additional questions about household composition and the channels that are received in the home. One major limitation to this method is that the viewing is tied to a set rather than to a person, so out-of home viewing may be significantly understated.

Radio audiences are also measured with diaries, but these diaries are supposed to accompany people rather than sets. That way, an individual can record listening that occurs outside the home. Figure 3.5 is an instruction page from an Arbitron radio diary. It begins at 5 A.M. and divides the day into broader dayparts

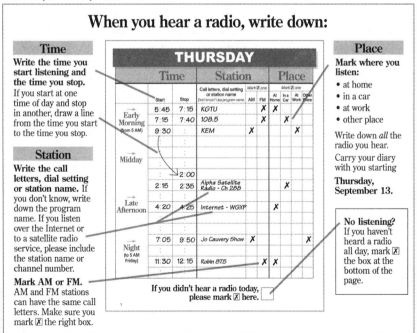

You count in the radio ratings!

No matter if you listen a lot, a little or not at all, you're important!
You're one of the few people picked in your area to have the chance to tell radio stations and other businesses what you listen to.
This is *your* radio diary. Please make sure you fill it out yourself.

Here's what we mean by "listening":
Listening is any time you can hear a radio – whether you choose the station or not. You may be listening to radio on AM, FM, the Internet or satellite. Be sure to include all your listening.

Any time you hear radio from **Thursday, September 13, through Wednesday, September 19,** write it down – whether you're at home, in a car, at work or someplace else.

When you hear a radio, write down:

Time
Write the time you start listening and the time you stop.
If you start at one time of day and stop in another, draw a line from the time you start to the time you stop.

Station
Write the call letters, dial setting or station name. If you don't know, write down the program name. If you listen over the Internet or to a satellite radio service, please include the station name or channel number.

Mark AM or FM.
AM and FM stations can have the same call letters. Make sure you mark ☒ the right box.

THURSDAY

Time		Station	Place				
		Call letters, dial setting or station name	Mark ☒ one		Mark ☒ one		
Start	Stop	Don't know? Use program name	AM	FM	At Home	In a Car	At Work	Other Place

	Start	Stop		AM	FM	At Home	In a Car	At Work	Other Place
Early Morning (from 5 AM)	5:45	7:15	KGTU	☒	☒				
	7:15	7:40	108.5		☒		☒		
	9:30	:	KEM	☒				☒	
Midday		:2:00							
	2:15	2:35	Alpha Satellite Radio - Ch 288				☒		
Late Afternoon	4:20	4:25	Internet - WGXP			☒			
Night (to 5 AM Friday)	7:05	9:50	Jo Cauvery Show	☒				☒	
	11:30	12:15	Robin 87.5	☒	☒				

If you didn't hear a radio today, please mark ☒ here. ☐

Place
Mark where you listen:
• at home
• in a car
• at work
• other place

Write down *all* the radio you hear.
Carry your diary with you starting **Thursday, September 13.**

No listening?
If you haven't heard a radio all day, mark ☒ the box at the bottom of the page.

© 2012 Arbitron Inc.

Questions? Call us toll-free at 1-800-638-7091. Visit our website: www.arbitronratings.com

FIGURE 3.5. Sample of Arbitron Diary
Reprinted by permission of Arbitron.

than the rigid quarter-hour increments of the television diary. Because a radio diary is a personal record, the diary keeper does not note whether other people were listening. The location of listening, however, is recorded. Keep in mind, though, that the diary as a method of data collection in radio is being replaced in more and more markets by the *portable peoplemeter* (PPM).

Diary placement and retrieval techniques vary, but the usual practice goes something like this. The ratings company calls members of the originally designated sample on the phone to secure the respondent's cooperation and collect some initial information. Those who are excluded (e.g., people living in group quarters) or those who will receive special treatment (e.g., those needing a diary in a special language) are identified at this stage. Follow-up letters may be sent to households that have agreed to cooperate. Diaries are, then, either mailed or delivered to the home in person by field personnel. Incidentally, although respondents are asked to cooperate, diaries can be distributed to those who say they are not interested in cooperating. Quite often, a modest monetary incentive is provided as a gesture of goodwill, but the incentive may change in markets with traditionally lower response rates. During the week, another letter or phone call may encourage the diary keeper to note his or her media use. Diaries are often designed to be sealed and placed directly in the mail, which is typically how the diary is returned to the ratings company at the end of the week. Occasionally, a second monetary reward follows the return of the diary. In some special cases, homes are called and the diary information is collected over the telephone.

Diaries have some significant advantages that account for their continued popularity. They are a relatively inexpensive method of data collection. Considering the wealth of information that a properly filled-out diary contains, few of the other techniques we discuss here are as cost-effective. Most importantly, they report which people were actually in the audience. In fact, until the introduction of peoplemeters in the 1980s, diaries had to be used in conjunction with more expensive metering techniques to determine the demographic composition of national television audiences. In some places, that meter/diary combination is still in use. And in many smaller markets, with less advertising money at stake, diary-only data collection may be the only method that makes economic sense.

Despite their popularity, there are a number of problems associated with the use of diaries—problems of both nonresponse and response error. We have already discussed nonresponse error in the context of sampling. It should be noted, however, that diaries are particularly troublesome in this regard. Response rates on the order of 20 percent are common, and in some markets the rate will drop below that. These might be improved with larger incentives or more elaborate recruitment, but that would drive up costs. Obviously, diary keepers must be literate, but methodological research undertaken by the industry suggests that those who fill out and return diaries are systematically different in other ways. Younger people, especially younger males, are less responsive to the diary technique. Some minorities, too, are less likely to complete and return a diary. There is also some evidence that those who return a television diary are heavier users of the medium than are nonrespondents.

There are a number of response errors typical of diary data as well. Filling out a diary properly is a good deal of work. There is a fair amount of anecdotal evidence that diary keepers frequently do not note their media use as it occurs but instead try to recollect it at the end of the day or the week. To the extent that entries are delayed, errors of memory are more likely. Similarly, it appears that diary keepers are more diligent in the first few days of diary keeping than the last. This *diary fatigue* may artificially depress viewing or listening levels at the end of the week. Children's use of television is also likely to go unreported if they watch at times when an adult diary keeper is not present. Using media late at night, using media for short durations (e.g., surfing channels with a remote), and using secondary sets (e.g., in bedrooms, etc.) are typically underreported. Conversely, people are more apt to overstate watching or listening to popular programs or stations.

These are significant, if fairly benign, sources of response error. There is less evidence on the extent to which people deliberately distort reports of their viewing or listening behavior. Most people seem to have a sense of what ratings data are and how they can affect programming decisions. Again, anecdotal evidence suggests that some people view their participation in a ratings sample as an opportunity to "vote" for deserving programs, whether they are actually in the audience or not. While diary data may be more susceptible to such distortions than data of other methods, instances of deliberate, systematic deception, although real, are probably limited in scope.

A more serious problem with diary-based measurement techniques has emerged in recent years. As we noted earlier, the television viewing environment has become increasingly complex. Homes that subscribe to cable or satellite services have hundreds of channels, and often a DVR or an STB with VOD is available. In addition, remote control devices are in virtually all households. These technological changes make the job of keeping an accurate diary more burdensome than ever. A viewer who has flipped through dozens of channels to find something of interest may not know or report the network he or she is watching. Compared with more accurate methods, diaries report longer periods of continuous viewing but detect fewer sources or channels being viewed. Hence, diary-based measurement is likely to favor larger, more-established outlets at the expense of smaller, less-popular cable outlets.

Meters. Meters have been used to measure audiences as long as any technique except telephone surveys. The first metering device was Nielsen's Audimeter, which went into service in 1942. Today they are several kinds of meters in use around the world, and they are generally preferred to other measure techniques when resources allow.

Modern *household meters* are essentially small computers that are attached to all of the television sets in a home. They perform a number of functions, the most important of which is monitoring set activity. The meter records when the set is on and the channel to which it is tuned. This information is typically stored in a separate unit that is hidden in some unobtrusive location. The data it contains can be retrieved through a telephone line and downloaded to a central computer.

For years, that was the scope of metering activity. And as such, it had enormous advantages over diary measurement. It eliminated much of the human error inherent in diary keeping. Viewing was recorded as it occurred. Even exposure of brief duration could be accurately recorded. Members of the sample did not have to be literate. In fact, they did not have to do anything at all, so no fatigue factor entered the picture. Because information was electronically recorded, it could also be collected and processed much more rapidly than paper-and-pencil diaries. Reports on yesterday's program audiences, called the *overnights,* could be delivered.

There were two major shortcomings to this sort of metering. First, it was expensive. It cost a lot to manufacture, install, and maintain the hardware necessary to make such a system work. Second, household meters could provide no information on who was watching, save for what could be inferred from general household characteristics. The fact that the television could be on with no one watching meant that household meters then overreport total television viewing. More importantly, they provided no "people information," with which to describe the composition of audience. This has caused most audience measurement companies to opt for peoplemeters whenever the revenues can justify the expense.

With that, you might imagine that the use of household meters was quickly becoming a thing of the past. But, as we noted in the section on sampling, digital STBs (including devices like TiVo) are now in a great many homes. If they are properly programmed, they can be turned into the functional equivalent of household meters. In principle, they can record when a set is turned on and the channel to which it is tuned. The good news, from a measurement perspective, is that it is possible to do this in millions of homes. The bad news is that, just like conventional household meters, STBs have a number of limitations. For example, they cannot measure who is watching, just that the set is in use. STBs also have no way to determine what content is on the screen, although scheduling information can be added to behavioral data after the fact. STBs also have a unique limitation, sometimes called the "TV-Off" problem. People frequently turn their television set off without turning off the STB, which falsely continues to report viewing. All of these problems can be addressed in one way or another, which we discuss in the section on production.

Peoplemeters are the only pieces of hardware that affirmatively measure exactly who within households is viewing the set. They were introduced in the United States and much of Europe in the 1980s and have since been adopted as the preferred method of television audience measurement in much of the world. These devices do everything that conventional household meters do, and more. Although the technology and protocols for its use may vary from one measurement company to another, peoplemeters essentially work like this. Every member of the sample household is assigned a number that corresponds to a push button on the metering device. When a person begins viewing, he or she is supposed to press a preassigned button on the meter. The button is again pressed when the person leaves the room. When the channel is changed, a light on the meter might flash until viewers reaffirm their presence. Most systems have hand-held units, about the size of a remote control device, that allow people to button push from some remote location in the room.

These days, television sets are often display devices for a variety of media. They show regular linear programming, on-demand video, DVDs, video games, and, increasingly, content from the Internet. State-of-the-art meters often identify that content directly, rather than relying on scheduling information. For example, Nielsen uses an active/passive, or "A/P," meter. Electronic media frequently carry an identifying signature, or "watermark." Often, this is an unobtrusive piece of code embedded in the audio or video signal. If it has that identifying piece of code, the A/P meter will passively detect it. If the material is uncoded, the meter will actively record a small piece of the signal and try to identify it against a digital library. Modern peoplemeters report that information, along with a minute-by-minute record of what each member of the household (and visitors) watched, over telephone or wireless connections.

Peoplemeters have also been designed to go beyond these "basic" functions. Figure 3.6 shows a peoplemeter developed by GfK Telecontrol, a Swiss company with peoplemeters in many countries around the world. This particular model has a remote control and a display unit. The remote features the usual buttons for people to signal their presence in front of the set, but it has another set of buttons on the right. These allow respondents to rate what they are seeing in response to a prompt or question on the display unit. Of course, these functions might make the peoplemeter even more obtrusive than it ordinarily would be. But it does demonstrate how the technology could be used to measure something other than exposure.

Peoplemeters can suffer from response error. Most notably, the meters are believed to underrepresent the viewing of children. Youngsters, it turns out, are not terribly conscientious button pushers. But even adults sometimes fail to push buttons. A ratings company can, for example, see instances when a set is in use and no one has indicated they are watching. Depending on the edit rules of the company, that household might need to be temporarily eliminated from the sample. If that happens, the home is said to *fault out*, which effectively reduces the size of the in-tab sample. Generally, these problems can be corrected with a little coaching. Still, button-pushing fatigue can be a problem. Nielsen

FIGURE 3.6. Telecontrol Peoplemeter

used to keep household meters in homes for 5 years. Because of the extra effort required by peoplemeters, Nielsen turns these households over every 2 years.

For a long time, the "Holy Grail" of television measurement has been what is called a *passive peoplemeter*. Such a device would require no effort on the part of sample participants. The meter would be unobtrusive but somehow know which people were in the audience. In the late 1980s, Nielsen began work on a passive peoplemeter. It used a "facial image recognition" system to identify family members. The system worked, but it was never deployed, perhaps because it was too intrusive for many people's tastes. However, some of the newest television sets now have a front-facing camera, just like many computer screens. They are intended to recognize viewers so they can offer appropriate programming. But, some industry observers claim the image recognition technology could be used to see who is actually watching a program or an ad and, by reading expressions, determine how they reacted. So, passive peoplemeters might once again be on the horizon.

So far, all of the meters we have described—passive or not—are tied to particular sets in particular locations. As such, they cannot see what users are doing in other locations or on other platforms. To address that problem, measurement companies have developed *PPMs* that overcome some of the limitations of household-bound meters. Arbitron has the most widely deployed PPM system, which it uses to produce radio ratings in the 50 largest U.S. cities. Arbitron's PPM is also licensed for use in several countries around the world.

PPMs are small devices that a sample of willing participants wear or carry with them throughout the day. Arbitron's PPM looks like a pager. Another device by Telecontrol looks like a wristwatch. The PPM "listens" for the audio portion of a television or radio program, trying to pick up an inaudible code that identifies the broadcast. If it detects the code, the participant is assumed to be in the audience. At night, the PPM is put in a docking station, where it is recharged and its record of media exposure is retrieved electronically. Figure 3.7 shows the Arbitron "PPM 360," a name that connotes comprehensiveness in measuring audiences for all available platforms.

PPMs have also been adapted in an effort to measure exposure to print media. One strategy is to embed RFID chips in print media that the meter can detect. Another is design the meter in such a way that respondents can simply report what they have read. Figure 3.8 shows the Telecontrol Mediawatch with a screen for entering such information.

Much of the functionality we associate with PPMs need not be built into dedicated devices. In principle, smartphones can be programmed to do most of the same things. They can be "instructed" to listen for those inaudible codes and report what they hear. They can ping users at various times to ask questions about media use. And users typically carry their smartphones around all the time. Some companies have tried to harness these tempting possibilities to turn them into PPMs, but the practical problems are considerable. First, smartphone users might not want you tampering with their device. Second, you could not measure those without smartphones unless you gave them a device, which might alter their behavior and drive up expenses. Third, smartphones use many different operating systems, so developing and updating programs for all those devices would be quiet a chore. Nonetheless, smartphones remain a resource that might be tapped in the future.

With the growth of the Internet as an advertising medium, it has become important to track who is visiting which sites and seeing which pages. What we call *computer meters* are a way for organizations like comScore and Nielsen

FIGURE 3.7. Arbitron's PPM 360

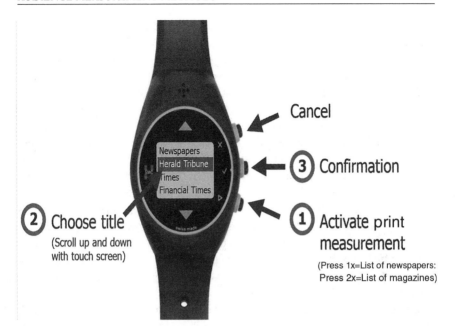

FIGURE 3.8. Telecontrol's Mediawatch

to monitor online computer use. This is still a user-centric approach to measurement. Respondents agree to load software on their own machines that will record Web and other Internet activity. These data are sent back to a central location for processing. Because this method of data collection is relatively inexpensive, it allows companies to create very large samples. That's a good thing, because no medium offers more possibilities for audience fragmentation than the Internet. Between the big samples and the click-by-click granularity of the information being collected, these systems generate an enormous amount of information, which is condensed into a variety of reports for subscribers.

One disadvantage of this method is that users might be reluctant to allow software to run on their computers. Privacy is a significant concern when every action is monitored with such precision. It is very likely that people who would allow this technology on their computer will differ from people who do not want it installed. And even if they do not differ in terms of demographic profile, the presence of this monitoring technology might influence their choices when they use the Internet. Another problem is that a great deal of Internet use occurs in the workplace. If employers are reluctant to allow this software to run on their equipment, then truly random samples of workplace or university users are compromised.

Nonetheless, with the Internet serving as the platform for more and more media services, like YouTube or Hulu, measurement companies have been hard pressed to figure out how to capture information on Internet use and tie it to other forms of media consumption, especially television. Toward that end, Nielsen has introduced installed computer monitoring software in the households of people in the national U.S. peoplemeter panel. By doing so, they can track individuals as they move back and forth between those platforms. That kind of measurement makes possible the "extended screen" ratings we mentioned earlier.

Servers. Servers are a relatively new tool with which to measure audiences. Servers power the Internet and other broadband distribution systems, offering new ways to see and quantify audiences. Some servers offer content or services directly to users. These include web "publishers" like YouTube or NYTimes. com, as well as most cable and satellite systems that serve digital content to subscribing households. We have seen, for example, how STBs are used to describe the size and composition of television audiences. Some servers manage people's access to the Internet, allowing a company like Hitwise to aggregate all the traffic reported by Internet service providers to estimate how many people visit different websites. Still other servers, operated by ad networks, deliver advertising to other websites and are able to count the number of clicks or impressions to provide a kind of commercial rating.

Server-centric data need not be confined to describing audience behavior. Analyses can also focus on how users navigate within a particular website. In fact, there is an entire field of study called *web analytics* devoted to this subject. Among other things, these researchers are in a position to mount unobtrusive experiments, referred to as *A/B testing*, that can manipulate site content to see how users react to different offers, recommendations, and page layouts (Christian, 2012). Google, for example, is constantly experimenting with how to deliver search results in an effort to refine its search algorithm. Still other server-centric analyses are attempts to target just the right message to just the right people at just the right time. This happens on large websites like Facebook, Amazon, or Google, which keep track of user information and activities, and so provide marketers with powerful tools to sell goods and services. Any one of these uses of server-centric data could be, and often is, the subject of a book-length treatment. But to conclude our discussion of measurement techniques, we make a few generalizations.

Servers collect enormous amounts of data. This is the product of tracking millions of users as they click their way through websites, sometimes offering up additional information as they go. Servers record all of these actions with ease, at virtually no cost to the operator and in a way that probably goes unnoticed by most users. One result is a phenomenon that is sometimes called "big data." As one study reported:

> In July 2011, Facebook's 750 million worldwide users uploaded approximately 100 terabytes of data every day to the social media platform. Extrapolated against a full year, that's enough data to manage the U.S. Library of Congress' entire print collection—*3,600 times over.* (Winterberry, 2011, p. 3, emphasis in original)

To some it seems like a treasure trove of information just waiting to be mined. But before you can really make sense of it, you have to be clear about the answers to two familiar questions: Who is it you are studying? What are exactly are you measuring?

Every time a server receives a request for a file (e.g., a web page), it is called a *hit*. In the 1990s, that was one of the principal metrics used to describe site use. Unfortunately, it is difficult to interpret. One hundred hits could mean an audience of 100 people, or just one person who had made 100 requests. It was hard to know who was a return visitor. In 1994, Netscape addressed that problem by using a *cookie*, which was a small text file that the server placed on each visitor's browser. With cookies, servers could not only recognize return visitors, but they could also see what they did on their last visit. That information gave researchers a better idea of who they were studying. However, using cookies to track users has several limitations; we discuss these in chapter 6. But cookies are an important tool for tracking web use. And they are not the only way researchers learn about the identity of users.

Servers will typically note the IP address of the visitor, which can sometimes reveal their location. People using apps on their mobile phones are often leaving a rather precise record of their locations throughout the day. Researchers will often begin to make inferences about the visitor based on their actions. What do they look at? Is it characteristic of someone young or old, rich or poor? Google has been described as collecting a "database of intentions" (Batelle, 2005, p. 1). Searches may indicate a person's interests or intentions to buy. That says a lot about visitors and is one reason why "paid search" has been so lucrative for Google. There are also ways to entice users to divulge personal information in exchange for free services or special privileges. Social media sites often know an enormous about their users. The key to Facebook's value is its data on users. As the *New York Times* noted:

> Every time a person shares a link, listens to a song, clicks on one of Facebook's ubiquitous "like" buttons, or changes a relationship status to "engaged," a morsel of data is added to Facebook's vast library. It is a siren to advertisers hoping to leverage that information to match their ads with the right audience. (Sengupta & Rusli, 2012)

Server operators might also share or buy data from other sources, to construct more complete dossiers on users, although these practices can run afoul of privacy policies—a topic we address later. In any event, even though users may think of their web use as anonymous, their identities may be more apparent than they realize, giving researchers a pretty good idea of whom they are studying.

The second question to answer is exactly what is being measured. For the most part, servers record behaviors. These include site visits, page views, time spent viewing, click-throughs, downloading, linking, buying, voting, "retweeting"—the list goes on and on. Many of these behaviors can be construed as exposure, in the same less-than-perfect way that tuning in is construed as exposure with more traditional electronic media (see MRC, 2007). So much of what we know about people's exposure to the Internet comes from harnessing these measures. It might also be possible to infer something beyond mere exposure. A look at behaviors over time might reveal people's loyalties and levels of engagement. Measures of time spent viewing or repeat viewing have been interpreted as indications of liking, involvement, or stickiness. Rentrak, for instance, uses STB data to construct a "stickiness index" for programs, which is the average percentage of a program viewed divided by the average for all programs of similar duration.

Using behaviors to reveal preferences is a common practice in the social sciences, especially economics. However, it is not without its problems. For example, maybe you do not like everything you buy. You might purchase a book on Amazon only to decide it is awful. But Amazon only has a record of you buying a book, which it takes as indicative of liking and then causes it to recommend it to other people "like you." Unfortunately, for researchers, behaviors are not always simple reflections of preferences.

Servers also capture more "qualitative" declarations from users. Voting for or against something, often in the form of a "like" button, is arguably measuring some sort of affect. Social media sites like Twitter or Facebook are often full of text-based commentaries that tell others what the writer thinks. A number of companies now harvest these data and quantify them to provide some indication of social buzz. Some are able to automatically scan the text to measure the incidence of positive or negative comments. These kinds of analyses have the potential to offer new insights into engagement. But once again, some caution is merited. For example, is the volume of tweets about some topic the result of a few fanatics or a broadly based phenomenon? Researchers are still trying to figure out what exactly is being measured and reach some consensus on how the data are best used (Proulx & Shepatin, 2012).

Beyond these questions of interpretation, servers have other limitations. Quite often, the server has no way of seeing what users are doing on other platforms. Cookies might reveal something about movement from one server to another, but they will not tell you what television, radio, and print media are consumed—at least until everything migrates to the Internet. Therefore, server-centric measurement can often create a "siloed" kind of information. It is easier to design user-centric approaches to capture anytime/anywhere media use. Servers also raise thorny legal, ethical, and business issues about privacy. Typically, people do not affirmatively "opt-in" to measurement. Yet vast amounts of information can be collected and used without their knowledge. Many companies offer privacy policies that provide users some protections, but the ultimate question is who should own and control that data. The answer varies by country. At this writing, the United States has begun using "do-not-track" buttons that can be enabled in a user's browser (Angwin, 2012). European nations have been the most protective of user privacy. In fact, some have advocated for a "right to be forgotten," which would oblige companies to purge the data of such a person. As servers become ever more central to modern life, these issues of privacy are likely to be a continuing source of consternation for all involved.

The principal methods of audience measurement in the electronic media are summarized in Table 3.1. Obviously, the chart does not exhaust the possibilities for data collection. New techniques, or refinements of old ones, are being introduced and tested all the time.

PRODUCTION

The issues that arise in sampling and measurement are well known to survey researchers. We have, in these areas, some well-established criteria with which to judge the quality of the ratings data. But sampling and measurement alone do not make audience estimates. The data that are collected must undergo a production process, just as any other raw material is turned into a product. Here, standards of what is or is not appropriate may be harder to come by. Yet, no discussion of audience research methods would be complete without mention of the production process. Every research company processes data a little differently, but generally production involves three activities. First, companies must edit the data, cleaning up errors and putting it into a form that can be analyzed. Second, they often adjust the data to correct for known defects. Third, they supplement the data by combining it with other sources of information.

Editing Data

Audience measurement companies are continually flooded with data that must be summarized and turned into a useful product. Servers and metered panels can generate information by the terabyte, but it inevitably contains glitches that need to be identified and reconciled. The process of getting clean, accurate, complete data ready to be processed is called *editing*. It can be a laborious activity, and, despite efforts at quality control, editing is one place where *production error* can occur.

Diaries are one of the messier sources of data. Hundreds of thousands of hand-written diaries arrive at audience measurement companies each year. They must be checked for accuracy, logical inconsistencies, and omissions.

TABLE 3.1
Summary of the Major Methods of Audience Measurement

	Advantages	*Disadvantages*
Telephone recall	Relatively fast turnaround Relatively inexpensive Personal contact with respondent No literacy requirement	Memory problems Deliberate misrepresentation Limited times when researcher can call the home Biased sample—some homes do not have phones
Telephone coincidental	Relatively fast turnaround Personal contact with respondent No literacy requirement No memory problems	Limited times when researcher can call the home Biased sample—some homes do not have phones Costly, labor-intensive method of data collection
Diaries	Relatively inexpensive Potential to collect very detailed information including demographics Can be carried to measure out-of-home media use Completed at respondents' convenience	Time lag to collect and process the data Memory problems Bias in favor of popular, memorable programs Deliberate misrepresentation Literacy requirement Error prone in complex media environments Lower response rates
Household meters (traditional and STB)	Fast turnaround Accuracy—records actual set tuning activity No literacy requirement Does not require any effort on the part of respondent Continuous measurement allows for analysis of very short time periods The same households can be studied for several years With STBs potentially very large samples	Cost—expensive to make, install, and maintain systems Household-level data offer limited demographic information Reconciliation with other sources of data a possible source of error With STBs, compensating for "TV-off" phenomenon

TABLE 3.1 *Continued*

	Advantages	Disadvantages
Peoplemeters	Fast turnaround Accuracy—records actual exposure to content with electronic codes No literacy requirement Continuous measurement allows for analysis of very short time periods Demographic data available	Cost—expensive to make, install, and maintain Requires active participation on the part of respondents Button pushing, especially by children, may be unreliable Sample must be turned over more rapidly than with household meters Can require cooperation of media to embed identifying codes
Portable Peoplemeters	Fast turnaround Accuracy—records actual exposure to content with electronic codes Can record use of multiple media No literacy requirement Requires relatively little effort on part of respondent Captures out-of-home media use Demographic data available	Cost—expensive to make High sample turnover compared to household-bound meters Respondents fail to carry or wear meter Can require cooperation of media to embed identifying codes
Computer Meters	Fast turnaround Relatively inexpensive since it uses respondent's computers Provides continuous, accurate record of Internet (or Web) activity Demographic data available Very large samples are possible	Awareness of metering may alter respondents' behavior Monitoring computers in businesses can be problematic
Servers	Fast turnaround Accurate measurement of user actions Unobtrusive Ease of data collection Census-level numbers of respondents	Information on respondent traits can be limited Limited ability to see behavior beyond server or network Potential legal or ethical problems with privacy

Diary editing involves a number of activities. First, diaries must be evaluated for inclusion in the tabulations. They are excluded if respondents filled them out during the wrong week, mailed them back too late, or submitted excessively incomplete or inconsistent information. Measurement companies often capture a digital image of all the pages in a diary and then keystroke the information into a machine-readable form. Computers can then screen the data for logical inconsistencies like reports of nonexistent stations or programs on the wrong channel. Strict editing procedures usually prescribe a way to resolve these discrepancies.

Metered data can also suffer from errors or omissions. These are sometimes referred to as *faults* in the data and they can be of two sorts. First, there may be a hardware failure. In some parts of the world, power outages or surges make meters especially prone to faulting. In late October 2012, Hurricane Sandy caused prolonged power outages on the eastern seaboard of the United States. The disruption was so severe that Nielsen decided not to produce any November ratings for New York. Because this DMA is so large, these power outages also affected national ratings.

The second source of faulting occurs when respondents fail to do their part. For example, a peoplemeter might record that a set was in use with no one entering a corresponding button push. In either event, editing rules may cause the offending household to fault out, at least until the problem can be corrected. Fault rates compound the problem of nonresponse and have the effect of further lowering the in-tab sample. Ratings companies sometimes measure the combined effect of nonresponse and faulting with a statistic called a *sample performance indicator* (SPI). The lower the SPI, the more concern you should have that the sample does not represent the population.

While measurement companies try to automate as much of the data collection process as possible, people are still involved in the process of entering and judging data. Diaries must be deciphered and typed into computerized records. Even digital media record keeping and data management involve a surprising amount of manual labor. With that comes the possibility of error. As one expert on digital media noted:

> First, every time a human touches a piece of data, the chances of human error go up. Second, manual labor is slower than machine labor—which means there are orders of magnitude *fewer* computations that can happen when you don't have machines doing the grunt work. Combine those two points, and you get media management that's less data-rich, and more accident-prone, than is good for gathering good metrics. (Wise, 2011)

Editing also can involve more subjective questions of definition. As data-gathering techniques capture ever-more-granular behaviors, different definitions of something as basic as program viewing or website usage become possible. We alluded to these in the section on what's being measured. For example, should a person who watches a channel for 1 minute be included in the audience? Should a person who looks at a website for 5 seconds be considered a visitor? Similarly, should a program audience include people who see replays across other non-linear platforms? If so, must that viewing occur within a certain period of time? Sometimes ratings services provide relatively unedited data streams to customers and let them decide. But to produce industry-wide estimates, which might function as currency, someone has to decide what constitutes exposure. Typically there are no clear right or wrong answers, only what the affected industries accept as the agreed-on definition.

Adjusting Data

Audience data can contain known defects or biases. These could include missing values or in-tab samples that deviate from the composition of the population they are supposed to represent. Measurement companies often apply mathematical adjustments in an effort to address these potential problems. Here, too, we can encounter production error. Usually, these are not mistakes like misreading a diary, although data-processing errors sometimes occur. Rather, these adjustments are used to remedy problems and make estimates more accurate. But they are essentially educated guesses, and to the extent that they produce results that deviate from reality, they are technically introducing error.

Suppose, for example, that someone sent in a diary that was almost complete but was missing one or two variables. Rather than throw out an otherwise usable diary, research companies often "fill in the blanks" through a process called *ascription*. These procedures typically use computer routines to determine an answer with the highest probability of being correct. If, for example, Nielsen receives a diary reporting a 31-year-old male head of household with no age recorded for female head of household, an algorithm might "guess" that her age would be 3 years less than her husband's (i.e., 28).

Ascription techniques are also used to reconcile household meters with diary data. In many markets, television use is still measured by household meters that do not collect people information. Under these circumstances, meters, which provide a more accurate measure of tuning behavior, tell us what is being viewed. Diaries are used to tell us who is viewing. The problem is, meters typically identify more sources being viewed and for shorter periods of time. That means you have instances where meters indicate viewing but there's no corresponding record in the diaries, a phenomenon called the "zero-cell" problem. Ascription techniques can be used to fill as many of those blank cells as possible. While these practices may seem suspect, ascription is a standard procedure in virtually all survey work and is typically based on systematic methodological research. But once again, it is an educated guess.

Ultimately, the research services must publish estimates of audience size and composition. They usually project these estimates from samples. Although the process is complex, we can illustrate the basic logic with a simple example of diary measurement. Suppose we choose a sample of 1,000 individuals from a population of one million. Each respondent would represent 1,000 people. If 50 people in our sample watch a news program, we could project the show's actual audience to be 50,000. That is essentially what the ratings services do. They determine the number of people represented by one in-tab diary and assign that diary an appropriate number. If people are the unit of analysis, the number is called *persons per diary value (PPDV)*. If households are the unit of analysis, the number is labeled *households per diary value (HPDV)*.

This illustration works quite well if we have perfect probability samples, in which all members of the population are proportionately represented. But as we have seen, that is never the case. Nonresponse can mean that some kinds of people are overrepresented, while others are underrepresented. Remember, also, that the most common remedy for this problem is to weight the responses of some sample members more heavily than others. Suppose, in the illustration above, that 18- to 24-year-old men were underrepresented in the in-tab sample. Let's say they constitute 4 percent of the sample but are known to be 8 percent of the population. Men in this group would receive a weight of 2.0 (i.e., 8 percent/4 percent = 2.0). Therefore, to project total audience size for this group, each young man should have a PPDV of 2,000 (i.e., 1,000 × 2.0), instead of 1,000. Conversely, overrepresented groups should have PPDVs of less than 1,000.

In practice, the weights that are assigned to different groups are rarely as extreme as in our illustration (i.e., they come closer to 1.0). Further, ratings services weight a single respondent on a number of variables besides age and gender to make a final determination. Although adjusting the data with mathematical weights can introduce error, it is very commonly done to make samples better conform to the known parameters of the population being described. But it is not uncontroversial. In 2010, Nielsen believed its peoplemeter sample overrepresented households with computers and broadband access. It wanted to give them less weight in audience estimates, but some networks feared that this change might favor some programs over others. As one client noted, "Even fractional declines in ratings can become costly over time" (Mandese, 2010).

Supplementing Data

Despite the enormous amounts of data collected by diaries, meters, and servers, such information alone might not be sufficient to produce audience estimates.

Other information is often added to these data to make a complete, research product. Historically, ratings companies have had to add information on program scheduling to their data. More recently, with the growth of server-centric measurement, researchers have used a variety of techniques to impute user characteristics that are not directly measured. And with the growing need for cross-platform data, measurement companies are combining different data sets in a process called *data fusion*.

Until relatively recently, most metered measurement systems had no way of knowing what exactly was being displayed on a television set. That is still true of at least some meters and most STB-based measurement. To attribute tuning behavior to a particular program, measurement companies have added program scheduling information collected in some other way. As more and more sources of both linear and nonlinear programming have become available, this approach has become increasingly burdensome and error prone. Moreover, in systems that produce commercial ratings like C3s, one needs to know the exact instant when a commercial appears. Fortunately, state-of-the-art meters now identify program content using embedded electronic codes or other means of detection. Even so, supplemental information about when programs and commercials air is still used to produce audience estimates.

While some sources of server-centric information, like Facebook, have a lot of information about individual user traits, most do not. These user characteristics can make an important difference in the value of a research product. Therefore, companies that do not directly measure user traits will often use techniques to estimate what those traits might be. We have noted STBs do not measure who is viewing. But STB systems can estimate the composition of the audience in other ways. For example, outside data suppliers know a lot about the characteristics of the homes in particular zip codes (size, income, owners' occupations, etc.). By combining that information with the home zip code of each STB household, it is possible to make an estimate of audience composition. Similarly, companies that record and summarize the buzz on social media like Twitter will sometimes estimate the characteristics of those making comments. For example, a Cambridge, Massachusetts–based company called Bluefin Labs uses each person's first name and tweet history to infer their gender. So, if someone named Henry refers to himself as a "dad," chances are good he is a male. Of course, not every case is so clear-cut. Systems that impute user traits with an algorithm can be pretty accurate, but they can also introduce error into the production process.

We have noted that, increasingly, people are consuming media across a variety of platforms. Most advertisers and media companies would like to be able to track the same users across television, radio, print, mobile devices, and the Internet. But true *single source* systems that accurately measure all forms of media use, product purchases, and other desirable users characteristics are expensive and uncommon. Most media measurement is still specific to a particular medium. To overcome that limitation in a cost-effective manner, research companies sometimes use a technique called *data fusion*. It has been widely used in Europe since the late 1980s and is now common in the United States as well. Basically, it is a way to integrate two or more separate sets of data with "linking variables" that are common to different respondents in each database. For example, Nielsen's peoplemeter panel has been fused with both its online Internet measurement sample and MRI's survey of print use and product purchase data. Successful data fusion depends on finding the right linking variables, which are often some combination of demographic and media use variables. It is a statistically complex process that results in something that looks like a single source set of data. But even its proponents recognize it is not the ideal. As Nielsen's primer on data fusion concludes, "No human endeavor is perfect and all research contains the potential for error and bias. Data fusion works within the realm of the possible, not the unattainable" (Nielsen, 2009, p. 8).

The same might be said of all the research methods we have reviewed in this chapter. Nothing is perfect, although some techniques clearly have advantages over others. If you can recognize good research practices, you will be better able to judge the quality of the information you have and how best to use it.

RELATED READINGS

Babbie, E. (2009). *The practice of social research* (12th ed.). Belmont, CA: Wadsworth.

Beville, H. M. (1988). *Audience ratings: Radio, television, cable* (rev. ed.). Hillsdale, NJ: Lawrence Erlbaum Associates.

Gunter, B. (2000). *Media research methods: Measuring audiences, reactions and impact.* London: Sage.

Iachobucci, D., & Churchill, G. A. (2009). *Marketing research: Methodological foundations* (10th ed.). Belmont, CA: South-Western College Pub.

Kaushik, A. (2010). *Web analytics 2.0: The art on online accountability & science of customer centricity.* Indianapolis, IN: Wiley.

Sissors, J. Z., & Baron, R. B. (2010). *Advertising media planning* (7th ed.). New York: McGraw Hill.

Russell, M. A. (2011). *Mining the social web: Analyzing data from Facebook, Twitter, LinkedIn, and other social media sites.* Sebastapol, CA: O'Reilly.

Turow, J. (2011). *The daily you: How the new advertising industry is defining your identity and your worth.* New Haven, CT: Yale University Press.

Wimmer, R., & Dominick, J. (2010). *Mass media research: An introduction* (9th ed.). Belmont, CA: Wadsworth.

Part II

Audience Analytics

CHAPTER 4

Understanding Audience Behavior

Audience measurement comes in many different forms and has a wide variety of applications. The wealth of data can be a bit overwhelming. How does one harness all that information to answer questions about the audience? For example, what factors influence media choices? Why are some things popular and others are not? What variables trigger audience loyalties? What are unusual or important features of media use and what are routine? In this chapter, we offer a framework for addressing such questions. Our emphasis is on generalizable concepts and theories. Our goal is to help readers understand the forces that shape and predict audience behavior. The best forms of audience analytics are grounded in that understanding.

The chapter is divided into four sections. First, we take a closer look at just what an analyst is typically trying to assess—exposure to media. We categorize and discuss the principal measurements of audience behavior. Second, we review the most common theories for explaining people's media choices. These rely heavily on people's preferences to explain what the audience is doing. Third, we introduce a number of other factors that are critical in understanding audience formation. Finally, we present a model of audience behavior that reflects all of these considerations and offers a more complete way to understand exposure to media. This is the key to interpreting audience information.

EXPOSURE TO MEDIA

It is best to begin this exercise by reminding ourselves of the central focus of audience measurement. The information collected by research firms may be vast in size and reported in a great many ways, but conceptually it is rather straightforward. At their core, most databases are simply a record of people's exposure to media. A record that is typically inferred from people's media choices (e.g., channel or program selections, page requests, etc.). As we noted in chapter 3, meters and servers collect a continuous stream of such behaviors but often not much else. The data do not say much about the effects of exposure. They usually do not explain people's motivations or levels of engagement, although social media are beginning to fill that void. An analyst, then, typically has a mountain of data on individual patterns of media consumption through time, accompanied by a modest amount of information about the traits of each individual (e.g., age, gender, etc.).

An experienced analyst also knows that whatever the source of data, it is going to contain some errors. But even experienced researchers, who are aware of error in the data, tend to take the numbers at face value in their day-to-day work. For the most part, that is our approach. When substantial methodological problems or biases suggest a qualified interpretation of the data, it is noted, but otherwise we treat the audience ratings as valid measures of exposure.

We have already encountered several ways to summarize media audience behavior. Some of these are routinely reported by the ratings services, others are routinely calculated by ratings users. The most basic of all audience metrics is a rating. That term is bandied about in the industry and serves as a kind of shorthand for many forms of audience data. Technically, a rating is a percentage of the population watching a channel or listening to a station. Two other measures, shares and "HUTs" (households using television), often accompany ratings. Figure 4.1 provides an illustration of how those metrics are calculated. In this imaginary world of 10 television households, 2 are watching channel A and 3 are watching channel B. So those channels have ratings of 20 and 30, respectively. But not all homes are watching television at any point in time. The number of homes with sets in use is expressed in the HUT level. In our example, it is 50 percent, or just 50. A share is a percentage based only on those who are actually watching. In our example, A has a 40 share and B has a 60 share. Because HUT levels are always less than 100 percent of the population, a channel's share is always larger than its ratings. In practice, there are all kinds of ratings, which describe different populations (male or female, young or old) or different media objects (programs, commercials, websites, etc.). We will describe these in detail in the following chapters.

It is useful, at this point, to draw a rather broad distinction between two basic types of audience metrics. We call one type *gross measures* and the other *cumulative measures*. The distinction has to do with whether they track the behavior of specific individuals over time. If an audience metric does not depend on tracking, it is a gross measure. If it does, it is cumulative. This temporal quality in the data defines a fundamental distinction that is carried through the rest of the book.

Gross Measures of the Audience

Gross measures of exposure include estimates of audience size and composition made at a single point in time. Examples include the ratings and shares we just described. Other gross measures include served impressions, views on YouTube,

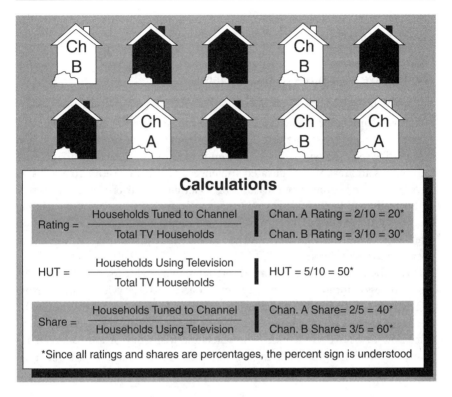

FIGURE 4.1. Simple Rating and Share Calculations

and movie ticket sales. In none of these instances do we have any clear sense of the number of "repeat customers" involved. In effect, these are snapshots of the population that indicate the popularity of a media product or outlet.

Electronic media can take these snapshots with great rapidity. Ratings services estimate how many people listen to a station in an average quarter hour or watch a program in an average minute. Projections of total audience size and estimates of the number of HUTs and persons using television (PUTs) belong in this category as well. Gross measures of exposure can also include secondary calculations derived from other gross measurements. Gross rating points (GRPs) are such calculations. GRPs are just a summation of individual ratings over a schedule. Simple cost calculations, like cost per ratings point (CPP) and cost per thousand (CPM), can, similarly, be thought of as gross measures. These measures are discussed thoroughly in chapter 5.

Gross measures are the most common summaries of audience, and most of the numbers reported in syndicated research reports are of this type. As a result, they are the best known and most widely used of audience measurements. Useful as they are, however, they fail to capture information about how individual audience members behave over time. That kind of behavior is expressed in cumulative measures.

Cumulative Measures of the Audience

The most familiar example of the second group of audience measurements is a station's cumulative audience, or *cume*. To report a weekly cume audience, a ratings company must sort through each person's media use for a week, and summarize the number that used the station at least once. Analogous audience summaries are: reach, unduplicated audience, and unique visitors to a website. A closely related cumulative measure that is familiar to advertisers is frequency, or how often an individual sees a particular advertising message over some period of time. Studies of program audience duplication, likewise, depend on tracking individual media users over time. You will read more about cumulative measurements in chapter 6.

With the exception of the cume ratings and unique visitors, cumulative measures are less commonly reported by syndicated research services than are gross measurements. Customized studies of audience duplication, however, may be useful in a variety of applications. For example, programmers studying audience flow or advertisers tracking the reach and frequency of a media plan are concerned with how the audience is behaving over time. Table 4.1 lists the most common gross and cumulative measures of media exposure.

Comparing Gross and Cumulative Measurements

To get a clearer picture of the difference between gross and cumulative measures, and to begin to appreciate the analytical possibilities offered by such data, consider Figure 4.2. Just like Figure 4.1, it uses households as the unit of analysis and television channels as the media object of interest. But conceptually, this is also how you might think of people visiting websites or seeing commercials

TABLE 4.1
Common Measures of Exposure to Media

Gross Measures	Cumulative Measures
Average ratings	Cume ratings
Market shares	Reach
Impressions	Unique visitors
Views	Frequency
Total sales	Audience duplication

at different points in time. The large box in the upper left-hand corner of the figure represents a simplified ratings database. The data are from a hypothetical sample of 10 households. These are numbered 1 through 10, down the left-hand column. The media use of each household is measured at 10 points in time, running from Time 1 to Time 10 across the top of the figure. Both types of measures can be generated for such a database.

In practice, of course, a ratings sample would be much larger, including hundreds or thousands of units of analysis. There also would be many more points in time. For example, a standard television diary divides each of 7 days into 80 quarter hours. That means that each person is measured across 560 (i.e., 7 × 80) points in time, rather than the 10 we have illustrated. Now try to imagine how many points in time we could identify in peoplemeter data that track viewing moment to moment over a period of years!

In Figure 4.2, we have assumed a three-station market, which means that each household can be doing one of four things at each point in time. It can be tuned to Channel A, Channel B, Channel C, or nothing at all. These behaviors are indicated by the appropriate letters, or a blackened box, respectively.

The most commonly reported gross measures of exposure are shown in the box directly under the database. Each column of data is like Figure 4.1, and is treated in the same way. Hence, Channel A has a rating of 20 and a share of 40 at Time 4. All one needs to do is look down the appropriate column. Unlike the calculation of a cume, whatever happened before or after that time period is irrelevant to the calculation of a rating.

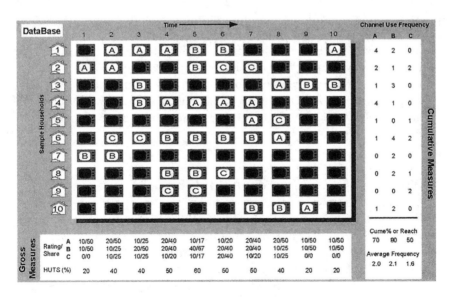

FIGURE 4.2. Gross Versus Cumulative Measures in Rating Data

The box on the right-hand side of the figure includes common cumulative measures. To calculate these, we must first examine each household's viewing behavior across time. That means moving across each row in the database. The first household, for example, watched Channel A four times and Channel B two times but never watched Channel C. Moving down each channel's column of cumulative viewing, we can then determine its reach, or cume. Each channel's cumulative audience is expressed as a percentage of the total sample that viewed it at least once over the 10 points in time. Therefore, the first household would be included in the cume of A and B but not C. Further, among those who did view a channel, if we compute the arithmetic average of the numbers in the column, we can report the mean frequency of viewing. This is essentially what an advertiser does when calculating reach and frequency, with the relevant points in time being determined by when a commercial message runs.

Studies of program audience duplication can also be executed from this database. For example, we might be interested in how well Station A retains an audience from one show to the next. We could determine that by seeing how many people who watched Station A at one point in time continued to watch the program that aired after it. For that matter, we could compare any pair of program audiences to assess repeat viewing, audience loyalty, and so on. In each case, however, we would have to track individual households across at least two points in time. Hence, we would be doing a cumulative analysis of exposure.

Depending on the kind of question they want to answer, ratings analysts would interpret gross measures, cumulative measures, or numbers that are derived from these two ways of defining exposure. As you will see, there are a large number of analytical techniques that can be organized in this way. In fact, these techniques are likely to maintain their usefulness even as the new technologies develop. Whether audiences are reached through the Internet, DBS, or traditional over-the-air broadcasting, the concepts of gross and cumulative measurements convey important information to programmers and advertisers. To exploit those analytical techniques to their fullest, however, we must develop a better understanding of the factors that shape audiences from moment to moment.

COMMON THEORIES OF MEDIA CHOICE

A question often asked by audience analysts is, "Why do people choose specific media content?" The answer most often given is, "They choose what they like." This kind of reasoning is typical of industry practice, communications policy, and most academic theories of choice. It suggests that people's preferences explain their choices, and hence audience behavior. This section reviews four of the most popular theories of media choice: the working theories used by industry practitioners; economic models of program choice; selective exposure theory; and uses and gratifications research. All rely very heavily, if not exclusively, on the idea of preferences. They provide a background against which our own framework can be better understood.

Working Theories of Program Choice

Working theories are the principles and assumptions used by media professionals in the conduct of their jobs. These "rules of thumb" may or may not have been subjected to systematic investigation. They may or may not correspond to the more academic theories of choice we review in the following sections. But they certainly deserve our attention. Programmers and media planners base these working theories on a day-to-day familiarity with the audience and how it responds to the media environment.

The people who craft media content are quite attentive to overall trends in popular culture as they try to anticipate what the audience will do next. Often, interest centers around the types of content people will like. We are all familiar with program "types." In television, we talk about cop shows, situation comedies, news, sports, and reality programs. In radio, we describe formats as contemporary hits, country, rap, news/talk, or music of a certain decade. These are familiar industry categories, but we can actually define program types in any number of ways. For example, content could be grouped as entertainment or information, adult or children's, and so on. In the United States, it is increasingly common to organize news and information into conservative and liberal categories, called "red" and "blue" media, respectively.

It is widely assumed that people will have consistent preferences for content of a type. We see anecdotal evidence of such reasoning in the operation of media industries. Popular movies are made into television series of the same sort. Hit television programs are imitated the following years, all apparently on the assumption that there is an audience out there that likes this kind of material. As one pundit phrased it, in television nothing succeeds like excess. Marketing researchers have conducted more formal studies to identify the content characteristics that seem to polarize people's likes and dislikes. What they have generally discovered is that commonsense industry categories come as close to a viewer-defined typology as anything. That is to say, the people who like one situation comedy do, in fact, tend to like other sit-coms, and so on. Similar patterns of preference for rap music, country and Western, opera, and most other types of music are also common (MacFarland, 1997).

An interesting facet of people's media preferences has emerged from this type of research. People's dislikes are more clearly related to program type than are their likes. In other words, what we like may be rather eclectic, but what we dislike is more readily categorized. You might test yourself on this point by writing down the five television shows you like most and the five you like least. For some people, it is hard to express dislikes in anything other than program types. It seems that program choice results in not only seeking out what you like but also avoiding what you dislike.

Another significant feature of program type preferences is the linkage that often exists between certain types of content and the demographic character-istics of the audience. In television, for example, it is well established that news and information draw an older audience. Similarly, men tend to watch more sports than do women, children are attracted to animation, and viewers are often drawn to programs that feature characters of their own race or ethnic-ity. In fact, in multicultural contexts, media choices often gravitate to "cultur-ally proximate" content, the most powerful dimension of which is language (Ksiazek & Webster, 2008). None of these associations is intended to suggest a lock-step connection between preferences and demographics; they are only ten-dencies. But working professionals should certainly be aware of their existence.

As important as preferences are in determining people's choice of media materials, programmers know full well that many other factors enter the pic-ture. In chapter 8, we describe how programmers analyze and try to manage audience flow. Radio and television programs are placed in a carefully crafted lineup. If a program is scheduled immediately after a popular show, it will enjoy a significant advantage in building an audience. Programming strategies such as lead-in effects and block programming all depend on this type of reasoning.

It is also important to consider when the audience is likely to be using the media, particularly linear media. The idea that total audience size is determined by things other than the available programming is common to both the conven-tional wisdom of programmers and to at least some formal theories of audi-ence behavior. In 1971, the late Paul Klein, then a researcher at NBC, offered a tongue-in-cheek description of the television audience. Struck by the amazing predictability of HUT levels, Klein suggested that people turn the set on out of habit, without much advance thought about what they will watch. After the set is on, they simply choose the *least objectionable program (LOP)* from available offerings.

In effect, this suggests audience behavior is often a two-stage process in which a decision to use a medium precedes the selection of specific content. The ten-dency of people to turn on a set without regard to programming is sometimes taken as evidence of a *passive audience*, although this seems a needlessly value-laden label. The conceptual alternative, a thoroughly *active audience,* appears to be unrealistic. Such an audience would turn on a set whenever favorite pro-grams were aired and turn off a set when they were not. We know, however, that daily routines (e.g., work, sleep, etc.) effectively constrain when we turn sets on. We also know that many people still watch or listen to programming they are not thrilled with, rather than turning off their sets.

Of course, this is a broad generalization about audience behavior. It is not intended to rule out the possibility that people can be persuaded to turn their sets on by media content. Major events, like the Super Bowl, royal weddings, or dramatic news stories, undoubtedly attract people to the media who would not otherwise be there. Heavy promotion and advertising can sometimes get the attention of potential viewers who then remember to tune in. It is also likely that levels of activity vary by medium. Print and the Internet may be intrinsically more engaging even though they require more effort on the part of media consumers. Moreover, levels of activity can vary over time. The same person might be choosy at one time and a "couch potato" the next. Overall, though, a two-stage process, including the role of habit, appears to explain audience behavior rather well.

Economic Models of Program Choice

Economic theory presents a formal model for explaining program choice. Although it is more abstract, it shares many of the elements embedded in the working theories we just reviewed. Peter Steiner (1952) is credited with groundbreaking work in this field. He, and those who have extended his work (e.g., Owen & Wildman, 1992), take the approach that a person's choice of programming is analogous to his or her choice of more conventional consumer products. Hence, older theories of product competition have served as the model for economic theories of program choice.

These theories make two important assumptions about the audience. First, they assert that there are program types that can be defined in terms of audience preferences. That means that people who like one program of a type will like all other programs of that type. Conversely, people who dislike a program will dislike all others of that type. Economic models generally leave these "program types" abstract and undefined. But as we have seen, there is some reason to believe people have systematic likes and dislikes when it comes to common program types.

Second, if programming is advertiser-supported the models assume that programs are a "free good" to the audience member. Theorists explicitly ignore both the opportunity cost of audience time and the potential increased costs of advertised products. Assuming that programs are like free products has an important, although often unspoken, implication. If programs have no price, it seems logical that the only thing left to explain audience choice is preference. The assumption that preference is a cause of choice is certainly in keeping with the other economic theories, and it is broadly consistent with much social scientific theory.

Economic models of program choice have differed in how they resolve the active-passive question that we discussed earlier. Steiner (1952) assumed a thoroughly active audience in which audience size was determined by the presence of people's preferred program types. According to Steiner 's model, when your favorite program type was not on, neither was your set. Subsequent models, however, have relaxed that rather stringent assumption and incorporated a two-stage process that allows for second and third choices, much like that proposed by Klein.

With these assumptions in place, it is possible to predict the distribution of audiences across channels. For example, if it is assumed that there is a relatively large audience for some particular type of programming, then two or more competing channels or stations will split that audience by offering programming of that type. This will continue to occur until that program type audience has been divided into small enough pieces that it makes sense for the next competitor to counterprogram with different types of shows. Consequently, when there are only a few competitors, similar programs tend to be offered across channels. According to this body of theory, as the number of competitors increases, media content becomes more differentiated. This creates what one commentator described as a "long tail" distribution, with popular offerings at one end and countless niches spread out along the other (Anderson, 2008). The availability of all this material sets the stages for the *audience fragmentation,* we described earlier.

Selective Exposure Theory

Selective exposure theory offers another way to explain people's use of media content. It has been developed by social psychologists, who, among other things, are interested in understanding the media's effect on audience members. In its earliest form, selective exposure theory assumed that people had certain attitudes, beliefs, or convictions that they were loath to change. These predispositions led people to seek out media that were consistent with their beliefs and to avoid material that challenged them. Simply put, people would "see what they wanted to see" and "hear what they wanted to hear."

This commonsense notion gained credibility in the 1950s and 1960s with the introduction and testing of formal psychological theories, like cognitive dissonance. Early studies seemed to indicate that people did select media materials that supported their existing belief systems, or cognitions. Hence, selective exposure to news and information appeared to be an important principle for understanding an individual's choice of programming. While work on selective exposure to news languished for a time, the profusion of news and entertainment outlets on television and the Internet, including some with ideological slants, has encouraged new work in this area (e.g., Prior, 2007; Stroud, 2011).

Research on selective exposure has also gone beyond the bounds of news and information. Here the causal mechanism is not dissonance reduction so much as it is pleasure seeking. For example, experimental studies have shown that people's choices of entertainment vary with their moods and emotions. Excited or overstimulated people are more inclined to select relaxing program fare, whereas people who are bored are likely to choose stimulating content. Emotional states, in addition to more dispassionate cognitions, all seem to influence our program preferences. These variations in selective exposure research sometimes go under the general heading of "mood management theory" (e.g., Hartmann, 2011; Zillmann, 2000).

Uses and Gratifications Theory

Gratificationist theory provides a closely related, if somewhat more comprehensive, perspective on audience behavior. Studies of "uses and gratifications," as they are often called, are also the work of social psychologists. This approach emerged in the early 1970s, partly as a reaction against the field's apparent obsession with media effects research. Gratificationists argued that we should ask not only "what media do to people" but also "what people do with the media." Katz, Blumler, and Gurevitch (1974) spelled out the research agenda of this approach. According to them, gratificationists:

> are concerned with (1) the social and psychological origins of (2) needs, which generate (3) expectations of (4) mass media or other sources, which lead to (5) differential patterns of media exposure (or engagement in other activities), resulting in (6) need gratifications and (7) other consequences, perhaps mostly unintended ones" (p. 20).

Since the early 1970s, gratificationist research and theory have attracted considerable attention. Under this perspective, patterns of media use are determined by each person's expectations of how well different media or program content will gratify their needs. Such needs might be short-lived, like those associated with mood states, or they might be relatively constant. In any event, it seems likely that the gratifications being sought translate rather directly into preferences for the media and their content.

Gratificationist theory, therefore, has much in common with economic models of program choice and theories of selective exposure. All of them cast individual preferences, however they have emerged, as the central mechanism for explaining exposure. This approach to explaining media choice has a great intuitive appeal. Why does the audience for hard rock music tend to be young men? Because that is the kind of music they like. Why do older people consume more news and information? It is because they have a preference for that type of content. How, then, can we explain audience behavior? All we need to do is understand people's preferences.

Unfortunately, the power of preferences to determine exposure to the media is not as absolute as many people assume. Theories that rely exclusively on preferences to explain audience behavior put all their "eggs in one basket." They are pitched at what we earlier called the "micro-level" of analysis. But audience behavior is a "macro-level" phenomenon. To explain what large numbers of media users are doing, we need to consider the structural features of both the audience and the media environment. Without those macro-level factors, we can only see half the picture.

TOWARD A COMPREHENSIVE UNDERSTANDING OF AUDIENCE BEHAVIOR

Exposure to media happens at the interface between the audience and the media. In this section we consider both sides of the equation: *audience factors* and *media factors*. Each has a substantial effect on patterns of exposure. Within each category, we make a further distinction between structural and individual factors. Although it is sometimes hard to distinguish between the two, they reflect different levels of analysis. The distinction also identifies a traditional division in research and theory on media exposure. By *structural determinants,* we mean factors that are common to, or characteristic of, populations. These macro-level variables typically describe markets, media delivery systems, or masses of people. Much marketing and industry research highlights the role of structural determinants, like program schedules or hyperlinks, in shaping audiences. *Individual determinants* describe a person or household. These are micro-level variables that vary from person to person. Much social psychological research, like the theories we just reviewed, highlights the role of individual differences. Taken together, these factors offer a more complete framework for identifying the forces that shape audience behavior.

Audience Factors

Structural Features of the Audience. The first structural feature of the audience that shapes exposure to media is the size and location of *potential audiences.* Sometimes, the potential audience is easy to determine, like the number of people living within reach of a broadcast signal. But the potential audience can also be more elusive. For example, something posted on the Internet is technically available to a worldwide audience, yet as a practical matter, many sites have a distinctly local character and following. Obviously, no form of media can have an audience larger than the size of the relevant market population. The population, in effect, sets an upper bound on the audience potential for any program service. The larger the potential, the more media organizations are willing to invest to win a "piece of the pie."

Dallas, TX 75212
serviceohio@hpb.com

Items:

Qty Title   Locator

1   Ratings Analysis: Audience Measu...   L01-2-11-004-001-278

Marketplace: AmazonMarketplaceUS
Order Number: 4169275
Ship Method: Expedited
Customer Name: Paige Olson
Order Date: 8/26/2019 2:52:33 PM
Marketplace Order #: 113-5604164-4013042
Email: bzsjvjdl9lmpg7c@marketplace.amazon.com

If you have any questions or concerns regarding this order, please contact us at   serviceohio@hpb.com

In broadcasting, ratings services often divide large countries into local market areas. In the United States, there are over 200 television markets, what Nielsen calls Designated Market Areas (DMAs; see Appendix A). In China, there are 31 provincial markets. Clearly, the potential audience for a station in one market can be vastly larger than the audience in another. This does not, of course, guarantee that large market stations will have larger audiences, especially since large markets tend to have more media outlets. Nevertheless, it sets the stage for bigger audiences and bigger audience revenues.

Potential audiences, however, are not just a matter of the sheer number of people living within reach of a medium. The composition of the population can have an impact on long-term patterns of exposure as well. As the demographic makeup of potential audiences changes, it is reasonable to expect that patterns of media exposure will change as well. Census data, for example, can reveal shifts in the relative size of populations with different occupations, the age of the population, and most notably in the levels of education throughout the population. Occupation, age, and education are often associated with the choice of certain types of programming. A far-sighted media operator will take population shifts, most of which are quite predictable, into account when planning for the future.

The growth of Spanish-language programming in the United States can be viewed, at least in part, as a result of newly emerging potential audiences. For example, in 1970 Latinos or Hispanics accounted for 4.5 percent of the U.S. population. By 1990 that figure had doubled. By some estimates, it will double again by 2025, with even higher concentrations in a number of U.S. markets. Rapid growth rates also characterize the U.S. Asian population. Such changes in ethnic or linguistic populations provide new markets for advertisers and the media, and are often accompanied by new and very distinctive patterns of media use.

The second structural attribute of audiences, and one of the most powerful determinants of exposure to linear media, is *audience availability*. While potential audiences set an absolute physical limit on audience sizes, our daily routines set a practical limit on how many people are likely to be using either radio or television at any point in time. It is widely believed that the number of people using a medium has little, if anything, to do with programming and almost everything to do with who is available. Most practitioners take the size of the available audience as given, just as they would the size of the population itself. Even the use of nonlinear media (like watching video on-demand or visiting websites) is powerfully influenced by the rhythms of daily life (Taneja et al., 2012). As a rule then, people use media platforms when they have the time and inclination to do so. This limits who is available at any point in time and therefore sets an upper bound on the total size of the platform's audience at that moment in time.

The size of the available audience, like other forms of mass behavior, is quite predictable. Three patterns are apparent: seasonal, daily, and hourly. Seasonal patterns of media use are more evident in television than in radio. Television use is heaviest in the winter months and lightest during the summer. This shift seems to occur because viewers have more daylight in the summer and pursue outdoor activities that take them away from the set. These seasonal changes mean lower HUT levels in the summer and higher HUT levels in the winter. But household-level data can mask important differences within demographic groups. For example, when school is out, daytime viewing among children and teenagers soars. The same vacation-time phenomenon appears to account for seasonal differences in movie theater attendance.

Audience size also varies by day of the week. In the United States, prime time television audiences are larger on weeknights and Sunday and smaller on Fridays and Saturdays. The late-night audience (e.g., midnight) on Friday and Saturday, however, is larger than it is during the rest of the week. This, too, seems to reflect a change in people's social activities on the weekends.

The most dramatic shifts in audience availability, however, occur on an hourly basis. It is here that the patterns of each day's life are most evident. Figure 4.3, shows how Americans allocate their time across media platforms during each half hour of the day. The data were collected in an unusual study sponsored by the Council for Research Excellence (CRE). In it, investigators followed former Nielsen panelists throughout the day, noting their activities and use of media. They labeled television viewing, including DVR use, as the

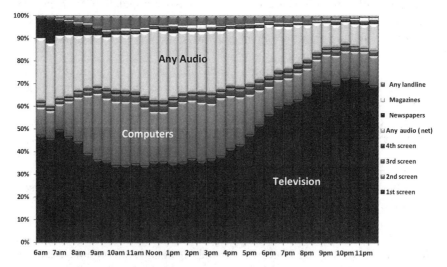

FIGURE 4.3. When Media Are Used

Source: Adapted from CRE (2008) *Video Consumer Mapping Study*. Permission Nielsen Company.

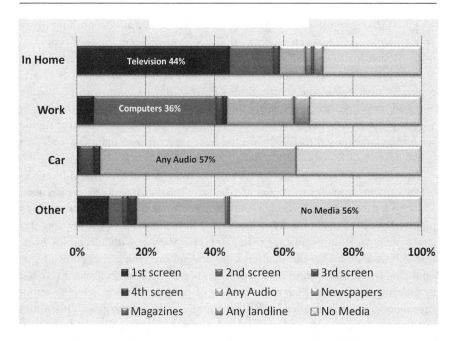

FIGURE 4.4. Where Media Are Used
Source: Adapted from CRE (2008) *Video Consumer Mapping Study.* Permission Nielsen Company.

"first screen." Computer use, including the Internet and software, was labeled "second screen." Using mobile devices for text, talk, or Internet was considered "third screen." And use of any other screen, like in cinema movies, was the "fourth screen." Television, radio, and, to a lesser extent, newspapers are people's media choices early in the day. Computers occupy a larger share of time during the workday. Throughout most of the day, audio use, including radio listening, is a steady presence until people return home from work. At about 5:00 p.m., television use begins to grow, and it becomes the dominant medium during the evening. It is during this time when HUT levels are at their highest in the United States and everywhere else in the world.

Media use also varies by the user's location. Figure 4.4 organizes the same CRE data by where media are used. The results are probably what you would expect. When people are at home, television is the dominant medium, followed by computers. When people are at work, computers are the most prominent, followed by some form of audio. In the car, audio—most likely radio—is the preferred platform. And in any one of these and other locations, there is a fair amount of time people spent using no media at all. All of these patterns in media use circumscribe what programs or media outlets a person is likely to encounter at any point in time.

Thus far, our approach to explaining exposure has had almost nothing to say about people's content preferences or the appeals of different kinds of programming. Remember, however, that we can characterize much audience behavior as a two-stage process. When people use different media platforms is clearly driven by their habits and the rhythms of day-to-day life. But once people are engaged with a particular medium, their needs and wants, likes and dislikes, as well as a number of other factors, play a more important role in determining what they are exposed to. These are the micro-level determinants of audience behavior.

Individual Audience Characteristics. The most important micro-level determinants of exposure to media are, broadly speaking, people's preferences. Much of a programmer's skill in building an audience comes from an ability to judge what people will or will not like. As we noted in the previous section, this strategy for explaining audience behavior is also popular with academics. Most research and theory on the relationship between preference and choice focus on the individual and assume that a person's preferences can be freely exercised in their media choices. Economic models of program choice, selective exposure theory, and gratificationist theories all rely on this assumption. It is often justified on the basis of studies done in laboratory settings that evaluate how individuals choose among limited options when they are alone. Unfortunately, in the real world at least two things interfere with the tidy relationship between a person's media preferences and what they actually choose. The first is the tendency of people to use media, especially television, in groups. The second is knowing which of a great many options is the best.

Group viewing mediates the relationship between individual preference and choice. Even today, when most households have more than one set, people still view in groups especially during prime time (CRE, 2008). What little research there is on the dynamics of group viewing suggests that negotiation among competing preferences is quite usual. Different members of the family seem to exercise more or less influence at different times of the day. For example, programmers take into account that children are often in control of the television set in the late afternoon when they return from school. Exposure to television programming, then, results not only from who is available and what they like, but who is actually making the program selections. People get their first choices some of the time but can be outvoted at other times. Even if they are overruled, however, they will often stay with the viewing group. Ask any parent of a young child whether they are watching more cartoons since the child's arrival. Ask children if they see more of the evening news than they would like. In effect, some of our exposure to media happens despite our preferences. Group viewing, or, for that matter, group music listening or group movie attendance, can constrain the relationship between preference and choice. More solitary forms of media use (e.g., reading or Internet) may offer a cleaner linkage between these factors.

An increasingly important factor that complicates the relationship between preference and choice is *awareness*. By awareness, we mean full knowledge of the media content or services that are available to you. Much theorizing about audience behavior assumes that people's choices reflect a perfect awareness of their options. This is very much in keeping with the "rational choice" models that underpin conventional economic theory. Although that assumption might be workable in very simple media environments, it is fraught with problems in the abundant media environments that confront most audience members.

People simply cannot be expected to know everything there is to know about their options. Nobel laureate Herbert Simon (1997) referred to this condition as "bounded rationality." There are two things that bound rational media choices. First, there is simply too much to choose from. Hundreds of television channels and millions of websites are usually just one click away. People can, and often do, use guides or search engines to help inform their choices, but these are time consuming and cannot provide perfect information. Second, media are typically "experience goods," meaning, you really do not know what they have to offer until you experience them. Even if a person chooses a familiar artist or television program, they will not know if a new offering is enjoyable until they have tried it. So, people can never be fully aware of which media will best satisfy their preferences at any point in time. They just do the best they can, something that Simon called "satisficing."

In addition to using guides to ease the problem of bounded rationality, media users rely on recommendations from other people. Communication researchers have known for a long time that interpersonal influence affects people's choices (Katz & Lazersfeld, 1955). But until recently, such influences flowed within relatively small social networks of friends and family. Today, social media have greatly expanded those networks. Facebook and Twitter provide platforms for gathering and aggregating opinions about what media are worthy of attention. Social news sites like digg poll users about what stories people should read. Often the process of recommendation is automated by "recommender systems," a topic we will address in the following section. Increasingly, though, social networks shape our media choices.

The role that audience preferences play in determining audience behavior, then, is more complex than many assume. For example, a small audience might indicate that people did not like a particular program, but it might also indicate that people were unavailable when it aired. A website or clip on YouTube that has only been viewed a few times might mean it is unappealing, or it could be that people do not know it exists. Any interpretation of media use should consider all the factors summarized in Table 4.2. But audience factors are only half the picture. The media themselves have an impact on patterns of exposure.

TABLE 4.2

Audience Factors Affecting Exposure

Structural	*Individual*
Potential Audiences	Preferences
Local v. National v. Global	Program Type Preferences
Demographic Trends	Tastes
Ethnic or Linguistic Populations	Gratifications Sought
Available Audiences	Group v. Solitary Media Use
Seasonal Variation	Awareness of Options
Weekly Variation	Social networks
Hourly Variation	

Media Factors

Like audience factors, media factors can be thought of as structural or individual in nature. The structural attributes of the media complement the structural features of the audience. They include market conditions and how media content and services are organized. Individual-level media factors define differences in the media environment from household to household.

Structural Features of the Media. The first structural characteristic of the electronic media is *coverage,* which is the extent to which people are physically able to receive a particular outlet or offering. In much of the world, broadcast signals are commonly available. Most households in developed countries now have cable or satellite services. High-speed access to the Internet is also becoming commonplace. But very few platforms are universally available, and the penetration of these technologies changes over time. Table 4.3 summarizes the growth of television systems in the United States since 1970. While television has been a fixture in virtually all homes over that period of time, cable has not. In fact, 10 percent of homes still get broadcast-only reception. But as you can see, new technologies can arise quickly. That changes the structure of the media environment. As the coverage of different media platforms grows or contracts, it opens or closes avenues for building audiences. Like population size, coverage sets a limit on what kinds of audiences are possible.

Even when national media are able to offer "free" content to everyone, local outlets may affect coverage by refusing to carry certain programs. In the United States, with the exception of a few television stations that are actually owned and operated (O&Os) by the networks, affiliates are independent businesses that act in their own self-interest. This means that an affiliate may not carry (or "clear") all of a network's programming if it believes some other programming strategy will be more profitable. They could drop an entire series or preempt a

TABLE 4.3
Penetration of TV Technologies in U.S. Households 1970 to 2012

Key: % of TV Households	'70	'75	'80	'85	'90	'95	'00	'05	'06	'07	'08	'09	'10	'11	'12
TV Households	96	97	98	98	98	98	98	98	98	98	98	98	98	99	97
Broadcast Only	—	—	—	—	—	—	—	—	—	—	12	11	9	10	10
Wired Cable	7	12	20	43	56	63	68	67	66	64	61	61	62	61	61
Cable Plus ADS	—	—	—	—	—	—	76	85	86	86	87	88	90	90	90
Cable Plus ADS w/Pay	—	—	—	26	29	28	32	42	41	45	45	46	52	50	52
Total ADS	—	—	—	—	—	—	—	19	21	23	27	28	29	30	31
Digital Cable	—	—	—	—	—	—	—	—	—	28	31	38	46	49	51
DBS	—	—	—	—	—	—	—	—	—	—	26	27	29	30	30
DVR	—	—	—	—	—	—	—	—	—	—	19	24	34	38	41
HD Receivable	—	—	—	—	—	—	—	—	—	—	14	18	43	59	67
HD Capable	—	—	—	—	—	—	—	—	—	—	17	23	46	60	67
HD Display Capable	—	—	—	—	—	—	—	—	—	—	25	32	53	64	70
Multi—Set	35	43	50	57	65	71	76	79	81	82	82	82	83	83	85
DVD	—	—	—	—	—	—	—	—	76	84	87	88	88	86	85
Video Games	—	—	—	—	—	—	—	—	39	41	39	38	41	43	44
VCR	—	—	—	14	66	79	85	90	89	85	79	72	65	60	57
PC Access-Home	—	—	—	—	—	—	—	—	—	—	—	80	81	83	85
PC Owner with Internet Access-Home	—	—	—	—	—	—	—	—	—	—	—	73	75	76	78

ADS-Alternate Delivery Service   DBS-Direct Broadcast Satellite   DVR-Digital Video Recorder   HD-High Definition   VCR-Video Cassette Recorder   PC-Personal Computer

Source: Nielsen (2011). The Television Audience 2010 and 2011.

single broadcast. These variations in *network clearance* mean that some broadcast network programs do not reach the entire population.

There are analogous phenomena with cable networks, syndicated programs, and the Web. Cable systems organize cable networks into exclusive tiers of service or they do not carry them at all. Syndicated programs are bought in some markets but not others, so very few approach the coverage of broadcast network programs. While websites can, in theory, reach anyone with Internet access, content owners may limit distribution to certain classes of users, like those who already have a cable television subscription. Some sites that offer free content at all are actively blocked. Businesses often do this on workplace computers. China is well known for having a "Great Fire Wall" that filters out unwanted content. Once again, this puts a cap on the total possible audience size.

Within any given medium, a number of other structural factors operate to affect audience behavior. The first consideration is the sheer number of options that confronts the audience. For most forms of media, that number has increased dramatically over the years. In the 1950s, the average U.S. television household could receive roughly four channels. Today, with cable and satellite television, it is common for homes to receive well over 100 channels. If you include nonlinear media like DVRs and VOD, not to mention the Internet, the choices seem almost limitless. We have noted how this contributes to audience fragmentation, but increased choice does not mean that all share equally in the audience.

We saw in Figure 2.2 that increased competition took a toll on broadcast network audiences, but we did not see how viewers spent the rest of their time. Even with abundant choices, some programs and outlets remain relatively popular while most must manage with small audiences. That discrepancy in audience size can be seen in what is called a *long tail* distribution. Figure 4.5 is a long tail distribution of television networks in the United States. It arranges media outlets along the horizontal axis from the most popular to the least popular. The vertical axis reports the size of each network's audience, in this case the monthly cume or reach. The light bars are the broadcast networks. While their audiences are not what they used to be, they still have far more viewers than their cable counterparts. This may be due, in part, to having better coverage of the population.

The Internet offers users even more choices. Figure 4.6 is a long tail distribution showing the monthly reach of the top 138 Internet "brands" (e.g., Google, Yahoo, Facebook). Although it assumes the same general shape of the television distribution, it is even more concentrated. That is, a relatively small number of websites dominate the medium, while audiences for the rest trail off quickly.

Long tail distributions, also called "power law" or "80/20" distributions, are commonplace in media consumption. It does not matter if you look at movies, music, or magazines, it is always the case that a relatively small number of the top sellers account for most of the audience. In fact, a medium with more choices like the Internet is often more likely to produce "winner-take-all" results.

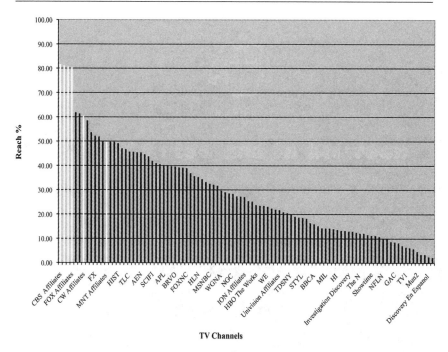

TV Channels

FIGURE 4.5. A Long Tail Distribution of U.S. Television Networks
Source: Webster & Ksiazek (2011)

Why this happens is a puzzle. It could be that best sellers are just of higher quality and therefore more popular. It could also be that people's desire to talk about media causes them to "herd" to a few visible offerings. Social media and recommendations systems probably help the herding along. While abundant choice clearly affects audience behavior, just how people make use of that abundance is not a simple matter (Anderson, 2006; Webster & Ksiazek, 2012).

The structural complexities of the media, however, go beyond the number of channels or outlets that are available. Different forms of media often have their own internal structures. Linear media, like radio and broadcast television, offer people a series of forced choices. It is quite possible to encounter situations in which two desirable programs are aired opposite one another, and the viewer has to choose between them. Had they been scheduled at different times, the viewer could have watched both. *Program scheduling,* within and across channels, therefore, has been an important factor in shaping the size, composition, and flow of audiences.

As we discuss in chapter 8, programmers use their knowledge of audience flow to encourage people to watch their programs rather than those of the competition. Indeed, there are well-documented patterns of audience duplication, such as inheritance effects, channel loyalty, and repeat viewing, that all seem to derive from structural factors (Goodhardt, Ehrenberg, & Collins, 1987;

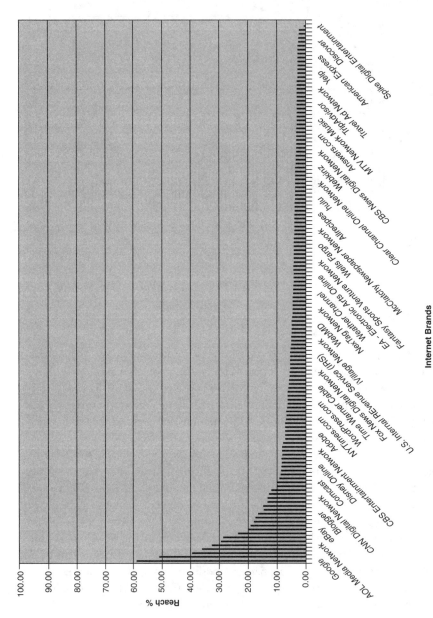

Internet Brands

FIGURE 4.6. Long Tail Distribution of Internet Brands.

Source: Webster & Ksiazek (2011)

Webster & Phalen, 1997). Despite the growing availability of nonlinear media like DVRs, these patterns persist in every country where they have be studied (Jardine, 2012; Sharp, Beal, & Collins, 2009; Yuan, 2010).

There are structural features built into the Internet as well. Many websites have hyperlinks that point visitors to other pages on the Web. These links make some things more visible and easily accessible than others, encouraging people to visit. The power of hyperlinks to direct traffic is built into search engines like Google, which ranks its recommendations by the number and importance of a sites inbound links (Battelle, 2005; Turow & Tsui, 2008). Search engines are one of many recommender systems that help people make choices in a world of bounded rationality. Some use simple head counts to report things like the most viewed videos or news stories. Others, like "social TV guides," use algorithms to recommend what "people like you" have chosen. As useful as these systems might be, they have their own biases. For example, most put a premium on personalizing results, encouraging people to consume more of the same. Virtually all of them steer users to the most popular options within categories (Webster, 2010). In doing so, they direct public attention to some things and away from others. They are yet another structure that, increasingly, shapes audience behavior.

But even these factors do not entirely exhaust explanations of variability in media environments. There are a few micro-level media factors that complete the picture.

Individual Media Environments. Factors like network coverage, program scheduling, and search engine results are generally beyond the control of any one audience member. But certain aspects of the media environment are within the individual's control. In fact, this is truer today than it has ever been. As new technologies and programming alternatives enter the marketplace, each of us has greater latitude in shaping a media environment to suit our purposes. These decisions can certainly affect our exposure to the media and are closely related to the micro-level audience factors we reviewed earlier.

One of the first considerations is the kind of *technologies owned* by individual audience members. Radio and television sets have been in virtually all U.S. households for decades, but more and more people have multiple sets throughout their homes. Set technology also changes over time. The latest televisions not only have big, high-definition screens, but they integrate access to the Internet. Every day seems to bring new electronic toys that entice consumers, whether it is the latest tablet computer or smartphone. A 2011 survey of online respondents in 56 countries around the world indicates how many have or intend to buy several kinds of newer media platforms. For example, only 12 percent report owning tablets, but another 19 percent said they plan on buying one. Similarly, 36 percent had smart phones, and another 21 percent intended to get one (Nielsen, 2011). Individuals presumably buy these technologies because they believe they will be useful—even if it is only to impress the neighbors. But owning any one of those platforms can change the way people use media and, in the aggregate, affect audience behavior.

Subscriptions are yet another decision that each person or household makes. People have long subscribed to different print media like newspapers or magazines. They now subscribe to Internet service providers (ISPs), cable or satellite systems, premium services like HBO or Netflix, as well as various online publications and services. These obviously enable differential patterns of exposure.

Individuals also have idiosyncratic habits that structure their media environments. Most media users must cope with an overwhelming number of choices. We have known for some time that, confronted with a large number of channels, television viewers develop a *channel repertoire* (Heeter & Greenberg, 1988). That is a small subset of the available channels that the viewer actively uses. For example, people who receive 100 channels generally use 15 or so on a regular basis. That pattern is typical around the world (e.g., Yuan & Webster, 2006). Similarly, confronted with overwhelming choices on the Web, people rely on "bookmarks." As media use now ranges across multiple platforms, audience analysts have begun to identify analogous "media repertoires" (e.g., van Rees & van Eijck, 2003). These can effectively preclude exposure to most channels and websites, even if they are only one click away. Moreover, technologies that allow people to preset favorites or "learn" and support a person's habits of use could further entrench repertoires. The net result is that, on a day-to-day basis, each media user makes choices from a surprisingly limited menu. These menus are tailored to each individual and may pose an effective barrier to more wide-ranging selections. Table 4.4 summarizes the media factors we have discussed.

TABLE 4.4
Media Factors Affecting Exposure

Structural	Individual
Coverage	Technologies owned
Household penetration	Radios and TV sets
Signal carriage	DVDs and DVRs
Clearance	Computers/phones
Content options	Subscriptions
Number of choices	Cable/satellite
Program schedules	Internet service
Hyperlinks	Premium services
Recommender systems	Repertoires
Search engines	Channel repertoires
Social media	Bookmarking

AN INTEGRATED MODEL OF AUDIENCE BEHAVIOR

Audience behavior is influenced by many things. We have defined and discussed most of them in the preceding sections but have not put the pieces of the puzzle together. It is useful, at this point, to step back and reflect on what has been presented as we construct a cohesive framework or model of audience behavior. A good model helps us ask the right questions and, in turn, guides the analysis of data.

Audience researchers have devoted considerable time and effort to understanding people's use of the electronic media. Ad agencies and the media themselves have done very pragmatic studies of audience formation, economists have developed rather abstract theories of program choice, and social psychologists have performed a seemingly endless succession of experiments and surveys to reveal the origins of media use. Despite progress in these, and many other fields, there has been an unfortunate tendency for each group to work in isolation from the others. Instances of collaborative work between theorists and practitioners or even across different academic disciplines are all too rare.

At the risk of greatly oversimplifying matters, two fairly distinct approaches to understanding the audience can be identified. The first emphasizes the importance of the individual factors. This perspective is typical of work in psychology, communication studies, and, to some extent, marketing and economics. It also has enormous intuitive appeal and is likely to characterize most commonsense explanations of the audience. After all, audiences are simply collections of individuals. Surely, if we can understand behavior at the individual level, then our ability to explain larger patterns of mass behavior will follow. When we conceptualize audience behavior at the individual level, we tend to look for explanations by thinking of those things that distinguish us as individuals. Above all, we have invoked preferences as a way to explain behavior. With this focus, however, we often miss seeing patterns that crystallize higher levels of analysis. For instance, it is doubtful that any one television viewer chooses to create an inheritance effect, yet night after night, we see that kind of audience flow. It is unlikely that people conspire to make long tail distributions, yet their actions create them with great regularity.

The second perspective emphasizes structural factors as key determinants of mass behavior. This approach is more typical in sociology, social network analysis, and at least some forms of marketing and advertising research. It downplays individual needs and wants and concentrates on things like market information, coverage areas, program schedules, and hyperlinks in an attempt to understand audience behavior. Although work in this area can be highly successful in creating statistical explanations of aggregated data, it often has a hollow ring to it. One is often tempted to ask, "What does this mean in human terms—what does it tell us about ourselves?" Such explanations are usually possible but not always apparent.

It is important to recognize that neither approach is right or wrong. They just have different way of seeing the audience. The first focuses on individual media users and tries to understand audiences from the inside out. The second focuses on structures and works from the outside in. Academics sometimes say these approaches emphasize either "agency" or "structure." And there is a school of thought that says you cannot have one without the other, something academics call a "duality" (Giddens, 1984; Webster, 2011). That is, people need structures to enact their desires and, in doing so, they reproduce and change those structures. Agency and structure are "mutually constituted," which is a productive way to think about audiences. For example, we call program schedules a structural factor, yet programmers constantly adapt these to the actions of viewers. Signal coverage is a structure, yet it depends on individuals buying technologies and subscribing to services. Similarly, recommender systems like search engines are structural, yet they build their recommendations by aggregating individual actions. The list goes on and on. The most comprehensive models of audience behavior recognize the roles of agency and structure, and the tensions between them (e.g., Cooper & Tang, 2009; Webster, 2011; Wonneberger, Schoenbach, & van Meurs, 2009; Yuan & Ksiazek, 2011).

The Model

The model presented in Figure 4.7 is intended to help organize our thinking about audience behavior as it is commonly defined in audience research. It suggests broad relationships, but it does not, in and of itself, provide hypotheses to be tested. It certainly falls short of being a mathematical model (although we use Figure 4.7 as a springboard for discussing several such models in chapter 6). The model focuses on short-term audience behaviors. Within that time frame, the structures we see are relatively rigid.

The central component of the model, the thing we are trying to explain, is exposure to media. As we argued in chapter 1, audience analysts are interested in macro-level behaviors. We saw earlier in this chapter that the most common measures of that behavior can be categorized as gross or cumulative. Two broad categories are shown as the causes of exposure: audience factors and media factors. The shape of the "boxes" indicates the direction of influence. For example, the model suggests that audience factors help determine ratings, not vice versa. There also are cause-and-effect relationships among the factors within each box. For instance, audience preferences probably contribute to patterns of availability, and cable subscription helps shape cable network coverage. We have opted to omit arrows suggesting all these interrelationships, to keep the model cleaner.

To use the model, you should identify the sort of audience behavior you wish to analyze. Are you concerned with the size of an audience at a single point in time (i.e., a gross measure), or are you interested in how audience members are

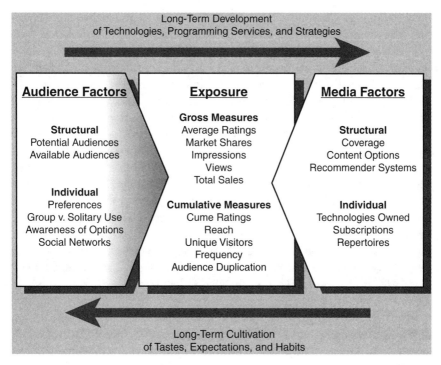

FIGURE 4.7. A Model of Audience Behavior

behaving across time (i.e., a cumulative measure)? To begin the process of evaluating, explaining, or predicting that behavior, consider the structural determinants first. There are three reasons why we recommend you look initially for structural explanations. First, like the measures of exposure you are analyzing, they are pitched at the macro-level of analysis. Second, they are more knowable. Information on program schedules, network coverage, and total audiences is typically in the research reports themselves. Individual factors, like audience awareness or the strength of user preferences, are a bit harder to pin down. Third, we know from experience that structural explanations work well with most forms of audience data. If they fail to provide a satisfying answer, however, begin the process of thinking through the individual-level factors on either side of the model.

Let's work our way through an example to get a better sense of the model. Keep in mind that it is not designed to provide a quick answer to difficult audience research questions but rather to guide the analyst in considering all the relevant factors. Consider, for instance, the ratings of a local television news program. Why do some stations have high ratings, and others have low ratings? What factors will shape a station's audience size in the future? Advertisers, as well as local station managers and programmers, would probably have an interest in this sort of analysis. Imagine that you work for a station and you want to assess its situation.

A rating, of course, is a gross measure of audience size. Local news ratings, in particular, have an important impact on station profitability. To explain the size of a station's news audience, we should first consider structural factors. If audience size is to be expressed as an absolute number, we would need to know the size of the potential audience defined by the population in the market. At the same time, we would want to consider the nature of the station's coverage area. Is it a VHF or a UHF station? If it is the latter, you're probably already at a disadvantage. Is there anything about the station's signal or local geography that would limit the station's ability to reach all of the potential audience? Next, we would want to know the size of the audience at the time when the news is broadcast. An analysis of share data, of course, might overlook this, but since we are interested in ratings, the bigger the available audience, the better are our chances of achieving a large rating. We might pay special attention to those segments of the audience that are more likely to be local news viewers. Experience tells us that these are probably going to be older adults. Next, we would consider a variety of program-scheduling factors.

The first scheduling consideration would involve assessing the competition. Just how many competitors are there? As they increase in number, your ratings are likely to decrease. Do other stations enjoy any special advantages in covering the market? What are your principal competitors likely to program opposite the news? Will you confront only news programs, or will the competition counterprogram with something different? The latter is much more likely if you are an affiliate facing other independent stations. If the available audience contains a large segment that is less likely to watch the news (e.g., children and young adults), that could damage your ratings. Consider the programming you have before and after your news. A highly rated lead-in is likely to help your ratings, especially if it attracts an audience of news viewers. If you are an affiliate, pay close attention to the strength of your network's news program. Research has shown that there is a very strong link between local and network news ratings.

More often than not, these structural factors explain most of the variations in local news ratings. A station can control some things, like lead-in programming. Other things, like the number of competitors it has, are beyond its control. Because a single ratings point might make a substantial difference in a station's profitability, however, consideration of individual factors may be warranted, especially if these are things a station can manipulate.

Among the most likely candidates for consideration are viewer preferences and awareness. Are there certain personalities or program formats that are going to be more or less appealing to viewers? Every year, consultants to stations— news doctors they are called—charge large fees to make such determinations.

It is possible that monitoring social media may give a lower-cost way to assess people's preferences and levels of engagement. But remember, these are self-selected commentators who may not represent the audience at large. In markets that are not measured continuously, stations often schedule sensationalist special reports to coincide with the ratings sweeps. A riveting investigative report is unlikely to boost a program's ratings, however, unless additional viewers are made aware of it. So stations must simultaneously engage in extraordinary promotional and advertising efforts. Here again, social media present new opportunities for building the program's brand or a conversation about stories, although it is sometimes difficult to manage that process. And all the stations in a market are probably doing the same thing. Therefore, although catering to audience preferences is important in principle, in practice it may not make a huge ratings difference. Even so, a small edge can be crucial to a program's profitability.

The analysis of Internet audience behavior follows along the same lines as television, except we typically define exposure in terms of unique visitors, page views, or impressions. Suppose, for example, you wanted to explain the flow of traffic from one website to another. This might reveal something about audience loyalties. The kind of behavior we are interested in is cumulative, and a study of audience duplication between websites is probably our best bet. Once again, begin by considering structural factors. If we were interested in global audience flows—after all, it is the "World Wide" Web—we would probably want to be mindful of the language used on the websites. Loyalties might well revolve around language and ethnic and national identities. Among the media structures to consider would be the nature of links among sites. Sites that are tied together by hyperlinks are more likely to share traffic. You would also want to assess the role of user information regimes in making some sites more salient than others. It is possible that a handful of structural factors will explain audience duplication across sites. If not, adding information about the kinds of sites (e.g., news, sports, entertainment, shopping, etc.) might better reflect the range of user preferences for content and help explain why some sites seem to cluster together.

In closing, we might comment briefly on the long-term nature of exposure to media. One danger of characterizing audience behavior as the result of nicely drawn arrows and boxes is that things are made to seem simpler than they really are. For instance, the model defines exposure as the result, but not the cause, of other factors. Over time, audience ratings can have a substantial effect on the structure of the media (e.g., Anand & Peterson, 2000; Napoli, 2011). Similarly, the model, as we have presented it, suggests a high degree of independence between audience and media factors. In the short term, that seems to be a workable assumption. Over the long haul, however, it could promote a distorted picture of audience behavior.

To at least acknowledge these issues, we have specified some long-term relationships between audience and media factors. For example, the growth of potential audiences and patterns of availability clearly affect the development of media services and programming strategies. Conversely, the structure and content of the media undoubtedly cultivate certain tastes, expectations, and habits on the part of the audience. These are important relationships but not central to our purpose. Bearing such limitations in mind, we hope the model provides a useful framework for evaluating audience data and exploiting the analytical techniques discussed in the remaining chapters.

RELATED READINGS

Anderson, C. (2006). *The long tail: Why the future of business is selling less of more.* New York: Hyperion.

Barwise, P., & Ehrenberg, A. (1988). *Television and its audience.* London: Sage.

Hartmann, T. (ed.). (2009). *Media choice: A theoretical and empirical overview.* New York: Routledge.

MacFarland, D. T. (1997). *Future radio programming strategies: Cultivating listenership in the digital age.* Mahwah, NJ: Lawrence Erlbaum Associates.

McPhee, W. N. (1963). *Formal theories of mass behavior.* New York: The Free Press.

McQuail, D. (1997). *Audience analysis.* Thousand Oaks, CA: Sage.

Owen, B. M., & Wildman, S. W. (1992). *Television economics.* Cambridge, MA: Harvard University Press.

Pariser, E. (2011). *The bubble filter: What the Internet is hiding from you.* New York: Penguin Press.

Prior, M. (2007). *Post-broadcast democracy: How media choice increases inequality in political involvement and polarizes elections.* Cambridge, UK: Cambridge University Press.

Rosengren, K. E., Wenner, L. A., & Palmgreen, P. (Eds.). (1985). *Media gratifications research: Current perspectives.* Beverly Hills, CA: Sage.

Stroud, N. J. (2011). *Niche news: The politics of news choice.* Oxford: Oxford University Press.

van Rees, Kees, and Koen van Eijck. "Media Repertoires of Selective Audiences: The Impact of Status, Gender, and Age on Media Use." *Poetics* 31, no. 5–6 (2003): 465–90.

Webster, J. G., & Phalen, P. F. (1997). *The mass audience: Rediscovering the dominant model.* Mahwah, NJ: Erlbaum.

Zillmann, D., & Bryant, J. (Eds.). (1985). *Selective exposure to communication.* Hillsdale, NJ: Lawrence Erlbaum Associates.

Zillmann, D., & Vorderer, P. (2000). *Media entertainment: The psychology of its appeal.* Mahwah, NJ: Lawrence Erlbaum Associates.

CHAPTER 5

Analysis of Gross Measures

As we noted in chapter 1, for many people who deal with electronic media, "audience research" means nothing more than "ratings research." While that view is certainly not held by everyone in the business, it is true that no other form of audience measurement so dominates the industry. For this reason, our focus in the next two chapters is on the analysis and interpretation of ratings information.

Once audience data are collected, edited, and reported, it is up to the analyst to interpret their meaning. Fortunately, there is no need to reinvent the wheel every time you are tasked with analyzing this kind of audience data; researchers in the media industries and in academia have already developed many useful analytical strategies. Learning these techniques has two important advantages. First, they have been tested, and their strengths and limitations are well known. Second, standardization of analytical techniques has many benefits. Comparisons of one sort or another play an important part in ratings analysis. If everyone calculated the cost of reaching the audience differently, for example, meaningful comparisons would be difficult or impossible to make, thus limiting the utility of the analysis. This has become a major concern for programmers and advertisers who want to compare the cost of media across different platforms. Standardization can help us build a systematic body of knowledge about audiences and their role in the operation of electronic media. If one study can be directly related to the next, progress and/or dead ends can be more readily identified.

In chapter 4, we defined *gross* and *cumulative measurements*. Following this distinction, we have organized analytical techniques into two chapters—those that deal with gross measures and those that deal with cumulative measures. We recognize that this distinction is not always obvious. Analyses of one sort are often coupled with the other; and there can be strict mathematical relationships between the two. However, this scheme of organization can help the reader manage a potentially bewildering assortment of ways to manipulate the data.

Within each chapter, we go from the least complicated analytical techniques to the most complicated. Unfortunately, as we make this progression, our language becomes increasingly complex and arcane, but we try to keep the technical jargon to a minimum. The majority of analytical techniques described require only an understanding of simple arithmetic. Some, however, involve the use of multivariate statistics.

BROADCAST-BASED METRICS

We begin by reviewing metrics that are commonly used in broadcasting. Many of these measures date back to the early days of radio. Gross measures can be thought of as snapshots of the audience taken at a point in time. Included in this category are the measures themselves (e.g., ratings and shares), any subsequent manipulations of those measures (e.g., totaling GRPs), or analyses of the measures using additional data (e.g., calculating the cost to reach 1 percent of the audience, the "cost per point" or CPP). Excluded from this category are audience measurements that require tracking individual audience members over time.

Throughout the book, we have made frequent use of terms like *ratings* and *share*. Although basic definitions of these terms were provided in chapter 4, they ignored a good many nuances that an analyst should know. In fact, it is important to recognize that these measures are themselves a kind of first-order data analysis. Ratings, shares, and gross audience projections are all the result of mathematical operations being applied to the database.

Projected audiences are the most basic gross measurements of the audience. In this context, "projection" means going from the sample to an estimate of what is happening in the population. It should not be confused with predicting future audiences. These projections are estimates of absolute audience size, intended to answer the question, "How many people watched or listened?" Audience projections can be made for specific programs, specific stations, or for all those using a medium at any point in time. Projections can be made for households, persons, or various subsets of the audience (e.g., the number of men aged 18–49 who watched the news). Most of the numbers in a ratings report are simply estimates of absolute audience size, whether for program content or for commercial content.

Projections are made from samples. The most straightforward method of projection is to determine the proportion of the sample using a program, station, or medium and then multiply that by the size of the population. For example, if we wanted to know how many households watched Program Z, we would look at the sample, note that 20 percent watched Z, and multiply that by the estimated number of television households in the market, say 100,000. The projected number of households equipped with television (TVHH) watching

Program Z would therefore be 20,000. That proportion is, of course, a rating. Hence, projected audiences can be derived by the following equation:

Rating (%) × Population = Projected Audience

For many years, this was the approach Nielsen used with its metered samples. It assumed that the in-tab sample, without further adjustments, adequately represented the population. Today, as Nielsen folds local peoplemeters (LPM) into its national sample to boost sample size, it weights respondents accordingly— a methodological fix that has been standard operating procedure in audience measurement for years. As we have noted, it is common to weight the responses of underrepresented groups more heavily than others; the specific variables used to weight the sample and the way these weights are combined vary from market to market. The end result is that the weighted responses of households or individuals are combined to project audience size. Unlike the simple procedure described previously, here projected audiences must be determined before ratings. In fact, if sample weighting or balancing is used, audience projections are actually used to calculate a rating, not vice versa.

Audience projections, used in the context of advertising, will sometimes be added to produce a number called gross audience or *gross impressions*. This is a summation of program or station audiences across different points in time. Those points in time are usually defined by an advertiser's schedule of spots. Table 5.1 is a simple example of how gross impressions, for women aged 18 to 49, would be determined for a commercial message that aired at four different times.

Gross impressions are just like GRPs, except they are expressed as a whole number rather than percentage points. They provide a rough estimate of total audience exposure to a particular message or campaign. They do not take frequency of exposure or audience duplication into account. As a result, 10,000 gross impressions might mean that 10,000 people saw a message once or that 1,000 people saw it 10 times

TABLE 5.1
Determining Gross Impressions

Spot Availability	Audience of Women Aged 18 to 49
Monday, 10 A.M.	2,500
Wednesday, 11 A.M.	2,000
Thursday, 4 P.M.	3,500
Friday, 9 P.M.	1,500
Total (gross impressions)	9,500

Ratings are the most familiar of all gross measures of the audience. Unlike projected audience, they express the size of the audience as a percentage of the total population, rather than a whole number. The simplest calculation for a rating, therefore, is to divide a station or program audience by the total potential audience. In practice, the "%" is understood, so a program with 20 percent of the audience is said to have a rating of 20.

The potential audience on which a rating is based can vary. Household ratings for the broadcast networks are based on all U.S. TVHH. But ratings can also be based on people, or different categories of people. Local market reports include station ratings for different market areas, like DMA and Metro. Some national cable and satellite networks might base their ratings not on all TVHH, or even all cable households, but only on those homes that can receive a network's programming. Although there is a rationale for doing that, such variation can affect our interpretation of the data. A ratings analyst should, therefore, be aware of the potential audience on which a rating is based.

In addition to ratings, it is frequently useful to summarize the total number of people using the medium at any point in time. When households are the units of analysis, this summary is called *households using television,* or *HUT level* for short. HUT levels are typically expressed as a percentage of the total number of television households in a market. As with ratings, though, it is possible to express them in absolute terms. If individuals are being counted, *persons using television,* or PUT, is the appropriate term. In radio, the analogous term is *persons using radio* (PUR).

There are several different kinds of ratings calculations. Their definitional equations are summarized in Table 5.2 (actual computations are much more complex). To simplify the wording in the table, everything is described in terms of television, with television households (TVHH) as the unit of analysis. Radio ratings, and television ratings using persons as the unit of analysis, would be just the same, except they would use slightly different terminology (e.g., PUT vs. HUT).

Also summarized in Table 5.2 are calculations for GRPs and HUT levels. These are analogous to gross impressions and HUTs, respectively. They carry essentially the same information as those projections of audience size, but they are expressed as percentages instead of whole numbers. They are also subject to the same interpretive limitations as their counterparts. Reporting HUT or PUT as percentages means they are a kind of rating. To avoid confusion, we will refer to them as such. In practice, however, these percentages are usually called HUTs or PUTs, without appending the word "rating."

Share, the third major gross measurement, expresses audience size as a percentage of those using the medium at a point in time. The basic equation for determining audience share among television households is:

$$\frac{\text{Number of TVHH Tuned to Station or Program}}{\text{HUT Level}} = \text{Share}$$

TABLE 5.2
Ratings Computations[a]

Basic rating (R)

$$R\,(\%) = \frac{\text{TVHH watching program or station}}{\text{Total TVHH}}$$

Quarter-hour rating (QH)

$$QH = \frac{\text{TVHH watching more than 5 minutes in a quarter hour}}{\text{Total TVHH}}$$

Average quarter-hour rating (AQH)

$$AQH = \frac{\text{Sum of quarter hour ratings}}{\text{Number of quarter hours}}$$

Average audience rating[b] (AA)

$$AA = \frac{\text{Total all minutes TVHH spend watching program content}}{\text{Program duration in minutes} \times \text{total TVHH or persons}}$$

C3 rating

$$C3 = \frac{\text{Total all minutes TVHH or persons spend watching commercial content in a program including 3 days of replay}}{\text{Total TVHH or persons}}$$

HUT rating (HR)

$$HR = \frac{\text{Projected HUT level}}{\text{Total TVHH}}$$

Gross rating points (GRP)

$$GRP = R_1 + R_2 + R_3 + R_4 + R_5 \ldots + R_n$$

[a] The precise method for computing a rating depends on whether the responses of sample members are differentially weighted. When they are, program audiences must be projected and then divided by the total estimated population. When the responses of sample members are not weighted, or have equal weights, proportions within the sample itself determine the ratings and subsequent audience projections.

[b] In this computation, the number of minutes each TVHH spends watching a program is totaled across all TVHH. This is divided by the total possible number of minutes that could have been watched, as determined by multiplying program duration in minutes by total TVHH. AA can also be reported for specific quarter hours within the program, in which case the denominator is 15 × total TVHH.

The calculation of person shares is exactly the same, except persons and PUT levels are in the numerator and denominator, respectively. In either case, the rating and share of a given program or station have the same number in the numerator. The difference is in the denominator. As we noted in chapter 4, HUT or PUT levels are always less than the total potential audience, so a program's share will always be larger than its rating.

Like ratings, audience shares can be determined for various subsets of the total audience. Unlike ratings, however, shares are of somewhat limited value in buying and selling audiences. Although shares indicate performance relative to the competition, they do not convey information about actual size of the audience, and that is what advertisers are most often interested in. The only way that a share can reveal information about total audience size is when it is related to its associated HUT level, as follows:

Program share × HUT = projected program audience

or

Program share × HUT rating = program rating

Audience shares can also be calculated over periods of time longer than program lengths. In local rating books, for example, audience shares are often reported for entire dayparts. When long-term average share calculations are made, the preferred method is to derive the average quarter-hour (AQH) share from the AQH rating within the same daypart. The following equation summarizes how such a daypart share might be calculated with television data:

$$\frac{\text{AQH rating}}{\text{AQH HUT rating}} = \text{AQH share}$$

Unlike AQH ratings, it is not appropriate to calculate AQH shares by adding a station's audience share in each quarter hour and dividing by the number of quarter hours. That is because each audience share has a different denominator, and it would distort the average to give them equal weight.

Defining audience size in these ways presents some interesting problems, many of which occur when households are the unit of analysis. Suppose that a household is watching two different programs on different sets. To which station should that home be attributed? Standard practice in the ratings business is to credit the household to the audiences of both stations. In other words, it counts in the calculation of each station's household rating and share. However, it will only be allowed to count once in the calculation of HUT levels. This means that the sum of all program ratings can exceed the HUT rating, and the sum of all program shares can exceed 100. This was an insignificant problem in the early days of television because most homes had only one television. In the United States, for example, close to 85 percent of all television households have more than one television set, and Nielsen estimates the national average is three sets per household.

Because households are typically collections of two or more people, household ratings tend to be higher than person ratings. Imagine, for example, that some market has 100 homes, with four people living in each. Suppose that one person in each household was watching Station Z. That would mean that Station Z had a TVHH rating of 100 and a person rating of 25. Some programs, like "family shows," do better at attracting groups of viewers, whereas others garner more solitary viewing. It is, therefore, worth keeping an eye on discrepancies between household and person ratings, because differences between the two can be substantial.

Even when people are the unit of analysis, aberrations in audience size can occur. Most ratings services require that a person be in a program or quarter-hour audience for at least 5 minutes to be counted. That means it is quite possible for a person to be in two programs in a quarter hour or to show up in several program audiences of longer duration. This creates a problem analogous to multiple set use at the household level. In the olden days, when person ratings could only be made with diaries and people had to get up to change the channel, it was not much of a problem. Today, with peoplemeters tracking a population that has remote control devices and dozens of channels from which to choose, the potential for viewers to show up in more than one program audience is considerably greater.

As if this were not complicated enough, technology is now drawing into question the very act of viewing itself. Nielsen used to credit people who taped a program with their VCR to the program audience and simply note the size of the VCR contribution. In effect, to tape a program was to watch it. Of course, many taped programs were never watched, but the total amount of taping was so limited that no one was particularly concerned. With the introduction of DVRs, however, the definition of *viewing* became problematic. DVR users can time-shift within a program on a near-live basis or stockpile content for later viewing. Nielsen will segregate all time-shifted viewing, even if a viewer pauses for a few seconds; any recorded material that is actually played within a 7-day period can be added back into the audience, producing a "live plus" rating. While syndicators have used ratings compiled from multiple airings for years, this type of system is still relatively new to networks. Obviously it has the potential to alter our understanding of overnights and even fundamental concepts like ratings, HUTs, and shares.

The most common way to extend the data reported in a typical ratings "book" (the term is still used even though most information is now digital) is to introduce information on the cost of reaching the audience. Cost calculations are an important tool for those who must buy and sell media audiences. There are two such calculations in wide use, and both are based on manipulations of gross audience measurements.

Cost per thousand (CPM), as the name implies, tells you how much it costs to reach 1,000 members of a target audience. It is a yardstick that can be used to compare stations or networks with different audiences and different rate structures. The standard formula for computing CPMs is:

$$\frac{\text{COST OF SPOT (\$)} \times 1000}{\text{PROJECTED TARGET AUDIENCE}} = \text{CPM}$$

The projected target audience is expressed as a whole number. It could simply be the number of households delivered by the spot in question, or it could also be men aged 18 to 49, working women, teens aged 12 to 17, and so on. CPMs can be calculated for whatever audience is most relevant to the advertiser, as long as the ratings data can be calculated to project that audience. Occasionally, when a large number of spots are running, it is more convenient to compute the average CPM for the schedule in the following way:

$$\frac{\text{COST OF SCHEDULE(\$)} \times 1000}{\text{TARGET GROSS IMPRESSIONS}} = \text{Average CPM}$$

CPMs are the most widely used measure of the advertising media's cost efficiency. They can be calculated to gauge relative costs within a medium or used to make comparisons across different media. In print, for example, the cost of a black-and-white page or a newspaper's line rate is divided by its circulation or the number of readers it delivers. Comparisons within a medium are generally easier to interpret than intermedia comparisons. As long as target audiences are defined in the same way, CPMs do a good job of revealing which spot is more cost efficient. There is less agreement on what is the magazine equivalent of a 30-second spot.

The electronic media have a unique form of cost calculation called cost per point (CPP). Like CPM, it is a yardstick for making cost-efficiency comparisons, except here the unit of measurement is not thousands of audience members but ratings points. CPP is computed as follows:

$$\frac{\text{Cost of spot (\$)}}{\text{Audience Rating}} = \text{CPP target}$$

An alternative method for calculating CPP can be used when a large number of spots are being run and an average CPP is of more interest than the efficiency of any one commercial. This is sometimes called the cost per gross ratings point (CPGRP), and it is calculated as follows:

$$\frac{\text{Cost of schedule (\$)}}{\text{Gross rating points}} = \text{CPGRP}$$

As you know by now, there are different kinds of ratings. In network television, C3 ratings are used to calculate the cost and efficiency of an advertising buy because they more accurately express the size of the audience at the moment a commercial is run. For ratings based on diary data in local markets, a quarter-hour rating is used. Television market reports also estimate station break ratings by averaging quarter hours before and after the break. This procedure gives buyers an estimate for the time closest to when a spot actually runs.

CPP measures are part of the everyday language of people who specialize in broadcast advertising. Stations' representatives, and the media buyers with whom they deal, often conduct their negotiations on a CPP basis. This measure of cost efficiency has the additional advantage of relating directly to GRPs, which are commonly used to define the size of an advertising campaign. CPPs, however, have two limiting characteristics that affect their use and interpretation.

First, they are simply less precise than CPMs. Ratings points are rarely carried beyond one decimal place. They must, therefore, be rounded. Rounding off network audiences in this way can add or subtract tens of thousands of people from the audience, causing an unnecessary reduction in the accuracy of cost calculations. Second, ratings are based on different potential audiences. We would expect the CPP in New York to be more than it is in Louisville because each point represents many more people. But how many more? CPMs are calculated on the same base—1,000 households or persons—so they can be used for intermarket comparisons. Even within a market, problems can crop up when using CPP. Radio stations whose signals may cover only part of a market should be especially alert to CPP buying criteria. It is quite possible, for example, that one station delivers most of its audience within the metropolitan area, whereas another has an audience of equal size located mostly outside the metropolis. If CPPs in the market are based on metropolitan ratings, the second station could be at an unfair and unnecessary disadvantage.

WEB-BASED METRICS

With more and more media being delivered over the Web and other digital networks, the foregoing review of broadcast-based metrics might seem a bit quaint. The Web, after all, is a vast, interactive, nonlinear medium that enables new forms of media use. Those behaviors are measured with servers or very large panels of metered computers, with a level of "granularity" that would have been unimaginable in the early days of radio. But, in many ways, broadcasting has established precedents that the Web is bound to follow. This happens for two interrelated reasons.

First, the Web is a victim of its own success. There is so much data that analysts parse in so many ways that the industry is awash in metrics. The result has been what the Interactive Advertising Bureau (IAB, 2011) called "a cacophony of competing and contradictory measurement systems." Not only are there a great many possible metrics to choose from, but even fairly common measures are defined and calculated in different ways. This happens, in part, because user-centric panels and servers record somewhat different kinds of information that affect the production of metrics. But even server-centric data alone are managed in idiosyncratic ways. Web analytics are typically done using computerized tools that access server data. Unfortunately, as Avinash Kaushik, an expert in the field noted, "each tool seems to have its own sweet way of reporting these numbers. They also tend to compute those numbers differently" (2010, p. 37). There are too many metrics with too little standardization. The result can be confusion about what the numbers mean and disagreement about which of them to use.

Second, remember that audience measurement always happens within an institutional context. The major players are the media themselves, who are trying to attract and sell audiences, and the advertisers who are trying to reach them. The system works best when there are straightforward, universally understood metrics that can function as the currency used to transact business. Broadcast-based metrics have done that. They guide the allocation of billions in ad spending around the world. They summarize the most relevant kinds of audience behaviors (audience size, composition, and loyalty). Media planners are, in turn, used to working with them. As other media arise, broadcast-based metrics offer a ready-made, if imperfect, template that can be extended to newcomers. Making "apples to apples" comparisons across media is increasingly critical as advertisers decide how to allocate their resources among platforms. Promoting that kind of standardization has been an important motivation for the IAB (2011), which hopes to "develop digital metrics and advertising currency that facilitate cross-platform measurement and evaluation of media." These forces will result in a standardization of Web metrics and, we suspect, one that favors measures that relate directly to existing broadcast-based metrics. We review only the most common Web-based metrics next.

Hits were among the first measures to indicate website popularity. A hit occurs each time a file is requested from a web server. The problem is that even a single web page might contain dozens of files, each one of which would be counted as a hit. As a result, most analysts now regard hits as largely meaningless. In fact, many joke the acronym "HITS" stands for "How Idiots Track Success."

A more useful gross measure is *page views*. Most websites allow users to visit specific pages. One common way to judge the popularity of a page is to count the number of times that it has been viewed. An analogous term is simply *views*. YouTube counts and reports the number of times each video has been watched. In neither case do you have any idea whether the count results from a few people viewing repeatedly, or many people viewing once. Nonetheless, views can function as a kind of currency. For that reason, YouTube goes to some lengths to authenticate the accuracy of its view counts.

There are many actions that can be counted in this way. *Clicks* occur when users follow a link from one page to another. Advertisers will often count the number of clicks an ad generates. Many voting schemes, where users indicate their likes and dislikes, allow people to vote multiple times. The same can true for measures of engagement that are built on counting "tweets." In all these instances, you have a gross measure of something but no idea how many people are actually responsible.

Visits constitute yet another way to measure popularity. Web users typically have a session on a website in which they look at many pages. Each session is regarded as a visit. If they stop looking at pages or do not take any action for a period of time (e.g., 30 minutes), the visit ends. If they return later, it is regarded as another visit. You can use the number of visits as a measure of how much traffic a website gets, but it does not tell you how many different visitors there were. The "unique visitors" count is a cumulative measure that we discuss in the following chapter.

Impressions are a widely used Web metric. In today's Web, ad servers often deliver display ads to multiple websites. These can appear as banner ads or some graphic element that might link you back to the advertiser. People do not always click on these ads, but they might see them. It is common to count and report the number of served impressions, which can be thought of as opportunities to see the ad. As we noted in chapter 3, many advertisers are not happy about counting served impressions, because those ads are not always placed on the page where users can see them. So there is a move in the industry to pare down the count to just "viewable impressions."

Impressions, viewable or not, are just like the gross impressions used in broadcast-based metrics. They provide a measure of the overall weight of an ad campaign, without really telling you anything about reach and frequency. And just like their broadcast counterparts, they are routinely combined with information on costs to create a hybrid measure called cost per impression. These are generally reported in the form on CPMs. That is, they tell you how much it costs to achieve a thousand impressions. The use of CPMs across media platforms allows marketers to make judgments about the cost-effectiveness of different advertising vehicles.

COMPARISONS

Comparing gross measures is, in fact, the most common form of ratings analysis. There are an endless number of comparisons that can be made. Some might show the superiority of one station over another, the relative cost efficiency of different advertising media, or the success of one program format as opposed to another. There are certainly more of these than we can catalog in this chapter. We can, however, provide illustrative examples of comparisons that may be useful in buying or selling time and programs, or simply reaching a better understanding of the electronic media and their audiences.

One area of comparison deals with the size and composition of the available audience. You know from chapter 4 that the nature of the available audience is a powerful determinant of station or program audiences. Therefore, an analyst might want to begin by taking a closer look at who is watching or listening at different times. This kind of analysis could certainly be of interest to a programmer who must be cognizant of the ebb and flow of different audience segments when deciding what programs to run. It might also be of value to an advertiser or media buyer who wants to know when a certain kind of audience is most available. The most straightforward method of comparison is to graph the size of various audience segments at different hours throughout the day.

As we noted earlier, the single most important factor affecting the size of broadcast audiences is when people are available to listen. Work hours, school, commuting, and meal times, as well as seasons of the year, are the strongest influences on when people are available and potentially interested in using mass media. There are no regular surveys that provide detailed information on such availabilities, but several older studies can be reconstructed to give a rough idea of the availability of men, women, teens, and children throughout the day (Figure 5.1A).

Holidays, special events, and coverage of especially important news stories can certainly alter these patterns of availability, but as a rule they translate rather directly into the patterns of media use depicted in Figure 5.1B. The instances when a single program, or big event, has influenced a rise in HUTs are relatively rare. The most famous such occasions were the assassination of President Kennedy, men landing on the moon, the verdict in the O. J. Simpson trial, the events of 9/11, and the inauguration of Barak Obama, the first African American U.S. president.

With few exceptions, though, the best indicators of how many people will use media at any given time are existing reports of total audience size. Any new program or network that plans to find an audience among those who are not already listening or viewing is very unlikely to be successful. New programs, formats, and program services, for the most part, divide the existing potential and available audiences into smaller pieces of the pie rather than cause new viewers to tune in. The most obvious evidence of this is the decline in national broadcast network share due to the increasing number of cable and DBS competitors.

Thus, to plot when various audience segments are using a medium in a market is a valuable starting point for the audience analyst. Radio market reports have a section of day-part audience estimates with people using radio (PUR)

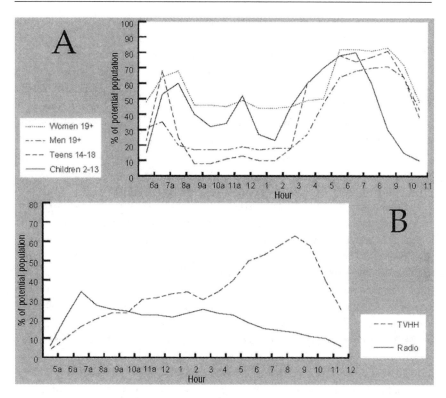

FIGURE 5.1. Hypothetical Audience Availabilities and Typical Patterns of Radio and Television Use

levels, as well as different station audiences. Television reports typically estimate audiences by the quarter hour or the half hour.

Advertisers, of course, must eventually commit to buying time on specific stations or networks. To do so, they need to determine the most effective way to reach their target audience. This relatively simple requirement can trigger a torrent of ratings comparisons. From the time buyer's perspective, the comparisons should be responsive to the advertiser's need to reach a certain kind of audience in a cost-efficient manner. From the seller's perspective, the comparisons should also show his or her audiences in the best possible light. Although these two objectives are not mutually exclusive, they can cause audience analysts to look at ratings data in different ways.

The simplest form of ratings analysis is to compare station or program audiences in terms of their size. This can be determined by ranking each program, station, or network by its average rating and, in effect, declaring a winner. One need only glance at the trade press to get a sense of how important it is to be "Number 1" by some measure. Of course, not everyone can be Number 1.

Further, buying time on the top-rated station may not be the most effective way to spend an advertising budget. Comparisons of audience size are typically qualified by some consideration of audience composition.

The relevant definition of audience composition is usually determined by an advertiser. If the advertiser has a primary audience of women aged 18 to 24, it would make sense for the analyst to rank programs by ratings among women aged 18 to 24 rather than by total audience size. In all probability, this would produce a different rank ordering of programs and perhaps even a different Number 1 program. For radio stations, which often specialize in a certain demographic, ranking within audience subsets can allow several stations to claim they are Number 1.

At this point, we should emphasize a problem in ratings analysis about which researchers are quite sensitive. Analysis or comparison of audience subsets reduces the actual sample size on which those comparisons are based. Casual users can easily ignore or forget this because published ratings seem so authoritative once they are published and downloaded to a desktop computer. But remember that ratings estimates are subject to sampling error, and the amount of error increases as the sample size decreases. That means, for instance, that the difference between being Number 1 and Number 2 among men aged 18 to 24 might be a chance occurrence rather than a real difference. A researcher in this case would say the difference was not statistically significant. The same phenomenon produces what people in the industry call *bounce,* which is defined as a change in station ratings from one book to the next that is a result of a sampling error rather than any real change in the station's audience size. An analyst should never be impressed by small differences, especially those based on small samples.

Having so cautioned, we must also point out that comparisons are sometimes made using statistics other than sheer audience size. Ratings data can be adjusted in a way that highlights audience composition and then ranked. This may produce very different rank orderings. There are two common techniques used to make these adjustments.

Indexing is a common way to make comparisons across scores. An index number simply expresses an individual score, like a rating or CPM, relative to some standard or base value. The basic formula for creating index numbers is as follows:

$$\frac{\text{Score} \times 100}{\text{Base Value}} = \text{Index Number}$$

Usually the base value is fixed at a point in time to give the analyst an indication of how some variable is changing. Current CPMs, for instance, are often indexed to their levels in an earlier year. Base values have been determined in other ways as well. Suppose a program has a high rating among women aged 18 to 24 but a low rating overall. An index number could be created by using the overall rating as a base value. That would make the target audience rating look strong by comparison. CPM indices are also created by comparing individual market CPMs to an average CPM across markets (see Poltrack, 1983).

Thus far, we have defined target audiences only in terms of two demographic variables: age and gender. These are the segmentation variables most commonly used to specify an advertiser's audience objectives. Age and gender, of course, may not be the most relevant descriptors of an advertiser's target market. Income, buying habits, lifestyle, and a host of other variables might be of critical importance to someone buying advertising time. Target audiences defined in those terms make effective sales tools. Unfortunately, this kind of specialized information is not reported in ratings books.

As we discussed in chapter 1, ratings services are capable of producing customized ratings reports. The widespread use of personal computers and Internet access to databases has made this sort of customization increasingly common. As a consequence, it is now possible to describe audiences in ways that are not reported in the syndicated ratings report.

For example, ratings services keep track of the zip code in which each member of the sample lives. Zip code information is valued because knowing where a person lives can reveal a great deal about that individual. Inferences can be made about household incomes, occupations, ethnicity, education levels, lifestyles, and so on. As long as sample sizes are sufficiently large, these inferences will be reasonably accurate on average. Several companies offer research that combines geography with demographic/psychographic characteristics. Nielsen acquired Claritas, a market leader in this type of analysis, and now offers its own product called NielsenPRIZM. The use of this information means that audiences can be defined and compared in a virtually unlimited number of ways.

Of course, these audience comparisons alone will not necessarily convince an advertiser to buy time. As with any product for sale, no matter how useful or nicely packaged, the question usually comes down to how much it costs. In this context, CPM and CPP comparisons are critical. Such comparisons might be designed to illuminate the efficiency of buying one program, station, or daypart as opposed to another. Table 5.3 compares CPMs for network and spot television across several dayparts. Note that gaining access to 1,000 homes during daytime is relatively inexpensive, while the same unit costs several times more during prime time. CPM levels for cable networks are generally lower.

Programmers use rating and share comparisons as well. Consider, for example, how they might use zip codes to segment and compare audiences. A radio station might compare its ratings across zip code areas within a market to determine whether ratings are highest in areas with the highest concentration of likely listeners. If a station places a strong signal over an area with the kind of

TABLE 5.3
Cost-per-thousand for Network and Spot TV 30-Second Units (2011–2012)

			Sex		Adults		
	Homes	Adults	Men	Women	18–34	18–49	25–54
Broadcast Networks							
Early A.M.	$12.55	$10.74	$27.26	$17.45	$49.17	$24.12	$20.75
Daytime	6.80	6.19	—	8.47	18.13	11.93	12.84
Early news	11.50	8.40	19.59	15.38	48.65	22.29	20.77
Prime	26.93	19.48	40.98	29.98	56.19	34.34	35.60
Late fringe	21.06	16.42	38.94	33.76	43.24	26.21	30.27
Syndication							
Daytime	5.35	4.88	—	6.89	16.96	9.58	10.85
Early fringe	12.73	10.05	22.29	15.17	33.47	17.82	17.15
Prime access	19.96	16.63	38.37	28.51	79.84	34.41	35.02
Late fringe	12.92	11.05	24.01	20.50	34.77	17.01	18.20
Cable Networks							
Daytime	3.66	3.50	8.09	5.90	11.86	7.55	7.12
Early/late fringe	8.63	8.21	18.67	13.72	24.10	13.45	14.77
Prime	13.26	10.61	24.24	19.80	39.39	22.77	19.26
Spot (100 Markets)[a]							
Daytime	6.60	6.22	---	8.29	22.78	12.47	12.14
Early fringe	7.83	6.89	16.97	11.03	26.21	14.36	13.73
Late fringe	11.41	8.56	18.56	15.04	27.17	14.17	14.10

[a]Since there is no upfront for spot, these estimates are more akin to network TV scatter CPMs.

Source: National TV ACES, a service of Media Dynamics, Inc. (national data only). Spot data are Media Dynamics, Inc. estimates. Used by permission, Media Dynamics, Inc.

population that should like its format but has few listeners, special promotions might be called for. One station that uses this kind of analysis placed outdoor advertising and conducted a series of remote broadcasts in the areas where it was underperforming.

Radio programmers may also find it useful to represent the audience for each station in the market on a special *demographic map*. This can be done by creating a two-dimensional grid, with the vertical axis expressing, for example, the percentage of males in each station's audience and the horizontal axis expressing the median age of the audience. Once these values are known, each station can be located on the grid. The station audiences could also be averaged to map formats rather than individual stations. Local radio market reports contain the information needed to determine these values, although a few preliminary calculations are necessary.

The most difficult calculation is determining the median age of each station's audience. The median is a descriptive statistic, much like an arithmetic average. Technically, it is the point at which half the cases in a distribution are higher and half are lower. If, for example, 50 percent of a station's audience is younger than 36 and 50 percent are older, then 36 is the median age.

To determine the median age of a station's audience, you must know the audience size of individual age categories reported by the ratings service. Table 5.4 contains these data for a single station in a single daypart, as well as the estimated

TABLE 5.4
Calculating Median Age and Gender of Station Audience

Age Group	Male (in 00's)	Female (in 00's)	Group Frequency (in 00's)	Cumulative Frequency (in 00's)
12–17	?	?	23	23
18–24	29	50	79	102
25–34	63	41	104	206
35–44	43	60	103	309
45–54	35	27	62	371
55–64	20	17	37	408
65+	8	16	24	432
Total 12+	?	?	432	
Total 18+	198	211	409	
Percent M-Fa	48%	52%		

a Because radio market reports do not ordinarily report the gender of persons 12 to 17, the male to female breakdown for a station's audience must be determined on the basis of those 18 and older. In this case, there are 409(00) persons 18+ in the audience.

numbers of men and women who are listening. The station has 43,200 listeners in an AQH. Because radio books report audiences in hundreds, it is more convenient to record that as 432 in the table. The number of listeners aged 65 and older must be inferred from the difference between the total audience aged 12 and older and the sum of all other categories (i.e., 432 − 408 = 24).

The median can now be located in the following way. First, figure out the cumulative frequency. This is shown in the column on the far right-hand side of the table. Second, divide the total size of the audience in half. In this case, it is 216 (i.e., 432/2 = 216). Third, look at the cumulative distribution and find the age category in which the 216th case falls. We know that 206 people are 34.5 or younger, and that there are 103 people in the next oldest group. Therefore, the 216th case must be between 34.5 and 44.5. Fourth, locate the 216th case by interpolating within that age group. To do that, assume that the ages of the 103 people in that group are evenly distributed. To locate the median, we must move 10 cases deep into the next age group. Stated differently, we need to go 10/103 of the way into a 10-year span. That translates into .97 years (i.e., $10/103 \times 10 = 0.97$). Add that to the lower limit of the category and, bingo, the median age is 35.47 (i.e., 34.5 + 0.97 = 35.47).

This procedure sounds more burdensome than it really is. Once you get the hang of it, it can be done with relative ease. It is simply a way to reduce a great deal of information about the age of the station's audience into a single number. Similarly, the gender of the audience is reduced to a single number by using the male/female breakdowns in each category. In the example just given, 48 percent of the audience was male. These two numbers could become coordinates that allow us to plot a point on a two-dimensional grid. Figure 5.2 shows how stations with different formats would look on a demographic map of radio stations.

Figure 5.2 is a fairly typical array of formats and the audiences associated with each one. As you can see, formats can vary widely in terms of the type of listener they attract. Both an album rock station and a contemporary hits station will tend to have young listeners, but they typically appeal differently to young men and women. A classical station tends to attract older listeners. Music syndicators often package radio formats designed to appeal to very specific demographics, and the pronounced differences in audience composition explain how different stations can be Number 1 with different categories of listeners.

This kind of demographic mapping can be used by programmers in a number of ways. For example, it can help identify "holes" in the market by drawing attention to underserved segments of the population. It can also offer a different way to look at the positioning of stations in a market, and how they do or do not compete for the same type of listeners. By creating maps for different dayparts, the programmer can look for shifts in audience composition.

A number of cautions in the interpretation of the map should, however, be kept in mind. First, it tells the analyst nothing about the size of the potential

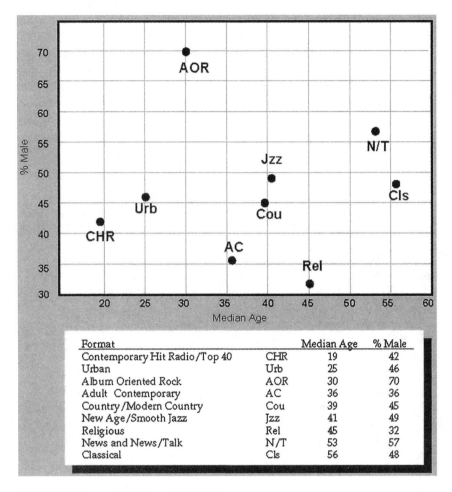

Format		Median Age	% Male
Contemporary Hit Radio/Top 40	CHR	19	42
Urban	Urb	25	46
Album Oriented Rock	AOR	30	70
Adult Contemporary	AC	36	36
Country/Modern Country	Cou	39	45
New Age/Smooth Jazz	Jzz	41	49
Religious	Rel	45	32
News and News/Talk	N/T	53	57
Classical	Cls	56	48

FIGURE 5.2. Demographic Map of Radio Stations

audiences involved. There may be a hole in the market because there are relatively few people of a particular type. Some markets, for example, have very old populations; others do not. Similarly, the map reports no information on the size of the station's actual audience, only its composition. Second, the analyst should remember that different types of listeners may be more valuable to advertisers, and hence constitute a more desirable audience. This could be attributable to their demographic composition, or the fact that many listen exclusively to their favorite station. Third, just because two or more stations occupy the same space on the map, it does not mean that they will share an audience. A country and Western station and a public radio station will often fall side-by-side on a map, but typically they have very little crossover audience. The tendency of listeners to move back and forth between stations can be more accurately studied by using the audience duplication section of the ratings book. We discuss such cumulative measurements later. Finally, remember that age and gender are not the only factors that might be related to station preferences. The map could look quite different if ethnicity or education were among the dimensions. Just such a map can be constructed when other demographic variables, such as education and income, are available.

Median age can also be a useful way to differentiate among television program sources. Table 5.5 shows a comparison of broadcast and cable networks on the

TABLE 5.5
Median Age of Network Audiences 2011–2012

CBS	56
ABC	52
NBC	49
Fox	46
CW	37
USA	52
LIFETIME	50
AMC	50
HISTORY	49
TNT	49
Syfy	47
A&E	46
WE	46
Food	46
DISC	43
TLC	43
Bravo	42
TBS	39
FX	38
E!	34
ABC Family	27
MTV	23

Data are from John Consoli, "A Random Sampling of Cable Networks' Median Age Audiences" in *Broadcasting & Cable* August 28, 2012. (Analysis of NielsenData) http://www.broadcastingcable.com/article/488919-A_Random_Sampling_of_Cable_Networks_Median_Age_Audiences.php median age of their audiences. Aside from the CW, which attracts a younger audience, the median age of broadcast network viewers is rising. Cable networks show an even wider range of median ages. MTV's is 23, while USA network's median age is 52. As you might expect, news networks occupy the other end of the spectrum. The FOX News prime time audience is 61.2, and CNN's is over 65.

The median age of networks can mask significant variation in programs, so it is also useful to look at averages for program types. According to Media Dynamics (2012, p. 211), the audience for primetime animated sitcoms has a median age of 31.4, much lower than the average of networks as a whole. Similarly, the median age for late night comedy / variety programs and for cable sports channels is a comparatively low 41.9. At the other end of the spectrum are early evening newscasts and syndicated game shows, which tend to skew much older (average ages of 60.8 and 61.1, respectively).

Ratings comparisons are also made longitudinally, over several points in time. In fact, most local market ratings reports will include data from previous sweeps under the heading of ratings trends. There could be any number of reasons for looking at audience trends. A radio programmer might want to determine how a format change had altered the composition of the station's audience, perhaps producing a series of maps like the one in Figure 5.2. A financial analyst might want to examine the ratings history of a particular media property. A policy-maker or economist might want to study patterns of audience diversion to assess the competitive positions of old and new media.

Modern metering devices also permit what might be called a "micro-longitudinal" study of audiences. Instead of comparing gross measures over a period of weeks or months, the analyst can assess audience behavior on a second-by-second basis. DVRs, like those sold by TiVo Inc., or set-top boxes (STBs) could become the functional equivalent of household meters—capturing a group of television sets playing moment to moment.

Figure 5.3 is a report of how households with TiVo watched Super Bowl XLVI (2012) on an aggregate, anonymous basis. The horizontal axis displays the time of the broadcast; the vertical axis represents an audience *index*, which compares viewing at a given point in time with the average audience over the course of the game. An index of 1.0 means the audience during that 30-second time period was the same as the average audience. If the index is higher than 1.0, the time period audience was higher than average; and if it is less than 1.0, the audience at that time was lower than average. Note that the index values on the left are scaled differently than the values on the right—the left axis represents live viewing, and the right represents time-shifted viewing.

This graph can be used to gauge audience interest in various parts of the Super Bowl broadcast. For example, the live audience grew steadily throughout the game but dipped slightly during commercials and during one segment of the halftime show. The viewers who time-shifted and watched the game any

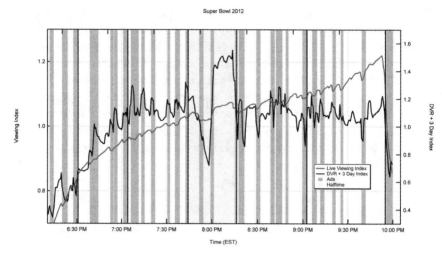

FIGURE 5.3. NFL Real-time Audience Size
Courtesy of TiVo Inc.

time during the next 3 days had more interest in the last segment of the half-time show than they did at any other point in the game. They zapped through the commercials they found boring and watched the ones they liked. This DVR audience shows much more variability in their viewing pattern.

Aside from offering a footnote to popular culture, such micro-longitudinal studies of program audiences can be of value to advertisers and programmers alike. The former can assess the attention-grabbing power of their commercials or, conversely, the rate at which DVR users are skipping the ads altogether. The latter can look at the same information the way they use "program analyzer" data—identifying those parts of the show that people want to skip or see again and again.

As you can surely tell by now, there are any number of ways to manipulate and compare estimates of audience size and composition. In fact, because the major ratings services now produce electronic ratings books that are read by a computer, the time involved in sorting and ranking ratings data can be drastically reduced. Both Arbitron and Nielsen sell software packages that will manipulate their data in a variety of ways. Some private vendors have also produced software that can turn ratings data into bar graphs, pie charts, and so on.

Although most of these developments are a boon to ratings analysts, a number of cautions should be exercised in either producing or consuming all the comparative statistics. Do not let the computational power or colorful graphics of these programs blind you to what you are actually dealing with. Remember that all gross measures of the audience are simply estimates based on sample information. Keep the following points in mind:

- Be alert to the size of the sample used to create a rating or make an audience projection. One consequence of zeroing in on a narrowly defined target audience is that the actual number of people on which estimates are based becomes quite small. That will increase the sampling error surrounding the audience estimates. A national peoplemeter sample might be big enough to break out the audience into narrow subsets. It does not follow that local market samples, which are smaller, can provide similar target estimates of equal accuracy.
- Techniques like indexing and calculating target efficiency can have you taking percentages of percentages, which tend to obscure the original values on which they are based. For example, comparing a 1.4 rating to a 0.7 rating produces the same index number (i.e., 200) as comparing a 14.0 to a 7.0. Sampling error, however, will be much larger relative to the smaller ratings. This means you should have less confidence in the first index value because even slight variations in its component parts could cause it to fluctuate wildly. The fact that the second index number is more reliable is not readily apparent with this sort of data reduction.
- Keep it simple. The ability to manipulate numbers in a multitude of ways does not necessarily mean that it is a good idea. This is true for two reasons. First, the more twists and turns there are in the analysis, the more likely you are to lose sight of what you are actually doing to the data. In other words, you are more likely to make a conceptual or computational error. Second, even if your work is flawless, more complex manipulations are harder to explain to the consumers of your research. You may understand how some special index was created, but that does not mean that a media buyer will have the time or inclination to sit through the explanation.

PREDICTION AND EXPLANATION

Most people schooled in quantitative research and theory are familiar with the concepts of prediction and explanation. In fact, the major reason for developing social scientific theory is to allow us to explain and/or predict the events we observe in the social world around us. In the context of ratings research, we can use the theories of audience behavior we explored in chapter 4 to help explain and predict gross measures of audience size and composition. Although prediction and explanation are certainly of interest to social theorists, they are not mere academic exercises. Indeed, predicting audience ratings is one of the principal activities of industry users.

It is important to remember that all ratings data are historical. They describe something that has already happened. It is equally important to remember that the buying and selling of audiences are always conducted in anticipation of future events. Although it is certainly useful to know which program had the largest audience last week, what really determines the allocation of advertising dollars is an expectation of who will have the largest audience next week or next season. Hence, ratings analysts who are involved in sales and advertising often spend a considerable portion of their time trying to predict ratings.

In the parlance of the industry, the job of predicting ratings is sometimes called pre-buy analysis (not to be confused with the pre-buy analyses done by financial planners and programmers when they evaluate a program acquisition). The buyer and seller of advertising time must each estimate the audience that will be delivered by a specific media schedule. The standard method of prediction is a two-stage process.

In the first stage, the analyst estimates the size of the total audience, as reflected in HUT or PUT levels, at the time a spot is to air. This is largely a matter of understanding audience availability. You will recall from our discussion in chapter 4 that total audience size is generally quite predictable. It varies by hour of the day, day of the week, and week of the year. It can also be affected by extremes in the weather (e.g., snowstorms, heatwaves, etc.), although these are obviously harder to know far in advance.

The simplest way to predict the total audience level for a future point in time is to assume it will be the same as it was exactly 1 year ago. This takes hourly, daily, and seasonal variations into account. A somewhat more involved procedure is to look at HUT/PUT over a period of months or years. By doing so, the analyst may identify long-term trends, or aberrations, in audience levels that would affect his or her judgment about future HUT levels. For instance, a 4-year average of HUT levels for a given hour, day, or month might produce a more stable estimate of future HUTs than would looking only at last year, which could have been atypical. In fact, to determine audience levels during months that are not measured, HUT levels should be interpolated by averaging data from sweeps before and after the month in question.

In the second stage, the analyst must project the share of audience that the station or program will achieve. Here, the simplest approach is to assume that an audience share will be the same as it was during the last measurement period. Of course, a number of factors can affect audience shares, and an analyst must take these into account. Programming changes can have a dramatic effect on audience shares. In radio, rival stations may have changed formats, making them more or less appealing to some segment of the market. In television, a competing station might be counterprogramming more effectively than in the past. Less dramatic, long-term trends might also be at work. Perhaps cable penetration has caused gradual erosion in audience shares that is likely to continue in the near future. Just as in estimating HUT levels, making comparisons across several measurement periods might reveal subtle shifts that would otherwise go unnoticed.

Once total audience levels and specific audience shares have been estimated, predicting an audience rating is simple. Multiply the HUT level you expect by the projected audience share, and you have a predicted rating. This formula is summarized as follows:

Estimated HUT × projected share (%) = predicted rating

In effect, it simply codifies the conventional wisdom expressed in Paul Klein's (1971) theory of the "least objectionable program." That is, exposure is best thought of as a two-stage process in which an already available audience decides which station or program to watch. The procedure to predict ratings for specific demographic subsets of the audience is the same, except that you must estimate the appropriate PUT level (e.g., men aged 18–49) and determine the program's likely share among that audience subset. In either case, there are now a number of computer programs marketed by the ratings companies and independent vendors that perform such pre-buy analyses.

Although these formulas and computer programs are useful, remember that predicting audience ratings is not an exact science. It involves experience, intuition, and an understanding of the factors that affect audience size. Unfortunately, we can only offer help in the last category. Our advice would be to consider the model of audience behavior in chapter 4. Systematically work your way through the structural and individual-level factors that are likely to affect audience size, and begin to test them against your own experience. Sometimes that will lead you to make modifications that just seem to work.

The DVR and the introduction of C3 ratings have affected the audience-prediction calculus. Now buyers and sellers have to take into account not only the differences between program and commercial viewership but also whether a recorded program will actually be played back within 3 days. Some programs like popular dramas have a high rate of time-shifted viewing, which adds to the C3 rating; others, such as live events, do not gain as much additional viewership over time.

One of the most difficult and high-stakes occasions for predicting ratings occurs during the upfront market in network television. Major advertising agencies and network sales executives must try to anticipate how the fall lineups will perform. This is especially tricky because new programs have no track record to depend on. At least one major agency has found, through experience, that it can predict network ratings more accurately if it bases those predictions not on total HUT levels but on network-only HUT levels. In other words, the first stage in the process is to estimate the total number of viewers who will watch broadcast network television. Why this results in better predictions is not entirely clear.

TABLE 5.6
Sweeps Used for Post-Buy Analysis[a]

February	January-February-March
May	April-May-June
July	July-August-September
November	October-November-December

[a]This schedule for post-buy analysis assumes the market is measured four times a year. Additional sweeps in January, March, and October would, if available, be used for post-by analysis in January, March, April and September-October, respectively.

Armed with share projections and predicted ratings for various segments of the audience, buyers and sellers negotiate a contract. Sellers are inclined to be optimistic about their ratings prospects, whereas buyers tend to be more conservative. In fact, the ratings projections that each brings to the table may be colored by the need to stake out a negotiating position. Eventually a deal is struck. Because most spot buys involve a schedule of several spots, the sum total of audience to be delivered is usually expressed in GRPs.

After a schedule of spots has run, both buyers and sellers want to know how well they did. Just as programmers and financial managers evaluate program buys, salespeople and buyers evaluate ratings predictions through a *post-buy analysis*. In markets that are continuously measured, it is possible to know exactly how well programs performed when a spot aired. Most local markets, however, are only surveyed during certain months. Consequently, precise data on ratings performance may not be available. Table 5.6 identifies the sweeps that are traditionally used for post-buy analysis in different months. The point is to use the best available data for evaluative purposes.

With the schedule of spots in one hand and the actual ratings in the other, the schedule is "re-rated." For example, it may be that the original contract anticipated 200 GRPs, but the actual audience delivered totaled 210 GRPs. If that is true, the media buyer did better than expected. Of course, the opposite could have occurred, resulting in an audience deficiency. In upfront deals, networks have traditionally made up such deficiencies by running extra spots. More often, however, it is simply the media buyer's bad luck.

Questions are often raised about how accurate ratings predictions are, or should be. The standard practice in the industry has been to view delivered audience levels within ±10 percent of the predicted levels as acceptable. There are three sources of error that can cause such discrepancies—forecasting error, strategic error, and sampling error. *Forecasting errors* are usually the first that come to mind. Included are errors of judgment and prediction. For example, the analyst might not have properly gauged a trend in HUT levels or foreseen the success of some programming strategy. *Strategic errors* are those errors deliberately introduced into the process at the time of contractual negotiations. A researcher might, for instance, honestly believe that a particular program will deliver a 5 rating while the person selling the program believes that it could be sold at 6 if a projection justified that number. To make a more profitable deal, the projection is knowingly distorted.

Sampling error can also affect the accuracy of ratings predictions, and should serve to remind us once again that these numbers are simply estimates based on sample information. As we saw in chapter 3, any rating is associated with a certain amount of sampling error. The larger the sample on which the rating is based, the lower is the associated error. In addition, the error surrounding small ratings tends to be rather large relative to the size of the rating itself. The same logic can be applied to a schedule of spots as expressed in GRPs. In the mid-1980s, Arbitron conducted an extensive study of the error (Jaffe, 1985) in GRP estimates. The principal conclusions were as follows:

- GRPs based on larger effective sample bases (ESB) had smaller standard errors. In effect, this means that GRPs based on large audience segments (e.g., men aged 18 and older) are more stable than those based on smaller segments (e.g., men aged 18–34). It also means that larger markets, which tend to have larger samples, will generally have less error than small markets.
- The higher the pairwise correlation between programs in the schedule, the higher the standard error. In other words, when there is a high level of audience duplication between spots in the schedule, there is a higher probability of error. This happens because high duplication implies that the same people tend to be represented in each program rating, thereby reducing the scope of the sample on which GRPs are based.
- For a given GRP level, a schedule with relatively few highly rated spots was less prone to error than a schedule with many low-rated spots.
- All things being equal, the larger the schedule in terms of GRPs, the larger the size of absolute standard error, but the smaller the size of relative standard error.

A more recent study by Nielsen (2005) reached similar conclusions. As a practical matter, all this means that a post-buy analysis is more likely to find results within the ±10 percent criterion if GRPs are based on relatively large segments of the market and programs or stations with relatively high ratings. A match of pre-buy predictions to post-buy ratings is less likely if GRPs are based on small ratings among small audience segments, even if forecasting and strategic error are nonexistent. As increased competition fragments radio and television audiences, and as advertisers try to target increasingly precise market segments, this problem of sampling error is likely to cause more postbuy results to fall outside the 10 percent range. For a thoughtful discussion of buying and selling predicted audiences, see Napoli (2003).

The method for predicting ratings we have described thus far is fairly straightforward, requires relatively little in the way of statistical manipulations, and depends heavily on intuition and expert judgment. There have, however, been a number of efforts to model program ratings in the form of mathematical equations. With either approach, the underlying theory of audience behavior is much the same. In attempts to model the ratings, however, many expert judgments are replaced by empirically determined, quantitative relationships.

Gensch and Shaman (1980) and Barnett, Chang, Fink, and Richards (1991) developed various models that accurately estimate the number of viewers of network television at any point in time. Consistent with our earlier discussions, they discovered that total audience size was not dependent on available program content but rather was a function of time of day and seasonality. Once the size of the available audience was predicted, the second stage in the process, determining each program's share of audience, was modeled independently. This is analogous to the standard method of prediction in the industry. For an excellent review of the state of the art in forecasting television ratings, see Danaher, Dagger, and Smith (2011).

A number of writers have developed integrated models of viewer choice, considering factors such as lead-in effects, counterprogramming, a program's rating history, program type, and even the demographic characteristics of cast members (e.g., Cooper, 1993; Danaher & Mawhinney, 2001; Shachar & Emerson, 2000; Rust, Kamakura, & Alpert, 1992; Weber, 2003; Webster & Phalen, 1997). In addition to these general predictive models, more specialized studies have also been done. Researchers have used correlational studies of gross audience measurements to assess the success of different programming strategies (e.g., Lin, 1995; McDowell & Dick, 2003; Tiedge & Ksobiech, 1986, 1987), to determine the cancellation threshold of network programs (Adams, 1993; Atkin & Litman, 1986), to assess the impact of media ownership on ratings performance (Parkman, 1982), and to examine the role of ratings in the evolution of television program content (McDonald & Schechter, 1988). In our judgment, these sorts of analyses represent a fertile area for further study. They are very helpful for historical and methodological insights.

RELATED READINGS

Balnaves, M., O'Regan, T., & Goldsmith, B. (2011). *Rating the audience: The business of media*. New York: Bloomsbury Publishing Plc.

Buzzard, K. (2012). *Tracking the audience: The ratings industry from analog to digital*. New York: Routledge.

Danaher, P. J., Dagger, T. S., & Smith, M. S. (2011). Forecasting television ratings. *International Journal of Forecasting, 27*(4), 1215–1240. doi:10.1016/j.ijforecast.2010.08.002

Katz, H. E. (2010). *The media handbook: A complete guide to advertising media selection, planning, research and buying* (4th ed.). New York: Routledge.

Kaushik, A. (2010). *Web analytics 2.0: The art on online accountability & science of customer centricity.* Indianapolis, IN: Wiley.

Media Dynamics. (2012). *TV dimensions.* Nutley, NJ: Author.

Napoli, P. M. (2003). *Audience economics: Media institutions and the audience marketplace.* New York: Columbia University Press.

Rust, R. T. (1986). *Advertising media models: A practical guide.* Lexington, MA: Lexington Books.

Sissors, J. Z., & Baron, R. B. (2010). *Advertising media planning* (7th ed.). New York: McGraw-Hill.

Webster, J. G., & Phalen, P. F. (1997). *The mass audience: Rediscovering the dominant model.* Mahwah, NJ: Lawrence Erlbaum Associates.

CHAPTER 6

Analysis of Cumulative Measures

Cumulative measures are routinely used for audience analysis. These metrics are distinguished from gross measures because they depend on tracking individual media users over some period of time. Historically, gross measures would summarize use over a week or a month. But with the increased use of meters and server-centric measurement, it is common to see time periods as brief as a session on the Web. As those time periods shrink and the number of cumulative measures grow, it can be difficult know whether a particular measure is technically gross or cumulative. As a rule, if it reflects knowledge of repeat customers or it reports characteristics of average users, chances are it is a cumulative measure.

Ultimately, the technical distinction is less important than what these metrics reveal about audience behavior. While gross measures are often the preferred measure of a program's or outlet's popularity, cumulative measures reveal more about audience loyalties and the extent to which people are exposed to advertising campaigns. They also form the basis of some measures of engagement. Analysts sometimes combine gross and cumulative measures to produce hybrid measures.

In this chapter, we identify the standard cumulative metrics used in the more traditional broadcast environment. We then look at a newer generation of metrics born of the Web. We review the concepts of reach and frequency, which are crucial to advertisers, and delve deeper into the concept of audience duplication, which can be a building block for many types of analyses. As we did in the last chapter, we provide some examples of how these metrics can be usefully compared and, finally, demonstrate how cumulative analysis can be used to explain patterns of audience behavior.

BROADCAST-BASED METRICS

Once again, we begin with broadcast-based metrics. These are used to summarize people's use of radio and most forms of television. They also set a precedent for the measurement of nonlinear media, including the Web-based metrics we review in the following section. Ultimately, the kinds of cumulative analyses that are possible depend on how the data were collected and exactly what information they contain. Most broadcast-based measures were initially derived from samples responding to questions or filling out diaries. The introduction of peoplemeters and servers made it possible to track users on a moment-by-moment basis and for longer periods of time.

Some cumulative measures appear routinely in ratings reports or the spreadsheets analysts use to manage aggregated data. Other, more specialized, metrics can be calculated by combining common summary statistics. Many other forms of cumulative analysis are possible if the analyst has access to the underlying, respondent-level, data sets.

Cume is the most common cumulative measure of the audience; it is the total number of different people or households who have tuned in to a station at least once over some period of time—usually a "daypart" (e.g., primetime), day, week, or even a month. The term *cume* is often used interchangeably with "reach" and "unduplicated audience." When a cume is expressed as a percentage of the total possible audience, it is called a *cume rating*. When it is expressed as the actual number of people, it is called *cume persons*. These audience summaries are analogous to the ratings and projected audiences we discussed in the previous chapters.

Like ordinary ratings and audience projections, variations on the basic definition are common. Cumes are routinely reported for different subsets of the audience, defined both demographically and geographically. For example, Arbitron reports a station's metropolitan cume ratings for men and women of different age categories. Cume persons can also be estimated within different geographic areas within the market. Regardless of how the audience subset is defined, these numbers express the total, unduplicated audience for a station. Each person or household in the audience can only count once in figuring the cume. It does not matter whether they listened for 8 minutes or 8 hours.

In addition to reporting cumes across various audience subsets, the ratings services also report station cumes within different dayparts. In the United States, radio ratings reports estimate a station's cume audience during so-called morning drive time (i.e., Monday through Friday, 6 A.M.–10 A.M.), afternoon drive time (i.e., Monday through Friday, 3 P.M.–7 P.M.), and other standard dayparts. Cume audiences can also be calculated for a station's combined drive-time audience (i.e., how many people listened to a station in A.M. and/or P.M. drive time).

If cumes are based on diary data, they run no longer than a week. In principle, household meters could produce household cumes, and peoplemeters could produce person cumes over any period of continuous operation (e.g., years). As a practical matter, cume audiences are rarely tracked for more than 1 month. These 4-week cumes are commonly reported with meter-based data, and they are particularly useful for television programs that air only once per week.

Two other variations on cumes are reported in radio. The first is called an *exclusive cume*. This is an estimate of the number of people who listen to only one particular station during a given daypart. All other things being equal, a large exclusive audience may be more saleable than one that can be reached over several stations. Arbitron also reports *cume duplication*. This is the opposite of an exclusive audience. For every pair of stations in a market, the rating services estimate the number of listeners who are in both stations' cume audiences. It is possible, therefore, to see which stations tend to have an audience in common.

The various cume estimates can be used in subsequent manipulations, sometimes combining them with gross measures of the audience, to produce different ways of looking at audience activity. One of the most common is a measure of *time spent listening* (TSL). The formula for computing TSL is as follows:

$$\frac{\text{AQH persons for daypart} \times \text{number of quarter hours in the daypart}}{\text{Cume persons for daypart}} = \text{TSL}$$

The first step is to determine the average quarter-hour (AQH) audience for the station, within any given daypart, for any given segment of the audience. This will be a projected audience reported in hundreds. Multiply that by the total number of quarter hours in the daypart. For A.M. or P.M. drive time, that is 80 quarter hours. For the largest daypart (Monday through Sunday, 6 A.M.–Midnight), it is 504 quarter hours. This product gives you a gross measure of the total number of person quarter hours people spent listening to the station. Dividing it by the number of people who actually listened to the station (i.e., the cume persons) tells you the average amount of time each person in the cume spent listening to the station. At this point, the average TSL is expressed as quarter hours per week, but it is easy enough to translate this into hours per day, in order to make it more interpretable. Table 6.1 shows how this exercise could be done to compare several stations.

TABLE 6.1
Calculating TSL Estimates Across Stations[a]

Station	AQH Persons	AQH persons × 504 QHs* =	Cume/ Persons	Total QHs/ Cume = weekly TSL	Weekly TSL/28 days = TSL hours per day
WAAA	500	252,000	3,500	72.0	2.57
WXXX	1,500	756,000	20,000	37.8	1.35
WBBB	6,500	3,276,000	40,000	81.9	2.93
WZZZ	1,000	504,000	12,000	42.0	1.5

[a]This sample calculation of TSL is based on estimated audiences Monday-Sunday from 6 A.M. to midnight. That daypart has 504 quarter hours (QHs).

As you will note, the average amount of time listeners spend tuned in varies from station to station. All things being equal, a station would rather see larger TSL estimates than smaller TSL estimates. Of course, it is possible that a high TSL is based on only a few heavy users, whereas a station with low TSLs has very large audiences. For example, compare the first two stations on the list in Table 6.1. In a world of advertiser support, gross audience size will ultimately be more important. Nonetheless, TSL comparisons can help change aggregated audience data into numbers that describe a typical listener, and so make them more comprehensible. Although TSLs are usually calculated for radio stations, analogous *time spent viewing* estimates could be derived by applying the same procedure to the AQH and cume estimates in the daypart summary of a television ratings report.

With direct access to the audience database it is possible to simply count the number of quarter hours a person spends watching television or listening to a particular station. Further, if the data are based on meters rather than diaries, you can count the actual minutes spent watching or listening. Since many large consumers of ratings information now pay for direct access to the data, a new kind of *cumulative share* calculation has become increasingly common, especially in studies of television audiences. Essentially what the analyst does is count the number of minutes that a given audience spends viewing a particular source (e.g., a network, station, or program) over some period of time and divides that by the total time they spend watching all television over the same time period. Recall Figure 2.2, which depicted the way in which big-three prime time audience shares had declined over the years. That pictured a succession of cumulative shares in each of the last 18 television seasons. Analogous share values could conceivably be computed for individuals by counting the number of minutes each person spent watching a channel and dividing by the total time they spent watching all television. The equation below shows the basic recipe for calculating cumulative shares. Be aware that the unit of analysis could be anything the analyst chooses (e.g., households, adults aged 18 and older, etc.), as could the programming source (e.g., channel, station, program, etc.).

$$\frac{\text{Time spent viewing channel}}{\text{Time spent viewing TV}} = \text{cumulative share}$$

Another combination of cume and gross measurements results in a summary called audience turnover. The formula of audience turnover is:

$$\frac{\text{Cume persons in a daypart}}{\text{AQH persons in a daypart}} = \text{Audience turnover}$$

Estimates of audience turnover are intended to give the analyst a sense of how rapidly different listeners cycle through the station's audience. A turnover ratio of 1 would mean that the same people were in the audience quarter hour after quarter hour. Although that kind of slavish devotion does not occur in the "real world," relatively low turnover ratios do indicate relatively high levels of station loyalty. Because listeners are constantly tuning into a station as others are tuning out, turnover can also be thought of as the number of new listeners a station must attract in a time period in order to replace those who are tuning out. As was the case with TSL estimates, however, the rate of audience turnover does not tell you anything definitive about audience size. A station with low cume and low AQH audiences could look just the same as a station with large audiences in a comparison of audience turnover. For a discussion of other inventive ways to use published data to measure radio station loyalty, see Dick and McDowell (2004).

Another fairly common way to manipulate the cume estimates that appear in radio ratings books is to calculate what is called *recycling*. This manipulation of the data takes advantage of the fact that there are cumes reported for both morning and afternoon drive time, as well as the combination of those two dayparts. It is, therefore, possible to answer the question, "Of the people who listened to a station in A.M. drive time, how many also listened in P.M. drive time?" This kind of information could be valuable to a programmer in scheduling programs or promotion. Estimating the recycled audience is a two-step process.

First, you must determine how many people listened to the station during both dayparts. Suppose, for instance, that a station's cume audience in morning drive time was 5,000 persons. Let's further assume that the afternoon drive time audience was also reported to be 5,000. If it was exactly the same 5,000 people in both dayparts, then the combined cume would be 5,000 people as well (remember each person can only count once). If they were entirely different groups, the combined cume would be 10,000. That would mean no one listened in both dayparts. If the combined cume fell somewhere in between those extremes, say 8,000, then the number of people who listened in both the morning and the afternoon would be 2,000. This is determined by adding the cume for each individual daypart, and subtracting the combined cume (i.e., A.M. cume + P.M. cume—combined A.M. AND P.M. cume = persons who listen in both dayparts).

Second, the number of persons who listen in both dayparts is divided by the cume persons for either the A.M. or P.M. daypart. The following formula defines this simple operation:

$$\frac{\text{Cume persons in both dayparts}}{\text{Cume persons in one daypart}} = \text{Recycled audience}$$

Essentially, this expresses the number of persons listening at both times as a percentage of those in either the morning or afternoon audience. Using the hypothetical numbers in the preceding paragraph we can see that 40 percent of the morning audience recycled to afternoon drive time (i.e., 2,000 / 5,000 = 40 percent).

Nearly all radio stations get their largest audiences during the morning hours when people are first waking up, so programmers like to compare that figure with those who listen at any other time of the day. It may also be useful to compare whether these same listeners tune in during the weekend, for example. In both television and radio, the promotion department can use data detailing when the most people are listening to schedule announcements about other programs and features on the station. Thus, stations hope to "recycle" their listeners into other dayparts—this builds a larger AQH rating for the station.

WEB-BASED METRICS

Unique Visitors, Visits, and Page Views. One of the most widely used Web metrics is *unique visitors*. It is a count of the number of different people who have visited a website over some period of time, often a month. It is a cumulative measure because users must be tracked over time to know if they are a new or returning visitor. The unique visitors metric is directly analogous to the cume measures used in broadcasting. Both count the number of unduplicated audience members. As is the case with cumes, unique visitors can be computed on different subsets of the audience (e.g., men, women, etc.) or over varying lengths of time. Many Web analytic tools allow researchers to look at daily unique visitors, weekly unique visitors, and so on.

If the measurement of unique visitors is based on a user-centric panel in which the identity of respondents known, then the computation is relatively straightforward. If, on the other hand, the metric is based on server-centric data, calculating unique visitors becomes more challenging. As we explained in chapter 3, servers typically identify returning visitors by using cookies, which have several limitations as a method of tracking audience behavior. For example, a single computer might be used by more than one person. Alternatively, one person might use different browsers on different platforms to access the Web (e.g., a desktop at work, a laptop at home, and a smartphone on the go). In either case one cookie cannot be clearly equated with one user. Further, many people reject or delete cookies on a regular basis. By one estimate, deletion rates range from 30 percent to 43 percent (Nielsen, 2011). Nonhuman agents, like robots or spiders, that search engines use to scour the Web also complicate the picture. The affected industries are studying these issues and possible solutions (e.g., IAB, 2009; MRC, 2007).

The IAB highlighted these difficulties in what they call the "Hierarchy of Audience Measurement Definitions in Census-Based Approaches" seen in Figure 6.1. Moving between each level in the hierarchy requires a mathematical adjustment to correct for over or under counting. The problem is, there are different ways to do that. None of them is without error. And each provider of server-centric measurement employs different algorithms to produce an estimate. Our purpose in pointing out these details is not to torture the reader with trivia, but to

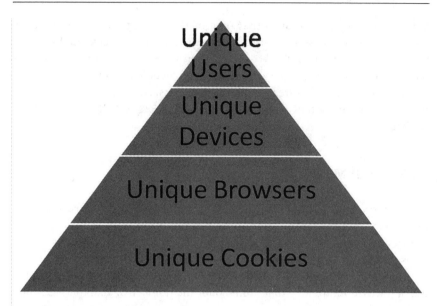

Unique Cookies are those unduplicated cookies that represent visits to Internet content or advertising during a measurement period.

Unique Browsers result from the count of Unique Cookies after adjustment for cookie deletion.

Unique Devices result from the count of Unique Browsers after multiple browser usage on an individual computer is accounted for.

Unique Users represent unduplicated people who have visited the Internet content or advertising during the measurement period. It is the most difficult measure for a census-based measurement organization to report, as the calculation required to reach this metric must include a component that is directly attributable to people, rather than computers or other mechanized devices.

FIGURE 6.1. Hierarchy of Audience Measurement Definitions in Census-based Approaches

demonstrate that with server-centric measurement, it is never as straightforward as one would think. The devil, as they say, is in the details.

Each visitor can, over a period of time, be responsible for one or more visits. As we noted, the sheer number of visits a site receives is another popular metric, but since it does not account for repeat customers, it is a gross measure. Visits will, therefore, always equal or exceed unique visitors. During a visit, or "session," users will view one or more pages and will spend varying amounts of time on each one. These behaviors are the foundation of two additional metrics: page views and time spent. For example, a particular page might have been 1,000 page views. The gross measure does not tell you whether that is the product of 1,000 different people or one person clicking on it 1,000 times. But page views and time spent can be tied to specific visitors, which results in averages that describe the typical user.

Average page views are reported and calculated in a variety of ways. It could be the average page views per visit, in which case you simply divide page views by visits, both of which are gross measures. It could be the average page views per visitor, which can be calculated as follows.

$$\frac{\text{Page views}}{\text{Unique Visitors}} = \text{Average Page Views Per Visitor}$$

Alternatively, it is possible to count the number of pages viewed by each user, resulting in respondent-level scores. Doing it that way, if your analytics program allows it, has the advantage of producing an average and letting you see the entire distribution. In this case you could tell whether visitors were all about the same, or highly variable in their use of pages.

Time Spent Viewing/Listening. In order to report time spent, the meters and servers must record how many minutes and seconds each site or page is viewed during each visit. These sessions are initiated when a user requests a page from a website. The session lasts as long as the user remains active. Of course, people will sometimes leave tabs open while they do something else, so most systems will end a session if there is no activity for 30 minutes. If they return after that time, it is recorded as another visit. Within a typical visit, users click from one page to the next, and each new request marks the end time for viewing the previous page.

Measuring this activity with meters is straightforward, since the metering software can be designed for that purpose. But once again, servers present a problem. Servers can see when a user requests a page. They can tell how long a user spends on that page by when the user requests another page. But most servers have no way of knowing when a user actually leaves the last page they view. So time spent on the last page is a mystery. That is potentially important, since their final destination might reveal what they were really after. Once again, various rules or algorithms must be used to "guestimate" the duration.

Like page views, *average time spent* metrics can be reported in various ways. It could be time spent per visit, per visitor, per site, per page, etc. Often these metrics appear as averages. But as was the case with page views, an analyst can get a better understanding of any time spent phenomenon if they can look at respondent-level scores. That is, he or she can generate time spent per whatever score, for each user. By doing so, you not only see what the average is, you can see differences among people. It might be that most people spent little time on a site, but a minority devotes hours. Knowing about those loyalists and what they do could provide an important insight into how to manage the site.

Conversion Rate. One metric that is near to the heart of many Web publishers and marketers is the conversion rate. A conversion rate is a percentage of the number of visitors who actually take some desired action like ordering or downloading a product. Avinash Kaushik (2010) argues that it is most appropriate to express it as a percentage of unique visitors. In which case, it is calculated as follows:

$$\frac{\text{Action or outcome}}{\text{Unique visitors}} = \text{Conversion Rate}$$

User Loyalty and Engagement. Cumulative measures are often used to assess user engagement. Because they track users over time, cumes offer a window into people's loyalties and the intensity with which they attend to something. In fact, a great many cumulative measures can be read as measures of engagement. They include the usual metrics of page views and time spent, along with the frequency of visits, all of which are best analyzed in respondent-level distributions. It is also worth noting that all these are ultimately based on measures of exposure. Because of that, analysts caution that these measures are better at suggesting the level of engagement rather than the kind of engagement. In other words, people who appear engaged, might love something, hate something, or simply find it bizarre and outlandish. Data on exposure cannot make that determination.

That is one reason the data harvested from social media sites like Facebook and Twitter are attracting the interest of media industries. These platforms allow people to comment, express their likes and dislikes, and share things with other people in their networks. All of these activities can be, and are, reduced to audience metrics. Facebook, which has close to a billion users worldwide, provides a service to page owners called "Page Insights." For each marketer who has a fan page, Facebook reports the number of self-declared fans, how many friends of fans there are, the number of "engaged users" (including measures of exposure like viewing photos) and "talking about this" (including the number of likes). Figure 6.2 is an example of what these data contain and how they are reported.

Some Observations About Web Metrics. The most important thing about these, or any, metrics is what they tell you about audiences and, in turn, how best to conduct your business. Just what all these metrics are telling us is debated, especially in the world of Web analytics. It is clear that they capture different kinds of behaviors and may constitute different measures of success. For example, a search engine might hope to have many unique users but expect to have relatively low page views or time-spent measures. After all, a really good search engine helps you find what you want and sends you on your way. Social networking sites, on the other hand, might hope to keep users engaged for long periods of time and would measure success in page views, time-spent metrics, or other measures of engagement.

Engaged Users

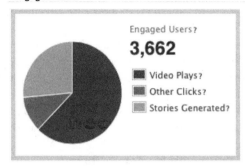

Video plays: The number of times the play button of your video was clicked on.

Photo views: The number of times your photo was viewed in its full size.

Link clicks: The number of time the link included in your post was clicked on.

Other clicks: The number of clicks on your post that are not counted in other metrics. These clicks can include clicks on people's names in comments, clicks on the like count, clicks on the time stamp, etc.

Stories generated: The number of stories that were created from your post. Stories include liking, commenting on or sharing your post, answering a question or RSVP-ing to an event.

Talking About This

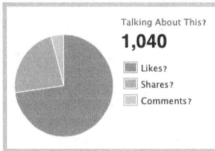

Likes: The number of likes on your post.

Shares: The number of times your post was shared.

Comments: The number of comments on your post.

Event RSVPs: The number of times people responded to your event.

Questions answered: The number of times your question was answered.

FIGURE 6.2. Measures of Engagement in Facebook: (a) Engaged Users and (b) Talking About This
Source: Facebook (2011). Facebook Page Insights: Product Guide for Page Owners. Used by permission.

REACH AND FREQUENCY

A somewhat different way to express cumulative measures is to talk of reach and frequency. These concepts are widely used by advertisers and media planners. One of their primary interests is how many different people have seen a commercial campaign and how often they have seen it.

The term *reach* is just another way to express a cumulative audience—that is, how many unduplicated people were exposed to the message. This is like a broadcaster wanting to know the station's cume, or a Web publisher wanting to know a site's unique audience. However, an advertiser wants to know the reach of an advertising campaign, which often that means counting exposures across multiple stations or websites. Historically, it has been difficult to measure reach across different media (e.g., combining reach across television and the Web), but newer services like Nielsen's "cross-platform campaign ratings" are designed to do just that. As is the case with cumes, reach can be expressed as the actual number of people or households exposed to a message, or it can be expressed as a percent of some population.

Although reach expresses the total number of audience members who have seen or heard an ad at least once, it does not say anything about the number of times any one individual has been exposed to that message. *Frequency* expresses how often a person is exposed, and is usually reported as the average number of exposures among those who were reached. For example, a media planner might say that a campaign reached 80 percent of the population, and it did so with a frequency of 2.5.

Reach and frequency, which are both cumulative measures of the audience, bear a strict mathematical relationship to gross rating points (GRPs). That relationship is as follows:

Reach × Frequency = GRPs

A campaign with a reach of 80 percent and a frequency of 2.5 would, therefore, generate 200 GRPs. Knowing the GRPs of a particular advertising schedule, however, does not give you precise information on the reach and frequency of a campaign. This is because many combinations of reach and frequency can add up to the same number of ratings points. Nonetheless, the three terms are related, and some inferences about reach and frequency can be made on the basis of GRPs. Additionally, analysts use algorithms to translate GRPs to estimates of reach and frequency. These calculations take into account the time of day and type of program, as well as any other variables that might affect the balance of reach and frequency.

Figure 6.3 depicts the usual nature of the relationship. The left-hand column shows the reach of an advertising schedule. Along the bottom are frequency and GRPs. Generally speaking, ad schedules with low GRPs are associated with relatively high reach and low frequency. This can be seen in the fairly steep slope of the left-hand side of the curve. As the GRPs of a schedule increase, gains in reach occur at a reduced rate, while frequency of exposure begins to increase.

The diminishing contribution of GRPs to reach occurs because of differences in the amount of media people consume. People who watch a lot of television are quickly reached with just a few commercials. The reach of a media schedule, therefore, increases rapidly in its early stages. Those who watch very little television, however, are much harder to reach. In fact, reaching 100 percent of the audience is virtually impossible. Instead, as more and more GRPs are committed to an ad campaign (i.e., as more and more commercials are run), they simply increase the frequency of exposure for relatively heavy viewers. That drives up the average frequency. These patterns of reach and frequency can be predicted with a good deal of accuracy across all types of media, including the

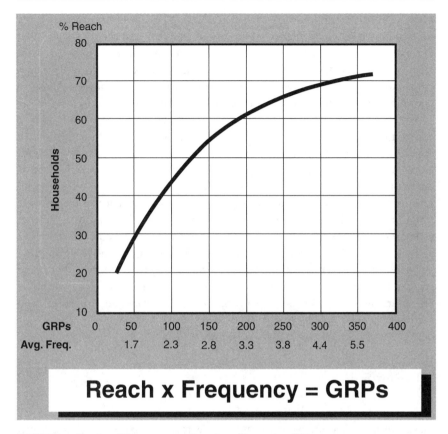

FIGURE 6.3. Reach and Frequency as a Function of Increasing GRPs

Internet. For a review of the various mathematical models used to estimate reach and frequency, see Cheong, Leckenby, and Eakin (2011).

As the preceding discussion suggests, reporting the average frequency of exposure masks a lot of variation across individuals. An average frequency of 2.5 could mean that some viewers have seen an ad 15 times and others have only seen it once. It is useful to consider the actual distribution on which the average is based. These distributions are usually lopsided, or skewed. The majority of households could be exposed to far fewer advertising messages than the arithmetic average, and a relatively small number of "heavy viewing" households might see a great many advertisements. In light of these distributions, advertisers often ask, "How many times must a commercial be seen or heard before it is effective?" "Is one exposure enough for a commercial to have its intended effect, or even be noticed?" "Conversely, at what point do repeated exposures become wasteful, or even counterproductive?" Unfortunately, there are no simple answers to these questions. For many years, the rule of thumb was that an ad had to be seen or heard at least three times before it could be effective. More recent research and theory suggest that one exposure, particularly if it occurs when a consumer is ready to buy, is sufficient to trigger the desired effect. That is one reason that paid search advertising is particularly appealing to advertisers. Whatever the number, the fewest exposures needed to have an effect is referred to as the *effective frequency*.

If one exposure, timed to hit the consumer when he or she is ready to buy, constitutes effective communication, then achieving reach becomes the primary concern of the media planner. This idea, sometimes called "recency theory," along with concerns about audience fragmentation and the variable cost of different advertising vehicles, caused advertisers to push for new ways to optimize reach. The solution came in the form of *optimizers*. These are computer programs that take respondent-level data from a research syndicator and cost estimates for various kinds of spots and identify the most cost-effective way to build reach. For example, instead of simply buying expensive prime-time spots to achieve reach, an optimizer might find a way to cobble together many smaller, less-expensive audiences to accomplish the same result. Today, optimizers, which tend to be expensive to run, are used by most big advertisers and media services companies to plan their advertising schedules.

COMPARISONS

As is the case with gross measures of the audience, it is a common practice to make comparisons among cumulative measures. Comparisons, after all, can provide a useful context within which to interpret the numbers. However, with cumulative measures, part of the impetus for comparing every conceivable audience subset, indexed in every imaginable way, is absent. As a practical matter, gross measures are used more extensively in buying and selling audiences than are cumulative measures, so there is less pressure to demonstrate some comparative advantage, no matter how obscure. Although some cume estimates, like reach, frequency, and unique visitors, can certainly be useful in buying and planning media, much of the comparative work with cumulative measures is done to realize some deeper understanding of audience behavior.

Interesting analyses have been performed by looking at the reach and time spent viewing of television stations. Barwise and Ehrenberg (1988) argued that television stations rarely have small-but-loyal audiences. Instead, it is almost always the case that a station that reaches a small segment of the audience is viewed by that audience only sparingly. This is sometimes labeled a *double jeopardy* effect because a station suffers not only from having relatively few viewers, but also from having relatively disloyal or irregular viewers. To demonstrate the double

jeopardy effect, they constructed a graph based on television ra
the United States and the United Kingdom. More recent studi
have been done in the United States, United Kingdom, and A
are depicted in Figure 6.4.

Along the horizontal axis of each is the weekly reach of the tu.
nels, expressed as a percent of the total audience. Along the vertical axis is .
average number of hours each channel's audience spent viewing in a week. As
you can see, the slope of each curve is remarkably similar despite reporting on
different countries during different decades. They are rather flat to begin with
but rise sharply as the reach of the channel increases. This means that, as a rule,
low reach is associated with low amounts of time spent viewing.

Many people find double jeopardy effects counterintuitive. After all, niche
media are often characterized as responding to audience loyalists by giving them
exactly what they want rather than "lowest common denominator" programming
(Anderson, 2006). But even media like movies and recorded music demonstrate
double jeopardy effects (Elberse, 2008). In television, there are two noteworthy exceptions. First, minority language channels often have small-but-loyal audiences.

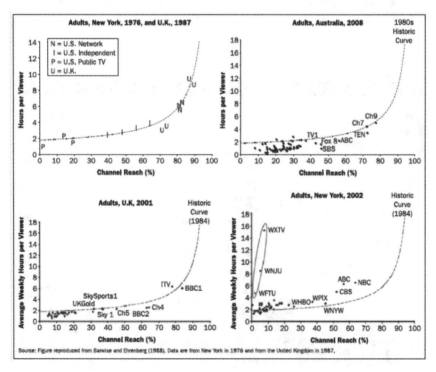

FIGURE 6.4. Comparing Reach and Average Time Spent Viewing in Multiple Countries
Source: Sharp, Beal, & Collins (2009)

ven the original work by Barwise and Ehrenberg (1988) noted this exception, and you can see evidence of it in the circled outliers in the lower right hand graph of Figure 6.4. Second, premium channels, like movie channels for which people pay an extra fee, generally have smaller audiences that spend a good deal of time watching them (Webster, 2005). Many people do not want to pay a premium to watch television, but those who do want to get their money's worth.

The newer video delivery platforms offered by the Web present new opportunities to understand audience behavior. Figure 6.5 presents a comparison of online video destinations using two cumulative measures. On the left are the most popular destinations as measured by the "unique viewers" watching video. This is like the unique visitors metric we just reviewed. You can see that YouTube is the number one destination, by a wide margin. On the right are video destinations ranked by the average time spent viewing per month. Here the number one platform is Netflix, by a similarly wide margin. This seems analogous to the premium channel exception to double jeopardy. YouTube, and many other online services, at present specialize in relatively short video clips. Netflix, which charges its subscribers, offers longer-form movies and television programs. Of course, that may change, and analysts should be able to see if those changes affect viewing behavior by comparing cumulative measures.

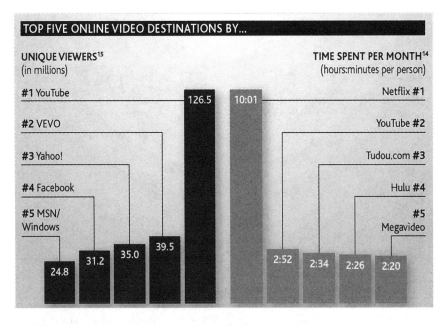

FIGURE 6.5. Comparing Cumulative Measures of Video Destinations
Source: Nielsen (2011). State of Media Consumer Usage Report 2011.

AUDIENCE DUPLICATION

One of the simplest, and most powerful, ways to understand cumulative audience behavior is to analyze *audience duplication*. Basically, analyses of audience duplication ask, "Of the people who were exposed to one program or outlet, how many were exposed to another?" This question can be asked in many ways. Of the people who watched one program, how many watched another? Of the people who visited one website, how many visited another? In each such comparison, we want to measure the size of the duplicated audience. That can help answer very pragmatic questions like, "Are the people who watch my program also going to my website?" And when you look at audience duplication across many different pairs of outlets, you can often see larger patterns of audience behavior. We will describe what studies of audience duplication reveal about audiences in the last section on explaining and predicting behavior. This section begins by concentrating on the basics.

Unfortunately, most questions of audience duplication cannot be answered by looking at the typical numbers in a ratings report. To observe that one television program has the same rating as its lead-in is no assurance that the same audience watched both. However, if the analyst has access to the respondent-level data on which the ratings are based, a variety of analytical possibilities are open. These days, that is often possible. Nielsen and other television ratings companies offer online tools that allow analysts to request data on audience duplication. Similarly, Internet measurement companies, like comScore, have online tools that report audience duplication and "source / loss" (which tells you where visitors to a site are coming from and going to). All of these begin with a straightforward statistical technique called cross-tabulation.

Cross-tabulation is described in detail in most books on research methods, and is a common procedure in statistical software packages. Cross-tabs, as they are sometimes called, allow an analyst to look at the relationship between two variables. If, for instance, we conducted a survey about magazine readership, we might want to identify the relationship between reader demographics and subscription (e.g., are women more or less likely than men to buy *Cosmopolitan*?). Each person's response to a question about magazine subscription could be paired with information on their gender, resulting in a cross-tabulation of those variables.

When cross-tabulation is used to study audience duplication, the analyst pairs one media-use variable with another. Suppose, for example, we had diary data on a sample of 100 people. We would then be in a position to answer questions like, "Of the people who watched one situation comedy (e.g., SC1), how many also watched a second situation comedy (e.g., SC2)?" These are two behavioral variables, among a great many, contained in the data. A cross-tabulation of the two would produce a table like Table 6.2.

TABLE 6.2
Cross-Tabulation of Program Audiences

(a)		Viewed SC1		
		Yes	**No**	**Total**
	Yes	5	15	20
Viewed SC2	No	15	65	80
	Total	20	80	100

(b)		Viewed SC1		
		Yes	**No**	**Total**
	Yes	O = 5	O = 15	20
Viewed SC2		E = 4	E = 16	
	No	O = 15	O = 65	80
		E = 16	E = 64	
	Total	20	80	100

The numbers along the bottom of Table 6.2a show that 20 people wrote "yes," they watched SC1, whereas the remaining 80 did not watch the program. The numbers in these two response categories should always add up to the total sample size. Along the far right-hand side of the table are the comparable numbers for SC2. We have again assumed that 20 people reported watching, and 80 did not. All the numbers reported along the edges, or margins, of the table are referred to as *marginals*. We should point out that when the number of people viewing a program is reported as a percentage of the total sample, that marginal is analogous to a program rating (e.g., both SC1 and SC2 have person ratings of 20).

By studying audience duplication, we can determine whether the same 20 people viewed both SC1 and SC2. The cross-tabulation reveals the answer in the four cells of the table. The upper-left-hand cell indicates the number of people who watched both SC1 and SC2. Of the 100 people in the sample, only 5 saw both programs. That is what is referred to as the *duplicated audience*.

Conversely, 65 people saw neither program. When the number in any one cell is known, all numbers can be determined because the sum of each row or column must equal the appropriate marginal.

Once the size of the duplicated audience has been determined, the next problem is one of interpretation. Is what we have observed a high or low level of duplication? Could this result have happened by chance, or is there a strong relationship between the audiences for the two programs in question? To evaluate the data at hand, we need to judge our results against certain expectations. Those expectations could be either statistical or theoretical/intuitive in nature.

The statistical expectation for this sort of cross-tabulation is easy to determine. It is the level of duplication that would be observed if there were no relationship between two program audiences. In other words, because 20 people watched SC1 and 20 watched SC2, we would expect that a few people would see both, just by chance. Statisticians call this chance level of duplication the *expected frequency*. The expected frequency for any cell in the table is determined by multiplying the row marginal for that cell (R) multiplied by the column marginal (C) and dividing by the total sample (N). The formula for determining the expected frequency is:

$$R \times C / N = E$$

So, for example, the expected frequency in the upper-left-hand cell is 4 (i.e., $20 \times 20 / 100 = 4$). Table 6.2b shows both the observed frequency (O) and the expected frequency (E) for the two sitcom audiences. By comparing the two, we can see that the duplicated audience we have observed is slightly larger than the laws of probability would predict (i.e., $5 > 4$). Most statistical packages (e.g., SPSS) will run a statistical test, like *chi-squared*, to tell you whether the difference between observed and expected frequencies is "statistically significant."

From one time period to another, audiences will overlap. For example, if 50 percent of the audience is watching television at one time, and 50 percent is watching later in the day, a certain percentage of the audience will be watching at both times. The statistical expectation of overlap is determined exactly as in the example just given, except now we are dealing with percentages. If there is no correlation between the time period audiences, then 25 percent will be watching at both times, just by chance (i.e., $50 \times 50 / 100 = 25$). We routinely observe a level of total audience overlap or duplication that exceeds chance.

It is here that second kind of expectation comes into play. An experienced analyst knows enough about audience behavior to have certain theoretical or intuitive expectations about the levels of audience duplication he or she will encounter. Consider those two sitcoms again. Suppose we knew that they were scheduled on a single channel, one after the other, at a time when other major networks were broadcasting longer programs. Our experience with "audience flow" would lead us to expect a large duplicated audience. If each show were watched by 20 percent of our sample, we might be surprised to find anything less than 10 percent of the total sample watching both. That is well above the statistical expectation of 4 percent. On the other hand, if the two shows were scheduled on different channels at the same time, we would expect virtually no duplication at all. In either case, we have good reason to expect a strong relationship between watching SC1 and SC2.

The research and theory we reviewed in chapter 4 should give you some idea of the patterns of duplication that are known to occur in actual audience behavior. You should be alert, however, to the different ways in which information on audience duplication is reported. The number of people watching any two programs, or listening to a station at two different times, is often expressed as a percentage or a proportion. That makes it easier to compare across samples or populations of different sizes. Unfortunately, percentages can be calculated on different bases. For each cell in a simple cross-tab, each frequency could be reported as a percent of the row, the column, or the total sample.

Table 6.3 is much like the 2 × 2 matrix in Table 6.2. We have decreased the size of the SC1 audience, however, to make things a bit more complicated. First, you should note that changing the marginals has an impact on the expected frequencies (E) within each cell. When SC1 is viewed by 10, and SC2 by 20, E equals 2 ($10 \times 20/100 = 2$). That change, of course, affects all the other expected frequencies. For convenience, let us also assume that we actually observe these frequencies in each box. We can express each as one of three percentages or proportions. Because our total sample size is 100, the duplicated audience is 2 percent of the total sample (T). Stated differently, the proportion of the audience seeing both programs is 0.02. We could also say that 20 percent (C) of the people who saw SC1 also saw SC2. Alternatively, we could say that 10 percent (R) of the people who saw SC2 also saw SC1.

Different expressions of audience duplication are used in different contexts. The convention is to express levels of repeat viewing as an average of row or column percentages. These are usually quite similar because the ratings of different episodes of a program tend to be stable. This practice results in statements like, "The average level of repeat viewing was 55 percent." Channel loyalty is

TABLE 6.3
Cross-Tabulation of Program Audiences with Expected Frequencies and Cell Percentages

	Viewed SC1		
	Yes	No	Total
Yes	E = 2	E = 18	20
	T = 2%	T = 18%	
	R = 10%	R = 90%	
	C = 20%	C = 20%	
	Viewed SC2		
No	E = 8	E = 72	80
	R = 10%	R = 90%	
	C = 80%	C = 80%	
	10	90	100

usually indexed by studying the proportion of the total sample that sees any pair of programs broadcast on the same channel. We will have more to say about this later on when we discuss the "duplication of viewing law." Audience flow, sometimes called inheritance effects, can be reported in different ways (Jardine, 2012; Webster, 2006). We will give you an example of how a major U.S. media company studies audience flow in chapter 8.

PREDICTION AND EXPLANATION

The audience behavior revealed in cumulative measurements can be quite predictable—at least in the statistical sense. We are dealing with mass behavior occurring in a relatively structured environment over a period of days or weeks, so that behavior can be approximated with mathematical models—often with great accuracy. This is certainly a boon to media planners attempting to orchestrate effective campaigns, especially because actual data on audience behavior is always after the fact. As a result, much attention has been paid to developing techniques for predicting reach, frequency of exposure, and audience duplication.

The simplest model for estimating the reach of a media vehicle is given by the following equation:

$$\text{Reach} = 1 - (1 - r)^n$$

where r is the rating of the media vehicle, and n is the number of advertisements, or insertions, that are run in the campaign. When applying this equation, it is necessary to express the rating as a proportion (e.g., a rating of $20 = 0.20$). Although straightforward, this model of reach is rather limited. In the early 1960s, more sophisticated models were developed based either on binomial or beta binomial distributions (e.g., Agostini, 1961; Metheringham, 1964). These and other techniques for modeling reach and frequency are described in detail by Rust (1986) and Cheong et al. (2011).

Although models of reach embody some assumptions about audience duplication, to predict duplication between specific pairs of programs, it is best to employ models designed for that purpose. One such model, called the "duplication of viewing law," was developed by Goodhardt et al. (1987). It is expressed in the following equation:

$$r_{st} = k r_s r_t$$

where r_{st} is the proportion of the audience that sees both Programs s and t, r_s is the proportion seeing program s, r_t is the proportion seeing program t (i.e., their ratings expressed as proportions), and k is a constant whose value must be empirically determined. When the ratings are expressed as percentages, the equation changes slightly to:

$$r_{st} = k r_s r_t / 100$$

The logic behind the duplication of viewing law is not as complicated as it might appear. In fact, it is almost exactly the same as determining an expected frequency in cross-tabulation. If we were trying to predict the percent of the entire population that saw any two programs, we could begin by estimating the expected frequency. Remember, that is determined by $E = R \times C / N$. If we are dealing with program ratings, that is the same as multiplying the rating of one program (s) by the rating of another (t), and dividing by 100 (the total N as a percentage). In other words, the general equation for expected frequency becomes $r_{st} = r_s r_t / 100$, when it is specifically applied to predicting audience duplication. That is exactly the same as the duplication of viewing equation, with the exception of the k coefficient.

Goodhardt and his colleagues compared the expected level of duplication with the actual, or observed, level of duplication across hundreds of program pairings. They discovered that under certain well-defined circumstances, actual levels of duplication were either greater or less than chance by a predictable amount. For example, for any pair of programs broadcast on ABC, on different days, it was the case that audience duplication exceeded chance by about 60 percent. In other words, people who watched one ABC program were 60 percent more likely than the general population to show up in the audience for another ABC program on a different day. To adapt the equation so that it accurately predicted duplication, it was necessary to introduce a new term, the k *coefficient*. If duplication exceeded chance by 60 percent, then the value of k would have to be 1.6.

The values of k were determined for channels in both the United States and the United Kingdom. American networks had a duplication constant of approximately 1.5 to 1.6, whereas English channels had a constant on the order of 1.7 to 1.9. These constants serve as an index of *channel loyalty;* the higher the value of k, the greater the tendency toward duplication or loyalty.

As more networks have become available, many catering to a particular segment of the audience, indices of channel loyalty have generally gone up. Recent research has reported k values more like 2.0. Increasing channel loyalty has implications for both programmers and advertisers. As Sharp et al. (2009) note:

> This rising channel loyalty is associated with increasing audience fragmentation and suggests that, when confronted with a large number of channel choices, viewers restrict their viewing to a small group of learned favorites. Channel loyalty is not necessarily good news for advertisers. It does suggest that spreading advertising across channels is increasingly important if they wish to gain high reach relative to frequency of exposure. (p. 216)

Noting deviations from levels of duplication predicted by the duplication of viewing law also serves as a way to identify unusual features in audience behavior. In effect, the law gives us empirical generalizations against which we can judge specific observations. One important deviation from the law is what Goodhardt et al. (1987) called *inheritance effects*. That is, when the pair of programs in question is scheduled back-to-back on the same channel, the level of duplication routinely exceeds that predicted by ordinary channel loyalty. There is now a considerable body of research on inheritance effects or "audience flow" (e.g., Adams, 1997; Eastman et al., 1997; Henriksen, 1985; McDowell & Dick, 2003; Tiedge & Ksobiech, 1986). Despite the increased use of remotes and non-linear media, inheritance effects appear to be as robust as ever (Jardine, 2012; Webster, 2006). Building a program audience is still affected by the channel that carries a show and the strength of the lead-in program.

The duplication of viewing law represents one way data on audience duplication can be analyzed to develop empirical generalizations about audience behavior. But it is not the only way. It has, in fact, been criticized for being inflexible (Headen, Klompmaker, & Rust, 1979; Henriksen, 1985). An alternative way to manage data on duplication is to define program pairs as the unit of analysis and treat the duplicated audience (e.g., r_{st}) as the dependent variable. The independent variables in this kind of analysis become attributes that describe the program pairs. Recall that the model of audience behavior we presented in chapter 4 identified both structural and individual-level factors that explain audience behavior. Many of those can be translated into variables that characterize a program pair. For example, structural factors could include things like, Are the programs on the same channel (Y/N), or are they scheduled back to back (Y/N)? Theories of program choice would suggest programs of the same type should have relatively high levels of duplication. So an individual-level factor might suggest program pairs be described as being of the same type (Y/N). With such an approach, all independent variables can enter a regression equation and the analyst can see their relative ability to explain audience duplication.

This way of handling pairwise audience duplication has become common, although the technical details vary from study to study (Headen, Klompmaker, & Rust, 1979; Henriksen, 1985; Jardine, 2012; Webster, 2006). Neither is this approach limited to television only. As media users move from platform to platform, it becomes important to understand the patterns of use that emerge across media. So, in principle, the pair could be a television network and a website, or a television program and a YouTube video. As long as the analyst has access to respondent-level data that track users across platforms, audience duplication across any pair of outlets or products is possible.

Yet another way to conceptualize and manage audience duplication is to think of media outlets as nodes in a network and levels of duplication as the strength of the links between those nodes. This strategy allows the analyst to use statistical procedures borrowed from social network analysis (see Ksiazek, 2011). That was the approach Webster and Ksiazek (2012) took to study audience fragmentation across platforms. They used Nielsen "convergence panel" data, which tracked the same panel members across television and the Internet using peoplemeters and metering software on personal computers. Figure 6.6 shows a portion of the outlets that they studied, visualized as a network. For example, it indicates that 48.9 percent of the audience watched NBC and visited a Yahoo website in the course of a month. That is a measure of audience duplication (essentially r_{st}) and it quantifies the strength of the link between those two nodes. Treating the data in this way allows the analyst to identify which, if any, nodes are central destinations and whether outlets (i.e., nodes) cluster together in some discernible way.

Audience duplication between any pair of media outlets, then, can be thought of as a building block for many different forms of cumulative analysis. These can include fairly conventional multivariate approaches, like multiple regression, and newer techniques like social network analysis. Since more and more research

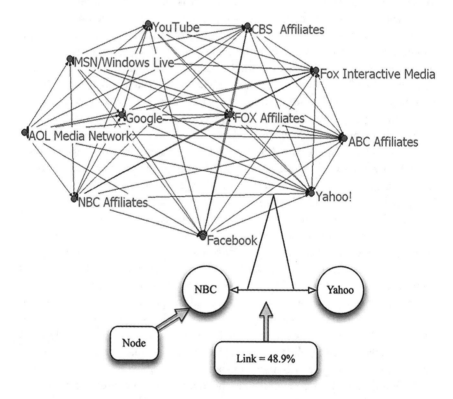

FIGURE 6.6. A Network of Television Channels and Internet Brands Defined by Audience Duplication
Source: Webster & Ksiazek (2012). Based on Nielsen TV/Internet Convergence Panel, March 2009.

syndicators are making data on audience duplication available through online tools, the building blocks should become more readily available to analysts. As long as analysts are guided by an integrated model of audience behavior, they will know the right questions to ask. That is over half the battle. Armed with the right data and analytical techniques, we should be able to explain and predict audience behavior as never before.

RELATED READINGS

Barwise, P., & Ehrenberg, A. (1988). *Television and its audience*. London: Sage.

Easley, D., & Kleinberg, J. (2010). *Networks, crowds, and markets: Reasoning about a highly connected world*. Cambridge, UK: Cambridge University Press.

Goodhardt, G. J., Ehrenberg, A. S. C., & Collins, M. A. (1987). *The television audience: Patterns of viewing*. Aldershot, UK: Gower.

Kaushik, A. (2010). *Web analytics 2.0: The art on online accountability & science of customer centricity*. Indianapolis, IN: Wiley.

Sissors, J. Z., & Baron, R. B. (2010). *Advertising media planning* (7th ed.). New York: McGraw Hill.

Rust, R. T. (1986). *Advertising media models: A practical guide*. Lexington: Lexington Books.

Webster, J. G., & Phalen, P. F. (1997). *The mass audience: Rediscovering the dominant model*. Mahwah, NJ: Lawrence Erlbaum Associates.

Part III

Applications

CHAPTER 7

Audience Research in Advertising

Throughout this book we have stressed that the business of commercial television is to sell audiences to advertisers. But, unlike subscription newspapers and magazines, electronic media do not have circulation numbers to tell them who is using their product. Instead, they depend on research firms to estimate the size and composition of "their" audiences. These estimates, the ratings, are the principal information used by media and advertisers to determine the monetary value of television time.

Advertisers are interested in capturing the attention of the viewer or listener to convey some message. The message might be as simple as introducing people to a new brand or reminding them of an old one, or it might involve trying to change their attitudes toward a person or product. Often advertisers attempt to influence viewer behavior on some level—from mundane product purchases to voting for a specific political candidate. Whatever the purpose, advertisers need access to audiences, if only for a moment, and they pay the media for this opportunity.

The need of advertisers to buy audiences, and the eagerness of broadcasters to sell them, brought the ratings services into being. As a consequence, advertisers have an enormous stake in the audience measurement business and wield considerable influence in shaping the form of ratings data. In fact, without advertiser support, electronic media ratings as we know them would not exist. Their *raison d'etre* is to give buyers and sellers the information they need to negotiate the price of advertising time.

For several decades after the widespread adoption of television as a form of popular entertainment, ratings services employed relatively static measurement structures to generate estimates of viewership. This "audience information system" evolved with technology—although it often had difficulty keeping pace. Cable, direct broadcast satellite, and the Internet all required changes in measurement methods in order to generate the audience information needed to support economic exchange. Today, viewers can use computers, tablets, and mobile phones to access video content, and they have DVRs to make time shifting easier than ever before. These modes of viewing require new adjustments to audience measurement methods, but whatever the technology used to watch television content, ratings data are needed to estimate the value of time to advertisers.

The buying and selling of audiences takes place at many levels. In the comparatively simple world of broadcast, cable, and satellite television, a large national market was dominated by a few broadcast and cable networks, syndicators, and major corporate advertisers. In local markets, individual stations sold to area merchants. National spot and regional markets provided access to specific geographic areas. While this is still the basic framework, technology has changed the options for reaching audiences, and these changes have affected the markets for advertising time.

Each marketplace has developed its own institutions and practices, which affect how audience data are analyzed and interpreted. The following section describes the major markets for electronic media audiences. We explain how the trade in audiences is carried out through the traditional media of network and local broadcasting, the newer medium of satellite television (DBS), and the online world characterized by nontraditional modes of viewing: computer, tablet, or mobile device.

Table 7.1 summarizes total ad revenues for each medium, illustrating patterns of market growth. In the United States alone, advertising is a $150 billion business. As more and more countries open their markets to private ownership and advertiser support of communications media, global ad expenditures are predicted to reach $522 billion by 2013. We focus here on the structures supporting economic exchange in the United States because, while the specifics of organization may vary across the globe, the basic transactional arrangements involving audience information are consistent.

NATIONAL MARKETS

Broadcast and Cable Networks and Alternate Delivery Systems

Broadcast Networks. For advertisers who need to reach vast national markets, legacy networks still have much to offer. On average, the major television broadcast networks still draw the largest audiences, although cable programs now compete very effectively—often garnering larger audiences than the legacy networks. As a practical matter, the network television market is divided into smaller markets called *dayparts,* which are defined by time of day or program content. Because each designation is associated with specific audience characteristics, the various dayparts appeal to different advertisers and generate different amounts of sales revenue.

TABLE 7.1
Advertising Revenues of Electronic Media[a]

Year	Radio[b]				Television[c]				Cable[d]		Internet[e]	Total
	Network	Spot	Local	Digital	Network	Spot	Local	Synd	Network	Spot/Local		
1950	$132	$119	$203		$85	$31	$55	$—	$—	$—	$—	$625
1960	45	208	402		820	527	280	—	—	—	—	2,282
1970	49	355	853		1,658	1,234	704	—	—	—	—	4,853
1980	158	746	2,643		5,130	3,269	2,967	50	50	50		15,063
1985	329	1,320	4,915		8,285	6,004	5,714	540	612	139		27,858
1990	433	1,626	6,780		9,863	7,788	7,856	1,109	1,802	737		37,994
1995	426	1,920	9,124		11,600	9,119	9,985	2,016	3,993	1,634		49,817
2000	1,029	3,596	15,223		15,888	12,264	13,542	3,108	10,673	4,124	8,087	87,534
2005	1,053	19,018			25,083	16,755		4,222	16,100	5,800	12,542	100,573
2009	1,048	13,203		480	25,342	12,922		4,229	18,700	5,500	22,661	104,085
2010	1,102	14,181		615	26,635	15,892		4,111	20,500	6,600	26,041	115,677
2011	1,136	14,060		709	26,513	15,160		4,746	22,100	6,600	31,735	122,759

Note: Fox was counted as syndication prior to 1990, and as network after 1990. UPN, WB, and PAX were counted as syndication after 1990. Reprinted by permission of Interactive Advertisers Association.

[a] Revenue in millions.

[b] Radio Advertising Bureau.

[c] Television Bureau of Advertising. ("TV Basics" based on TVB analysis of Kantar data)

[d] Cabletelevision Advertising Bureau. Spot/Local includes regional sports.

[e] Interactive Advertising Bureau/PricewaterhouseCoopers. ("IAB Internet Advertising Revenue Report")

Prime time, the most important of the network dayparts, includes all regularly scheduled programs from 8 P.M. to 11 P.M. EST, Monday through Saturday, and 7 P.M. to 11 P.M. on Sunday. Networks generate their highest revenues during prime time because they attract the largest audiences. Advertisers like this daypart because they can simultaneously reach a wide variety of people across the entire nation, including people who work during the day. Access to this mass market, however, is not cheap; the most popular prime-time programs are the most expensive.

Daytime is the second most lucrative daypart. For the networks, daytime extends from 7 A.M. to 4:30 P.M. EST, Monday through Friday. This audience is much smaller and, with the exception of early news programs, disproportionately female. As a result, it appeals most to advertisers who want to reach women, especially full-time homemakers. Companies selling household products like soap and food frequently buy spots in this time period, paying far less than prime-time advertisers.

The *sports* daypart is defined strictly by program content. Among the most important network sports programs are major-league games like those of the NFL or NBA. These events attract men to the audience and, as might be expected, advertisers who buy most heavily in this daypart include breweries, car and truck manufacturers, and companies that sell automotive products. The cost of advertising in sports varies widely—mostly as a function of audience size—all the way up to the Super Bowl, which cost an estimated $3.5 million per 30-second spot in 2012.

The *news* daypart is defined more by program content than by simple time periods, although there is a correlation between news and time of day. This daypart includes the network's evening news programs, weekend news programming, and news specials and documentaries. Excluded from this daypart are the morning news programs (considered daytime) and regularly scheduled prime time programs like *60 Minutes,* even though network news divisions might produce these programs. The news daypart tends to attract an older audience, so it is especially appealing to companies that sell products like pharmaceuticals, healthful foods, and luxury items.

Late night begins at 11:30 P.M. EST, Monday through Friday. Its best-known programs are *The Tonight Show With Jay Leno* and *Late Show With David Letterman,* which have dominated the time period for years. Not surprisingly, the audience during this daypart is small and almost entirely adult in composition.

Many public interest groups and regulators view the *children's daypart* as one of the most important electronic media markets. This market includes the Saturday and Sunday morning children's programs, a time period that critics once dubbed the "children's ghetto," as well as weekday programming aimed at children. Although children watch a great deal of television at other times, the children's daypart offers advertisers the most efficient way to reach this audience through broadcast television. Among the largest advertisers in daytime are cereal and candy makers and toy manufacturers. The cost of a 30-second spot varies as the demand changes by season. An advertising spot at Christmastime, for example, might cost three times as much as it would in the months that follow.

Although television networks, whether broadcast, cable, or satellite, command much of our attention these days, we should recall that the first networks were radio. Permanently established by the late 1920s, these radio networks set in place many practices and traditions that are evident in network television today. And even though television has moved to center stage in our lives, now commanding the lion's share of the advertising revenues, radio networks have been an important social and cultural force in American life. In fact, radio still offers advertisers an alternative to reach a national audience. This is especially true of satellite radio, although these services still do not have the reach of terrestrial networks.

Most national radio networks in operation today are controlled by a handful of companies. Arbitron measures audiences for six of these network operators: American Urban Radio Networks, Crystal Media Networks, Cumulus Media, Dial Global, Premiere Networks, and United Stations Radio Network. Each of these organizations offers multiple services including news, music, and political and sports talk programming. Syndicators, although not "networks" per se, provide specialized radio formats via satellite to a large number of stations all over the country. These formats include all types of popular music, call-in sports, and political conversation. Some feature well-known personalities like Rush Limbaugh and Don Imus and are carried by hundreds of radio stations simultaneously. Stations can receive news programs from news-gathering organizations like Associated Press, as well as cable services such as CNN, Fox News, and ABC's ESPN. And group owners can distribute programming to their own stations, essentially functioning as ad hoc networks.

Cable Networks and Alternate Delivery Systems. Table 7.2 shows a ranking of national cable television networks by their Persons 2+ audience. All of these services depend, at least in part, on advertising revenues to make money. However, even the oldest and most popular cable networks still reach fewer American homes than the major broadcast networks.

The most obvious competitive strategy employed by cable programmers is to target a particular kind of viewer. Note the number of networks in Table 7.2 that offer programming for just a part of the audience. MTV, for example, is designed for teens and young adults. Nickelodeon and the Cartoon Network appeal to children. Lifetime is a network for women; Spike TV is for men. BET targets African Americans. To the extent that cable networks offer media buyers these specific audiences, they may be a more efficient buy for an advertiser. Further, cable networks are often more willing to work with advertisers to develop special programming or promotional efforts to enhance the impact of commercials.

TABLE 7.2
Cable Networks 2012 Ranked by Average Audience 2+

Network	Households (000)	Coverage %
The Weather Channel	100,205	87.36%
TBS Network	100,025	87.21%
CNN / HLN	99,727	86.95%
Nick-at-Nite	99,664	86.89%
Nickelodeon	99,664	86.89%
Discovery Channel	99,604	86.84%
Food Network	99,601	86.84%
USA Network	99,301	86.57%
Adult Swim	99,159	86.45%
Cable News Network	99,156	86.45%
The Cartoon Network	99,159	86.45%
A&E Network	99,012	86.32%
Headline News	98,971	86.29%
Home and Garden TV	98,947	86.27%
Turner Network Television	98,921	86.24%
ESPN	98,903	86.23%
Lifetime Television	98,904	86.23%
Tlc	98,871	86.20%
ESPN2	98,806	86.14%
History	98,708	86.06%
Disney Channel	98,666	86.02%
Spike TV	98,623	85.98%
Comedy Central	98,607	85.97%
MTV: Music Television	98,591	85.96%
FX	98,052	85.49%
SYFY	98,006	85.45%
Fox News Channel	97,981	85.42%
VH1	97,944	85.39%
CNBC	97,497	85.00%
ABC Family	97,451	84.96%
E! Entertainment TV	97,414	84.93%
AMC	96,700	84.31%
Animal Planet	96,625	84.24%
TV Land	96,573	84.20%

TABLE 7.2 *continued*

Cable Networks 2012 Ranked by Average Audience 2+

Network	Households (000)	Coverage %
MSNBC	95,526	83.28%
Travel Channel	94,716	82.58%
Bravo	94,607	82.48%
TRU TV (Formerly Court TV)	92,315	80.48%
CMT	91,834	80.06%
Black Entertainment TV	91,516	79.79%
Hallmark Channel	87,373	76.18%
Lifetime Movie Network	84,453	73.63%
Golf Channel	84,436	73.61%
National Geographic Chnl	83,881	73.13%
Speed	81,449	71.01%
TV Guide Network	80,388	70.09%
Disney XD (Formerly Toon Disney)	79,785	69.56%
MTV2	79,655	69.45%
BBC-America	79,548	69.35%
Oxygen Media	79,500	69.31%
Investigation Discovery (Formerly Discovery Times)	79,491	69.30%
Oprah Winfrey Network (Formerly Discovery Health)	79,092	68.96%
We:womens Entertainment	78,783	68.69%
NBC Sports Network	78,063	68.06%
Style	77,714	67.75%
Science (Formerly Science Channel)	76,257	66.48%
WGN America (Formerly Superstation WGN)	75,965	66.23%
GSN	75,049	65.43%
Nick Jr (Formerly Noggin)	75,022	65.41%
ESPNEWS	74,680	65.11%
ESPNU	73,234	63.85%
Teennick (Formerly The N)	71,767	62.57%
The Inspirational Network	70,922	61.83%
MLB Network	69,861	60.91%
Biography Channel	69,426	60.53%
Soapnet	68,961	60.12%

TABLE 7.2 *continued*
Cable Networks 2012 Ranked by Average Audience 2+

Network	Households (000)	Coverage %
H2 (Formerly History International)	68,432	59.66%
Fox Business Network	68,407	59.64%
Independent Film Channel	67,060	58.47%
Galavision	65,469	57.08%
The Hub (Formerly Discovery Kids)	64,200	55.97%
Reelzchannel	63,893	55.70%
Great American Country	62,550	54.53%
G4	61,628	53.73%
Nicktoons	61,426	53.55%
VH1 Classic	60,962	53.15%
Military Channel	60,656	52.88%
NBA-TV	59,833	52.16%
Cooking Channel (Formerly Fine Living)	59,613	51.97%
Destination America (Formerly Planet Green)	59,596	51.96%
NFL Network	59,499	51.87%
Current TV	59,260	51.67%
DIY Network	57,793	50.39%
TV One	57,308	49.96%
National Geographic Wild	56,809	49.53%
Fuse	56,727	49.46%
Sprout	54,413	47.44%
GMC	52,179	45.49%
Ovation Network	51,400	44.81%
Logo	50,299	43.85%
Centric	48,921	42.65%
Discovery Fit & Health (Formerly Fit TV)	48,835	42.58%
Hallmark Movie Channel	47,262	41.20%
Chiller	43,486	37.91%
FX Movie Channel	42,485	37.04%
Velocity (Formerly HD Theater)	41,793	36.44%
Fox Soccer Channel	41,442	36.13%
RFD-TV	41,206	35.93%

TABLE 7.2 *continued*

Cable Networks 2012 Ranked by Average Audience 2+

Network	Households (000)	Coverage %
Encore	40,950	35.70%
Encore Primary	39,801	34.70%
Mun2 Cable	38,200	33.30%
Outdoor Channel	37,801	32.96%
Fuel	37,029	32.28%
Cloo (Formerly Sleuth)	36,528	31.85%
TR3S	33,616	29.31%
ESPN Classic	31,969	27.87%
HBO - The Works	31,014	27.04%
HBO Prime	30,562	26.65%
Sportsman Channel	30,288	26.41%
Nuvo TV	29,621	25.82%
Starz	27,828	24.26%
Starz Primary	27,040	23.57%
Showtime	25,071	21.86%
Showtime Prime	24,846	21.66%
Multimax	19,095	16.65%
Maxprime	18,864	16.45%
Discovery En Espanol	8,027	7.00%
Total Cable Plus	103,934	90.61%
Total Wired Cable	68,568	59.78%
Cable Plus W/ Pay	55,245	48.16%
Wired Cable W/ Pay	35,792	31.20%
ADS	36,170	31.53%
Total U.S.	114,700	

Not only do cable networks offer the prospect of fewer "wasted" exposures, they often sell access to their audiences for less than the networks charge. Broadcast networks, perhaps because of their greater reach or the prestige associated with hit programs, often command a premium in the marketplace. In recent years, however, cable-originated programming has become more popular, often surpassing competing broadcast programs in the ratings.

Like cable, Direct Broadcast Satellite (DBS) services can sell national advertising. And, like all its media competitors, DBS needs credible audience estimates to attract advertisers. In 2003, Nielsen agreed to develop a measurement system for rating satellite-delivered programming; DirecTV became its first client for the new service. Until then, commercial time on DirecTV was sold based on viewer estimates extrapolated from similar programming and distribution channels. True satellite ratings were a significant boost to the sales effort. Like cable, however, satellite programming has limited coverage compared with the broadcast networks. As a result, "national" ratings are generally lower than those for similar programs on the broadcast networks. Satellite services have, however, been able to gain an advantage by delivering more sports programming to subscriber households.

Buying and Selling Audiences in the National Market. We have considered three ways of thinking about "markets" when it comes to buying and selling advertising: by geography (national, local, and regional), by medium (broadcast, cable, or ADS); and by daypart (prime time, daytime, etc.). A third definition of market describes when the actual buying takes place. Transactions occur in different stages throughout the year, with some advertisers purchasing time well in advance of airdate and others purchasing time just a few months or weeks before broadcast. These different rounds in the buying process are called the *upfront* market, the *scatter* market, and the *opportunistic* market.

The upfront market begins in the spring when each network hosts advertisers and agencies for a decades-old ritual event to showcase new and returning programs. Network executives introduce buyers to their new programming lineups for fall, and advertisers commit billions of dollars to secure time for the coming season. In 2011, for example, the broadcast networks sold an estimated $9 billion in the upfront market. Although this method of buying ties up advertisers' budgets for months to come, the upfront gives them access to the best network programs. And because these companies make long-term commitments to the network, they generally get more favorable rates than will be available later in the year. In fact, to lessen the advertiser's risk, networks often give *audience guarantees* to ensure that the total audience estimates will be delivered, even if the networks have to run additional commercials, called *make-goods*, without charge to the advertiser. The process is complicated by uncertainty—no one knows exactly which audiences will watch new programs in the fall lineup. Even with guarantees, the upfront market is the occasion for much high-stakes gamesmanship.

The *scatter market* operates within a shorter time frame. Each television season is divided into quarters. In advance of each quarter, advertisers may wish to buy time for specific purposes such as advertising seasonal products or running some limited campaign, not envisioned during the upfront buying. Because advertisers are usually less flexible in the scatter market, and network buyers are generally at a disadvantage, prices in the scatter market are usually higher than they were in the upfront. At times, however, market conditions could favor the buyer. Programs that were high risks in the upfront market will have track records when scatter buying occurs—this means a less risky investment for the advertiser. Additionally, if the networks have a slow season, rates could actually be lower in scatter than in the upfront.

The *opportunistic market* occurs as the television season progresses. Although most of the networks' inventory is purchased during the upfront and scatter markets, some time might become available closer to airdate. Perhaps deals negotiated early in the season fell through as a result of cuts in an advertiser's budget or the implementation of new marketing strategies. Or perhaps changes in network lineups, such as the cancellation or rescheduling of a program or the addition of a special event, resulted in extra inventory. These changes would relieve advertisers of their commitments, and create opportunities for the last-minute purchase of airtime. The circumstances might favor the network, or they might give the advantage to an advertiser. Buyers and sellers often use such opportunities to settle debts from past business deals. For example, a salesperson with extra inventory might offer a low-cost spot to a particular buyer who has been an excellent customer. Or a buyer may purchase a spot to help the seller out because the salesperson has given him preferential treatment in the past.

The competitive landscape for national advertising continues to evolve as technology makes new forms of distribution possible. Broadcast and cable networks now compete with alternate delivery systems (ADS) like DirecTV and DISH Network, and with the Internet. More television households dropped cable subscriptions than signed up for new cable service in 2011. Some of this drop is due to ADS, and some is undoubtedly brought about by an increase in online viewing. Nationally, cable penetration is at 60.2 percent; ADS penetration is now at 31.2 percent. The near-universal coverage of broadcast networks still gives them an edge over cable and ADS in building the largest television audiences. Cable networks have, however, developed other strategies for selling their audiences.

Syndication

Stations are in constant need of programming. Even network affiliates must fill large blocks of time not programmed by the networks. To do this, broadcasters rely on a variety of program sources, including one that is particularly relevant to a discussion of advertising—*barter syndication*.

Barter syndication has fairly straightforward origins. Basically, advertisers found they could use a station's need for programming to get their message across to an audience. They could produce a program, place their advertisements in it, and offer it to stations without charging a license fee. Stations found this attractive because they acquired new programs without having to pay cash for them; they could even sell spots in the programs if the original sponsor did not use them. With the growth of satellite program distribution in the 1980s, this simple idea gave rise to a rapidly growing new advertising marketplace.

In general, the barter syndication market works like this. A distributor produces programs, owns the rights to existing shows, or works on behalf of another producer to sell programs to local stations. The sales arrangement could be "all barter," meaning that a station gives the syndicator all available commercial time to sell in the national market. Sometimes the agreement is a hybrid, called "cash-plus-barter," which, as the name suggests, requires stations to pay a fee for the program as well as accepting advertisements placed by the syndicator. Depending on the specific terms of the deal, stations might also sell some local spots in a cash-plus arrangement.

Syndicators determine the terms of a deal before they place a program in the marketplace. Trade publications print lists of these arrangements at the beginning of each calendar year, just before the National Association of Television Programming Executives (NATPE) conference. At NATPE syndicated programs are marketed intensely to potential buyers, especially those from medium and small markets. Table 7.3 reproduces part of this list of available programs for January 2012. Although barter terms may change to meet market demand, this list gives a good indication of the type of deals syndicators are seeking. Individual barter contracts may require stations to broadcast programs in a specific daypart, such as early fringe. Requirements like this are typical of popular programs that are especially desired by stations. Some of the programs listed in Table 7.3 are not scheduled to be available until a year or two after they are sold.

In addition to the terms of sale, program buyers are interested in the number of markets that have already purchased (or "cleared") the programs. The more stations that acquire a program, the larger is the potential audience. If one station in every market agrees to air a program, the distributor would, hypothetically, have the same reach as a major television network. As a practical matter, once a program is carried on enough stations to reach 70 percent of U.S. households, it is sold to advertisers in much the same way as network time.

Just like their network counterparts, the barter syndication firms approach national advertisers and their ad agencies to sell commercial time. They sell in the upfront, scatter, and opportunistic markets, and may even guarantee audiences like the networks. In fact, advertisers may use barter syndication as a supplement to their purchases of network time or as a substitute for it. Sometimes program environments are available through barter that are not offered by traditional broadcast networks. For example, game shows and talk shows are more likely to be available in syndication than on broadcast networks. Still, the major benefit of advertising on a barter program is reaching an audience at a somewhat lower cost than other national or regional alternatives.

Despite some similarities, buying time in barter syndication is not quite comparable to network advertising. Many programs, especially those produced for first-run syndication, are sent to all stations in the country at the same time, and at least run on the same day. But other types of programming, off-network syndication for example, may air at different times in different markets. Weekly syndicated programs might even air on different days, which complicates the process of predicting audiences.

Barter syndication and related ways to package advertising for national or regional audiences are almost certain to grow. Satellite communications have made the rapid, cost-efficient delivery of programs feasible. Stations pick up these syndicated program feeds if they perceive this to be in their best interests, perhaps even preempting more traditional networks. Assuming an effective way to buy and evaluate audiences, advertisers are likely to use these alternative routes for reaching the public. Such ever-changing syndicated networks are also likely to pose some of the most interesting challenges for audience analysts.

LOCAL MARKETS

Broadcast networks reach national markets by combining the audiences of local affiliated stations. Similarly, national cable networks aggregate the viewers of local cable systems. But an individual station or cable system can sell its own audiences to advertisers who want to reach their local customers. These audiences are attractive to businesses that trade in a concentrated geographical area and to national or regional marketers who want to advertise in specific markets. The former create a market for *local sales;* the latter take part in the *national spot market.*

Broadcast Stations

The physics of broadcasting are such that a station's signal has geographic limits. In light of this, the federal government decided to license radio and television stations to specific cities and towns across the country. Larger population centers have more stations. Naturally enough, people spend most of their time listening to nearby stations because the signal is clearest and the programs are of local interest. In television, the major ratings service uses this geographically determined audience behavior to define the boundaries of a local media market area. Nielsen calls these markets *Designated Market Areas* (DMAs).

Appendix A lists the 210 U.S. television markets designated by Nielsen. There are even more radio markets. In both cases, market size varies considerably. New York, for instance, has over 7 million television households, whereas Glendive barely has 4,000. Indeed, buying time on a major station in New York might

TABLE 7.3

Syndicated Programming: Sample of Programs Available in 2012

Type	Title	Distributor	Producer	Notes	Terms
First-run strips	America Now	Bellum Entertainment	Raycom, ITV Studios America	Two half-hours back-to-back, hosted by Leeza Gibbons and Bill Rancic	Cash only
	Katie	Disney-ABC Domestic Television	Disney-ABC Domestic Television	One-hour talker starring former Today and CBS Evening News anchor Katie Couric.	Cash plus barter (Cleared in more than 90% of the country)
	Steve Harvey	NBCUniversal Domestic Television Distribution	Endemol USA	One-hour talker featuring Harvey's comedic but real take on relationships and other topics	Cash plus barter (Sold in 85% of the U.S.)
	Dish Nation	Twentieth Television	Studio City Prods.	Half-hour strip, culled from the nation's funniest morning radio shows	Cash plus barter (Cleared in 60% of the country)
	Last Shot with Judge Gunn	Trifecta	Trifecta	Half-hour court show	All barter with four minutes national and four minutes local
	The Lawyers	CBS TV Distribution	Stage 29 Prods.	One-hour strip	Cash plus barter
Off-network sitcoms (2013)	Hot in Cleveland	CBS Television Distribution	Hazy Mills Prods. and Samjen Prods. in association with TV Land	Half hour sitcom starring Valerie Bertinelli, Wendie Malick, Jane Leeves, and Betty White	Cash plus barter

Show	Distributor	Production Companies	Notes
Parks and Recreation	NBCUniversal Cable and New Media Distribution / NBCUniversal Domestic Television	Deedle-Dee Prods., Fremulon, 3 Art Entertainment, Universal Television	Available for cable, digital, and broadcast platforms
Community	Sony Pictures Television	Sony Pictures Television, Krasnoff Foster Prods., Russo Bros., Harmonious Claptrap, Universal Media Studios	Being shopped to television stations, cable networks, and digital distributors for cash plus barter
Modern Family	Twentieth Television	Twentieth Century Fox Television, Lloyd-Levitan Prods.	Sold for cash plus barter to TV stations and for cash to USA Network. Cleared in 95% of U.S.
Castle	Disney-ABC Domestic Television Distribution	ABC Studios	Sold to TNT and being sold to TV stations in all-barter deals
30 Rock	NBC Universal Domestic TV Distribution	NBC Studios, Broadway Video, Little Stranger	Premiering simultaneously in broadcast syndication and on Comedy Central, WGN America
The Big Bang Theory	Warner Bros. Domestic TV Distribution	Warner Bros. Television	Half-hour sitcom, will simultaneously premiere on broadcast and on TBS

Note: Data are from *Daily Variety*, January 23 and 24, 2012.

deliver more viewers to an advertiser than a buy on national cable network. Conversely, many small-market radio stations might have audiences too small for a ratings company to measure economically. This point is best illustrated by the fact that regular radio ratings are available to fewer than half the stations in the country. Of course, measured stations account for the overwhelming majority of all radio listening.

These vast differences in audience size have a marked effect on the rates that local broadcasters can charge for a commercial spot. The price of a 30-second spot in prime time might be $400 in Des Moines and $4,000 in Detroit. Other factors can affect the cost of time, too. Is the market growing, or has it fallen on hard times? Is the population relatively affluent or poor? How competitive are other local media, like newspapers? Even factors like a market's time zone can affect the rates of local electronic media.

Other characteristics that vary with market size are the volume and sophistication of the ratings users who analyze audience information. Many radio markets are measured just twice each year. Audiences in major television markets, on the other hand, are measured continuously. Because of this, and the greater number of advertising dollars available in major markets, the buyers and sellers of media in those markets tend to be more experienced with and adept at analyzing ratings information.

In most markets, the largest buyers of local advertising include fast food restaurants, supermarkets, department stores, banks, and car dealers. Like network advertisers, these companies often employ an advertising agency to represent them. The agency can perform a number of functions for its client, from developing a creative strategy, to writing copy and producing the advertisements. Most important in this context, the agency's media department projects the audience for various programs, plans when the advertisements are to run, buys the time, and evaluates whether the desired audience was delivered. Smaller advertisers, or those in smaller markets, may deal directly with local stations.

Because of the different types of people and organizations involved, local time-buying decisions vary from intuitive judgments made by a merchant who thinks a certain number of advertisements on a local station will generate extra business, to choices based on complex analyses of ratings information. Indeed, many small radio stations and cable systems sell without using any ratings information at all. Increasingly, though, the process of buying and selling time depends on the use of ratings.

Although specific terminology may differ from organization to organization, the purchase of local time generally works like this. The advertiser or its agency issues a request for avails. In effect, the buyer is asking what spots are available for sale on the local stations. Avail requests typically specify the buyer's target audience, preferred dayparts, and estimated budget. Station salespeople respond by proposing a schedule of spots to deliver some or all of the requested audience.

At this point, the buyer and seller negotiate differences over the projected rating and the cost of a spot. Assuming the parties reach an agreement, buyers place an order and the spots air. After the campaign, the next available ratings information is analyzed to determine whether the expected audience was actually delivered. As in network buying, this last stage in the process is called *post-buy analysis*.

As noted earlier, national and regional advertisers participate in the national spot market when they buy spots on local stations. For example, a snow tire manufacturer might want to advertise only in northern markets. Similarly, a maker of agricultural products might wish to buy time in markets with large farm populations. In fact, such national spot buys constitute the largest single source of revenues for many television stations. The question is, how can so many local stations deal effectively with all these potential time buyers? It would be impractical for thousands of stations to have their own personnel trying to contact each and every national advertiser.

To solve this problem, an intermediary called a *station representative* (or *rep firm*) serves as the link between local stations and national advertisers. Rep firms for both television and radio stations are located in major media markets like New York and Chicago. Television reps usually represent only one client per market, in order to avoid any conflict of interest. Radio reps may serve more than one station in a market, as long as their formats do not compete for the same audience. Rep firms vary according to the number of stations they represent, and the types of services they offer to clients. Some firms provide stations with research services or advice on programming. Most importantly, though, rep firms monitor the media buys that national advertisers are planning, and they try to secure some portion of that business for their stations.

The station sales force and the salespeople at the rep firm under contract with the station are essentially selling the same commercial time. This can cause some conflicts. Local advertisers could be shut out of a daypart because national advertisers secure the inventory, or vice versa. In Las Vegas, for example, local businesses pay a premium to advertise in early news programs in order to reach visitors who are deciding where to go for the evening. This means that national advertisers cannot purchase time in local broadcast news without paying very high rates. Instead, they may turn to cable television to reach those audiences.

Local Cable Systems

Cable systems also offer local advertising opportunities. Usually, this involves inserting a local ad in a cable network, but it could also mean sponsorship of locally produced programs. There are two limitations to this process. First, just like cable networks, cable systems simply cannot reach every member of the available television audience. Second, as is the case with small market radio stations, the audience for most local cable systems is too small to measure economically. In this case, advertisers must guess at audience size and composition. However, Nielsen has been installing peoplemeters in the largest television markets, which could improve cable measurement by expanding sample sizes. Further, as more cable systems begin to provide programming via digital set-top boxes, they can access aggregate information about household viewing. While these improvements will help level the playing field in the local ad market, local cable is likely to be at a disadvantage for some time.

Eventually though, cable systems might enjoy an advertising advantage because they are not just local, they are "ultra-local." In many television markets, programming is fed to different neighborhoods by different headends. Each headend is capable of inserting advertisements for its own coverage area, so an advertiser can create a patchwork of small coverage areas to suit its needs. A local merchant could run a spot across a group of interconnected headends, reaching only those viewers who live in a certain part of town. Or a chain restaurant might run one commercial across the entire market but vary the address of the closest local outlet. Similarly, since cable franchise areas, almost by definition, conform to governmental boundaries within the market, cable seems a likely venue for political advertising. These potentials are being exploited more and more by cable rep firms.

ADVERTISING WORLDWIDE

Like the electronic media themselves, the advertising marketplace is constantly evolving. Two major developments that deserve comment are the growth of advertising worldwide and the challenges and opportunities posed by advertising through newer communication technologies. Table 7.4 provides total advertising expenditures by region through 2011, with projections to 2014. In most regions advertisers continue to spend more money each year; the exception is the Middle East and North Africa.

Advertising in the United States is a relatively large and stable marketplace with a dollar volume of activity closely tied to the overall health of the economy. The same is true of other mature industrialized nations, especially those of Western Europe. One significant difference, however, is the way commercial media evolved. In the United States, radio and television systems began as commercial ventures; in many other countries media were largely or completely government supported for years. Different models of commercial support are still evolving and the precise configurations vary by country. This evolution does not mean, however, that governments are uninvolved in steering the development of media. As Straubhaar (2007) observes, television systems are often "stubbornly national," which means advertisers must tailor "global" media plans to the regulatory policies and cultural expectations of individual countries.

TABLE 7.4

Global Advertising Expenditures and Projections Through 2014: Advertising Expenditure by Region

	2010	*2011*	*2012*	*2013*	*2014*
North America	162,165	165,202	171,203	177,930	186,513
Western Europe	106,078	108,232	108,694	111,571	115,042
Asia/Pacific	124,760	132,144	141,016	150,498	162,440
Central and Eastern Europe	23,980	25,906	27,510	29,987	32,944
Latin America	32,065	35,364	38,117	41,936	45,731
Middle East & North Africa	4,881	4,155	4,198	4,313	4,412
Rest of world	9,812	10,443	11,218	12,265	13,496
World	**463,741**	**481,446**	**501,956**	**528,500**	**560,578**

Source: ZenithOptimedia

Note: Major media (newspapers, magazines, television, radio, cinema, outdoor, Internet).

$US million current prices. Currency conversion at 2011 rates. Used by permission.

One need is consistent, however, no matter which country we consider. In order for commercial television to expand, media and advertisers need credible audience data to assign value to airtime. Each country has its own unique challenges when it comes to developing an audience information system that can provide these data. For many, a completely independent third-party ratings provider is neither familiar nor desirable. Legacy research services, such as BARB in the United Kingdom, BBM in Canada, and GfK in Germany, are either formed by, or hired by, a consortium of representatives from media, advertisers, and advertising agencies. Joint Industry Committees (JICs), Media Owner Committees (MOCs), or Tri-partite Research Company Contracts (TRCCs) determine the official audience ratings provider(s) for the country. They not only control the measurement of audiences, but the distribution of audience information as well.

Although antitrust regulations prevent these types of organizations from forming in the United States, there are four reasons that they have become institutionalized worldwide. The first has to do with history—if a media system has been totally or mostly controlled by government, the transition to commercial broadcasting is fraught with uncertainty. Not only are the public interest responsibilities of media owners at stake, but the perceived responsibility of government to ensure quality programming could also be compromised. Second, in countries with a culture of consensus, joint decision-making in such an important business sector is a desirable process. Third, the advanced technologies of larger countries could give foreign suppliers an advantage over indigenous companies when competitive forces determine the outcome; joint committees can factor localism into their decisions. And fourth, when one entity is making decisions for an entire industry, it has the power to unseat one company in favor of another every time contracts expire. This means that research companies have the motivation to provide their best services year after year because there is no presumption of contract renewal.

Evolving Communication Technologies

At a time when more people seek access to media audiences, a range of evolving communication technologies present new challenges. As we noted previously, the average U.S. television household receives over 100 channels of programming. With remote control devices, viewers can skip commercials by changing channels, perhaps even choosing noncommercial pay services. More disconcerting from the advertiser's perspective are digital video recorder (DVRs), like TiVo, that allow viewers to prerecord programs with advertising, then skip the commercials altogether. Of course, some segments of the audience may avoid the clutter of advertisements on radio and television by opting for interactive media like video games. Taken together, these technologies empower viewers in a way that seems to threaten the entire system of advertiser-supported media. In response to changes in technology, Nielsen has adjusted its method for calculating and reporting audience data. As we explained earlier, audiences are now calculated on the basis of "live-plus" viewing, which can include playback same day, 3 days, or 7 days.

As a result, advertisers are using alternate strategies to bring their messages to the public's attention. One tried-and-true technique that has received renewed interest is *product placement,* a strategy that has been used for some time in the film industry. If people won't watch a commercial for some product, then place the product in the program itself. You may remember the movie *E.T.: The Extraterrestrial,* in which E.T. was lured by Reese's Pieces. On television we have seen judges for *American Idol* sipping cups of Coca-Cola, Don Draper pitching Kodak on *Mad Men,* and characters on *Seinfeld* enjoying Junior Mints. Hundreds of millions of dollars are now spent on product placement in television, and it is expected the practice will soon exceed $1 billion in the United States alone. Planners use audience ratings as well as storylines to identify the best placements for their client's products; agencies have even developed models to estimate the monetary value of these placements. In some countries this practice has been slowed by Joint Industry Commissions that fear the overcommercialization of television and radio content. For example, paid product placement in U.K. programming was banned on broadcast stations until 2010 when Ofcom decided to allow it. Broadcasters still, however, have to adhere to a set of rules that limit the practice.

In a similar vein, advertisers are being more deliberate about placing logos and slogans in sporting events. Billboards in a baseball outfield, or surrounding a soccer pitch, can produce valuable exposures. In fact, chroma-key technology can create "virtual billboards" that only exist in the televised images of a game. NASCAR seems to have sold every available square inch on drivers' cars and uniforms. Messages woven into the fabric of a program or event are difficult for viewers to miss. And ratings companies, like Nielsen Media Research, now offer services that estimate the size and composition of the audience that is actually exposed to those images.

Marketers are also exploring less-traditional advertising options. Although European movie theaters have shown advertisements for some time, this practice has met resistance in the United States. But the captive movie audience is proving hard for advertisers to resist, and cinema advertising is one of the most rapidly growing ad venues in North America. Advertisers can buy spots in the short program before a feature film, and show either the same commercials they use for television, or new ones produced specifically for the film-going audience. A trade association, the Cinema Advertising Council (CAC), performs the same kind of promotion and lobbying tasks as its electronic media counterparts: the Television Bureau of Advertising (TVB), the Cable Advertising Bureau (CAB), the Radio Advertising Bureau (RAB), the Interactive Advertising Bureau (IAB), the Syndicated Network Television Association (SNTA), and the Open Mobile Video Coalition (OMVC). Nielsen Media Research, partnering with cinema advertising sales organizations, launched a service to measure and quantify theater audiences. Nielsen's "gross cinema points," roughly analogous to television's "gross rating points," allow cinema sales reps to compete with broadcasting and the Internet for a share of the advertising market.

Advertisers are also testing the effectiveness of commercials in video games. This gives them better access to young men, who are a desirable, and often hard to reach, segment of the market. Initial research indicates that gamers actually like the presence of advertisements and identifiable products in their games, because they enhance the realism of the gaming environment. As you might expect, Nielsen is measuring audiences/users for this new advertising venue.

Internet

Although the Internet does not conform to the "local versus national" distinction that has defined traditional media markets, advertisers are able to target Internet users by demographic group and by location. In the latter half of the 1990s, advertising dollars started pouring into the Web; the momentum slowed in the early 2000s but reached nearly $32 billion in 2011 (IAB Internet Advertising Revenue Report, 2011). Just like radio and television, however, the viability of Internet advertising requires that there be independent audience measurement firms verifying the number and characteristics of Web users.

The Internet audience research business has developed along the same lines as broadcast audience measurement. Concepts like "impressions," "reach," "frequency," and "audience duplication" are used to summarize and evaluate Internet users. Just as their broadcast counterparts, Web sites are represented in the advertising market by rep firms, which provide a variety of services for the sites they represent. Foremost among them, though, is soliciting advertising revenue for their clients.

There are some major differences between broadcasting and the Internet that affect the ways audiences can be tracked. The most important difference is that everyone who visits a website is being sent content directly from a server. This computer can keep track of everyone who accesses a website. The server can, in principle, produce a census of all users, eliminating the need for sampling altogether. In fact, one of the first ways to measure Internet audiences was to count the number of hits that the server received. But, as we discussed in chapter 5, hits are very imprecise measurements. For the Internet to become a viable advertising medium, marketers needed audience/user data comparable to the estimates they had for broadcasting and cable.

Advertisers are increasingly interested in reaching audiences via digital technologies. Two major audience measurement companies vie for supremacy in the field of Internet measurement: Nielsen Online and comScore Media Metrix. Both maintain very large samples of Internet users, at home and at work, who have agreed to report information about themselves and to have their Web surfing behavior recorded. These data are aggregated into various reports, which are available to clients willing to pay for independent estimates of the size and composition of website audiences.

An interesting, and dramatic, change in the way advertisers reach audiences came with the introduction of Internet-connected tablets and mobile phones. Ad placement is no longer about a single distribution technology and content type matched to a single screen (i.e., broadcast or cable television viewed on stationary television sets, Internet accessed on desktop or laptop computers). If they can connect to the Web, viewers can watch television or browse websites on different types of screens, from the home-bound television set to the smallest of mobile phones. The challenge for the audience research industry is to discover ways to capture content consumption across all screens so producers and distributors can sell their audiences to advertisers.

Another powerful, but not yet fully realized, potential of the Internet is *addressable advertising*. Because Internet advertisements can be served independently of Web page content, advertisers can target individual users with specific advertising appeals, regardless of which content they choose. At present, most targeting occurs by linking the content of Web pages to a complementary ad (e.g., a travel website carries an ad for an airline). But more precise targeting is, in theory, possible. At some point in the future, advertisements are likely to reach the right consumer at the right time, no matter what content the consumer has chosen to view. When this scenario becomes a reality, the rules for programming advertiser-supported media will have to be rewritten.

RESEARCH QUESTIONS

Obviously, the buying and selling of audiences happens in a number of different places and involves people with different motivations and levels of sophistication. There are, nonetheless, a handful of recurring research questions that transcend these differences. By distilling these from the previous discussion we can see more clearly how ratings data are used in the context of advertising. The four basic questions users ask of the ratings data concern the size and composition of the audience and the cost to reach potential customers.

How Many People Are in the Audience?

More than any single factor, the size of the media audience determines its value to advertisers and, in turn, its value to the media. Local radio audiences are usually counted in the hundreds of people. Television audiences are numbered in the thousands at the local level, and in the tens of thousands or millions at the national level. In the day-to-day buying and selling of advertising, these audiences are expressed as ratings—in fact the term is so widely recognized that we chose to use it in the title of this book.

In the national market, ratings estimates can be directly compared within each distribution channel. A 5 rating among persons aged 18 and older on NBC represents the same number of viewers as a 5 rating among persons aged 18 and older on CBS or AMC or FX—as long as the rating is based on the same population. This is also true of radio networks. However, ratings are not the best measure for inter-market comparisons between DMAs. The reason, of course, is that each market has a different total population—a 25 rating in Denver does not represent the same number of people as a 25 rating in Los Angeles. In this context, projected audiences are more useful.

Advertisers typically run a series of advertisements over a period of days or weeks. In some ways, then, the audience for a single commercial is less important than total audience exposure over the entire campaign. To provide some assessment of total exposure, ratings for each individual commercial can be summed across a campaign to generate the GRPs we discussed in chapter 5. The term is used quite commonly in advertising, and almost nowhere else.

Audiences are consuming television content on a number of different platforms, which makes tracking viewership more complicated. Figure 7.1 illustrates the range of viewing options used by audiences in 2012 during the U.S. collegiate

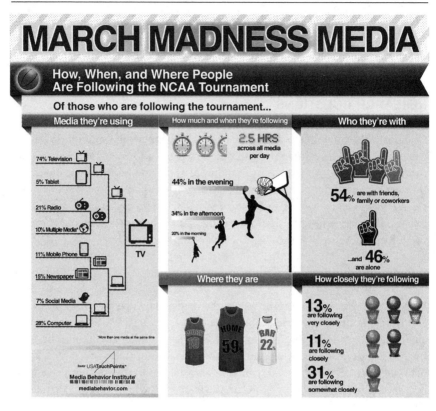

FIGURE 7.1. Viewing Options Used by Audiences During March Madness

basketball tournament, commonly known as "March Madness." As you can see, basketball fans watched across a number of different screens from television sets to tablets to computers to mobile phones. This graphic shows that 74 percent watched on television sets, 28 percent on computers, and 11 percent on mobile phones. These numbers add up to more than 100% because some viewers used different platforms at the same time—10 percent watched more than one screen simultaneously. On average, fans spent 2.5 hours per day, across all media, watching the tournament, and they viewed at work, at home, and in bars. The media would like to "monetize" this content by credibly measuring these audiences, assigning monetary value to them, and selling their attention to advertisers.

How Often Do the Same People Show Up in the Audience?

Advertisers are, understandably, interested in how many different people see their message and how often they see it. These concerns are addressed by measures of reach and frequency, respectively. Certain media are better at achieving large cumulative audiences than others. Prime time broadcast television, for example, produces considerable reach for a commercial message, since its audiences tend to be quite large. Further, many people only watch television during prime time and, therefore, are reachable only in that daypart. As a result, advertisers are often willing to pay a premium for prime time spots. Cable networks, on the other hand, are limited by the penetration of cable systems, and so cannot hope to achieve penetration levels as high as their broadcast counterparts.

The second factor of interest is the frequency of exposure. The question here is how many times on average did an audience actually see or hear the message? Some programs and dayparts tend to attract relatively small audiences, which means a GRP goal would be achieved through low reach and high frequency (remember, GRPs = reach × frequency). If, for example, you wanted to market a product to Spanish-speaking audiences, buying time on a Spanish language station might produce a low cume but a high frequency of exposure. Similarly, radio can be an effective medium for achieving high frequency, since the audiences for many stations and satellite networks tend to be loyal to station formats. The optimum balance between reach and frequency depends on the goals of the advertiser.

Table 7.5 summarizes reach estimates for different GRP levels on broadcast television and cable. Reading across the row for each daypart, it is clear that reach does not increase proportionally as the GRP levels go up; this means that

TABLE 7.5

Estimated 4-Week Reach Attained by Various Forms of Television at Differing GRP Levels

		Adult Target GRPs (Total U.S.)						
		25	*50*	*75*	*100*	*150*	*200*	*300*
Broadcast TV								
Early A.M.	Net	13	18	22	25	27	28	29
Daytime[a]	Net	14	21	25	28	30	32	33
Early news	Net	17	28	35	39	42	44	46
Prime	Net	21	36	44	51	57	62	66
Cable[b,c]								
5-Channel buy		17	27	36	42	46	49	51
10-Channel buy		19	31	39	45	50	54	57
15-Channel buy		20	34	42	48	54	58	61

Source: Media Dynamics, TV Dimensions 2012, p. 150, Used by permission.

[a] Women targets only.

[b] It should be noted that cable's "wired" penetration is only 61% of U.S. TV homes; however, another 27% to 28% of U.S. TV homes view via direct TV (satellite).

[c] All dayparts.

the combination of reach and frequency differs across dayparts. For example, doubling the number of GRPs from 50 to 100 in prime time on a broadcast network does not double the reach—it adds 15 points (an increase of about 42 percent). The same GRP change in daytime will add 7 reach points (an increase of 33 percent). Note that each daypart builds reach differently. At 100 GRPs, prime time broadcast networks will deliver a reach of about 51 percent of all adults. During the early news broadcast, these networks will deliver a reach of 39 percent at the same GRP level. Note also that to reach half of all adults via cable, the advertiser would have to buy 300 GRPs in a 5-channel schedule and 150 GRPs with a schedule of 10 cable channels.

Who Are the Audience Members?

Throughout this book we have referenced the need for different advertisers to reach different kinds of audiences. If the size of the audience is the most important determinant of its value, the composition of the audience is not far behind. In fact, advertisers are increasingly interested in presenting their messages to specific subsets of the mass audience, a strategy called *market segmentation*. This strategy plays a very important role in advertising and, in turn, has a major impact on the form that ratings data take. Audiences are segmented according to the traits of viewers or listeners. Almost any attribute can become a segmentation variable, as long as it is reasonably well defined. In practice, viewer or listener attributes are usually grouped into one of four categories.

Demographic variables are the most commonly reported in ratings data. By convention, we include in this category such attributes as race, age, gender, income, education, marital status, and occupation. Of these, age and gender are the most frequently reported audience characteristics, and the standard reporting categories featured in ratings books. So, for example, advertisers and broadcasters will often buy and sell "women 18 to 49," "men 18 to 34," and so on. Most buying and selling of audiences is done on the basis of demographic variables.

Demographics have much to recommend them as segmentation variables. For one thing, everyone in the industry is used to working with them. When you talk about an audience of women or 18- to 34-year-olds, everybody knows exactly what you are talking about. On the other hand, there may be important differences between two women of the same age, differences that are potentially important to an advertiser. Therefore, additional methods of segmentation are used.

Geographic variables offer another common way to describe the audience. We have already encountered one of the most important, designated market areas or DMAs. Just as people differ from one another with respect to their age and gender, so, too, they differ in terms of where they live. Every television viewer or radio listener in the country can be assigned to one particular market area. Obviously, such distinctions would be important to an advertiser whose goods or services have distinct regional appeal.

Other geographic variables that are commonly used in ratings research are county and state of residence (including breakouts by county size) and region of the country. Political advertisers rely heavily on this kind of information. Because areas like congressional districts do not conform exactly to the DMAs for which ratings are readily available, media planners analyze audiences by county. A television station that earns the highest DMA ratings might not be the one that gets the advertising from a particular campaign. Instead, planners will suggest whichever station(s) have the highest ratings in the counties of interest. Table 7.6 shows a comparison of county-level ratings by daypart for broadcast stations in the New York DMA. The index compares county ratings to DMA ratings. An index of 100 means the ratings in the counties of interest were the same as the rating for the entire market; an index of 50 means the county ratings were half as large as the market rating. As you can see, of the three broadcast-network-owned stations, WABC consistently gets higher daytime viewership in Orange and Putnam counties.

Tracking a person's zip code is another popular tool of geographic segmentation. With such finely drawn areas, it is often possible to make inferences about a person's income, lifestyle, and station in life. These zip-code–based techniques of segmentation are commonly referred to as *geodemographics*.

Behavioral variables draw distinctions among people on the basis of their behaviors. The most obvious kind of behavior to track is media use. We need to know who watched a particular program before we can estimate the size of its audience. With this kind of information, it is possible to describe an audience not only in terms of age and gender, but also in terms of what else they watched or listened to. Such audience breakouts, however, are only occasionally provided by the ratings service.

The other behavioral variables that weigh heavily in an advertiser's mind are product purchase variables. Because most advertisers want to reach the audience that is most likely to buy their product, what better way to describe an audience than by purchase behaviors? For example, we could characterize an audience by percentage of heavy beer drinkers, or the average amount of laundry soap purchased. One ratings company has called such segmentation variables *buyer-graphics*. As you might imagine, advertisers like this approach to audience segmentation.

Combining media usage data with other types of variables is particularly useful to marketers targeting potential customers who fit narrower definitions than specific age and gender. However, this information can be very expensive to obtain. Only those organizations that pay subscription fees can use this data in their sales or buying efforts.

TABLE 7.6
Comparison of County-Level Ratings by Daypart for Broadcast Stations in the New York DMA

| | | | Report Period: 04/26/2012–05/23/2012 Timeshifting: Live + Same Day Service: NSI Persons 35+ | | | | | | Report Period: 09/19/2011–11/23/2011 Timeshifting: Live + Same Day Service: NSI Persons 35+ | | | | | | | | |
| | | | New York DMA | | | Orange+Putnam, NY | | | New York DMA | | | Orange+Putnam, NY | | | | | |
Daypart	Stn	Affl	RTG	SHR	IMPS	RTG	SHR	IMPS	RTG	SHR	IMPS	RTG	SHR	IMPS	avg ny dma	avg orange+putn	index
M-F 5:00A.M.–6:00A.M.	WNBC	NBC	0.68	7.46	73,764	0.50	2.43	1,233	0.81	9.16	87,980	0.35	3.35	995	0.75	0.43	57%
	WABC	ABC	0.92	10.06	99,482	6.53	32.05	16,273	0.88	9.93	95,387	2.47	23.90	7,105	0.90	4.50	500%
	WCBS	CBS	0.77	8.41	83,210	1.40	6.89	3,496	0.87	9.84	94,539	0.90	8.67	2,577	0.82	1.15	140%
M-F 6:00A.M.–7:00A.M.	WNBC	NBC	1.74	12.55	188,036	1.37	6.08	3,440	1.77	13.64	191,892	0.35	2.37	1,005	1.76	0.86	49%
	WABC	ABC	1.79	12.90	193,262	6.02	26.76	15,150	1.92	14.81	208,327	4.37	29.66	12,585	1.86	5.20	280%
	WCBS	CBS	1.44	10.39	155,580	1.70	7.54	4,269	1.52	11.76	165,424	1.81	12.29	5,212	1.48	1.76	119%
M-F 7:00A.M.–9:00A.M.	WNBC	NBC	2.56	15.36	277,062	3.59	14.27	9,045	2.41	15.25	261,847	1.56	7.58	4,488	2.49	2.58	104%
	WABC	ABC	2.17	13.02	234,807	5.58	22.19	14,059	2.09	13.23	227,184	4.55	22.12	13,099	2.13	5.07	238%
	WCBS	CBS	0.97	5.81	104,751	1.51	6.02	3,812	0.94	5.97	102,455	1.07	5.19	3,073	0.96	1.29	135%

Daypart	Station														
M-F 9:00AM–10:00AM	WNBC NBC	1.70	10.77	184,198	1.87	8.11	4,712	1.59	10.56	172,219	1.52	8.72	4,371	1.65	1.70	103%
	WABC ABC	2.11	13.36	228,551	2.85	12.37	7,185	2.02	13.45	219,422	2.67	15.34	7,683	2.07	2.76	134%
	WCBS CBS	0.97	6.13	104,836	1.06	4.60	2,669	0.92	6.13	100,012	0.31	1.75	878	0.95	0.69	72%
M-F 10:00A.M.–11:00A.M.	WNBC NBC	1.21	7.79	131,000	0.85	4.85	2,134	1.03	7.16	112,353	0.76	5.13	2,186	1.12	0.81	72%
	WABC ABC	1.18	7.56	127,066	1.88	10.75	4,725	1.07	7.41	116,372	2.08	14.07	5,996	1.13	1.98	176%
	WCBS CBS	1.19	7.65	128,687	0.24	1.35	594	1.12	7.78	122,046	0.20	1.32	564	1.16	0.22	19%
M-F 11:00A.M.–12:00P.M.	WNBC NBC	0.61	3.74	66,287	0.23	1.28	574	0.49	3.20	53,107	0.08	0.61	235	0.55	0.16	28%
	WABC ABC	2.60	15.83	280,891	1.72	9.63	4,333	2.54	16.61	275,733	2.53	18.75	7,282	2.57	2.13	83%
	WCBS CBS	1.76	10.73	190,394	0.06	0.31	139	1.61	10.55	175,090	0.06	0.47	184	1.69	0.06	4%
M-F 12:00P.M.–1:00P.M.	WNBC NBC	0.52	3.12	56,338	0.62	3.19	1,554	0.36	2.30	39,010	0.05	0.36	136	0.44	0.34	76%
	WABC ABC	2.74	16.36	295,704	3.03	15.66	7,618	2.45	15.71	266,314	2.28	17.37	6,576	2.60	2.66	102%
	WCBS CBS	1.83	10.97	198,234	0.00	0.00	0	1.49	9.56	162,133	0.03	0.25	96	1.66	0.02	1%

Psychographics draw distinctions among people on the basis of their psychological characteristics. While definitions of what belongs in this broad and amorphous category vary, they typically include things like people's values, attitudes, opinions, motivations, and preferences. One type of psychographic variable that has attracted attention recently is variously labeled *viewer loyalty, involvement,* and/or *engagement.* The idea here is that, as new technologies empower audience members with ever more choices, it is increasingly important for advertisers to know which people are particularly committed to which media products. Some evidence suggests that those who are very engaged with a program (e.g., its fans) are more attentive to the advertisements contained within. Although such traits can, in principle, be very valuable in describing an audience, psychographic variables are often difficult to define and measure precisely.

How Much Does It Cost to Reach the Audience?

Advertisers and the media, as well as middlemen like ad agencies and station reps, all have an interest in what it costs to reach the audience. Those on the selling side of the business try to maximize their revenues, whereas buyers try to minimize their expenses.

Although it is true that broadcasters and other forms of electronic media sell audiences, it would be an oversimplification to suggest that audience factors alone determine the cost of a commercial spot. Certainly, audience size and composition are the principal determinants, but several factors have an impact. Advertisers pay a premium, for example, to have their message placed first in a set of advertisements (a *commercial pod*). We have already pointed out that advertisers who buy network time early in the upfront market can get a better price. Similarly, advertisers who agree to buy large blocks of time can usually get some sort of quantity discount. Remember that these transactions happen in a marketplace environment. The relative strengths and weaknesses of each party, their negotiating skills, and, ultimately, the laws of supply and demand all affect the final cost of time.

These factors are represented in the rates that the media charge for commercial spots. It is common practice for an individual station to summarize these in a *rate card,* which is usually a table or chart that states the price of spots in different dayparts or programs. The rate card is a planning guide, but the actual rates are subject to negotiation. Although the estimated cost of a commercial spot is important to know, from the buyer's perspective, it is largely uninterpretable without associated audience information. The question the buyer must answer is, "What am I getting for the money?" This cannot be answered without comparing audience ratings to the rates that are being charged. Advertisers use either cost-per-thousand or cost-per-point calculations to analyze the value of advertising time.

Ratings are the currency that drives the economics of commercial electronic media audiences. But the media are complex organizations that can and do use audience information in a variety of ways. Similarly, those who want to study or regulate mass communication have found that the data gathered for the benefit of advertisers can offer many insights into the power and potential of the electronic media. In the chapters that follow, we discuss many of these applications. First we turn to the use of audience data in programming.

RELATED READINGS

Albarran, A. (2012). *Management of electronic and digital media* (5th ed.). Belmont, CA: Wadsworth.

Albarran, A. (2010). *The media economy.* New York: Routledge.

Alexander, A., Owers, J., Carveth, R., Hollifield, C. A., & Greco, A. (Eds.). (2004). *Media economics: Theory and practice* (3rd ed.). Mahwah, NJ: Lawrence Erlbaum Associates.

Baron, R. B., & Sissors, J. Z., (2010). *Advertising media planning* (7th ed.). Chicago: McGraw-Hill.

Bogart, L. (1996). *Strategy in advertising: Matching media and messages to markets and motivations* (3rd ed.). Lincolnwood, IL: NTC Business Books.

Poltrack, D. F. (1983). *Television marketing: Network, local, cable.* New York: McGraw-Hill.

Turow, J. (1997). *Breaking up America: Advertisers and the new media world.* Chicago: University of Chicago Press.

Warner, C. (2009). *Media selling: Television, print, Internet, radio* (4th ed.). Malden, MA: Wiley-Blackwell.

CHAPTER 8

Audience Research in Programming

To give value to commercial time, the electronic media must attract audiences. Broadly speaking, that is the job of a programmer, who may be anyone from the president of a huge media conglomerate to someone working for a radio station in a small rural community. In the world of advertiser-supported media, the programmer effectively sets the "bait" that lures the audience. In order to do this, he or she must know a great deal about audiences; after sales and advertising, the most important application of audience data is in programming.

Programming involves a range of activities. A programmer must determine where to obtain the most appropriate programs. Sometimes that means playing an active role in developing new program concepts and commissioning the production of pilots. For most television stations, it means securing the rights to syndicated programs, some of which have already been produced. In this capacity, the programmer must be skillful in negotiating contracts and in predicting the kinds of material that will appeal to prospective audiences. Programmers are also responsible for deciding how and when that material will actually air on the station or network. Successful scheduling requires knowing when different kinds of audiences are likely to be available, and how those audiences might decide among the options offered by competing media. Finally, a programmer must be adept at promoting programs. Sometimes that involves placing advertisements and promotional spots to alert the audience to a particular program or personality. With the growth of social media, it can mean promoting favorable word-of-mouth, triggering information cascades, although these are notoriously difficult to manage. It can also involve packaging an entire schedule of programs in order to create a special station or network "image." In all of these activities, ratings play an important role.

The way in which these programming functions take shape, and the priorities facing individual programmers, differs from one setting to the next. Occasionally, in small stations, the entire job of programming falls on the shoulders of one person. In larger operations, however, programming involves many people.

Often the job of promoting programs and developing an image is turned over to specialized promotions departments, especially in an increasingly competitive media marketplace.

The most significant differences in how programmers function depend on the medium in which they work. In the early 1950s, television forced radio to adapt to a new marketplace. No longer would individual radio programs dominate the medium. Instead, radio stations began to specialize in certain kinds of music or in continuous program formats. The job of a radio programmer became one of crafting an entire program service. Further, the vast supply of music from the record industry meant that stations could be less reliant on networks to define that service. In contrast, television built audiences by attracting them to individual programs. Although some cable networks now emulate radio by offering a steady schedule of one program type (e.g., news, music, weather, financial and business information, or comedy), most television programmers still devote more attention to the acquisition, scheduling, and promotion of relatively distinct units of content.

In the case of broadcast network affiliates, most program development and acquisition is done at the network level. However, affiliated stations do program certain dayparts, such as news, early fringe, and late night. There are also some independent television stations that program the entire broadcast day. In order to explain how audience research is used in programming, we consider the specific programming practices of each form of electronic media.

RADIO PROGRAMMING

Although facing increased competition from evolving audio technologies, traditional radio is still a significant medium in the United States. Arbitron estimates that radio reaches 93 percent of all persons aged 12+ in the course of an average week. There are more than 13,000 commercial radio stations in the United States and another 2,500 noncommercial educational ones, each offering different— sometimes only slightly different—programming and each reaching unique audiences. Most radio stations, from the smallest to the largest markets, have a *format*. A format is an identifiable set of program presentations or style of programming. Some stations, particularly those in smaller markets with fewer competitors, may have wider ranging formats that try to include a little something for everyone. Most stations, however, zero in on a fairly specific brand of talk or music.

Radio stations use formats for two related reasons. First, radio tends to be very competitive. In any given market, there are far more radio stations than television stations, daily newspapers, or almost any other local advertising medium. To avoid being lost in the shuffle, programmers use formats to make their station seem unique or special so it will stand out in the minds of listeners and induce them to tune in. This strategy is called *positioning* the station. Second, different formats are known to appeal to different kinds of listeners. Because most advertisers want to reach particular kinds of audiences, the ability to deliver on a certain demographic is important in selling the station's time.

Radio formats run the gamut from classical to country to pop contemporary hits. Radio programmers, consultants, and analysts have fairly specific names for dozens of different formats. However, most of these are usually grouped in about 20 categories. The most common labels, ranked by weekly cume, are shown in Table 8.1.

Format popularity varies by listener demographics, including age, gender, and ethnicity. For example, women listen to more adult contemporary and religious stations than men do; and men are more likely to listen to sports and album-oriented rock. While country is popular across all age groups, older adults prefer news/talk and information and adult contemporary; and young adults and teenagers consume more pop contemporary hit radio. Comparing the ethnic composition of audiences for radio, urban adult contemporary and urban contemporary are the formats ranking high with African Americans; Spanish adult hits, Mexican regional, and Spanish contemporary rank highest with Hispanics. There are different ways to program a radio station. Some stations do all of their own programming. They identify the specific songs they will play, and how often they will play them. They may also hire highly visible—and highly paid—disc jockeys, who can dominate the personality of the station during certain dayparts. This kind of customized programming is particularly common in major markets, and it is often accompanied by customized research. Not only do these stations buy and analyze syndicated ratings, they are also likely to engage in a variety of nonratings research projects.

The most typical nonratings research includes *focus groups,* which feature intensive discussions with small groups of listeners, and *call-out* research which involves playing a short excerpt of a song over the telephone to gauge listener reactions. Consultants also conduct customized research to investigate how radio audiences react to potentially offensive material, to assess listener awareness of particular program services, to measure the impact of advertising (for example, on bus cards, billboards, or television spots), and to judge the popularity of particular personalities or features (news, traffic, weather, contests, etc.) on the station.

Many stations, however, depend on a syndicated program service or network to define their format. Sometimes, large group owners like Clear Channel and Cumulus provide programming to their stations on a regional or format basis. Some stations rely on prepackaged material for virtually everything they broadcast, except local advertising and announcements. To do this they subscribe to a program service, usually provided to the station by a satellite feed. Other stations

TABLE 8.1
Radio Station Formats Ranked by Weekly Cume

Formats Ranked by Weekly Cume *Mon–Sun, 6 A.M.–Mid,* *Persons 12+, Fall 2010*		Gender Composition by Format *Mon–Sun, 6 A.M.–Mid,* *Persons 12+, Fall 2010*		
	Cume		*Women*	*Men*
Adult Contemporary	76,623,400	Adult Contemporary	63%	37%
Pop CHR	68,391,800	Contemporary Christian	62%	38%
Country + New Country	65,569,700	Hot Adult Contemporary	62%	38%
News/Talk/Information	58,258,600	Pop CHR	61%	39%
Classic Hits	42,444,300	Religious	61%	39%
Hot Adult Contemporary	41,237,200	Urban Adult Contemporary	56%	44%
Classic Rock	38,630,300	Spanish Contemporary	53%	47%
Rhythmic Contemporary Hit Radio	35,479,000	Country + New Country	52%	48%
All Sports	26,947,500	Rhythmic Contemporary Hit Radio	52%	48%
Adult Hits + 80s Hits	24,345,500	Urban Contemporary	52%	48%
Alternative	23,381,200	Oldies	50%	50%
Urban Adult Contemporary	21,176,300	Classic Hits	47%	53%
Urban Contemporary	19,757,300	Adult Hits + 80s hits	47%	53%
Active Rock	18,896,900	Adult Album Alternative	45%	55%
Contemporary Christian	18,305,900	All News	45%	55%
Album Oriented Rock	15,053,700	Spanish Adult Hits	44%	56%
All News	14,130,700	News/Talk/Information	41%	59%
Mexican Regional	14,026,100	Mexican Regional	37%	63%
Adult Album Alternative	12,784,100	Alternative	37%	63%
Oldies	11,780,500	Classic Rock	30%	70%
Spanish Contemporary	11,672,300	Active Rock	27%	73%
Religious	8,261,100	Album Oriented Rock	27%	73%
Spanish Adult Hits	8,138,500	All Sports	16%	84%

Note: Due to rounding, totals of gender composition percentages may not add to 100.

Source: Format definitions are supplied to Arbitron by the radio stations. Data come from TAPSCAN™Web National Regional Database. Fall 2010.

Source: Arbitron Radio Today, 2011. Reprinted by permission of Arbitron.

do some of their own original programming during the most listened-to morning hours and use syndicated services during the remaining hours of the day.

Most radio stations do not worry about ratings research because the majority are located in small to very small communities. Arbitron defines and measures radio listening in more than 270 market areas, the smallest with a population of less than 80,000. Even at that, the company publishes audience estimates for only about one third of the nation's more than 13,000 radio stations. Of course, measured stations account for the vast majority of the industry's listening and the lion's share of its revenues.

Noncommercial radio outlets also use quantitative audience estimates. National Public Radio (NPR) stations, for example, receive ratings, even though they are not listed in the ratings book alongside their commercial counterparts. In some markets they are even among the highest rated local stations. While audience data are not used in quite the same way, they may be important for fund-raising. Many of the larger stations have the functional equivalent of a sales department that regularly uses audience estimates to attract underwriting. Ratings are also used by programmers to make many of the same decisions a commercial station does about program popularity, scheduling, and promotion.

One of the most significant changes in radio audience measurement came with the introduction of PPMs in 2010. Although the majority of radio markets are still measured with diaries, close to 50 of the largest ones now receive estimates based on the PPM.

Traditional radio now competes with online audio and with satellite radio. According to the Pew Research Center (2012), roughly a third of Americans are listening to online audio services (including streaming AM/FM stations). And, although SiriusXM radio does not yet provide appreciable competition in any single radio market, some industry experts think satellite radio will impact the industry the way FM affected AM or the way cable affected broadcast television. In 2011, satellite radio had 22 million subscribers (Pew Research Center, 2012). Carmakers are installing satellite receivers as standard or optional equipment, and the acquisition of several important radio personalities, including Howard Stern, along with the ability to provide local market traffic and weather information, could lead to large subscription increases over the next few years.

TELEVISION PROGRAMMING

Broadcast

At the other end of the spectrum is the business of programming a major television network. Although television programmers share some of the same concerns as radio programmers, they are confronted with a number of different tasks. One important difference is the extent to which a network programmer is involved in the creation of new programs. Ratings data are certainly valuable for this task, but program development relies especially on talents for anticipating popular trends and tastes, and setting in motion productions that will cater to those tastes. Network programmers who have that talent are as well known in the business as any on-screen celebrity.

The studios, whose job it is to finance and produce programs and sell them to the networks, also rely on ratings information. The premiere of a show gives a snapshot, but the subsequent few weeks are really critical for the show's future. In order to convince networks to keep a show on the air, studio research departments study the ratings from different angles to look for signs that a show is trending upward. A decline in ratings might mean cancellation, but it could also motivate adjustments to program content. Programmers might request changes in program elements such as casting, storylines, or character development if they think these changes will increase viewership.

Programmers at local television stations spend less time on the actual production of new programs, and more time on purchasing them in the syndication market. Several kinds of syndicated programs are available, and new ones enter the pipeline every season. *Off-network* syndicated programs are those that originally aired on a broadcast network and are now available to individual stations. In general, they are among the most desirable of all syndicated programming from the standpoint of ratings potential.

Off-network programs work well in syndication for a number of reasons. They typically have high production values—something that viewers brought up on network fare have come to expect. They also have a track record of drawing audiences, which can be reassuring for the prospective buyer. In fact, only network series that have been on-air for at least 4 or 5 years usually make it to syndication. One reason for this is that local programmers schedule reruns as strips, airing different episodes Monday through Friday at the same time of day. To sustain stripped programming over several months, they must own a good number of programs. In general, this means that there must be 100 episodes before a series is viable in syndication; only the most popular network shows stay on the air that long.

Once they reach syndication, however, off-network programs can continue to attract new audiences for decades. *M*A*S*H*, for example, was enormously successful on CBS when it aired in the 1970s, and it has been successful in syndication for more than 30 years. Newer off-network programs, some available even before their original run ends, get the most desirable time slots, while older series get displaced to less desirable times. Nevertheless, with so many stations and cable outlets with so many hours to fill, even older programs, especially those that were very popular or have semi-cult status, still seem to find an audience. The durability of off-network series means they have an extensive ratings history, which is especially useful in programming. Prospective buyers can compile detailed information from many different markets, analyzing the relative success of one program versus another, or the flow of audience from one program to and from another.

During the late 1990s and early 2000s, networks started to rely on *reality programs* like *Survivor, American Idol,* and *The Voice.* These unscripted shows affect the syndication market by decreasing the number of off-network series that can draw audiences in syndication. Unlike scripted comedies and dramas, reality programs do not attract large audiences when they are repeated. After all, the fun of reality programs is to find out who wins—once that is known, audiences lose interest in viewing the series.

Syndication has also been affected by the trend toward vertical and horizontal integration in the media industries. A single owner can now have substantial financial interest in the production of programs, their distribution through syndication, and the stations or cable networks to which they can be sold. In the case of broadcast syndication, this means first priority will usually be given to the co-owned stations. In turn, these stations will usually comply with the seller's scheduling requirements. This situation presents a challenge for stations that have to find new sources of programming, and for independent syndicators who have to fight for fewer available time slots.

In recent years, cable has become a significant player in the syndication market. Some cable networks depend almost exclusively on reruns of old programs. Others complement their schedule of new programs and films with vintage series that are likely to appeal to specific target audiences. Mystery fans can watch *Perry Mason* on the Hallmark Channel or *Murder, She Wrote* on A&E. *Saturday Night Live* fans can watch reruns on Comedy Central, and science fiction fans can watch the earliest episodes of *The Twilight Zone* on the Sci Fi channel. An *off-cable* syndication market has also emerged, with pay cable series like *The Sopranos* and *Sex and the City* finding homes on basic cable networks.

Some programs are produced directly for syndication. Traditionally, these "first-run" syndication programs have included game shows and talk shows that cost relatively little to produce. More recently, courtroom reality series like *Judge Judy* have become very successful in first-run syndication.

There are other sources of programming, like movie packages or regional networks, but whatever their origin, the acquisition of syndicated programming is one of the toughest challenges a television programmer has to face. Usually the deal involves making a long-term contractual agreement with the distributor, or whoever holds the copyright to the material. For a popular program, that can mean a major commitment of resources. A mistake can cost an organization millions of dollars, and the programmer a job.

Buying and selling syndicated programming is often accompanied by an extensive use of ratings data. Distributors use the ratings to promote their product, demonstrating how well it has done in different markets. These data are often prominently featured in trade magazine advertisements. Buyers use the same sort of data to determine how well a show might do in their market, comparing the cost of acquisition to potential revenues. This is discussed in greater detail in chapter 9.

Once a network or a station commits to program production or acquisition, television programmers at all levels have more or less the same responsibility. Their programs must be placed in the schedule so as to achieve their greatest economic return. Usually that means trying to maximize each program's audience, taking into consideration the competition each show faces in the market. For affiliates, the job of program scheduling is less extensive than for others, simply because their network assumes the burden for much of the broadcast day. Even affiliates, though, devote considerable attention to programming before, during, and just after the early local news. The prime access daypart, just before network prime time, is usually very lucrative for an affiliate. Audience levels rise through the evening and the station need not share the available commercial spots with its network.

In television, as in radio, program production companies, network executives, and stations use a variety of nonratings research to sharpen their programming decisions. This may include the use of one or more measures of program or personality popularity. Marketing Evaluations, for example, produces a syndicated research service called TVQ that provides reports on the extent to which the public recognizes and likes different personalities and programs. Scores like these can be used by programmers when they make scheduling decisions. Knowing the appeal of particular personalities might tell them, for example, whether a talk show host would fare well against the competition in a fringe daypart.

Increasingly, the chatter or buzz on social media is being turned into metrics that help guide program decision-making. For example, a company called Bluefin Labs collects the comments people make on Twitter and other social networks. These are tied to particular programs and aggregated to create measures of engagement. Those measures are not always correlated ratings (i.e., popular programs are not always the most talked about). In some instances, analysts can judge whether comments are positive or negative and determine the gender of the persons making those comments. Optimedia, a major media buyer, combines such measures of buzz with convention ratings to create what it calls "content power ratings."

Other program-related research includes theater testing, which involves showing a large group a pilot and recording their professed enjoyment with voting devices of some sort. All networks and most program producers use some type of testing research in the program production process. One of the largest program testing facilities is in Las Vegas. Strange as it may seem, researchers recruit audiences—between the swimming pool and the lobby—of a large hotel. Pilots, commercials, and other program material are shown while respondents, seated at a computer, record data about themselves and give periodic reactions to the material being shown. This method, which identifies individual and cumulative responses to program elements, traces its origins back to the original Stanton–Lazarsfeld Program Analyzer of the late 1930s. Program executives can see this information almost instantly on their office computers in Los Angeles, New York, or anywhere. Ultimately, however, ratings are a programmer's most important evaluative tool. A classic quote from a network executive sums this up nicely, "Strictly from the network's point of view a good soap opera is one that has a high rating and share, a bad one is one that does not" (Converse, 1974).

Cable

As we implied previously, programming for some cable networks is similar to radio, and for others it is more like over-the-air television. Cable networks like WGN and TBS, for example, began as local stations and became national *super stations* by distributing their service via satellite. These and others like them often include a variety of programs in their lineups, much like television stations. The major difference between cable and local television though is that cable programmers seek more narrowly targeted audiences than do television broadcasters. Lifetime is programmed for women; ESPN and Spike for men; and the Cartoon Network and Nickelodeon for children. Some cable services concentrate on one type of content, such as news, talk, travel, cooking, and weather. You'll often find, however, that even specialized services use some variety of formats to broaden their audience. For example, virtually all have tried different forms of documentary programming as part of their schedule.

Programming strategies can be visualized on a continuum from traditional broadcast scheduling to newer forms of cable or narrowcasting. While programming patterns for each service have remained relatively distinct throughout most of television's history, some programmers are now testing alternative approaches. Broadcasters, for example, are using programming models that originated on public television or cable, such as repeating popular programs within the same week. Some original network programs are repeated on cable channels, usually co-owned networks, soon after their first run. To further complicate the situation, the growing ability of viewers to build their own schedules with various recording and on-demand technologies is likely to change the role of the programmer altogether. Although services like HBO and Showtime do not need audience estimates to sell advertising, pay cable ratings are still a valuable commodity. High ratings generate interest from media critics, analysts of pop culture, journalists, potential subscribers, and, importantly, media outlets interested in purchasing off-cable syndication rights. When pay cable series like *The Sopranos* earn higher ratings than some broadcast competitors, they attract the attention of Hollywood and Wall Street. Successful production efforts generate revenue for re-investment into new programming.

Pay cable's business model depends on recruiting at least one subscriber in a household and convincing him or her to renew a subscription year after year. Programmers maintain the quality of the schedule by offering theatrical movies, often before anyone else has the rights. They are able to secure this early *window* by making long-term deals with various studios. They also use promotional campaigns to create demand for, and buzz about, the channel's original programming. HBO's yearly Emmy nominations certainly prove how well they have succeeded on this front.

As cable channels, from basic to premium, gain popularity and take ratings away from commercial networks, broadcasters complain that the playing field is uneven. Due to differences in regulation and societal expectations, cable is able to address themes that are banned from over-the-air television. In fact, "edgy" content on cable networks usually means more sex and violence than on broadcast television.

THE INTERNET

As we saw in the previous chapter, the Internet has created new opportunities for advertisers to reach audiences. This means the content of Web pages has become increasingly important. "Programming" on the Web can mean anything from the simplest personal Web page to the most sophisticated corporate sites, to multimedia programs that viewers watch on their computer, tablet, mobile, and television screens. For many radio stations it means making the station available to a much wider audience. Most television networks make programs available on the Internet the day after their original broadcast—along with older programs they hope will capture the viewer's attention.

Sites like Hulu and Netflix gained popularity by streaming licensed videos to subscribers. Both services began making deals for original programming in the early 2010s, which put them in direct competition with traditional media outlets, especially pay cable. Netflix plans new episodes of *Arrested Development*, and the company outbid HBO and AMC for the right to produce *House of Cards*. Hulu began offering original series like *Battleground* and *Spoilers* in 2012. Whether the production of new programs develops into full-fledged competition with traditional media outlets remains to be seen.

Just like the more traditional electronic media, Internet content must be planned to attract audiences in the first place and to hold their attention. Research suggests that Internet users build a set of favorite Web resources, just as radio listeners and cable television viewers develop a set of favorite channels that they watch repeatedly. There are a few major differences, though. Content on the Web can be personalized in a way that was never before possible. If users allow cookies to be stored on their computers, a programmer could theoretically serve very individualized messages—a capability that interests Web advertisers. There is also an immediate feedback mechanism with the Internet that allows programmers and producers to interact with viewers.

The relationship between the more traditional electronic media and the Web continues to evolve. Broadcast networks and stations maintain Web sites that offer additional services to the viewers they already reach over the air, and to new viewers who make initial contact via the Web. They often provide advertising availabilities on these sites to enhance the value of broadcast advertising. Networks have experimented with showing trailers for films on their websites, an option that media buyers for the studios find attractive.

In whatever way the Internet evolves, and whatever connections form between old media and new, the need for audience information is certain. Programmers need ratings-type data to track the most popular sites and determine the services most valued by particular audiences.

RESEARCH QUESTIONS

Many of the research questions that a programmer tries to answer with ratings data are, at least superficially, no different than those asked by a person in sales and advertising: How many people are in the audience? Who are they? How often do the same people show up in the audience? This convergence of research questions is hardly surprising because the purpose of programming commercial media is, with some exceptions, to attract audiences that will be sold to advertisers. The programmer's intent in asking these questions, however, is often very different. Programmers are less likely to see the audience as some abstract commodity, and more likely to view ratings as a window on what "their" audiences are doing. They need to understand not only the absolute size of a program audience, but why they are attracting particular audiences and what could be done to improve program performance.

Did I Attract the Intended Audience?

Because drawing an audience is the objective of a programmer, the most obvious use of ratings is to determine whether the objective has been achieved. In doing so, it is important to have a clear concept of the intended, or target, audience. Although any programmer would prefer an audience that is larger to one that is smaller, the often-quoted goal of "maximizing the audience" is usually an inadequate expression of a programmer's objectives. More realistically, the goal is maximizing the size of the audience within certain constraints or parameters. The most important constraint has to do with the size of the available audience. That is one reason why programmers are particularly alert to audience shares.

Increasingly, however, it is not the programmer's intention to draw even a majority of the available audience. In other words, the programmer's success or failure is best judged against the programming strategy being employed.

Radio programmers, and increasingly those at cable networks, are largely concerned with cultivating well-defined target audiences. An experienced radio programmer can fine-tune a station's demographics with remarkable accuracy. Much of this has to do with the predictable appeal that a certain kind of music, and talk, has for listeners of different ages and gender. Table 8.2 lists some of the more common station formats and percent of their total audiences in different age categories. Obviously, you cannot expect to attract many young people with Oldies music, or many older listeners with Alternative rock.

Television programmers, like their counterparts in radio, may devote their entire program service to attracting a particular demographic. This is most evident in some of the highly specialized cable networks. MTV and Nickelodeon, for example, are programmed to draw certain age groups that their owners believe will be attractive to advertisers.

Even those conventional television stations that offer a variety of program types must gauge the size and composition of program audiences against the programming strategies they employ. One common strategy is called *counter-programming*. This occurs when a station or network schedules a program that has a markedly different appeal than the programs offered by its major competitors. For example, independents tend to show light entertainment (e.g., situation comedies) when the affiliates in the market are broadcasting their local news. The independents are not trying to appeal to the typical, often older, news viewer, and their ratings should be evaluated accordingly. Programmers may try counter-programming stunts to attract viewers who are not interested in the special events covered by other stations in the market. One station in Chicago, for example, broadcast a lineup of romantic dramas that it called "The Marriage Bowl" to compete with the college football games on New Year's Day.

One way to increase the likelihood of attracting the intended audience is through the use of promotional spots. Ratings data can be very useful in identifying programs with similar demographic profiles so that promotional announcements appealing to a particular audience can be scheduled when members of that target group are watching.

Noncommercial media also care about attracting an audience. Public broadcasters in the United States, or public service broadcasters around the world for that matter, must ultimately justify their existence by serving an audience. This can only be done if an audience is identified and measured. Therefore, many public stations use ratings as well. National Public Radio (NPR), with the Corporation for Public Broadcasting (CPB), has provided audience estimates to NPR stations since 1979. The Public Broadcasting Service (PBS), which distributes much of the programming to noncommercial stations, subscribes to

TABLE 8.2
Radio Station Formats by Age and Gender

AQH Share by Demographic

Mon–Sun, 6 A.M.–Mid, AQH Persons 12+, Fall 2010

Persons 35–44		*Persons 45–54*		*Persons 55–64*		*Persons 65+*	
Country + New Country	12.2%	Country + New Country	13.1%	News/Talk/Information	18.4%	News/Talk/information	27.3%
Adult Contemporary	9.6%	News/Talk Infomation	11.8%	Country + New Country	13.8%	Country	15.3%
News/Talk/Information	8.5%	Adult Contemporary	10.9%	Adult Contemporary	11.0%	Adult Contemporary	9.9%
Pop CHR	8.0%	Classic Rock	8.0%	Classic Hits	7.8%	Classic Hits	4.3%
Classic Rock	6.0%	Classic Hits	6.8%	Classic Rock	4.8%	All Sports	2.8%
Hot AC	5.2%	Urban AC	5.0%	Urban AC	4.8%		
Urban AC	4.4%	Pop CHR	4.4%	All Sports	3.9%		
All Sports	4.2%	All Sports	4.1%	Hot AC	2.6%		
Classic Hits	4.2%	Hot AC	4.0%	Contemporary Christian	2.4%		
Mexican Regional	3.9%	Contemporary Christian	3.2%	Pop CHR	2.2%		
Contemporary Christian	3.4%	Adult Hits + 80s Hits	2.7%	Adult Hits + 80s Hits	1.9%		
Rhythmic CHR	3.4%	Mexican Regional	1.9%	Mexican Regional	1.3%		
Active Rock	3.2%	Active Rock	1.7%	Urban Contemporary	1.0%		
Adult Hits+ 80s Hits	3.1%	Urban Contemporary	1.7%	Rhythmic CHR	0.8%		
Urban Contemporary	3.0%	Rhythmic CHR	1.6%	Active Rock	0.7%		
Alternative	2.7%	Alternative	1.5%	Alternative	0.7%		

Source: Arbitron Radio Today, 2011. Men and women include only listeners 12+ years old. Reprinted by permission of Arbitron.

Note: Top 16 formats listed.

Source: Format definitions are supplied to Arbitron by the radio stations. Data come from TAPSCAN™ Web National Regional Database, Fall 2010.

national ratings for several months of each year to judge the attractiveness of its programming. And many individual stations subscribe directly to Nielsen or indirectly through research consultants who analyze the data for them.

Although they do not have sponsors in the traditional sense, public broadcasters care very much about reaching, even maximizing, their audiences. For one thing, many organizations that put up the money for programming are interested in who sees both their programs and the underwriting announcements. The more viewers there are, the happier the funding agency is. Further, public stations are heavily dependent on donations from viewers. Only those who are in the audience will hear the solicitation. Thus, many public television broadcasters pay considerable attention to their cumes and ratings.

Even if one has no funding concerns in mind, programmers in a public station well might ask a question like "How can I get maximum exposure for my documentary?" Often documentaries and "how-to" programs can earn the same or a higher rating when repeated during weekend daytime or late night than they do during the first run in prime time. A careful analysis of audience ratings data could reveal when the largest number of those in the target audience are available to view, or whether the intended audience really saw the program.

How Loyal Is My Audience?

Like the concept of "engagement," audience loyalty is difficult to define precisely because it means different things to different people. Typically, *channel loyalty* is the extent to which audience members stick with, or return to, a particular station, network, program, or website. Loyalty is something that manifests itself over time. Despite all the positive images the word connotes, we should point out that audience loyalty is quite different from audience size—the attribute most valued by time buyers. Programmers are interested in audience loyalty for a number of reasons. First, in the most general sense, it can give them a better feel for their audience and how they consume the programming that is offered to them. This knowledge can guide other scheduling decisions. Second, audience loyalty is closely related to advertising concepts like reach and frequency, so it may affect the way an audience is sold. Finally, it can provide an important clue about how to build and maintain the audience you do have, often through a more effective use of promotions.

Radio programmers use a number of simple manipulations of ratings data to assess audience loyalty. Although the heaviest radio listening is in the morning when people wake up and prepare for the day, listeners turn their radios on and off several times during the day. They also listen in their cars or at work. To maintain ratings levels, a radio station must get people to tune in as often as possible and to listen for as long as possible. Radio programmers use two related measures, *time spent listening* (TSL) and *turnover*, to monitor this behavior. Using a simple formula based on the average ratings and cume ratings that are in the radio book, one can compute TSL for any station in any daypart. Turnover is the ratio of cume audience to average audience, which is basically the reciprocal of TSL.

If you listen to just about any radio station you can hear how they try to keep you tuned in—naming the songs or other items coming up, running contests, and playing a certain number of songs without commercial interruption. To programmers, these tricks of the trade are for *quarter-hour maintenance*—that is, trying to keep listeners tuned in from one quarter-hour to the next. The 15-minute period is important, because it is the basic unit of time used to compute and re-port ratings in diary markets. By tracking TSL and audience turnover measures, the programmer can see how well the audience is being retained.

The importance of TSL varies according to the specific format of a station. All would like to keep their listeners tuned as long as possible—but that is more likely for stations with narrower, more specialized formats such as country, urban, Spanish, or religious—although these formats may share audience if there are several similar stations in the market.

Another common measure of loyalty in radio programming is called *recycling*. Because ratings books routinely report station audiences for morning and afternoon drive time combined, it is possible to determine how many people listened at both times. This can be a useful insight. If the number is relatively small, for example, stations may offer similar programming, or they may do more promotion.

The same basic research question is relevant to television programmers as well. Do the people who watch the early evening news on a particular station return to watch the late news? If the answer is no, especially if the early news is successful, it would make sense to promote the later newscast with the early news audience.

What Other Stations or Programs Does My Audience Use?

In some ways, this is just the opposite of the preceding question. Although there are some people who will listen to one, and only one, station, it is more common for audience members to change from one station to another. In radio, we noted that no two stations are programmed precisely alike or reach exactly the same audience, but several stations in a large market may have very similar, or complementary, formats. For example, listeners who are interested in news and information in the morning might prefer a more relaxing dose of "lite rock" on the drive home, and so use two different stations almost equally. Or, listeners might not like a so-called "shock jock" on the station in the morning but are attracted to another comic talker in the afternoon. Whatever the reasons, many people listen to at least two stations each day. Programmers know that many of their listeners hear four or five other stations in a week. Radio listeners may have favorite times for choosing different formats, for example, news in the morning or jazz at night. It is important for a programmer to be able to assess the use of other stations.

In the largest markets, a station may be one of 60 or more radio signals available to listeners. However, the important competitors for most programmers are the other stations trying to reach a similar target audience. These are likely to be stations with similar formats. In general, advertisers only buy one or two stations deep to reach the specific demographic target they seek most. Knowing as precisely as possible where your listeners spend the rest of their radio time is very important.

The use of ratings information and a few tabulations will enable a programmer to know all the other stations with which he or she shares listeners. Two types of information are most relevant. The first is the *exclusive cume,* or the number of people who listened to just one particular station during specific dayparts. Although this is actually a measure of station loyalty, when it is compared with the total cume, it reveals the proportion of a station's audience that has also used the competition. That does not tell you which stations they are, however. This information is conveyed through a statistic called *cume duplication,* which reveals the extent to which the audience for one station also tunes to each of the other stations in the market.

While many listeners have a favorite station that they attend to most of the time, they may also try other stations with similar formats or try something completely different. That there is so much overlap among stations suggests that people have varied tastes and that they might like other fare during different times of the day or week. It is clear, however, that stations share the most listeners with stations of similar appeal.

To get a detailed look at how home listeners tune to different stations, programmers can study tuning to their station in great detail using a computer program such as Arbitron's Maximi$er. Researchers can use this program to tabulate persons in the sample who heard any given station—your station—by all the categories of demographics. You can see which other stations your listeners tune in, and when they are likely to do so. It is possible to see whether your cume audience consists of listeners who used it as their primary station, or heard it only occasionally. Further, the program gives demographic information about each reported listener and the zip code in which they live. The zip code data are often used by stations to find "holes" in their signal area or places to do more advertising—billboards, for example. You can customize a presentation to an advertiser showing precisely what type of listener you can offer, based on demographics and other lifestyle and consumption variables.

This kind of information is valuable to television organizations as well as to radio stations. In fact, the average television viewer undoubtedly watches more channels than the average listener uses stations. Programmers can use promos for the station most effectively by knowing when different kinds of viewers are tuned in. Sometimes that will mean paying attention to the geodemographics of the audience, just like an advertiser. But it is especially important to know when people who watch a competitor's program are watching your station. That can be the perfect opportunity to entice those viewers with promotional messages.

How Do Structural Factors Like Scheduling Affect Program Audience Formation?

One of the recurring questions a television programmer must grapple with is how to schedule a particular program. Often, scheduling factors are considered at the time a program is acquired. In fact, some programs sold in barter syndication require stations to broadcast them at a particular time. As we saw in chapter 7, that is because the syndicators also sell time to advertisers, and only certain scheduling arrangements will allow them to deliver the desired audience. In any event, how and when a program is scheduled will have a considerable impact on who sees it.

Programmers rely on a number of different "theories"—really just strategies—for guidance on how to schedule their shows. Unfortunately for the student, there are nearly as many of these theories as there are programmers. A few of these notions have been, or could be, systematically investigated through analyses of ratings data. Among the more familiar programming strategies are the following.

A *lead-in* strategy is the most common, and the most thoroughly researched. Basically, this theory of programming stipulates that the program that precedes, or leads into, another show will impact the second show's audience. If the first program has a high rating, the second show will benefit from that. Conversely, if the first show has low ratings, it will handicap the second. This relationship exists because the same viewers tend to stay tuned, allowing the second show to inherit the audience. In fact, this feature of audience behavior is sometimes called an *inheritance effect* (see Webster & Phalen, 1997). The ratings differential between *The Late Show* with David Letterman and *The Tonight Show* with Jay Leno is attributed, in part, to strength of their lead-in ratings.

Network programmers have to consider not only lead-in strategies within their own schedules, but the strength of their prime-time lead-in to affiliate news programs. In 2009 NBC scheduled *Leno* at 10 P.M., expecting its unique (and less costly) content to compete more effectively with scripted programs on the other networks. But NBC's audience ratings declined in the time period, and affiliates complained that the weaker lead-in hurt ratings for local news. Less than 6 months after the change, Leno moved back to *The Tonight Show* at 11:35 P.M. Early news experienced the same kind of ratings loss when *The Oprah Winfrey Show* went off-air. ABC affiliates had been used to the strong lead-in for the news; suddenly ratings in the time period dropped precipitously.

Another strategy that depends on inheritance effects is *hammocking*. As the title suggests, hammocking is a technique for improving the ratings of a relatively weak, or untried, show by "slinging" it between two strong programs. In principle, the second show enjoys the lead-in of the first, with an additional inducement for viewers to stay tuned for the third program. CBS used this strategy by scheduling *2 Broke Girls* after *How I Met Your Mother* and before *Two and a Half Men*—both highly successful comedies. Likewise, ABC's *Suburgatory* benefitted from its placement between hit comedies *The Middle* and *Modern Family*.[1] Hammocking works especially well when each program runs promotional spots for the upcoming show.

Block programming is yet another technique for inheriting audiences from one program to the next. In block programming, several programs of the same general type are scheduled in sequence. The theory is that if the viewers like one program of a type, they might stay tuned to watch a second, third, or fourth such program. Public broadcasting stations have used this strategy to build weekend audiences by scheduling blocks of "how-to" programs. In many cases, this block earned some of the highest ratings for stations. A variation on block programming is to gradually change program type as the composition of the available audience changes. For example, a station might begin in mid-afternoon when school lets out by targeting young children with cartoons. As more and more adults enter the audience, programming gradually shifts to shows more likely to appeal to adults, thereby making a more suitable lead-in to local news. Basic cable channels, like TVLand, sometimes do "stunts" that resemble block programming. For example, they may schedule marathons in which many, or all, of the episodes of a program are aired over a period of days. Mini-marathons may show 6 or more hours from one program.

All of the strategies described here attempt to exploit or fine-tune *audience flow* across programs. Incidentally, many of these programming principles were recognized soon after the first ratings were compiled in the early 1930s. Then, as now, analyses of ratings data allowed the programmer to investigate the success or failure of the strategies. Basically, this means tracking audience members over time—the cumulative measurements we discussed in chapter 6. Conceptually, the analytical techniques needed to do that are just the same as those used to study the loyalty, or "disloyalty" of a station's audience.

Figure 8.1 shows the results of a flow study analyzing the adult 18–34 audience for ABC's Wednesday night programming. The first row identifies the sources of audience flow; arrows connect each box to the corresponding program in the second row. The third row identifies where audiences went after they viewed each program on ABC. The horizontal arrows between programs tell us how much of the first program's audience stayed with ABC to watch the next show—expressed as a percentage and as rating points.

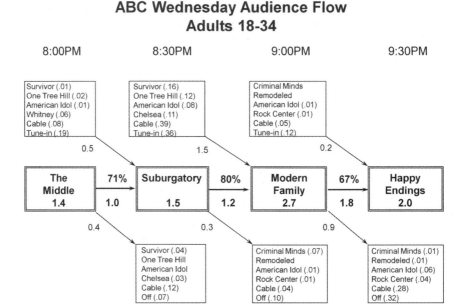

FIGURE 8.1. ABC Wednesday Audience Flow, Adults 18–34
Source: Turner Research from The Nielsen Company data. A18–34 Live Data 2/15/2012 & 2/22/2012.

The chart tells us, for example, that 71 percent of *The Middle*'s audience stayed tuned for *Suburgatory*, contributing 1.0 rating to *Suburgatory*'s 1.5 rating. This raises other questions. First, where did 29 percent (0.4 rating) of *The Middle*'s viewers go? The bottom row tells us that the "missing" 0.4 rating from *The Middle* was distributed among several different programs, and 0.07 turned off the set. The second question we want to answer is, from where did *Suburgatory* gain the 0.5 rating that was not delivered by its lead-in? For this information we look at the box in the top row that points toward *Suburgatory*. The 0.5 rating came from several different programs, but the biggest single source of viewers was people tuning in at 8:30 P.M. (0.19 of the program's rating is from tune in).

Should We Continue to Produce This Program?

When Will a Program's Costs Exceed Its Benefits?

Ultimately, programming decisions must be based on the financial resources of the medium. Although some new stations or networks can be expected to operate at a loss during the start-up phases of operation, in the long run the cost of programming must not exceed the revenues that it generates. This hard economic reality enters into a programmer's thinking when new programming is being acquired or when existing programming must be canceled. Because ratings have a significant impact on determining the revenues a program can earn, they are important tools in working through the costs and benefits of a programming decision.

When stations assess the feasibility of a new television program, whether syndicated or locally produced, it is typical to start with the ratings for the program currently in that time period. Based on current ratings and station rates, analysts calculate the revenue that can be generated in that time period. This can become very complex because many factors, including uncertainty about the size and composition of a new program's audience, affect the revenues a program generates.

If a programmer is not evaluating programs to acquire, he or she may have to worry about when a program should be canceled. Much of the press about television ratings has been over network decisions to cancel specific programs that are well liked by small, often vocal, segments of the audience. Ordinarily, a program will be canceled when its revenue-generating potential is exceeded by costs of acquisition or production.

The cost of 1 hour of prime time programming has risen steadily. Today, 1 hour of prime time drama can easily cost over $1 million to produce. *Terra Nova*, a dinosaur-filled series produced by Steven Spielberg for the 2011–2012 season, cost an estimated $4 million per episode (Dumenco, 2011). Despite having reasonably good ratings (3.6 among adults 18–49), its cost caused Fox to cancel it after just one season. As a rule though, ratings go a long way toward determining which series are renewed. And with increased audience fragmentation, the "cancellation threshold" has been falling. In the mid-1970s, networks routinely canceled programs when their ratings fell into the high teens. By the mid-1990s, programs with ratings in the low teens could remain in the schedule (see Atkin & Litman, 1986; Hwang, 1998). Nowadays, not even the top 10 programs consistently deliver ratings in the double digits; the average prime time household rating for ABC, CBS, and NBC ranges between 6.0 and 9.0. In fact, many programs on broadcast networks now survive with ratings in the 2.0 to 4.0 range.

Dwindling ratings, which are the result of increased competition for the viewer's attention, can be tolerated for a number of reasons. First, the total size of the television audience has increased, so one ratings point means more viewers. Second, CPMs have increased. Third, the FCC now allows networks to own the programs they broadcast, which enables them to make money in off-network syndication. And fourth, ratings do not tell the cost/benefit story unless they are evaluated relative to production costs, as the *Terra Nova* example illustrates.

The job of programming is probably more challenging today than at any time in the past. There is certainly more competition among electronic media than there has ever been, making the task of building and maintaining an audience more difficult. Television programmers, in particular, must contend with more stations, more networks, and newer technologies. As they face these challenges, programmers will continue to rely on analysis of ratings data to understand the audience and its use of media.

RELATED READINGS

Carroll, R. L., & Davis, D. M. (1993). *Electronic media programming: Strategies and decision making*. New York: McGraw Hill.

Eastman, S. T., & Ferguson, D. A. (2013). *Media programming: Strategies and practices* (9th ed.). Boston, MA: Wadsworth.

Ettema, J. S., & Whitney, C. D. (Eds.). (1982). *Individuals in mass media organizations: Creativity and constraint*. Beverly Hills, CA: Sage.

Fletcher, J. E. (Ed.) (1981). *Handbook of radio and TV broadcasting: Research procedures in audience, program and revenues*. New York: Van Nostrand Reinhold.

Fletcher, J. E. (1987). *Music and program research*. Washington, DC: National Association of Broadcasters.

Gitlin, T. (1983). *Inside prime time*. New York: Pantheon Books.

Lotz, A. (Ed.) (2009). *Beyond prime time: Television programming in the post-network era*. New York: Routledge.

MacFarland, D. T. (1997). *Future radio programming strategies: Cultivating listenership in the digital age* (2nd ed.). Mahwah, NJ: Lawrence Erlbaum Associates.

Newcomb, H., & Alley, R. S. (1983). *The producer's medium*. New York: Oxford University Press.

CHAPTER 9

Audience Research in Financial Analysis

While the most obvious uses of audience data are in sales and programming, ratings are also helpful to financial managers and economists who analyze media markets. In effect, media analysts cannot estimate future revenues without estimating future audiences.

The value of the audience commodity should be apparent by now. Audiences are a critical component in the media's ability to make money, and they frequently determine whether a particular media operator succeeds or fails. As the principal index of the audience commodity, ratings data are often used in day-to-day financial planning, as well as in more theoretical studies of industry economics. In these applications, audience information is used to answer questions that are somewhat different from those posed by advertisers or programmers.

Media owners and managers are most immediately concerned with the financial implications of ratings data. Advertiser-supported media are in business to make a profit, and in order to do that they try to minimize their expenses while maximizing their revenues. We have already seen how the profit motive affects programming decisions. But business expenses also include salaries, servicing the firm's debt, and a host of mundane budget items. Reducing these expenses boosts profit, but there is a limit to how much cost cutting can be done. The only other way to improve profitability is to increase revenues.

For commercial media, increasing revenues generally implies increasing income from advertising sales. Broadcast stations generate virtually all of their revenues from time sales. In radio, the majority of this income is generated from local advertisers; in television, the split between local and national spot revenue varies. Some stations, especially those in large markets, might get roughly equal amounts of revenue from each source, while others depend more heavily on local advertising than on national spot. Networks also depend heavily on advertising revenues, although cable networks typically derive additional income through direct payments from cable systems. And program syndicators can realize substantial revenues from selling barter time to national advertisers.

The financial analysis of media markets concerns people who work for media companies as well as those not directly involved in buying and selling audiences. Media organizations generally have separate finance departments to conduct ongoing analysis for planning, monitoring, and evaluating business decisions. These analysts rely heavily on the expertise of their research departments to evaluate and predict ratings. Wall Street analysts project the financial health of media firms in order to evaluate investments. Trade organizations, such as the National Association of Broadcasters (NAB), the National Cable & Telecommunications Association (NCTA), and the Internet Advertising Bureau (IAB), conduct financial analyses to assess the economic health of their industries and to lobby on behalf of their clients. Economists from industry and academia study the characteristics of economic transactions in media markets. And policy organizations like the FCC conduct financial analyses to determine the impact of their policies on the marketplace.

We consider first the more applied questions characteristic of corporate financial managers. Our goal is not to explain financial management in detail, as that is done elsewhere (e.g., Albarran, 2012, 2010), but rather to show the critical importance of audience ratings in financial planning. Of course, specific processes and procedures vary across firms and even within departments at a given company. We are more concerned with the factors that remain more or less constant across organizations so that the reader can focus on the concepts rather than the formats of particular analyses.

Within media organizations, financial analysis cuts across all functional areas. For example, the sales department projects advertising revenue and sets prices for advertising time, while the programming department analyzes the costs and income potential of programs. Both groups have to work together because decisions made in one department affect decisions in the other. However, each contributes a very different expertise and often a different set of priorities. A finance department will typically use information from all areas of the organization to generate its own analyses and financial projections. If the organization is part of a group, as is occurring more and more with widespread consolidation in the radio and television industries, a corporate finance department affects the process. We will say more about the effects of consolidation on financial planning later in the chapter.

The quantitative reports from services such as Nielsen and Arbitron offer financial analysts the most important audience data. The reason is straightforward—ratings provide an index to revenues. While the correlation is not perfect, the ratings represent an excellent predictor of advertising income. In fact, although financial analysts may use audience data in different ways, they need the same understanding of ratings as do programmers and sales managers.

There are, of course, dozens of questions related to finance that can be asked of ratings data. We concentrate on broad questions that illustrate their use in assessing the ongoing economic activity of the firm, planning expenditures, determining the value of media firms, and specifying the relationship between audiences and revenues.

RESEARCH QUESTIONS

How Effectively Does the Organization Compete for Market Revenues?

Monitoring the financial performance of an organization requires ongoing analysis of both the sales effort and market conditions. In its simplest form, this analysis involves comparing revenues earned with the potential revenues available in the marketplace. Because revenues are heavily determined by audience size and composition, a station's share of market revenue should reflect its share of audience. A statistic called the *power ratio* (also called the *conversion ratio*) expresses this relationship. The calculation is very simple:

$$\text{Power ratio} = \frac{\text{Share of market revenue}}{\text{Share of audience}}$$

This calculation estimates the percent of revenue your station earns for every audience share point. Audience share information, which comes from ratings services, is readily available to Nielsen and Arbitron subscribers. The revenue part of the equation is more problematic. A media firm knows its own sales figures, obviously, but would not ordinarily have access to data from competing organizations. There are organizations that routinely collect this information, such as Kantar Media or Nielsen Monitor-Plus, but such data are subject to error. Usually these services rely on self-reports of prices based on the word of buyers and salespeople. Both groups have an incentive to give false information. Sellers would want to estimate the highest prices possible so that their clients would not think that they overpaid, and buyers would want to estimate the lowest prices possible so that they would not appear to have made bad deals. Consequently, such data have serious limitations in terms of estimating total market revenues.

This problem has been addressed in some media markets by independent auditing firms that conduct confidential market share analyses. These firms collect sales data directly from media clients and report those figures in monthly, quarterly, or yearly reports. These reports are available only to the clients who take part in the analysis. Usually the organizations that subscribe to the services find out only the overall market revenue and their own share of that revenue, although in some markets they have access to competitors' data as well. Table 9.1 shows the kind of information that typically appears in a broadcast market-share report.

TABLE 9.1
Radio Revenue Report (in US$ thousands)

December, 2004

Revenue category	Sample city			WCPA										
	Revenue			Revenue			Revenue share		Rank		Nearest shares			
											Dec-04		Dec-03	
	Dec-04	Dec-03	% chg.	Dec-04	Dec-03	% chg	Dec-04	Dec-03	2004	2003	above	below	above	below
Local	4,577	4,351	5%	351	264	33%	7.7%	6.1%	6	6	8.0%	7.2%	6.1%	5.9%
National	601	600	0%	53	39	36%	8.8%	6.5%	6	7	10.1%	8.8%	6.8%	4.2%
Network	58	45	29%						8	6	5.2%		6.7%	
Total Cash Sales	5,236	4,996	5%	404	303	33%	7.7%	6.1%	6	7	8.1%	7.6%	6.6%	5.7%
Trade	460	380	21%	31	50	38%	6.7%	13.2%	8	3	8.0%	5.4%	14.7%	12.6%
Total Sales	5,696	5,376	6%	435	353	23%	7.6%	6.6%	6	7	7.8%	7.5%	7.3%	5.8%

Source: Adapted from sample report provided in Hungerford, Aldrin, Nichols, and Carter, *The Hungerford Radio Revenue Report: Users Guide.* Reprinted by permission of Hungerford, Aldrin, Nichols, & Carter, P.C., CPAs and Consultants.

In the sample city's local market, the total radio advertising revenue in December was $4,577,000. Of that total, $351,000 went to the hypothetical radio station WCPA—a figure representing 7.7 percent of the market's radio advertising during the month. The next highest share of revenue was 8.0 percent, and the next lowest was 7.2 percent (note that the stations garnering those shares are not identified). WCPA can calculate its power ratio with this information. If Arbitron shows an audience share of 7 percent, for example, then WCPA's power ratio is 1:1. This means that the station earns 1.1 percent of total advertising revenue for every 1 percent of audience share. Generally the Arbitron shares are adjusted to reflect share of audience only among those stations that report revenue figures. The value of this system is that it allows the media to evaluate their sales effort without compromising proprietary information.

The power ratio can be calculated on the basis of any demographic. If a radio station format were designed to appeal to men aged 18 to 49, then the sales department would want to know its share against that group. The statistic can also be calculated on any daypart for which information is provided by the auditing firm. However, the conversion ratio by itself conveys very little information. Analysts also look at trends in the daypart to find out whether the share of revenue is increasing or decreasing and determine whether this is a result of audience share differences or changes in overall sales revenue. Results must also be compared with historical data on the performance of particular formats in a market, because different formats can be expected to garner different shares of sales revenue.

What Is the Value of a Programming Investment?

After its investment in personnel, a broadcast station's largest cost item is generally programming. Each program purchase is evaluated according to its potential to generate revenue for the station. Analysts must determine how much money the programs will earn for the station and how much revenue will be lost by displacing other programs from the schedule. This may involve fairly straightforward analysis of costs and revenues, or it could involve complex analysis of properties such as sports rights.

Several factors determine the balance of costs and benefits in a program purchase decision. In general, these include the license fee that the seller is asking, the amount of time available for local advertising sales, the likely price that spots in a program will command in the advertising marketplace, the opportunity cost of purchasing the program, and the revenue that the program is likely to generate over the life of the contract. Because programs are often purchased 3 or 4 years before stations can air them, analysts need to generate planning estimates for 3 to 5 years into the future. The information needed to conduct this analysis requires input from several departments in the organization.

When a program property becomes available, financial decision makers put together a *pre-buy analysis*. Although the format will differ from organization to organization, the information needed is essentially the same. One of the most important elements in the revenue projection is the estimated audience the program will attract. As we noted in chapter 5, predicting an audience is both art and science, involving historical data as well as experienced judgment. The historical data are in the form of ratings.

In the case of an off-network syndicated television program, for example, analysts are interested in how a program performed in its original run on the network. The national ratings indicate its popularity and the composition of its audience. However, a program might have earned poor ratings nationally but perform well in an individual market. Several factors explain this difference. The show might have a distinct cultural appeal in certain parts of the country, or it might simply have been carried on stronger stations in some markets than in others. The difference could also be attributable to different demographic profiles of potential audiences across DMAs. Whatever the reasons, analysts must take local market characteristics and preferences into account when they project program ratings.

Analysts are able to study the performance of programs in previous syndication runs because some syndicated programs are sold for two or more cycles. If a program is being considered in its second cycle, the ratings earned in its first cycle would be of major importance. Using syndication ratings sources, analysts could compare how the program did in its original network run with how it performed in syndication. They could use this information to predict how it might do a third time around.

Analysts might also look at ratings for programs that are similar in content to the one being evaluated. This strategy is especially important in cases like first-run syndication, where there are no historical track records to consult. If analysts assume the program will attract audiences similar to others of its type, they can project ratings based on those audiences. The savvy user of audience data will, of course, consider not only program content but also the scheduling patterns of those programs.

Predicted rating also depends on the place in a schedule that the program is likely to occupy. Competition varies by daypart, by season, and by day of the week. Also, as we explain in chapter 4, time periods command different levels of available audience, so ratings vary considerably across dayparts. Programmers consider all of this when they decide on a schedule; financial analysts factor the information into their revenue calculations.

Some large media organizations may have all the resources in-house to make these kinds of predictions, but most firms will rely on information supplied by services such as rep firms. Programmers at rep firms may even be involved in program purchase decisions, helping programmers and general managers evaluate and negotiate deals. More often, they serve a consulting role, providing ratings information that they collect for their clients. They can share not only the ratings data but also the experience gained in various markets. This expertise can be very valuable to financial planners.

Revenue projections also take into consideration the number of spots available for sale in a given program. This availability depends on the program length and on commitments to other uses for those spots. A barter program, for example, will have less time available for local sale than a syndicated program purchased with cash. Stations might also reserve spots for promotional announcements, making this inventory unavailable to the sales staff. These variables affect the number of units sold to advertisers, and thus the revenue generated from time sales.

Just as researchers use historical ratings information and experience to project the likely audience for a program, salespeople use historical data and their firsthand knowledge of market conditions to estimate a *cost per point* (CPP) that the program will earn. The way a program is scheduled will have a significant effect on the prices that the advertising sales staff can charge. Even if a program is projected to earn a very high rating, it cannot be sold at a prime-time cost per point if it is scheduled in late fringe.

Table 9.2 illustrates a sample pre-buy analysis for a fictitious program called *Family Time*. Due to space constraints, the table covers only the first 3 years of a 6-year analysis, but it is sufficient to illustrate many of the factors we have discussed. The first columns give information about the season and likely scheduling patterns. Programmers determined that *Family Time* should start in early fringe, probably maintaining that time slot for the first few years. Subsequent columns report estimates that affect quarterly revenue projections.

Working with other departments at the station, financial analysts estimate the ratings that the program will achieve, the likely price it will command in the advertising marketplace, and the predicted sell-out percentage (percentage of available advertising time sold). In this case they estimated that the program would get a 6.0 household rating in the first year when it airs at 5:30 P.M. In the second and third years of the contract the rating drops to 5.0, and by the end of the year 2007 the program is projected to earn a 4.0. This drop in projected ratings is based on the assumption that some of the available audience has already seen the series, and that competing stations might offer more recent or otherwise more attractive programming. Although the data are not shown in Table 9.2, programmers plan to move *Family Time* to the early afternoon toward the end of the contract, which brings the estimated audience down to a 3.0.

The cost per point varies by quarter, and the cost per spot (also called *average unit rate*) varies according to the estimated rating and the CPP. These figures represent the value that salespeople think the program has in the marketplace. Sellers offered the program on a cash-plus-barter basis, asking for 1 minute of

TABLE 9.2
Prebuy Analysis

KZZZ Family Time prebuy (analysis for first 3 years of contract)

Primary run Qtr	Year	Time period	HHRtg	CPP($$)	Average Unit Rate ($$)	Avails*	SO%	Airings	Net Rev. ($000)
3rd/4th	2004	MF 5:30 P.M.	6.0	110.00	660	11	95%	85	586.2
1stQ	2005	MF 5:30 P.M.	6.0	80.00	480	11	95%	65	326.0
2nd Q	2005	MF 5:30 P.M.	6.0	120.00	720	11	95%	65	489.1
3rdQ	2005	MF 5:30 P.M.	6.0	90.00	540	11	95%	65	366.8
4thQ	2005	MF 5:30 P.M.	5.0	114.40	572	11	95%	65	388.5
1stQ	2006	MF 5:30 P.M.	5.0	83.20	416	11	95%	65	282.6
2nd Q	2006	MF 5:30 P.M.	5.0	124.80	624	11	95%	65	423.9
3rdQ	2006	MF 5:30 P.M.	5.0	93.60	468	11	95%	65	317.9
4thQ	2006	MF 5:00 P.M.	5.0	119.00	595	12	90%	65	417.7
1stQ	2007	MF 5:00 P.M.	5.0	86.50	432	12	90%	65	303.6
2nd Q	2007	MF 5:00 P.M.	5.0	129.80	649	12	90%	65	455.6
3rdQ	2007	MF 5:00 P.M.	5.0	97.30	486	12	90%	65	341.5
4thQ	2007	MF 5:00 P.M.	4.0	123.80	495	12	90%	65	347.6
1stQ	2008	MF 5:00 P.M.	4.0	90.00	360	12	90%	65	252.7

*Avails = Gross avails-barter-promos (one spot is reserved for promotional announcements in this program). This analysis assumes a 4% annual growth rate. This is reflected in the Cost Per Point.

barter time for the first 2 years of the contract. Note that the station is selling 11 avails through the third quarter of 2012, when it regains the minute of barter time it gave to the syndicator as part of the original contract. The station estimates that 95 percent of the available spots will be sold during the first 2 years of its run, dropping to 90 percent in year 3. The last column, net revenue, is calculated by combining the advertising cost and sell-out information with the total number of times the program is aired.

This analysis is completed, quarter by quarter, for the life of the contract. Financial analysts projected that *Family Time* would generate close to $7.1 million in revenue, while costing the station only about $1.6 million in license fees. This means that the program would make a profit of $5.5 million over its 6-year contract—attractive, but highly unlikely in the real world. Most programs are likely to show a much smaller margin of profit.

The revenue that a program will generate is only part of the financial calculation. Analysts also need to consider the alternative uses of airtime, and whether these alternatives would be more profitable for the station. Perhaps a different program scheduled in the same time slot would sell at a higher cost per point. Or a program with more local avails would be more profitable than an all-barter program. The question that has to be answered in each instance is whether the benefits of acquiring a property justify the lost revenue from other options. Another way of phrasing this is that financial planners must consider the *opportunity cost* of scheduling one program instead of another. This consideration affects all levels of the analysis.

Another factor in assessing the costs and benefits of acquiring a program is its effect on the rest of the schedule. High-profile programs, such as popular off-network dramas or major sporting events, might attract new viewers and create promotional opportunities to build audiences for other parts of the schedule. They could provide large lead-in audiences to locally produced programs, such as news. Or the schedule might benefit from a *halo effect* that brings viewers to the channel. Higher ratings for these other programs would translate into higher revenues overall.

There is no standard threshold that determines whether a program is acquired after the pre-buy analysis. Different types of programs have vastly different profit margins. In the off-network syndication market, for example, a blockbuster program often earns less for the station in direct advertiser revenue because so much of the advertising time is given up for national barter. But, for the image reasons listed previously, the program could be an excellent asset. Other shows might be projected to attract comparatively small audiences but with the sale of all local availabilities would generate higher profits. Usually, financial managers and programmers will seek a mix of both kinds of shows.

Sports-rights deals require a more complex analysis than regular programs or series. They also require, in the opinion of some industry professionals, more "instinct." Deal structures vary widely, from a team purchasing a 3-hour block from a station and selling the time themselves to deals that share production costs and leave the media organization to sell the time. Arrangements such as revenue sharing are not uncommon. This means that the same types of questions are asked about ratings predictions and opportunity costs, but there are additional considerations specific to the sports property. One complicating factor is that the times and lengths of games often fluctuate from week to week. This means that the regular schedule will be interrupted in inconsistent ways, which could drive regular viewers from the channel. It also means that advertisers in these regular programs might be bumped if a game goes late, and this has repercussions for the way the time is sold. However, while the analysis will differ based on the proposed terms of the deal, the basic question remains the same: What can I earn with one option compared with another? We have seen that the likely audience each option will attract is a key factor in assessing whether the balance of revenue lost and gained is in the organization's favor.

We noted earlier that group ownership affects financial planning at local media organizations. The corporate culture of a group owner, as well as its long-term image goals, is likely to affect decision making at the station level. Stations that used to function on their own before the consolidation of ownership might be subject to corporate approval in decisions such as program purchases. For example, a station might determine, based on a pre-buy analysis, that a sports programming opportunity is not in the best interests of the local sales effort. This decision would not be in the best interests of a group owner that wanted to create a national image as a "sports broadcaster." The national goals of the company would have to figure into the cost/benefit calculation made by the individual station.

Consolidation of businesses might also mean consolidation of financial expertise. As corporate financial analysts gain experience across many different markets, they can incorporate that knowledge into pre-buy analyses for individual group-owned outlets. Ordinarily, a smaller organization that is unaffiliated with a media group would not have access to this kind of expertise on a regular basis. In any case, group ownership means that program acquisition decisions are no longer made in isolation. Financial analysts at the newly acquired company might be accountable to financial managers at the corporate office. Program purchase decisions may require corporate approval or, in some instances, come from corporate programmers to the local stations as a *fait accompli*.

The results of financial analyses are used by program directors and general managers when they negotiate deals. The information gives them an indication of reasonable program prices and the highest price they should be willing to pay. It also helps them negotiate specific terms, such as the amount of barter time given to the syndicator. Because the value that local television stations attach to a spot could be very different than the value syndicators assess, stations might want to keep more time for local advertising sales. We should note that this example is hypothetical. Buyers in most markets do not have the option to negotiate the amount of barter time, although some of the smaller markets can still do this.

Although all departments have to cooperate in financial analysis, there is frequently tension among them. Agendas and priorities differ significantly. For example, the program director wants to build an audience over the course of a day, while the sales account executive wants inventory to sell potential clients. These programs may or may not fit the program director's strategies. From time to time a programmer may decide to preempt regular programming to cover a particularly important news event. This creates problems for the sales staff. If regular programs are continually preempted, then advertisers need *make-good* spots to compensate for lost audiences. The finance department is likely to be aware of all these priorities but has to remain focused on bottom-line considerations that benefit the company as a whole.

We have centered this discussion on the acquisition of syndicated programs, but the same principles apply to program production and distribution decisions. Before producing a 1-hour first-run syndication program, for example, the production company would have to look at audience information for similar 1-hour shows. They would estimate the clearance that they would be able to achieve and the likely audience shares they would garner. The supply of similar programming would also be a consideration, because supply and demand affects prices in both the program and advertising markets. Syndicators develop detailed projections to estimate the net profit or loss they can expect from a new program. This involves predicting ratings in all markets, the average cost per thousand that advertisers will pay, and the likely revenue from license fees. Analysts also factor in the estimated cost of promotion efforts and publicity as well as agency commissions and other expenses.

This type of analysis also takes place with the introduction or change of locally produced programs. For example, a station might want to add a half-hour of local news. Financial analysts would look at other markets or similar stations to determine the profitability of expanding news operations. They would have to predict the audience for a new schedule, and determine whether the benefits justify a potential loss of viewers.

In order to assess the accuracy of the financial planning process, financial analysts may conduct a *post-buy analysis* after a program runs. The process is similar to the one described in chapter 5 for advertising post-buys. Basically, the planning procedure is repeated after the "real" data are collected, and the results are compared with the predictions prior to investment. If any significant discrepancies are found, further analysis identifies whether the error was due to faulty audience projections, unforeseen changes in viewing patterns or market conditions, or lower than expected advertising rates.

We have used syndication to explain the factors involved in projecting and evaluating program revenues. A similar process takes place at cable and broadcast networks; managers need to know the contribution to revenue made by each program in their schedule. Finance analysts work with their research departments to estimate ratings, cost per thousand, and the number of spots that will be sold to advertisers. In this calculation, they factor in the number of times a program will run and they deduct the ad agency commission to reflect net income from ad sales. In the case of networks with owned and operated stations, analysts do the same kind of calculation to estimate the revenue each program will earn for local stations.

What Is the Value of a Media Property?

Many media companies are publicly traded, meaning that individual or institutional investors can go to a stock exchange and buy shares in the company. Just as investors would study the prospects of any potential acquisition, a thorough financial analysis is critical for decisions involving media concerns. This is likely to include an inspection of a company's ratings performance— past, present, and future. Even if shares in a media company are not traded on exchanges, investors can buy properties directly. Stations are brokered much like houses. Here again, investors must determine whether the property to be acquired will generate sufficient revenues to make the acquisition worthwhile. Projecting audience ratings is a critical element in making those judgments.

Financial analysts also recognize that, although audiences are an important determinant of media revenues, there may well be some discrepancy between a media property's share of the audience and its share of market revenues. They must consider many other factors. This can have practical implications for evaluating the desirability of different acquisitions. Table 9.3 illustrates how a financial analyst might go about evaluating the long-term revenue potential of a television station.

TABLE 9.3
Station Revenues Based on Audience Share Projections

	2004	2005	2006	Maturity
Net market revenue	$70 million	$74 million	$80 million	X
Station audience share	21%	22%	23%	25%
Over/under sell factor	0.80	0.83	0.86	0.90
Station revenue share	16.80%	18.30%	19.80%	22.50%
Station revenue	$11,760 million	$13,540 million	$15,840 million	X(.225)

The top line across the table represents the net market revenue for all television stations in the market. This number is likely to be a function of the overall market economy, especially the annual volume of retail sales. It is estimated by looking at historical trends in the market, and making some carefully considered judgments about the economic outlook for those sectors of the economy that are especially important. The second line represents the station's current and estimated share of the television audience. Here again, the analyst would consider recent trends and the chances that the station's overall ratings performance will improve or decline. As we saw in chapter 4, there are many factors that affect a station's ability to attract an audience. In this particular example, the analyst estimated that the station would eventually be able to attract and hold 25 percent of the audience.

But this does not necessarily mean that the station can expect to capture 25 percent of total market revenues. In fact, this station has regularly commanded a smaller share of market revenues than its share of the audience. In other words, it undersells its audience share. That factor is recognized in the third line across the table. The analyst believed that the undersell factor could be improved, but to be conservative, projected that share of revenue would always fall short of audience share.

Once these factors have been estimated, it is possible to make a reasonable projection of station revenues. When these revenue estimates are compared with projected operating expenses, the analyst can determine whether this property would have sufficient cash flow to cover its debt, and provide the owners with an acceptable return on their investments.

Another way ratings are used to estimate the value of a media property is in negotiations for *retransmission consent*. Broadcast stations have the legal right to either allow cable systems to carry (retransmit) their over-the-air signal for free in the local market or to charge the system a fee for the right to do so. Broadcasters argue that they bring larger audiences to cable systems than many of the program services cable operators pay a premium to carry. ESPN, for example, charges about $5.00 per subscriber; local market television stations are generally paid less than a $1.00 per subscriber. Broadcasters argue that higher ratings should mean higher retransmission fees.

Disagreements between cable/satellite distributors and local television stations can threaten audiences with the loss of popular programming. In 2012, Gannett Co. demanded significantly higher retransmission fees from Dish Network to carry its 19 local stations. Gannett also demanded that the network disable AutoHop, a DVR feature that allowed viewers to automatically skip commercials. This was one of dozens of high-profile retransmission stalemates that year. While most were settled in a reasonable timeframe before the threatened "blackout" of stations, the terms of these deals were not generally made public. Industry researcher SNL Kagan estimates, however, that broadcast retransmission fees will grow from just over 7 percent of all carriage fees paid by cable systems in 2012 to 10.7 percent of the total in 2015 (W. Friedman, 2012).

What Determines the Value of an Audience?

While the station's salespeople and financial analysts are very good at reading market signals, they may not be as concerned with quantifying the more abstract determinants of economic value. We have noted that, under a system of advertiser-supported media, audiences are really a commodity. They are bought and sold just like other commodities. They are "perishable," and their supply is unpredictable—but that hardly distinguishes them from other goods in the marketplace. Analysts have tried to figure out what determines their value, just as they do with other commodities. Knowing the determinants of a commodity's price is certainly of practical value to those who do the buying and selling, but it can also help us understand the operation of media industries.

The economic value of an audience is largely determined by supply and demand. Corporations and other organizations demand advertising time, and the media supply it. Generally speaking, when the U.S. economy is strong, and corporate profits are high, demand increases and advertising expenditures rise. While such macroeconomic variables establish an overall framework for prices, a number of factors operate within that framework to determine the value of specific audiences.

On the demand side, some companies cannot curtail their advertising expenditures as easily as others. For instance, the makers of many nondurable goods, like soft drinks, cosmetics, and fast foods, fear significant losses in market share if they stop advertising. Consequently, they may continue to advertise heavily, even if times are hard. Local merchants, on the other hand, will quite often cut advertising budgets to reduce expenses. For these reasons, during an economic downturn, local advertising markets may "soften" more readily than national markets, driving down the price of local audiences.

We have already noted that different advertisers demand different sorts of audiences, and that this interest in market segmentation has had a marked effect on the ratings. Audiences are routinely categorized by their demographic and geographic attributes. Increasingly, they are segmented by psychographics and product-purchasing behavior. Not all audience segments, however, are as easily supplied as others. Some kinds of people spend more time in the audience, and are therefore more readily available to advertisers. Other kinds of people constitute a tiny part of the population (e.g., executives earning more than $500,000) and are, therefore, rare. This tends to make them a more valuable commodity.

All these aspects of supply and demand come into play when determining the value of an audience. Ultimately, such factors are represented in cost calculations (e.g., CPMs) for the electronic media. In fact, advertisers will sometimes make trade-offs between print and electronic media based on the relative cost of audiences. Table 9.4 summarizes recent CPMs for the major

TABLE 9.4
Average CPM US$ (Adults) in Selected Countries[a]

	Television	Radio	Newspapers	Magazines
Syria	155.60	6.6	2.8	6.6
Lebanon	86.20	0.17	43.9	9.9
Argentina	69.7	0.7	15.5	9.2
Panama	48.6	3.1	13.4	11.9
Portugal	33.0	4.7	22.6	32.9
Hong Kong	32.2	1.8	22.4	32.1
Singapore	28.4	1.0	9.4	22.6
Australia	26.4	9.6	37.2	23.2
Belgium	22.5	9.2	(color) 61.1	19.6
Spain	21.8	12.2	28.4	28.3
Czech Republic	19.6	4.1	41.6	37.9
USA	19.5	N/A	71.4	15.4
Mexico	19.2	0.1	82.4	86.3
Romania	17.8	17.1	11.2	24.5
China	17.1	8.2	9.6	11.4
Italy	15.9	3.9	135.5	43.7
Philippines	15.3	N/A	4.0	27.9
Canada	15.0	10.9	74.6	14
Taiwan	11.9	N/A	8.9	13.5
France	10.3	16.1	58.8	12.7
Sweden	10.3	N/A	57.9	23.5
Vietnam	10.3	N/A	2.2	3.1
Ireland	8.3	6.1	58.3	41.6
U.K.	7.2	3.0	18.2	22.0
South Korea	7.1	2.1	29.2	12.4
Russia	6.6	3.7	2.1	9.7
Lithuania	4.3	2.0	18.3	12.2
Kazakhstan	4.1	0.7	33.1	55.5
Bulgaria	3.9	5.8	13.0	N/A
Greece	3.3	8.3	39.9	30.4
Indonesia	2.8	0.2	24.1	13.7
Turkey	2.1	0.1	9.1	28.7
Poland	1.3	1.2	19.1	14.5
Jordan	1.1	1.2	12.1	70.9
Brazil	N/A	5.7	181.1	106

[a] Television, 30-second peak time; newspaper, B/W; magazine, color.

N/A, not available in this report.

Source: ZenithOptimedia Market and MediaFact Reports 2011 Edition.

advertiser-supported media in several countries. Keep in mind that these figures are averages for an entire year; as such they give a very general estimate of CPMs. Although such contrasts can be an apples and oranges comparison, the price of competing media is another factor that determines the market value of a television or radio audience. This is especially true in local advertising where newspapers can provide stiff competition for the electronic media.

Table 9.4 indicates the ways different countries vary in the relative costs of advertising across media. The reasons for these differences include the size of each market, the ownership of media organizations, historical development of print and electronic media, the availability of technologies in homes, and supply relative to demand for each form of communication. In some countries, Taiwan and Romania, for example, advertisers pay comparable prices to reach consumers through print and broadcast. In others, like Argentina, Canada, Lebanon, and Syria, the discrepancies are quite large—and the differences are not consistent country to country.

What Contribution Do Ratings Make to Revenues?

The preceding discussion runs the risk of suggesting that audiences have some inherent value that translates directly into revenues. A number of factors can account for the fact that there is not a lock-step relationship between audience size and revenues. These may be of considerable importance to both economic and financial analysts.

The first thing to remember is that audiences of the electronic media are, themselves, invisible. The only index of this commodity is ratings data—an estimate of who is probably out there. In a very real sense, rating points, not audiences are bought and sold. As long as such audience estimates are the only way to know the size and shape of the audience, they effectively become that commodity. Although ratings companies are under considerable pressure to produce accurate audience measurements, certain biases and limitations do exist. Some may be inherent in research methods; others reflect the way ratings businesses have responded to marketplace demands. In any event, the media must generally operate within the constraints imposed by the ratings, and that may be a hindrance to selling certain audiences. In effect, the ratings data themselves can distort the link between audience size and audience revenues.

For example, we have noted that cable has gradually eroded the audience for broadcast television. The cable industry, however, has had some difficulty marketing that audience because historically the ratings business has been geared to estimating broadcast audiences. With the introduction of the peoplemeter, and their expansion into many local U.S. markets, Nielsen is now in a better position to provide cable ratings. The shifts in share of revenue illustrate how that change has affected the placement of advertising. Table 9.5 shows how

TABLE 9.5
Share of Total Television/Radio Advertising Revenue[a]

	Radio	Broadcast TV	Cable TV	Internet
1950	73%	27%	0%	
1960	29%	51%	0%	
1970	26%	74%	0%	
1980	24%	75%	1%	
1990	23%	70%	7%	
2000	23%	51%	17%	9%
2010	14%	40%	23%	23%
2011	13%	38%	23%	26%

Source: Based on advertising revenue estimates provided by the Radio Advertising Bureau, Television Bureau of Advertising, Cabletelevision Advertising Bureau, and Interactive Advertising Bureau.

advertising expenditures have changed over the years. While radio's share of revenue has remained fairly steady since the early 1980s, cable has claimed an increasing share at the expense of broadcast television. Once Internet became a viable advertising medium, ad revenues for radio and broadcast television dropped, and the growth of cable advertising slowed.

The second thing to remember is that audiences are made available to advertisers in the form of spot announcements, and these spots are limited in number. A broadcaster could exhaust the inventory of available spots before meeting the demand for audiences. If demand is high early in the buying season, and broadcasters sell out, then even those advertisers who would pay a premium to reach the intended audiences would be unable to purchase spots. The result is that some audience revenues would go unrealized.

The amount of advertising time sold by electronic media is affected by several factors. By tradition, certain dayparts have more commercials than others. Prime time, for instance, has fewer spot announcements than late night or daytime television. The type of station also affects the amount of commercial inventory. Network affiliates have less time to sell to local advertisers than independents, because network programming reduces the size of their inventories. Inventories can be increased by adding commercial time to a program or reducing the duration of spots (e.g., from 30 to 15 seconds), but like cost cutting, there is a practical limit to how much can be done without being counterproductive. Indeed, broadcasters sometimes argue about how much commercial time can be sold within each hour before listeners might be driven away to another station. Stations frequently try to lure listeners to a new, or revised, format by presenting very few commercials or guaranteeing X commercial-free minutes.

Even if ratings data were completely accurate and inventories more flexible, audiences are not the only factor in determining revenues. A sales force must take audience data into the marketplace and persuade advertisers to buy the commodity. Selling is a very human, and often imperfect, process. Some sales managers are more aggressive than others in their approach to time buyers. Some salespeople are more effective than others in dealing with clients. In addition, no two advertisers are alike. Some, for example, may purchase heavy schedules early in the season and routinely receive quantity discounts. The net result is that two audiences that seem to be identical may sell for different amounts of money.

Economists have devoted a good deal of attention to the relationship between audience ratings and audience revenues. In addition to the factors we have already described, there are other, less benign, explanations for a discrepancy between an audience's size and its market value. If, for instance, there are relatively few competitors in a market, they may be tempted to collude and set prices above competitive levels. Although we know of no cases of such collusion, the potential exists. What is clear, however, is that demand does affect price. Advertiser demand for television has been, and will probably remain, high. This has meant higher rates (proportional to the audience delivered) in markets with fewer stations. In less concentrated markets, the cost of audiences tends to be lower, but studies of this sort have not been conclusive.

RELATED READINGS

Albarran, A. (2012). *Management of electronic and digital media* (5th ed.). Belmont, CA: Wadsworth.

Albarran, A. (2010). *The media economy*. New York: Routledge.

Alexander, A., Owers, J., Carveth, R., Hollifield, C. A., & Greco, A. (Eds.). (2004). *Media economics: Theory and practice* (3rd ed.). Mahwah, NJ: Lawrence Erlbaum Associates.

Napoli, P. M. (2003). *Audience economics: Media institutions and the audience marketplace*. New York: Columbia University Press.

Owen, B. M., & Wildman, S. S. (1992). *Video economics*. Cambridge, MA: Harvard University Press.

Picard, R. G. (2011). *The economics and financing of media companies* (2nd ed.). New York: Fordham University Press.

Turow, J. (2012). *The daily you: How the new advertising industry is defining your identity and your worth*. New Haven: Yale University Press.

Veronis Suhler Stevenson. (2012). *Communications industry forecast and report*. New York: Author.

Vogel, H. L. (2011). *Entertainment industry economics: A guide for financial analysis* (8th ed.). Cambridge: Cambridge University Press.

CHAPTER 10

Audience Research in Social Policy

Electronic media play a central role in modern economic and social life. They facilitate the exchange of goods and services, help elect political candidates, and open or close the *marketplace of ideas* that is so essential to democracies. They may even shape our perceptions of reality. Given the powers commonly attributed to media, it is no surprise that they have been studied by social scientists from a wide variety of disciplines.

Since the earliest days of radio broadcasting in the 1920s, proponents and critics wondered how the medium would affect society. By the 1930s, a high-powered government committee on social trends appointed by President Hoover listed more than 150 effects of radio, from homogenizing regional cultures to encouraging morning exercise (Ogburn, 1933). Newly formed networks also began assessments of the radio audience, and academicians, especially from psychology, sociology, marketing, and education, became interested in researching the new medium.

Frank Stanton, a pioneer in communications research who later became president of CBS, published one of the first scholarly studies of the radio audience in 1935. Academics took an immediate interest, especially in the use of media for political purposes in the United States and Germany. They began to examine the use of radio by Franklin Roosevelt, as well as various religious and political demagogues, and they studied the manipulation of motion pictures by Adolf Hitler. In 1935, Hadley Cantril and Gordon Allport of Harvard University published *The Psychology of Radio,* reporting many of their early findings on topics such as these.

Cantril and Stanton eventually secured a grant from the Rockefeller Foundation to study radio audiences. By the time funds were available, however, Stanton was unable to head the project because he had become director of research at CBS. Instead, they asked social psychologist Paul Lazarsfeld to serve as director. The resulting Princeton Radio Research Project lasted 2 years before moving to Columbia University and becoming the Bureau of Applied Social Research.

The Bureau, often in collaboration with industry, conducted a string of studies that many regard as the real foundation of communications research in the United States. This new field of radio research, especially audience measurement, established Lazarsfeld as one of the founders of the scientific study of communications. In fact, the emergence of ratings research prior to World War II was intertwined with broader developments in the new field of mass communications and the growth of social/behavioral research in general. But electronic media audiences eventually emerged as appropriate subjects for communications research in their own right.

Today, audience data play an important, if underappreciated, role in social policy. They often figure in the work of policymakers, social advocacy groups, and academicians who use them to justify policy positions in the most contentious debates about mass media and society. Ratings data are a particularly appealing tool because they are the heart of the media's power. Ask yourself: Why do electronic media have economic value? Because they attract an audience. Why do news and entertainment programs have any social impact? Because they attract an audience. Why do political ads influence elections? Because they attract an audience. Even though ratings information alone cannot reveal the effects of media on society, they can frequently index the potential. As we have emphasized throughout this book, ratings are the currency with which media operate, and because of their wide and continuous availability, they are useful for analyzing communications law and social policy.

Among the individuals and institutions most likely to use audience data are (a) the federal government, (b) industry, and (c) the public. The dynamic interactions among these interested parties can determine the course of public policy.

GOVERNMENT

By the mid-1920s, it became apparent that broadcasting could not be left to operate as an unregulated marketplace. Demand for broadcast frequencies far exceeded the supply. The U.S. Congress addressed the problem by creating the Federal Radio Commission (FRC), which was replaced by the Federal Communication Commission (FCC) in 1934. The Commission was tasked with licensing stations to ensure that broadcasters operated in the public interest. Although definitions of "public interest" have changed over the years, three interrelated objectives have endured. First, commissioners have tried to limit certain undesirable social effects, especially among children. Second, they have tried to promote greater diversity in media content by taking steps like structuring markets in a way that makes them more responsive to audience demand. And third, like many other regulators, they have passed rules to ensure the overall economic health of the industry they regulate.

The FCC, however, does not have a free hand to implement whatever policies it chooses. Other institutions within the federal government are often involved. The president, the courts, and especially the Congress can and do make their wills known from time to time. In 1996, for example, Congress passed what many call the most sweeping legislation covering communications services since the original Communications Act of 1934. The *Telecommunications Act of 1996* affected many areas of the business, from ownership to content. It required the FCC to review long-standing rules and revise anything that had become outdated.

Other independent agencies, like the Federal Trade Commission (FTC) or the Copyright Royalty Board, also deal with matters of communications policy. Some executive branch offices, such as the Department of Commerce or the Department of Health and Human Services, may also enter the picture. In the early 1970s, for example, the surgeon general oversaw a massive study of the impact of television violence. Studies like this often influence legislators to vote for (or against) particular bills.

The United States government is not alone in using audience metrics to address questions of public policy. Since the 1980s, when reliable peoplemeter systems were put in place, audience data and patterns of media use have affected how European governments address various regulatory issues (e.g., Helberger, 2011; Just, 2009). For example, in 2012, the British Secretary of State for Culture, Olympics, Media and Sports commissioned a report on "Measuring Media Plurality." Plurality is analogous to the U.S. concern about diversity (e.g., Napoli, 2007). The report concluded that three categories of metrics were relevant to assessing plurality, "but the consumption metrics, especially reach, share and multi-sourcing, are the most important" (Ofcam, 2012, p. 1).

INDUSTRY

Many nongovernmental interests also weigh heavily in the policymaking process. The organizations with the most direct interest in communications policy are the media themselves. To advance their interests, some companies, such as large media conglomerates, might act as their own representatives in Washington. Often, however, D.C.-based trade associations do this for them. The most significant trade association for broadcasters has been the National Association of Broadcasters (NAB). The NAB serves commercial broadcasters by lobbying Congress and the FCC, testifying before congressional committees, filing briefs in the relevant judicial proceedings, and participating in rulemakings and inquiries at government agencies. In many of these activities, the NAB submits research that bears on the issue at hand. In fact, the association has a special department of research and information that performs policy studies using ratings data. Additionally, two important committees, the Committee on Local Television

Audience Measurement and the Committee on Local Radio Audience Measurement, monitor the quality of audience research on behalf of the industry.

The National Cable & Telecommunications Association (NCTA) represents the cable industry. The NCTA engages in the same sorts of activities as the NAB, including policy research. And the Interactive Advertising Bureau (IAB) represents major media and technology companies in the online advertising market. Other trade associations, like the Motion Picture Association of America (MPAA), will occasionally use ratings data as well.

THE PUBLIC

Although government and industry have a major influence on the formation of public policy, they do not completely control it. The public itself enters the process in a number ways. Most directly, we elect government representatives. Occasionally, one of these officials takes the lead on a matter of communications policy, inviting us to either support or reject that position. More highly organized public participation comes in the form of public interest groups. Some, like Action for Children's Television (ACT), were formed specifically to affect policymaking. Until its closing in the mid-1990s, ACT drew the attention of Congress and the FCC to problems of consumerism in children's television. Other organizations, like the Parent/Teacher Association (PTA) or the American Medical Association (AMA), express occasional interest in the social control of media even though regulation is not their central focus.

We should also note that the academic community contributes to policymaking. Professors with an interest in broadcasting and the electronic media have been attracted to policy questions dealing with the media's social and economic impact. They can affect policy in several ways. Most notably, they publish research relevant to questions of public policy. Because they are often viewed as experts, and relatively objective, university-based researchers may carry some special influence with the government. Academicians may also work as consultants for other participants in the policymaking process, exercising direct influence in a less public, and usually less objective, manner. Finally, of course, they can indirectly affect policy through their students. Many professionals who are involved in determining communications policy today would credit certain professors with influencing their views on matters of law, regulation, and social responsibility.

RESEARCH QUESTIONS

The range of applications for audience ratings in the formation of social policy is reasonably broad. Ratings stand apart from other types of social scientific data because they can be interpreted, or "read," in so many different ways.

Nevertheless, ratings are generally used in policymaking to answer one of three broad questions. The questions correspond to the long-term concerns of the FCC that we mentioned earlier: (a) limiting the undesirable effects of media, (b) promoting more diverse and responsive programming, and (c) tending to the economic condition of its client industries.

What Do the Media Do to People?

Policymakers must answer this "effects question" if they hope to limit undesirable effects. As a policy concern, the question certainly predates broadcasting. In the early 1930s, sociologists tried to determine the impact that movies had on young people. Later in the decade, psychologists studied the effects of wartime propaganda, and marketing researchers questioned the effect of press coverage on voter behavior. More recent studies focus on issues such as television's ability to distort perceptions of social reality and the role video games play in promoting violence.

Central to these, and all other effects questions, is the cause-and-effect relationship. In its general form, the question is, "Does exposure to the media (cause), make other things happen (effect)?" This is an extremely difficult question for social scientists to answer. An important starting place, however, is knowledge of what people listen to or watch. This is because, by definition, any direct media effect must begin with audience exposure to media messages.

Although an encounter with the media may not determine a particular outcome (again, the effect), hearing or seeing a message does define a certain potential. If many people use a medium, or see an item of content, the potential for effects is great. Advertisers have long realized this fact, and so have paid dearly for access to audiences. The value of this potential is also obvious in the frequently recurring debate over free airtime for political candidates. The opportunity to reach the electronic media audience is perceived by many as a kind of "right" that candidates should enjoy. They assume that citizens' voting behavior will be influenced by exposure to campaign messages. Conversely, if no one is exposed to a message, its impact is never felt.

Academics, too, have recognized that exposure is the wellspring of media effects (e.g., Bryant & Oliver, 2009). One of the most outspoken scholars has been George Gerbner, a proponent of *cultivation analysis*. Gerbner argued that television content is so uniform, and people are so unselective, that researchers need only compare heavy and light television viewers to determine the medium's social impact. Usually, these arguments are buttressed with data on the sheer amounts of time Americans spend watching (Gerbner, Gross, Morgan, Signorielli, & Shanahan, 2002).

Other academic researchers posit a greater degree of audience selectivity. In fact, studies of *selective exposure,* which we reviewed in chapter 4, have an important place in the history of media research. Although varied in their origins, these studies assume that audience members are capable of discernment and use it in their consumption of media content. Effects depend on the kinds of content they choose. In the surgeon general's report on television violence, for example, Israel and Robinson (1972) used viewing diaries to assess how much violence was consumed by various segments of the population. They assumed that heavy viewers of violence-laden programming would be more likely to show its ill effects. Whether one considers specific content or, like Gerbner, television viewing in general, exposure clearly sets the stage for subsequent media effects.

Government regulators also have used audience information to assess the media's potential to create socially undesirable effects. The FCC uses them, for example, to guide its effort to limit indecent language in broadcasting. Although the Commission might tolerate certain excesses when adults are listening, the presence of young children creates a problem. Some policymakers have tried to channel offensive language away from time periods when children are likely to be in the audience. They use ratings to identify those time periods. Hence, the detrimental effects that might result from exposure to indecent content are, at least, limited by the size of the child audience.

Limiting the potentially harmful effects of advertising on children is a concern for regulators worldwide. Rules that reflect this concern often use audience research estimates as a benchmark for policy. In the United States, advertisements for alcohol on television are restricted to programs with an audience profile made up of at least 70 percent viewers aged 21 and older. Additionally, these advertisements cannot run before 9 P.M. This latter restriction is a surrogate for audience demographics—many countries use time periods to restrict the advertising of tobacco, alcohol, and pharmaceuticals (ZenithOptimedia, 2011).

Based on its long history of encouraging *localism* in broadcasting, the FCC has also expressed concern about the audience for local news and public affairs programming. Their effort has been motivated, at least in part, by a desire to keep people informed about issues of public importance. They were convinced, for example, that cable television would pose a threat to localism by diverting audiences from broadcast stations. In a 1979 report on the relationship between cable and broadcasting, the Commission noted:

> Television may have an important effect in shaping the attitudes and values of citizens, in making the electorate more informed and responsible, and in contributing to greater understanding and respect among different racial and ethnic groups. . . . Historically, the FCC has encouraged particular types of programming—local news, public affairs, instructional programs—on these grounds. To the extent that a change in broadcast-cable policy would dramatically change the amount by which these programs are not only broadcast but also viewed, these issues could be an important component of a policy debate. (Federal Communications Commission, 1979, p. 639)

In some ways, this line of reasoning is a complement to the logic supporting the indecency rules. Instead of people being harmed by exposure to something that is bad for them, the FCC expressed concern that undesirable social consequences might flow from people *not* watching something that is good for them. Audience measurement can be a significant factor in these evaluations. In 2011, for example, the FCC commissioned a white paper about the consumption of local news on the Internet. Based on a quantitative analysis of comScore data, the study found that online news accounted for a very small percentage of Web traffic (Hindman, 2011).

Today, with the expansion of media options, understanding what people consume or manage to avoid is increasingly important. In 1980, the average household could view nine television stations. Thirty years later, a typical household could get 120 channels of television, not to mention everything available on DVDs, satellite radio, and the Internet. In fact, in 2010 Nielsen stopped reporting the number of "channels" because the digital, multichannel media environment means the term is no longer consistent across households. This abundance has caused some social critics to worry that people will choose to hear only like-minded speech and retreat into the media equivalent of "gated communities" (Sunstein, 2001, 2009; Turow, 1997). If people do, in fact, hear only what is agreeable and never encounter dissident voices, it could have undesirable social consequences. Tracking audience behavior offers a useful way to monitor these developments (e.g., LaCour, 2012; Webster, 2005; Webster & Ksiazek, 2012).

What Do People Want?

Another important goal of communications policy has been to provide the public with diverse media content. This objective seems very much in keeping with our First Amendment ideals and the benefits that are thought to result from a free marketplace of ideas. But how does one achieve diversity? Although policymakers have different opinions on that subject, the most popular solution has been to structure media industries so that a large number of firms can compete for the attention of the audience. In theory, competitors respond to audience demand by catering to likes and dislikes as expressed in program choices. The more competitors, the more likely it is that various niches will be served. Under this system, ratings can be thought of as a kind of feedback mechanism. Arthur Nielsen Jr. (1988) has described the link between ratings and preferences as follows:

> Since what the broadcaster has to sell is an audience to advertisers, it follows that in order to attract viewers, the broadcaster must cater to the public tastes and preferences. Ratings reveal these preferences. (p. 62)

Many commentators find the industry's argument that they only give the people what they want to be self-serving and deceptive. Most media, they point out, respond to the demands of advertisers, not audience members. Consequently, audiences that are less valuable to advertisers are underserved. Additionally, the advertiser-supported media system requires no measure of the extent to which viewers actually like a particular program, only that they have elected to use it. As we explained in chapter 4, a number of other factors complicate the link between preference and choice. Nevertheless, a considerable body of theory in both psychology and economics assumes that choice is a function of preference, and this provides adequate justification for the use of ratings in policymaking.

The most relevant of these theories has been developed in the study of *welfare economics,* a branch of the discipline that is concerned with how we can maximize the welfare, or overall well-being, of society. Like other branches of economics, it assumes that people are rational beings who will attempt to satisfy their preferences when choosing goods and services—at least insofar as their pocketbooks allow. Economists refer to this notion as the "theory of revealed preference" (e.g., Varian, 2006). Indeed, they make a case that deducing preferences from behavior may be superior to direct questions about a person's likes and dislikes. Because advertiser support imposes no direct costs on viewers (i.e., they do not pay a per-program fee), viewer preferences can be freely expressed in program choices. These concepts, and their consequences for how public policy might maximize viewer satisfaction, are fully discussed in Owen and Wildman (1992).

Welfare economists, therefore, have used ratings data to address questions of communications policy. One category of FCC rules that has received intense scrutiny is media ownership. The commission has historically sought to limit certain classes of media (e.g., local newspapers and radio) from owning local television stations, based on the assumption that different owners will contribute different viewpoints to the marketplace of ideas. Unfortunately, existing media may be more adept than newcomers at offering local programming that appeals to viewers. Parkman has, consequently, argued the following:

> If these classes of owners produce more popular programming than other classes of owners, the reduction in popular programming should be taken into consideration as cost of the diversification policy. To determine if certain newsgathering organizations are more successful than others in attracting viewers, we can look at the end result that these organizations produce as judged by the viewers, i.e., the ratings. (1982, pp. 289–290)

After analyzing the ratings of local television news programs, Parkman concluded that the commission's policy imposed "costs on individual viewers by forcing them to choose programs considered by them as less desirable" (p. 295).

The FCC itself has relied on ratings as a kind of "revealed preference." One notable example is the commission's designation of stations as *significantly viewed.* This concept was introduced into FCC rules in the early 1970s and was used to determine the popularity of a signal in a given geographical area. Its definition has affected many areas of regulation, such as must-carry, syndicated exclusivity, effective competition, and compulsory copyright. Although the definition changed somewhat over the years, a station was deemed significantly viewed in a market if it achieved a weekly 2 percent share of audience, and 5 percent weekly circulation in non-cable homes. Estimates like these are made from diary data in most markets, which means they are subject to the kinds of errors we describe in chapter 3. Problems occur when regulators ignore the error estimates and treat these numbers as reliable.

Assessing "what people want" begs the question "Which people are we measuring." In 2012 Arbitron faced legal action in California because of its sampling procedures with the PPM. The company was accused of undercounting African American and Latino audiences. The complaint claimed that when the PPM technology was introduced, "radio stations that serve African-American and Hispanic audiences lost a disproportionately large segment of rated radio listenership, resulting in a decline in advertising revenue to those radio stations, layoffs, and potential bankruptcy" (Complaint for Equitable Relief and Civil Penalties, 2012, p. 1–2). Arbitron had to reevaluate its sampling procedures and assure California's attorney general that minority audiences would be fairly represented.

What Are the Economic Implications of Various Policies?

A number of government laws and regulations affect the financial condition of the media and related industries. Because these policies have an impact on the "bread-and butter "—or in some cases the Mercedes and BMWs—of those businesses, they attract the attention of many participants in the policymaking process. Even the FCC, which in recent years has favored increased competition in the media, must remain alert to the economic consequences of various policies. After all, the commission is responsible for seeing to it that broadcasting serves the public interest. If broadcasters are driven out of business by some ill-conceived government policy, the commission's mandate might be compromised.

Financial statements that describe the media's revenues, expenses, and profitability are one obvious source of information on the economic condition of the industry. But, for a number of reasons, these data are not always used. For one thing, the commission stopped collecting financial statements from broadcasters many years ago, so the data are not readily available. For another, the harm might be too far advanced to correct economic injury by the time it shows up on company ledgers. A common alternative to a dollars-and-cents measure of economic impact is to use audience ratings. Because ratings measure the commodity that the media sell, policies that adversely affect a station's audience will damage its economic health. Even though ratings and revenues are not perfectly correlated, evidence of lost audiences is often taken as an indication of lost revenues.

Ratings information has been used in several studies to demonstrate audience diversion from established media. Such analyses are frequently used in skirmishes between broadcasters and the cable industry. Early on in the development of cable, broadcasters claimed economic injury to encourage policies that would restrict cable's growth. They argued that allowing cable to enter a market would threaten the survival of stations by siphoning off valuable audiences. In 1970, Rolla Park at the Rand Corporation assessed this threat through an analysis of local market ratings data. The results of this study helped shape the FCC's 1972 rules on cable television.

Again in the late 1970s, the commission considered the economic relationship between cable and broadcasting. And again, Park (1979) and a number of interested parties assessed the state of audience diversion through rather sophisticated analyses of audience ratings information. The FCC made extensive references to these studies in its final report.

The Commission also encountered claims of audience diversion in the context of its rules on *syndicated exclusivity*. First adopted in the early 1970s, Syndex rules ensured that broadcasters who bought exclusive rights to syndicated programming would not have to compete with cable systems that imported the same program on a distant signal. The imported signal, it was argued, would divert audiences that rightly belonged to the local station. In subsequent debates over the rule, the parties at interest (e.g., NAB, NCTA) submitted analyses of ratings data to show that audience losses did or did not occur in the absence of the rule. Although the rule was dropped for some time, the FCC reimposed it, reasoning that "the ability to limit diversion means broadcasters will be able to attract larger audiences, making them more attractive to advertisers, thereby enabling them to obtain more and better programming for their viewers" (Broadcasting, 1988, p. 58).

More recently, ratings data have been used in policy research to analyze television ownership restrictions. The Telecommunications Act of 1996 granted owners of UHF stations special consideration with regard to total audience reach. As stipulated in the Act, the combined audience reach of all stations owned by a single person or entity cannot exceed 35 percent of the total United States. However, because UHF stations have traditionally operated at a disadvantage compared with VHF stations, lawmakers allowed UHF owners to "discount" their reach estimates. They can count just half of the total station coverage towards the 35 percent total. Thus, a group owner of all UHF stations might have potential coverage of more than 50 percent of all television households, but under the FCC rules that would count as only 25 percent. To counter a challenge to this arrangement, the NAB prepared a report showing that UHF stations consistently drew smaller audiences because they operate on the UHF band. After accounting for other factors that could cause lower ratings, the NAB found that channel assignment was related to lower ratings. For example, UHF stations affiliated with Fox earned an average of 1 rating point lower than their VHF counterparts, and NBC affiliates demonstrated a difference of 3.6 ratings points between UHF and VHF stations (Everett, 1998).

Ratings data also have had a substantial impact on the distribution of fees from the *compulsory copyright license*. These fees are paid by cable and satellite systems for the right to carry broadcast signals. Those with a claim on the resulting revenues are copyright holders including program suppliers, commercial broadcasters, public broadcasters, and Canadian broadcasters. It is logical that audience shares would figure in the computation of awards. After all, the economic value of a program or program service rests largely on its ability to attract an audience.

The uses of audience information in legal or regulatory proceedings are considerable. Despite these, and many other applications of the data, it appears to us that social scientists have only scratched the surface of the analytical possibilities. For the most part, these uses of the ratings have dealt with gross measures of audience size. Perhaps that should not be surprising, because such estimates are the most readily available. Indeed, that is what the ratings are. Using ratings to track individuals over time, engaging in what we call cumulative analyses, would seem a logical next step for social scientific inquiry.

Take, for example, the question of media effects. Although the size of the audience exposed to a message may suggest something about its potential effect, so too does the regularity of exposure. Advertisers recognize this concept as frequency—the average number of times audience members see or hear a message. Effects researchers might similarly ask how often people see or hear a particular kind of programming. For example, do all children see about the same amount of violence on television, or do some consume more? Is some segment of the child audience violence junkies? If so, who are those children? Do they come from poor or affluent families? Do they watch alone or with others? The answer to such questions, all of which can be gleaned from audience data, might contribute much to our understanding of the impact of televised violence. Similar questions could be asked about the audience for news and information (e.g., Kim & Webster, 2012; Ksiazek, Malthouse, & Webster, 2010; Prior, 2007).

Studies of audience duplication might reveal more about people's preferences for programming as well. Does a particular program have a small-but-loyal following, or is it just small? Programmers and marketing researchers have long recognized a certain feature of audience duplication called channel loyalty. Religious, Spanish language, and at least some news channels are among the kinds of programming that seem to attract small-but-loyal audiences. Does this intensity of use suggest something about how the audience values a service above and beyond the number that uses it at any point in time?

Factors other than size and composition also affect the economic value of an audience. Advertisers may specify reach and frequency objectives in their media plans. Those who seek a high frequency of exposure might be willing to pay a premium for that small-but-loyal audience. In a similar vein, channel loyalty and inheritance effects undoubtedly contribute to the audience of a syndicated program. If a station adds value to the program by delivering an audience pre-disposed to watch, then perhaps the station should have a greater share of credit for a program's success.

Even media critics who distrust social scientific methods might learn more about audience experience with media through inventive uses of ratings data. For instance, analysts of popular culture have become increasingly interested in how people make sense of television programming. One insight from this line of research is that viewers experience the medium not as discrete programs, but as strips of textual material called *flow texts*. The emergence of flow texts could be studied through analogous research on audience flow.

All of these analyses, and many more, could be realized through the application of commercial audience data. Unfortunately, the effective use of such data in the social sciences and related disciplines has been uneven. In part, that is because the proprietary nature of syndicated research makes it too expensive for strictly academic analyses. Some academicians, however, may fail to exploit the data that are available, simply because they do not recognize the analytical possibilities.

RELATED READINGS

Baker, C. E. (2002). *Media, markets, and democracy*. Cambridge: Cambridge University Press.

Bryant, J., & Oliver, M. B. (Eds.). (2009). *Media effects: Advances in theory and research* (3rd ed.). New York: Routledge.

Comstock, G., & Scharrer, E. (1999). *Television: What's on, who's watching, and what it means*. San Diego: Academic Press.

Lowery, S., & DeFleur, M. L. (1995). *Milestones in mass communication research* (3rd ed.). White Plains, NY: Longman.

Napoli, P. M. (2007). *Media diversity and localism: Meaning and metrics*. Mahwah, NJ: Lawrence Erlbaum.

Owen, B., & Wildman, S. (1992). *Video economics*. Cambridge, MA: Harvard University Press.

Sunstein, C. R. (2001). *Republic.com*. Princeton, NJ: Princeton University Press.

Sunstein, C. R. (2009). *Going to extremes: How like minds unite and divide*. Oxford: Oxford University Press. 2009.

Turow, J. (1997). *Breaking up America: Advertisers and the new media world*. Chicago: University of Chicago Press.

Appendix A: DMA Market Rankings

Here are the latest local television market estimates from Nielsen for the 2012–2013 broadcast season that began on September 24, 2012.

Note that for the second year in a row, the total TV households in the United States are down, from 114.6 million households in 2011–2012 to 114.2 million households in 2012–2013.

TABLE A01

Rank	Local Market	TV Homes	% of US
1	New York	7,384,340	6.47%
2	Los Angeles	5,613,460	4.92%
3	Chicago	3,484,800	3.05%
4	Philadelphia	2,949,310	2.58%
5	Dallas-Ft. Worth	2,588,020	2.27%
6	San Francisco-Oak-San Jose	2,502,030	2.19%
7	Boston (Manchester)	2,366,690	2.07%
8	Washington, DC (Hagrstwn)	2,359,160	2.07%
9	Atlanta	2,326,840	2.04%
10	Houston	2,215,650	1.94%
11	Detroit	1,845,920	1.62%
12	Seattle-Tacoma	1,818,900	1.59%
13	Phoenix (Prescott)	1,812,040	1.59%
14	Tampa-St. Pete (Sarasota)	1,806,560	1.58%
15	Minneapolis-St. Paul	1,728,050	1.51%
16	Miami-Ft. Lauderdale	1,621,130	1.42%
17	Denver	1,566,460	1.37%
18	Cleveland-Akron (Canton)	1,485,140	1.30%

TABLE A01 *continued*

Rank	Local Market	TV Homes	% of US
19	Orlando-Daytona Bch-Melbrn	1,453,170	1.27%
20	Sacramento-Stkton-Modesto	1,387,710	1.22%
21	St. Louis	1,243,490	1.09%
22	Portland, OR	1,182,180	1.04%
23	Pittsburgh	1,165,740	1.02%
24	Raleigh-Durham (Fayetvlle)	1,150,350	1.01%
25	Charlotte	1,136,420	1.00%
26	Indianapolis	1,089,700	0.95%
27	Baltimore	1,085,070	0.95%
28	San Diego	1,075,120	0.94%
29	Nashville	1,014,910	0.89%
30	Hartford & New Haven	996,550	0.87%
31	Kansas City	931,320	0.82%
32	Columbus, OH	930,460	0.81%
33	Salt Lake City	917,370	0.80%
34	Milwaukee	902,190	0.79%
35	Cincinnati	897,890	0.79%
36	San Antonio	881,050	0.77%
37	Greenvll-Spart-Ashevll-And	846,030	0.74%
38	West Palm Beach-Ft. Pierce	794,310	0.70%
39	Grand Rapids-Kalmzoo-B.Crk	720,150	0.63%
40	Las Vegas	718,990	0.63%
41	Oklahoma City	718,770	0.63%
42	Birmingham (Ann and Tusc)	717,530	0.63%
43	Harrisburg-Lncstr-Leb-York	716,990	0.63%
44	Norfolk-Portsmth-Newpt Nws	709,730	0.62%
45	Austin	705,280	0.62%
46	Greensboro-H.Point-W.Salem	695,100	0.61%
47	Albuquerque-Santa Fe	691,450	0.61%
48	Louisville	670,880	0.59%
49	Memphis	662,830	0.58%
50	Jacksonville	659,170	0.58%
51	New Orleans	641,550	0.56%

TABLE A01 *continued*

Rank	Local Market	TV Homes	% of US
52	Buffalo	632,150	0.55%
53	Providence-New Bedford	606,400	0.53%
54	Wilkes Barre-Scranton-Hztn	581,020	0.51%
55	Fresno-Visalia	576,820	0.51%
56	Little Rock-Pine Bluff	561,760	0.49%
57	Richmond-Petersburg	553,390	0.48%
58	Albany-Schenectady-Troy	540,050	0.47%
59	Tulsa	526,960	0.46%
60	Mobile-Pensacola (Ft Walt)	525,990	0.46%
61	Knoxville	520,890	0.46%
62	Ft. Myers-Naples	502,050	0.44%
63	Dayton	498,270	0.44%
64	Lexington	485,630	0.43%
65	Charleston-Huntington	455,490	0.40%
66	Wichita-Hutchinson Plus	450,300	0.39%
67	Flint-Saginaw-Bay City	446,010	0.39%
68	Roanoke-Lynchburg	445,470	0.39%
69	Green Bay-Appleton	441,800	0.39%
70	Tucson (Sierra Vista)	438,440	0.38%
71	Honolulu	437,790	0.38%
72	Des Moines-Ames	427,860	0.37%
73	Spokane	420,640	0.37%
74	Springfield, MO	414,570	0.36%
75	Omaha	414,060	0.36%
76	Toledo	409,550	0.36%
77	Columbia, SC	398,510	0.35%
78	Rochester, NY	395,680	0.35%
79	Huntsville-Decatur (Flor)	390,590	0.34%
80	Portland-Auburn	389,530	0.34%
81	Paducah-Cape Girard-Harsbg	388,340	0.34%
82	Shreveport	384,410	0.34%
83	Champaign&Sprngfld-Decatur	378,720	0.33%
84	Syracuse	377,550	0.33%

TABLE A01 *continued*

Rank	Local Market	TV Homes	% of US
85	Madison	376,670	0.33%
86	Harlingen-Wslco-Brnsvl-McA	364,160	0.32%
87	Chattanooga	353,710	0.31%
88	Waco-Temple-Bryan	349,540	0.31%
89	Colorado Springs-Pueblo	343,990	0.30%
90	Cedar Rapids-Wtrlo-IWC&Dub	342,610	0.30%
91	El Paso (Las Cruces)	339,130	0.30%
92	Savannah	334,750	0.29%
93	Jackson, MS	331,500	0.29%
94	Baton Rouge	329,620	0.29%
95	South Bend-Elkhart	319,860	0.28%
96	Tri-Cities, TN-VA	319,060	0.28%
97	Burlington-Plattsburgh	316,910	0.28%
98	Charleston, SC	316,080	0.28%
99	Davenport-R.Island-Moline	303,800	0.27%
100	Greenville-N.Bern-Washngtn	303,280	0.27%
101	Ft. Smith-Fay-Sprngdl-Rgrs	297,590	0.26%
102	Johnstown-Altoona-St Colge	288,100	0.25%
103	Myrtle Beach-Florence	285,550	0.25%
104	Evansville	284,040	0.25%
105	Lincoln & Hastings-Krny	276,790	0.24%
106	Tallahassee-Thomasville	273,120	0.24%
107	Tyler-Longview(Lfkn&Ncgd)	268,150	0.23%
108	Reno	265,600	0.23%
109	Ft. Wayne	265,390	0.23%
110	Youngstown	260,000	0.23%
111	Boise	259,090	0.23%
112	Sioux Falls(Mitchell)	258,460	0.23%
113	Augusta-Aiken	257,730	0.23%
114	Springfield-Holyoke	252,950	0.22%
115	Lansing	251,140	0.22%
116	Peoria-Bloomington	244,050	0.21%
117	Fargo-Valley City	243,890	0.21%

TABLE A01 *continued*

Rank	Local Market	TV Homes	% of US
118	Montgomery-Selma	241,930	0.21%
119	Traverse City-Cadillac	241,800	0.21%
120	Macon	241,170	0.21%
121	Eugene	235,570	0.21%
122	SantaBarbra-SanMar-SanLuOb	231,950	0.20%
122	Yakima-Pasco-Rchlnd-Knnwck	231,950	0.20%
124	Lafayette, LA	229,320	0.20%
125	Monterey-Salinas	224,240	0.20%
126	Bakersfield	221,740	0.19%
127	Columbus, GA (Opelika, AL)	216,920	0.19%
128	La Crosse-Eau Claire	211,670	0.19%
129	Corpus Christi	203,730	0.18%
130	Amarillo	197,110	0.17%
131	Chico-Redding	191,500	0.17%
132	Wilmington	188,420	0.17%
133	Columbus-Tupelo-W Pnt-Hstn	184,990	0.16%
134	Wausau-Rhinelander	179,450	0.16%
135	Rockford	179,240	0.16%
136	Topeka	176,160	0.15%
137	Monroe-El Dorado	175,960	0.15%
138	Columbia-Jefferson City	173,640	0.15%
139	Duluth-Superior	169,610	0.15%
140	Medford-Klamath Falls	167,820	0.15%
141	Beaumont-Port Arthur	167,110	0.15%
142	Lubbock	159,840	0.14%
143	Wichita Falls & Lawton	158,500	0.14%
144	Salisbury	157,830	0.14%
145	Anchorage	156,280	0.14%
146	Erie	155,190	0.14%
147	Sioux City	154,830	0.14%
148	Palm Springs	154,560	0.14%
149	Joplin-Pittsburg	151,200	0.13%
150	Albany, GA	150,110	0.13%

TABLE A01 *continued*

Rank	Local Market	TV Homes	% of US
151	Minot-Bsmrck-Dcknsn(Wlstn)	150,000	0.13%
152	Odessa-Midland	147,730	0.13%
153	Rochestr-Mason City-Austin	143,330	0.13%
154	Terre Haute	139,600	0.12%
155	Bangor	138,040	0.12%
156	Bluefield-Beckley-Oak Hill	134,410	0.12%
157	Binghamton	133,420	0.12%
158	Wheeling-Steubenville	130,110	0.11%
159	Panama City	129,390	0.11%
160	Biloxi-Gulfport	128,300	0.11%
161	Sherman-Ada	126,930	0.11%
162	Idaho Fals-Pocatllo(Jcksn)	125,710	0.11%
163	Gainesville	123,430	0.11%
164	Abilene-Sweetwater	114,080	0.10%
165	Yuma-El Centro	113,230	0.10%
166	Missoula	113,010	0.10%
167	Hattiesburg-Laurel	109,950	0.10%
168	Billings	109,730	0.10%
169	Dothan	107,110	0.09%
170	Clarksburg-Weston	106,480	0.09%
171	Quincy-Hannibal-Keokuk	103,520	0.09%
172	Utica	102,890	0.09%
173	Rapid City	98,020	0.09%
174	Elmira (Corning)	95,530	0.08%
175	Lake Charles	94,610	0.08%
176	Jackson, TN	93,090	0.08%
177	Watertown	92,590	0.08%
178	Harrisonburg	90,260	0.08%
179	Alexandria, LA	89,280	0.08%
180	Marquette	84,640	0.07%
181	Jonesboro	80,740	0.07%
182	Bowling Green	78,780	0.07%
183	Charlottesville	74,340	0.07%

TABLE A01 *continued*

Rank	Local Market	TV Homes	% of US
184	Laredo	72,590	0.06%
185	Grand Junction-Montrose	70,580	0.06%
186	Meridian	68,860	0.06%
187	Butte-Bozeman	67,180	0.06%
188	Greenwood-Greenville	66,410	0.06%
189	Lafayette, IN	66,240	0.06%
190	Great Falls	65,930	0.06%
191	Twin Falls	64,100	0.06%
192	Bend, OR	62,950	0.06%
193	Parkersburg	62,620	0.05%
194	Eureka	59,610	0.05%
195	Cheyenne-Scottsbluff	56,350	0.05%
196	San Angelo	55,820	0.05%
197	Casper-Riverton	55,270	0.05%
198	Mankato	52,530	0.05%
199	Lima	51,240	0.04%
200	Ottumwa-Kirksville	46,730	0.04%
201	St. Joseph	46,180	0.04%
202	Fairbanks	37,920	0.03%
203	Zanesville	32,940	0.03%
204	Victoria	31,560	0.03%
205	Presque Isle	29,250	0.03%
206	Helena	28,260	0.02%
207	Juneau	26,320	0.02%
208	Alpena	16,910	0.01%
209	North Platte	14,720	0.01%
210	Glendive	4,050	0.00%
	NSI Total U.S.	114,173,690	100.00%

Glossary

AAAA (American Association of Advertising Agencies): trade association of U.S. advertising agencies.

Active Audience: term given to viewers who are highly selective about the programming they choose to watch. Active audiences are sometimes defined as those who turn a set on only to watch favored programs, and turn the set off when those programs are unavailable. Activity can also mean being goal-directed in media selections, or cognitively engaged with the media. See *LOP, passive audience.*

Adjacency: advertising opportunity immediately before or after a specific program.

ADI (Area of Dominant Influence): term once used by Arbitron to describe a specific market area. Every county in the United States was assigned to one, and only one, ADI. See *DMA.*

Advertising Agency: company that prepares and places advertising for its clients. Agencies typically have media departments that specialize in planning, buying, and evaluating advertising time.

Adware: program secretly placed on a user's computer that redirects the browser to selected sites and / or launches pop-up ads.

Affiliate: broadcast station that has a contractual agreement to air network programming.

Algorithm: computational procedure in which data are reduced, usually through a number of steps. Algorithms are used to produce audience metrics and recommendations to media users.

AMOL (Automated Measurement of Lineups): system that electronically determines the broadcast network programs actually aired in a local market.

ANA (Association of National Advertisers): trade organization of major national advertisers responsible for creating the first broadcast ratings service. See *CAB.*

A/P Meter (Active/Passive Meter): type of peoplemeter developed by Nielsen that has the ability to either detect a code embedded in a television program or actively identify its audio signature, thus identifying the programming on the set.

App: short for "application," it is a piece of software designed to help users perform a specific task (e.g., play a game, fetch a particular type of information, etc.). Apps are popular on mobile devices like smartphones and tablets.

AQH (Average Quarter Hour): standard unit of time for reporting average audience estimates (e.g., AQH rating, AQH share) within specified dayparts.

ARB (Audience Research Bureau): ratings company established in 1949 that was the predecessor of the Arbitron Company.

Arbitron: major supplier of local market and national network radio ratings.

Area Probability Sample: type of random sample in which geographic areas are considered for selection in some stage of the sampling process. See *probability sample, cluster sample.*

ARF (Advertising Research Foundation): trade organization of advertising and marketing research professionals in the United States and Canada advancing the practice and validity of advertising research.

Arianna: software program that handles television ratings; joint venture between Nielsen and AGB.

Ascription: procedure for resolving confused, inaccurate, or missing data entries.

Audience Appreciation (AA) data: supplemental data collected by some TAM systems that asks viewer to rate how much they like or appreciate a program. AA data are often collected through meters, though other survey techniques can be used.

Audience deficiency (AD): failure to deliver the numbers and kinds of audiences agreed to in a contract between time sellers and buyers. Sellers will often remedy audience deficiencies by running extra commercials, called "make-goods."

Audience duplication: cumulative measure of the audience that describes the extent to which audience members for one program, channel, or website are also in the audience of another program, channel, or website. Audience duplication data are a building block for many forms of cumulative audience analysis. See *audience flow, channel loyalty, inheritance effect, repeat viewing, recycling.*

Audience flow: extent to which audiences persist from one program or time period to the next. See *audience duplication, inheritance effects.*

Audience fragmentation: phenomenon in which the total audience for a medium is widely distributed across a large number of outlets. Cable is said to fragment the television audience, resulting in a decreased average audience share for each channel. Audience fragmentation contributes to problems of sampling error.

Audience polarization: phenomenon associated with audience fragmentation, in which the audiences for outlets or specific types of content use them more intensively than an average audience member. See *channel loyalty, channel repertoire.*

Audience turnover: phenomenon of audience behavior usually expressed as the ratio of a station's cumulative audience to its average quarter-hour audience.

Audimeter: Nielsen's name for several generations of its metering device used to record set tuning. See *SIA.*

Availabilities: advertising time slots that are unsold, and therefore available for sale. Sometimes called *avails.*

Available audience: total number of people who are, realistically, in a position to use a medium at any point in time. It is often operationally defined as those actually using the medium (i.e., PUT or PUR levels).

Average: measure of central tendency that expresses what is typical about a particular variable. An arithmetic average is usually called a *mean.* See *mean, median.*

Average audience rating: rating of a station or program during an average time interval over a specified period of time. Metered data, for example, allow reports of audience size during an average minute of a television program.

Average time per page: measure of the average time spent with a Web page across however many pages are examined in a single visit.

Away-from-home listening: estimates of radio listening that occurs outside the home. Such listening usually takes place in a car or place of work. Also called out-of-home.

Banner advertising: form of display advertising on the Internet, in which a box containing the advertiser's message appears on a portion of the page being viewed. Banner advertising often allows users to be linked to the advertiser's Web site.

BARB (Broadcasters' Audience Research Board): A joint industry committee that oversees the production of TAM data in the United Kingdom. See *JIC.*

Barter: type of program syndication in which the cash expenditure for programming is reduced, sometimes to zero, because it contains national or regional advertising that is sold by the syndicator.

Basic cable: programming services provided by a cable system for the lowest of its monthly charges. These services typically include local television signals, advertiser-supported cable networks, and local access.

BBM Canada: nonprofit entity established by Canadian broadcasters and advertisers to conduct audience measurement.

Birch: research company that once provided syndicated radio rating reports in competition with Arbitron.

Block programming: practice of scheduling similar programs in sequence in order to promote audience flow. See *inheritance effect*.

Bounce: tendency of a station or network's ratings to fluctuate over time due to sampling error, rather than real changes in audience behavior. Bounce is most noticeable for outlets with low ratings.

Bounce rate: is the percent of website visitors who leave without taking any further action on the site (e.g., clicking on another page).

Broadband: term describing the channel capacity of a distribution system. A common label for multichannel cable service, it is also applied to digital networks capable of delivering full motion video. See *cable system*.

Browser: computer program that allows users to gain access to pages on the World Wide Web. Browser can be set to accept or reject cookies, which are important in measuring Web use. See *cookies*.

Buffer sample: supplemental sample used by a rating company in the event that the originally designated sample is insufficient due to unexpectedly low cooperation rates.

C3: See *commercial rating*.

Cable Advertising Bureau (CAB): U.S. trade organization formed to promote advertising on cable television.

Cable penetration: extent to which households in a given market subscribe to cable service. Typically expressed as the percent of all television households that subscribe to basic cable.

Cable system: video distribution system that uses coaxial cable and optical fiber to deliver multichannel service to households within a geographically defined franchise area.

Call-back: practice of attempting to interview someone in a survey sample who was not contacted or interviewed on an earlier try. The number of call-back attempts is an important determinant of response rates and nonresponse error. See *nonresponse error*.

Cash-plus-barter: type of barter syndication in which the station pays the syndicator cash, even though the program contains some advertising. See *barter*.

CATV (Community Antenna Television): acronym for cable television, used in many early FCC proceedings.

Census: study in which every member of a population is interviewed or measured. Every 10 years, the federal government conducts a census of the U.S. population. Server-centric measurement sometimes claims to provide a census of media use.

Channel loyalty: common feature of television audience behavior in which the audience for one program tends to be disproportionately represented in the audience for other programs on the same channel. See *audience duplication, inheritance effects*.

Channel repertoire: set of channels from which a viewer chooses—typically much fewer than the total number of channels available.

Cinema Advertising Council (CAC): U.S. trade organization to promote the sale of commercial time in theaters.

Circulation: total number of unduplicated audience members exposed to a media vehicle (e.g., newspaper, station) over some specified period of time. See *cume, reach*.

Clearance: (1) the assurance given by a station that it will air a program feed by its affiliated network; (2) the sale of syndicated programs to individual markets.

Click: when the user of a Web page interacts with (i.e., clicks on) a message.

Click fraud: any method of artificially inflating the number of clicks on a Web site.

Click rate: percentage of advertising responses as a function of the number of clicks.

Clickstream: record of all http requests made from a browser.

Click-through: or click-through-rate (CTR) is a measure of Web ad effectiveness that tracks how many Web users actually click on the ad they see.

Cluster sample: type of probability sample in which aggregations of sampling units, called *clusters,* are sampled at some stage in the process. See *probability sample*.

CMSA (Consolidated Metropolitan Statistical Area): type of metropolitan area, designated by the U.S. Office of Management and Budget, often used by ratings companies to define a media market's metropolitan area.

Codes: (in survey research) the numbers or letters used to represent responses in a survey instrument like a diary. Coding the responses allows computers to manipulate the data.

Cohort: type of longitudinal survey design in which several independent samples are drawn from a population whose membership does not change over time. See *longitudinal*.

Coincidental: type of phone survey in which interviewers ask respondents what they are watching or listening to at the time of the call. Coincidentals, based on probability samples, often set the standard against which other ratings methods are judged.

Collaborative Filtering: sophisticated way to make recommendations that uses computer algorithms to compare a person's past actions to those of users with a similar profile.

COLRAM (Committee on Local Radio Audience Measurement): committee of the NAB concerned with a range of local radio measurement issues.

COLTAM (Committee on Local Television Audience Measurement): committee of the NAB concerned with a range of local television measurement issues.

COLTRAM (Committee on Local Television and Radio Audience Measurement): committee of the NAB which, in 1985, was divided into COLRAM and COLTAM.

Commercial rating: measure of the number of people or households who have been exposed to commercial messages. In the United States commercial ratings, called C3, are an average across all commercials in a program plus three days of replay.

Confidence interval: in probability sampling, it is the range of values around an estimated population value (e.g., a rating) with a given probability (i.e., confidence level) of encompassing the true population value.

Confidence level: in probability sampling, it is a statement of the likelihood that a range of values (i.e., confidence interval) will include the true population value.

Convenience sample: nonprobability sample, sometimes called an accidental sample, that is used because respondents are readily available or convenient.

Conversion rate: number of desired actions (e.g., placing an order on a website) divided by the number of visits or unique visitors.

Cookies: small text file sent by a server to a user's browser that serves to identify users and provide a record of their actions. Cookie counts help measure unique visitors, but must typically be adjusted with algorithms to avoid over- or under-counting users. They also provide a basis for serving targeted advertising. Cooperative Analysis of Broadcasting (CAB): first ratings company in the United States. Formed in 1930 by Archibald Crossley, it ended operations in 1946.

Correlation: statistic that measures the strength and direction of the relationship between two variables. It may range in value from +1.0 to −1.0, with 0 indicating no relationship.

Counterprogramming: programming strategy in which a station or network schedules material appealing to an audience other than the competition. Independents often counter-program local news with entertainment.

Coverage: potential audience for a given station or network, defined by the size of the population that is reached, or covered, by the signal.

CPA (cost per action): measure the cost of an Internet ad based on how many users take some action in response to an ad divided by the cost of the ad.

CPI (cost per impression): measure of the cost of an ad based on the number of impressions divided by the cost of the ad.

CPM (cost per thousand): measure of how much it costs to buy 1,000 audience members delivered by an ad. CPMs are commonly used to compare the cost efficiency of different advertising vehicles.

CPP (cost per point): measure of how much it costs to buy the audience represented by one rating point. The size of that audience, and therefore its cost, varies with the size of the market population on which the rating is based.

Cross-sectional: type of survey design in which one sample is drawn from the population at a single point in time. See *longitudinal*.

Cross-tabs: technique of data analysis in which the responses to one item are paired with those of another item. Cross-tabs are useful in determining the audience duplication between two programs. See *audience duplication*.

Cume: short for *cumulative audience*, it is the size of the total unduplicated audience for a station over some specified period of time. When the cume is expressed as percent of the market population it is referred to as *cume rating*. See *circulation, reach*.

Cume duplication: percentage of a station's cume audience that also listened to another station, within some specified period of time. See *exclusive cume*.

Daypart: specified period of time, usually defined by certain hours of the day and days of the week (e.g., weekdays vs. weekends), used to estimate audience size for the purpose of buying and selling advertising time. Dayparts can also be defined by program content (e.g., news, sports).

Data fusion: method of combining data from two of more separate samples by pairing individual respondents based of similarities in their sociodemographic and behavioral profiles. Data fusion is often used as an alternative way of studying cross-platform media use when no single source dataset is available.

Demographics: category of variables often used to describe the composition of audiences. Common demographics include age, gender, education, occupation, and income.

Diary: paper booklet, distributed by ratings companies, in which audience members are asked to record their television or radio use, usually for 1 week. The diary can be for an entire household (television) or for an individual (radio).

Direct Broadcast Satellite (DBS): mode of television distribution that uses signals transmitted via satellite to provide programming directly to subscriber households.

Display advertising: category of advertising. In newspapers it includes larger advertisements run by retailers and is often contrasted with classified ads. On the Internet, it includes banner ads and is often contrasted with paid search advertising.

DMA (Designated Market Area): term used by Nielsen to describe specific market areas in the United States. Every county belongs to one, and only one, DMA.

Domain consolidation level: consolidation of multiple domain names and/or URLs associated with a main site.

Domain name level: consolidation of multiple URLs associated with the same domain name.

DST (differential survey treatment): special procedures used by a ratings company to improve response from segments of the population known to have unusually low response rates. These may include additional interviews and incentives to cooperate.

DVR (digital video recorder): electronic device that records video programming on a hard drive. Sometimes called a personal video recorder (PVR), it empowers viewers with the ability to easily record, fast forward, replay programming, and skip commercials. TiVo is the best known DVR system.

EACA (European Association of Communications Agencies): European trade association of advertising agencies and related media specialists.

Early fringe: in television, a daypart in late afternoon immediately prior to the airing of local news programs.

EBU (European Broadcasting Union): An international trade association of radio and television broadcasters in over 50 countries across Europe, North Africa, the Middle East and other regions.

Editing: procedures used by a ratings company to check the accuracy and completeness of the data it collects. Editing may include techniques for clarifying or eliminating questionable data. See *ascription*.

Effective exposure: concept in media planning stipulating that a certain amount of exposure to an advertising message is necessary before it is effective. Often used interchangeably with the term *effective frequency*. See *frequency*.

Engagement: broad, ill-defined, term encompassing measures designed to assess user's liking of or involvement with various media products and services. Sometimes these are derived from more conventional measures of exposure (e.g., repeat viewing or time spent metrics). Sometimes they are derived from actions taken on social media sites (e.g., comments, sharing, etc.). Sometimes engagement is measured directly with dedicated surveys.

Enumeration survey: large-scale survey of the population designed to provide population estimates that can be used to adjust or weight data provided by ratings panels.

ESF (expanded sample frame): procedure used by Arbitron to include in its sample frame households whose phone numbers are unlisted. See *sample frame*.

ESOMAR (European Society of Opinion and Marketing Research): global association of marketing professionals and opinion pollsters.

ESS (effective sample size): size of a simple random sample needed to produce the same result as the sample actually used by the rating company. ESS is a convenience used for calculating confidence intervals. Also called effective sample base, or ESB.

Ethnography: term that describes any one of several qualitative research techniques. Audience ethnographies include in-depth interviews or group discussions, studying what people post on the Internet, and a variety of observer and participant observer techniques.

Exclusive cume audience: total size of the unduplicated audience that listens exclusively to one station within some specified period of time.

Exit rate: measure of how many visitors left a website from a particular page.

Fault rates: measure of the extent to which installed meters are not providing useable data. Faulting can result for hardware failures or respondents failing to enter data.

FCC (Federal Communications Commission): U.S. independent regulatory agency, created in 1934, that has primary responsibility for the oversight of broadcasting and cable.

Format: style of programming offered by a radio station. Common formats include MOR (middle of the road), news/talk, and adult contemporary.

Frequency: in advertising, the average number of times that an individual is exposed to a particular advertising message.

Frequency distribution: way of representing the number of times different values of a variable occur within a sample or population.

Fringe: in television, dayparts just before prime time (early fringe) and after the late news (late fringe).

Fusion: See *data fusion.*

Geodemographics: type of variable that categorizes audiences by combining geographic and demographic factors. For example, organizing audiences by zip codes with similar population age and income.

Grazing: term describing the tendency of viewers to frequently change channels, a behavior that is presumably facilitated by remote control.

Gross impressions: total number of times an advertising schedule is seen over a period of time. The number of gross impressions may exceed the size of the population, since audience members may be duplicated. See *GRP.*

Group quarters: dormitories, barracks, nursing homes, prisons, and other living arrangements that do not qualify as households, and are, therefore, not measured by ratings companies.

GRP (gross rating point): gross impressions of an advertising schedule expressed as a percentage of the population. GRPs are commonly used to describe the overall size or media weight of an advertising campaign. GRPs = reach × frequency.

Hammocking: television programming strategy in which an unproven or weak show is scheduled between two popular programs in hopes that viewers will stay tuned, thereby enhancing the rating of the middle program. See *audience flow, inheritance effect*.

Headend: part of a cable system that receives television signals from outside sources (e.g., off-the-air, satellite) and sends them through the wired distribution system. See *cable system*.

Head of household: common, if somewhat dated, term used in TAM that denotes the adult with main responsibility for the household. By convention, in married households, it is the husband. There is only one head per household.

Hit: once common, gross measure of website popularity. A hit occurs anytime a user requests a file from a Web server. Since a single Web page might contain many different files, counting hits can greatly overstate page views. The number of visits, visitors, or page views are now more widely accepted as measures of popularity.

Home county: county in which a station's city of license is located.

Home market: market area in which a station is located.

Home station: any station licensed in a city within a given market area.

Household: identifiable housing unit, such as an apartment or house, occupied by one or more persons. See *group quarters*.

HPDV (households per diary value): number of households in the population represented by a single diary kept by a sample household. Used to make audience projections. See *projected audience*.

HUT (households using television): term describing the total size of the audience, in households, at any point in time. Expressed either as the projected audience size, or as a percent of the total number of households.

Hypoing: any one of several illegal practices in which a station, or its agent, engages in an attempt to artificially inflate the station's rating during a measurement period. Also called *hyping*.

IAB (Interactive Advertising Bureau): U.S. trade association promoting the Internet and other interactive technologies as advertising media.

Impression: basic gross measure of audience. It is the counts the number of times a program or ad is seen by audience members. Online, it is the number of times an Internet ad is successfully served to a user's browser.

Independent: commercial television station that does not maintain an affiliation with a broadcast network.

Inertia: description of audience behavior that implies viewers are unlikely to change channels unless provoked by very unappealing programming.

Inheritance effect: common phenomenon of television audience behavior, in which the audience for one program is disproportionately represented in the audience of the following program. Sometimes called *lead-in effects*, audience inheritance can be thought of as a special case of channel loyalty. See *audience duplication, audience flow, channel loyalty.*

In-tab: term describing the sample of households or persons actually used in tabulating or processing results.

Internet: network of computer networks around the world that makes possible services like e-mail and the World Wide Web.

Interview: method of collecting data through oral questioning of a respondent, either in person, or over the phone.

Interviewer bias: problem of introducing systematic error or distortions in data collected in an interview, attributable to the appearance, manner, or reactions of the interviewer. See *response error.*

IP address: bit of computer code specified under an "Internet protocol" identifying your computer to servers on the Internet. IP addresses can be static, meaning they never change, or dynamic, meaning they are assigned each time you log on.

ISP (Internet Service Provider): company providing access to the Internet. These can include dial-up services, phone companies providing DSL and mobile devices, and cable systems offering high-speed modems.

JIC (Joint Industry Committee): common way to arrange for audience measurement services outside the United States. Affected industries (e.g., the media and advertisers), create a committee that specifies what services are needed, bids and awards a multiyear contract.

Keyword search: kind of advertising on the Web in which advertisers bid to have their site appear in response to a user's search request. Also called pay-for-placement or paid search advertising.

Late fringe: in television, a daypart just after the late local news (11 P.M. EST).

Lead-in: program that immediately precedes another on the same channel. The size and composition of a lead-in audience is an important determinant of a program's rating. See inheritance effect.

Lead-in effect: See *inheritance effect.*

Linear media: media systems that deliver content on a fixed schedule. Broadcast radio, television and cable are linear delivery systems. These are in contrast to nonlinear media that allow users to retrieve specifics items when they wish.

Longitudinal: type of survey designed to collect data over several points in time. See *cross-sectional.*

LOP (least objectionable program): popular theory of television audience behavior, attributed to Paul Klein, that argues that people primarily watch television for reasons unrelated to content, and they choose the least objectionable programs. See *passive audience.*

LPM (local peoplemeter): simply a peoplemeter installed to provide local market audience measurement.

Market segmentation: practice of dividing populations into smaller groups having similar characteristics or interests in order to market goods and services more precisely. See *demographics.*

Mean: measure of central tendency determined by adding across cases, and dividing that total by the number of cases. See *average, median, mode.*

Measure: procedure or device for quantifying objects (e.g., households, people) on variables of interest to the researcher.

Measurement: process of assigning numbers to objects according to some rule of assignment.

Measurement error: systematic bias or inaccuracy attributable to measurement procedures.

Mediametrie: private research company owned by French broadcasters and advertisers providing audience measurement services. See *JIC, TRCC.*

Median: measure of central tendency defined as that point in a distribution where half the cases have higher values, and half have lower values. See *average, mean, mode.*

Meter: measuring device used to record the on-off and channel tuning condition of a television set. See *SIA, peoplemeter.*

Metro area: core metropolitan counties of a market area as defined by a ratings service. Metros generally correspond to MSAs.

Metro rating: program or station rating based on the behavior of those who live in the metropolitan area of the market. See *rating.*

Metro share: program or station share based on the behavior of those who live in the metropolitan area of the market. See *share.*

Minimum reporting standard: number of listening or viewing mentions necessary for a station or program to be included in a ratings report.

Mode: measure of central tendency defined as the value in a distribution that occurs most frequently. See *average, mean, median.*

Mortality: problem of losing sample members over time, typically in longitudinal survey research.

MRC (Media Rating Council): U.S. industry organization responsible for accrediting the procedures used by ratings companies and monitoring the improvement of ratings methodologies.

MSA (Metropolitan Statistical Area): urban area designated by the Office of Management and Budget, often used by ratings companies to define their metro areas.

MSO (multiple system operator): company owning more than one cable system.

Multiset household: television household with more than one working television set.

Multi-stage sample: type of probability sample requiring more than one round of sampling. See *cluster sample, probability sample.*

NAB (National Association of Broadcasters): U.S. industry organization representing the interests of commercial broadcasters.

Narrowcasting: programming strategy in which a station or network schedules content of the same type or appealing to the same subset of the audience. See *block programming.*

NATPE (National Association of Television Program Executives): U.S. industry organization of media professionals responsible for television programming.

NCTA (National Cable and Telecommunications Association): industry organization representing the interests of the cable industry.

Net audience: See *cume, reach.*

Net weekly circulation: cume or unduplicated audience using a station or network in a week. See *cume.*

Network: organization that acquires or produces programming and distributes that programming, usually with national or regional advertising, to affiliated stations or cable systems.

Network analysis: approach to managing and visualizing data. It is useful in analyzing complex systems in which the component parts (referred to as nodes) are linked and interdependent. Because the units of analysis are not independent it uses specialized statistical procedures.

Nonlinear media: media systems that deliver content as it is requested. Digital video recorders (DRVs), video on demand (VOD), and websites that allow users to view or download media are nonlinear media. See *linear media.*

Nonprobability sample: kind of sample in which every member of the population does not have a known probability of selection into the sample. See *convenience sample, purposive sample, quota sample.*

Nonresponse: problem of failing to obtain information from each person originally drawn into the sample.

Nonresponse error: biases or inaccuracies in survey data that result from nonresponse. See nonresponse.

Normal distribution: kind of frequency distribution that, when graphed, forms a symmetrical, bell-shaped curve. Many statistical procedures are premised on the assumption that variables are normally distributed. See *skew*.

NPower: package of computer programs offered by Nielsen that affords clients access to its national peoplemeter database. It performs a wide range of customized analyses of gross and cumulative audience behavior.

NSI (Nielsen Station Index): reports local television market ratings in the United States.

NTI (Nielsen Television Index): reports national television network ratings in the United States.

Off-network programs: programs originally produced to air on a major broadcast network, now being sold in syndication.

O&O (owned & operated): broadcast station that is owned and operated by a major broadcast network.

Opportunistic market: buying and selling of network advertising time on short notice, as unforeseen developments (e.g., cancellation, schedule changes) create opportunities. See scatter market, upfront market.

Optimizers: any one of several computer programs used by large advertisers or ad agencies that take respondent-level peoplemeter data as input to create advertising schedules that optimize campaign reach while minimizing costs.

Overnights: label given to ratings, based on meters, that are available to clients the day after broadcast.

Oversample: deliberately drawing a sample larger than needed in-tab to compensate for nonresponse, or to intensively study some subset of the sample.

OzTAM: private Australian company owned by the major commercial broadcasters that provides television audience measurement. See *JIC, TRCC*.

Page rank: method for scoring websites developed by Google that ranks them according to the number and importance of their inbound hyperlinks.

Page views: number of Web pages viewed by users in a given time period.

Paid search advertising: popular form of advertising offered by search engines, in which advertisers bid for the right to place advertisements in response to certain search terms. Advertisers then pay on the basis on how many users click on their ads (i.e., pay-per-click). Keyword search and pay-for-placement are other terms describing this practice.

Panel: type of longitudinal survey design in which the same sample of individuals is studied over some period of time. For example, meters are placed in a panel of television households. See *cross-sectional, longitudinal, trend analysis.*

Passive audience: term given to viewers who are unselective about the content they watch. Passive audiences are thought to watch television out of habit, tuning to almost anything if a preferred show is unavailable. See *active audience, LOP.*

Pay cable: programming services provided by a cable system for a monthly fee above and beyond that required for basic cable. Pay cable may include any one of several "premium" services like HBO, Showtime, or The Disney Channel.

Pay-for-placement: see *paid search, keyword search.*

Pay-per-click: pricing model in which advertisers pay based on the number of users who click on their ad. See *paid search.*

Pay-per-impression: pricing model in which advertisers pay based on the number of impressions delivered by ad servers.

Peoplemeter: device that electronically records the on-off and channel tuning condition of a television set, and is capable of identifying viewers. If viewers must enter that information by button pressing, the meter is called *active;* if the meter requires no effort from viewers, it is called *passive.*

Periodicity: problem encountered in systematic sampling in which the sampling interval corresponds to some cyclical arrangement in the list.

Phone recall: type of survey in which a phone interviewer asks the respondent what they listened to or watched in the recent past, often the preceding day. See *coincidental.*

Placement interview: initial interview to secure the willingness of the respondent to keep a diary or receive a meter.

Platform: technological system for delivering content to users. Broadcast television, cable, the Internet and mobile devices are all referred to as platforms.

PMSA (Primary Metropolitan Statistical Area): urban area designated by the U.S. Office of Management and Budget that is often used in defining ratings areas.

Pocketpiece: common name given to Nielsen's weekly national television ratings report.

Pod: group of commercials, often numbering six to eight, that are aired one after the other. An ad's position in the pod is sometimes negotiated.

Population (or "universe"): total number of persons or households from which a sample is drawn. Membership in a population must be clearly defined, often by the geographic area in which a person lives.

Portable peoplemeter (PPM): metering system in which respondents wear a small device (e.g. wrist watch or page-like) that detects an inaudible code embedded in a broadcast signal. When the meter "hears" the code it ascribes the respondent to the audience.

Post-buy analysis: analysis conducted after a program runs. It could refer to (1) a financial analysis to determine whether the price paid for the program was appropriate, or (2) the analysis of ratings performance to determine whether the predicted rating was correct.

Power ratio: statistic that expresses the relationship between share of revenue and share of audience. Also called the conversion ratio, or home market share ratio.

PPDV (persons per diary value): number of persons in a population represented by a single diary kept by a member of a ratings sample. PPDV is used to project an audience. See *projected audience.*

Preempt: action, taken by an affiliate, in which programming fed by a network is replaced with programming scheduled by the station. Certain types of commercial time can also be "preempted" by advertisers willing to pay a premium for the spot.

Prime access (in local television): first hour of prime time, prior to network programming. Local stations generally schedule syndicated programs or local productions during prime access.

Prime time: television daypart often from 7 P.M. to 11 P.M. EST. Due to FCC regulations, U.S. broadcast networks typically provide prime time programming to affiliated stations from 8 P.M. to 11 P.M. EST.

Probability sample: kind of sample in which every member of the population has an equal or known chance of being selected into the sample. Sometimes called *random samples,* probability samples allow statistical inferences about the accuracy of sample estimates. See *confidence interval, confidence level, sampling error.*

Processing error: source of inaccuracies in ratings reports attributable to problems inherent in the mechanics of gathering and producing the data. See *ascription, editing.*

Program type: category of programming usually based on similarities in program content. Ratings companies often use standardized program types to report and summarize program audiences.

Projectable: quality describing a sample designed in such a way that audience projections may be made. See *projected audience, probability sample.*

Projected audience: total size of an audience estimated to exist in the population, based on sample information. See *HPDV, PPDV, probability sample.*

Psychographics: category of variable that draws distinctions among people on the basis of their psychological characteristics, including opinions, interests, and attitudes.

PTAR (Prime Time Access Rule): FCC regulation, effective from the 1970s through the early 1990s, limiting the amount of network programming that affiliates could carry during prime time, and preventing affiliates in the top 50 markets from airing off-network reruns during prime access.

PUR (persons using radio): term describing the total size of the radio audience at any point in time. See *HUT, PUT.*

Purposive sample: type of nonprobability sample, sometimes called a *judgment sample,* in which the researcher uses his or her knowledge of the population to "handpick" areas or groups of respondents for research.

PUT (persons using television): term describing the total size of the television audience, in persons, at any point in time. See *HUT, PUR.*

PVR (personal video recorder): another name for digital video recorders (DVRs), which has fallen into disuse.

Qualitative ratings: numerical summaries of the audience that not only describe how many watched or listened, but their reactions including enjoyment, interest, attentiveness, and information gained. See *engagement.*

Qualitative research: any systematic investigation of the audience that does not depend on measurement and quantification. Examples include focus groups and participant observation. Sometimes used to describe any nonratings research, even if quantification is involved, as in "qualitative ratings."

Quota sample: type of nonprobability sample in which categories of respondents called *quotas* (e.g., males), are filled by interviewing respondents who are convenient. See *nonprobability sample, probability sample.*

RAB (Radio Advertising Bureau): U.S. industry organization formed to promote advertising on radio.

RADAR (Radio's All Dimension Audience Research): Arbitron's syndicated ratings service for U.S. radio network audiences.

Random digit dialing (RDD): in phone surveys, a technique for creating a probability sample by randomly generating phone numbers. By using this method, all numbers including unlisted have an equal chance of being called.

Random sample: See *probability sample.*

Rate card: list of how much a station will charge for its commercial spots. Rate cards are sometimes incorporated with ratings data in computer programs that manage station inventories.

Rate of response: percentage of those originally drawn into the sample who provide useable information. See *in-tab.*

Rating: in its simplest form, the percentage of persons or households tuned to a station, program, or daypart out of the total market population.

Ratings distortion: activity on the part of a broadcaster designed to alter the way audience members report their use of stations. See *hypoing.*

Reach: total number of unduplicated persons or households included in the audience of a station or a commercial campaign over some specified period of time. Sometimes expressed as a percentage of the total market population. See *cume, frequency.*

Recency theory: idea that an ad is most effective if it hits consumers when they are ready to buy. This places a premium on reach and timing, rather than frequency of exposure.

Recycling: extent to which listeners in one daypart also listen in another daypart. See *audience duplication.*

Relative standard error: means of comparing the amount of sampling error in ratings data to the size of different ratings. It is the ratio of the standard error to the rating itself. See *sampling error.*

Relative standard error thresholds: size of a rating needed to have a relative standard error of either 25% or 50%. Often published in market reports as a means of judging ratings accuracy. See *relative standard error.*

Reliability: extent to which a method of measurement yields consistent results over time.

Repeat viewing: extent to which the audience for one program is represented in the audience of other episodes of the series. See *audience duplication.*

Replication: study repeating the procedures of an early study to assess the stability of results. In audience measurement, replications involve drawing subsamples from a parent sample to assess sampling error.

Respondent: sample member who provides information in response to questions.

Response error: inaccuracies in survey data attributable to the quality of responses, including lying, forgetting, or misinterpreting questions. See *interviewer bias.*

RFID (Radio Frequency Identification): tiny chip or tag, often embedded in products, that emits a signal that can be picked up by a scanner. RFIDs might offer a way to measure exposure to print media.

Rich media: type of Web advertisement that features more dynamic, eye-catching, content. Such advertisements often require Web connections with greater bandwidth to be effective.

ROI (return on investment): commercial benefits attributable to the money spent to generate those benefits. Marketers, for example, try to assess the sales attributable to advertising. See *conversion rates, pay-per-click*.

Rolling average: ratings level based on the average of several successive samples. As new sample data become available, the oldest sample is dropped from the average. A rolling average is less susceptible to sampling error. See *bounce*.

ROS (run of schedule): method of buying and scheduling advertisements in which the advertiser allows the station or network to run commercials at the best time that happens to be available.

Sample: subset of some population. See *probability sample*.

Sample balancing: see *sample weighting*.

Sample frame: list of some population from which a probability sample is actually drawn.

Sample weighting: practice of assigning different mathematical weights to various subsets of the in-tab sample in an effort to correct for different response rates among those subsets. Each weight is the ratio of the subset's size in the population to its size in the sample.

Sampling distribution: hypothetical frequency distribution of sample statistics that would result from repeated samplings of some population.

Sampling error: inaccuracies in survey data attributable to "the luck of the draw" in creating a probability sample.

Sampling rate: ratio of sample size to population size.

Sampling unit: survey element (e.g., person or household), or aggregation of elements, considered for selection at some stage in the process of probability sampling.

Satellite radio: mode of radio signal transmission that uses satellites to send digital quality programming to individual subscriber receivers.

Scatter market: period of time, just in advance of a given quarter of the year, during which advertisers buy network time. See *opportunistic market, upfront market*.

Search engine: Web site specifically designed to help Internet users find specific pieces of information on the World Wide Web.

Segmentation: practice of dividing the total market into subsets, often related to the needs of a marketing plan or the programming preferences of the population. See *target audience*.

Server-centric measurement: approach to estimating audiences based on gathering information from server logs. See *user-centric measurement*.

Servers: powerful computers that host and provide services to multiple clients. These include the computers that (1) provide media content and services to Web users, (2) manage access to the Internet, and (3) serve ads to visitors across websites.

Sets-in-use: total number of sets turned on at a given point in time. As a measure of total audience size, it has become outdated since most households now have multiple sets. See *HUT.*

Share: in its simplest form, the percentage of persons or households tuned to a station or program out of all those using the medium at that time.

SIA (Storage Instantaneous Audimeter): later version of Nielsen's original audimeter that allowed the company to retrieve electronically stored information over phone lines.

Simple random sample: one-stage probability sample in which every member of the population has an equal chance of selection. See *probability sample.*

Single source: term used to describe a data set that measures all the desired variables (e.g., metered media use across platforms, product purchases, demographic and lifestyle variables) across a single sample of respondents. See *data fusion.*

Skew: measure of the extent to which a frequency distribution departs from a normal, symmetrical shape. In common use, the extent to which some subset of population is disproportionately represented in the audience (e.g., "the audience skews old").

SMSA (Standard Metropolitan Statistical Area): former governmental designation of an urban area, once used by ratings companies to define local market areas. See *MSA.*

SPI (Sample Performance Indicator): measure that reports the percentage of people who were asked to join the sample and are providing usable data. It is a conservative measure that reflects both response rates and day-to-day fault rates.

Spill: extent to which nonmarket stations are viewed by local audiences, or local stations are viewed by audiences outside the market.

Spin-off: programming strategy in which the characters or locations of a popular program are used to create another television series.

Spyware: program secretly placed on a user's computer that sends data on surfing activities back to an advertiser or other business.

SRDS (Standard Rate and Data Service): service that publishes the station rate cards and other information useful in buying commercial time. See *rate card.*

Standard deviation: measure of the variability in a frequency distribution.

Standard error: standard deviation of a sampling distribution. It is the statistic used to make statements about the accuracy of estimates based on sample information. See *confidence interval, confidence level, relative standard error.*

Station rep: organization that represents local stations to national and regional advertisers, selling the station's time and sometimes providing research information useful in programming.

Station total area: Nielsen term meaning the total geographic area upon which total station audience estimates are based. The total area may include counties outside the NSI area.

Statistical significance: point at which results from a sample deviate so far from what could happen by chance that they are thought to reflect real differences or phenomena in the population. By convention, significance levels are usually set at .05 or lower, meaning a result could happen by chance only 5 times in 100. See *confidence level*.

STB (set-top box): small, computer-like box that satellite and cable systems use to assemble digital input into programming displayed on a subscriber's television set. When loaded with the appropriate software, STBs can record and report the channel switching behavior of the set, forming the basis of audience measurement.

Stratified sample: type of probability sample in which the population is organized into homogeneous subsets or strata, after which a predetermined number of respondents is randomly selected for each strata. Stratified sampling can reduce the sampling error associated with simple random samples.

Stripped programming: programming practice in which television shows are scheduled at the same time on 5 consecutive weekdays. Stations often strip syndicated programs.

Superstation: independent television station whose programming is widely carried on cable systems around the country.

Sweep: in television, a 4-week period of time during which ratings companies are collecting the audience information necessary to produce local market reports for November, February, May, and July.

Syndicated Network Television Association (SNTA): U.S. trade association that supports syndicators' efforts to sell commercial time.

Syndication: selling a standardized product to many clients. A syndicated program is available to stations in many different markets. A syndicated ratings report is also sold to many users.

Systematic sample: kind of probability sample in which a set interval is applied to a list of the population to identify elements included into the sample (e.g., picking every 10th name).

TAM (Television Audience Measurement): acronym widely used around the world.

Target audience: any well-defined subset of the total audience that an advertiser wants to reach with a commercial campaign, or that a station wants to reach with a particular kind of programming.

TARP (Target Audience Ratings Points): gross ratings points attributable to a specific target audience. See *GRP*.

Television household (TVHH): common unit of analysis in ratings research, it is any household equipped with a working television set, excluding group quarters.

Terrestrial TV: television that is received directly from an over-the-air broadcast signal.

Theory: tentative explanation of how some phenomenon of interest works. Theories identify causes and effects, which make them amenable to testing and falsification.

Tiering: practice of marketing cable services to subscribers in groups or bundles of channels called *tiers*.

Time buyers: anyone who buys time from the electronic media for purposes of running commercial announcements.

Time period averages: size of a broadcast audience at an average point in time, within some specified period of time.

Time spent: any one of several metrics that report the amount of time users devote to media products or outlets, including time spent listening, time spent viewing, time spent per visit, time spent per page, etc.

Total audience: all those who tune to a program for at least 5 minutes. Essentially, it is the cumulative audience for a long program or miniseries.

TRCC (tripartite research company contract): A kind of industry-wide organization in which the firm letting the contract is itself an audience measurement company. It typically has tripartite ownership including the media, advertisers and agencies. They are not unlike JICs, except that they typically provide at least some of their own measurement services. See *JIC, mediametrie*.

Trend analysis: type of longitudinal survey design in which results from repeated independent samplings are compared over time.

TSL (time spent listening): cumulative measure of the average amount of time an audience spends listening to a station within a daypart.

Turnover: ratio of a station's cumulative audience to its average quarter hour audience within a daypart.

TvB (Television Bureau of Advertising): U.S. industry organization formed to promote advertising on broadcast television.

TVQ: ratings system that assesses the familiarity and likability of personalities and programs.

UHF (ultra high frequency): class of television stations assigned to broadcast on channels 14 through 80.

Unduplicated audience: number of different persons or households in an audience over some specified period of time.

Unique visitors: unique Web users that visited a site over the course of the reporting period. See *cume, unduplicated audience.*

Unit of analysis: element or entity about which a researcher collects information. In ratings, the unit of analysis is usually a person or household.

Universe: see *population.*

Unweighted in-tab: actual number of individuals in different demographic groups who have returned usable information to the ratings company.

Unwired networks: organizations that acquire commercial time (usually in similar types of programming) from stations around the country and package that time for sale to advertisers.

Upfront market: period of time several months in advance of the new fall television season during which networks, barter syndicators, and major advertisers agree to the sale of large blocks of commercial time for the broadcast year.

URL (uniform resource locator): unique address for each document and resource on the World Wide Web. The system was developed in 1994 by Tim Berners-Lee.

User-centric measurement: approach to estimating audiences based on gathering information from a sample of willing respondents, often members of a panel. See *server-centric measurement.*

Validity: extent to which a method of measurement accurately quantifies the attribute it is supposed to measure.

Variable: any well-defined attribute or characteristic that varies from person to person, or thing to thing. See *demographic.*

VHF (very high frequency): class of U.S. television stations assigned to broadcast on channels 2 through 13.

View-through: measure of Web ad effectiveness that tracks how many Web users take action within some period of time (e.g., 30 days) after having seen an ad. See *click-through.*

Views: gross measure of the audience based on a count of the number of times a particular Web page or video has been seen.

VOD (video on demand): technology for delivering video (i.e., television programs, movies) in response to a viewer's request. Cable systems and some websites support VOD services. See *nonlinear media.*

VPVH (viewers per viewing household): estimated number of people, usually by demographic category, in each household tuned to a particular source.

Web analytics: practice of collecting and analyzing the data produced by the servers that power the World Wide Web. Analysts often use software packages to study the behavior of visitors to a particular website, with the purpose of managing the site to the owner's benefit. See *server-centric measurement.*

Web page: electronic document that can contain several files (e.g. text, pictures, links, etc.). Websites often contain many pages, each of which typically has its own URL. Pages form the basis of many Web metrics including pages views, time spent per page, etc. See *URL*.

Website: specific location on the World Wide Web offering information, entertainment, and/or advertising.

Weighted in-tab: number of individuals in different demographic groups who would have provided usable information if response rates were equivalent. See *sample weighting*.

Weighting: process of assigning mathematical weights in an attempt to correct overrepresentation or underrepresentation of some groups in the unweighted in-tab sample. See *sample weighting*.

WFA (World Federation of Advertisers): A trade association advocating for major companies engaged in global marketing.

WWW (World Wide Web): system of protocols and programs that enables Internet users to access pages of information on computer servers around the world. See *URL*.

Zapping: practice of using a remote control device to avoid commercials or program content by rapidly changing channels. Often used interchangeably with zipping.

Zipping: practice of using the fast-forward function on a VCR or DVR to speed through unwanted commercials or program content. Often used interchangeably with zapping.

Bibliography and Additional Sources

Adams, W. J. (1993). TV program scheduling strategies and their relationship to new program renewal rates and rating changes. *Journal of Broadcasting and Electronic Media, 37,* 465–474.

Adams, W. J., Eastman, S. T., Horney, L. J., & Popovich, M. N. (1983). The cancellation and manipulation of network television prime-time programs. *Journal of Communication, 33*(1), 10–27.

Advertising Research Foundation. (1954). *Recommended standards for radio and television audience size measurements.* New York: Author.

Agostini, J. M. (1961). How to estimate unduplicated audiences. *Journal of Advertising Research, 1,* 11–14.

Agostino, D. (1980). Cable television's impact on the audience of public television. *Journal of Broadcasting, 24,* 347–363.

Albarran, A. (2001). *Management of electronic media* (2nd ed.). Belmont, CA: Wadsworth.

Albarran, A. (2012). *Management of electronic and digital media* (5th ed.). Belmont, CA: Wadsworth.

Albarran, A. (2010). *The media economy.* New York: Routledge.

Albarran, A., & Arrese, A. (Eds.). (2003). *Time and media markets.* Mahwah, NJ: Lawrence Erlbaum Associates.

Albarran, A., & Chan-Olmsted, S. (Eds.). (1998). *Global media economics: Commercialization, concentration and integration of world media markets.* Ames: Iowa State Press.

Alexander, A., Owers, J., Carveth, R., Hollifiend, C. A., & Greco, A. (Eds.). (2004). *Media economics: Theory and practice* (3rd ed.). Mahwah, NJ: Lawrence Erlbaum Associates.

Allen, C. (1965). Photographing the TV audience. *Journal of Advertising Research, 5,* 2–8.

Allen, R. (1981). The reliability and stability of television exposure. *Communication Research, 8,* 233–256.

American Research Bureau. (1947, May). *Washington DC market report.* Beltsville, MD: Author.

Anand, N., & Peterson, R. A. (2000). When market information constitutes fields: Sensemaking of markets in the commercial music industry. *Organization Science, 11*(3), 270–284. doi:10.1287/orsc.11.3.270.12502

Anderson, C. (2006). *The long tail: Why the future of business is selling less of more.* New York: Hyperion.

Anderson, J. A. (1987). *Communication research: Methods and issues.* New York: McGraw-Hill.

Ang, I. (1991). *Desperately seeking the audience.* London: Routledge.

Angwin, J. (2012, February 23). Web firms to adopt 'no track' button. *Wall Street Journal.* Retrieved February 23, 2012, at http://online.wsj.com/article/SB100014 24052970203960804577239774264364692.html?mod=rss_whats_news_us&utm_ source=feedburner&utm_medium=feed&utm_campaign=Feed%3A+wsj%2Fx ml%2Frss%2F3_7011+%28WSJ.com%3A+What%27s+News+US%29&utm_co ntent=Google+Feedfetcher#articleTabs%3Darticle

Arbitron. (annually). *A guide to understanding and using radio audience estimates.* New York: Author.

Atkin, D., & Litman, B. (1986). Network TV programming: Economics, audiences, and the ratings game, 1971–1986. *Journal of Communication, 36*(3), 32–51.

Austin, B. A. (1989). *Immediate seating: A look at movie audiences.* Belmont, CA: Wadsworth.

Babbie, E. (2003). *The practice of social research* (10th ed.). Belmont, CA: Wadsworth.

Babbie, E. (2009). *The practice of social research* (12th ed.). Belmont, CA: Wadsworth.

Babrow, A. S., & Swanson, D. L. (1988). Disentangling antecedents of audience exposure levels: Extending expectancy-value analyses of gratifications sought from television news. *Communication Monographs, 55,* 1–21.

Baker, C. E. (2002). *Media, markets, and democracy.* Cambridge: Cambridge University Press.

Balen, R. E. (1995). *The new rules of the ratings game.* Washington, DC: National Association of Broadcasters.

Balnaves, M., O'Regan, T., & Goldsmith, B. (2011). *Rating the audience: The business of media.* New York: Bloomsbury Publishing Plc.

Banks, M. (1981). *A history of broadcast audience research in the United States, 1920–1980 with an emphasis on the rating services.* Unpublished doctoral dissertation, University of Tennessee, Knoxville.

Banks, S. (1980). Children's television viewing behavior. *Journal of Marketing, 44,* 48–55.

Barnes, B. E., & Thompson, L. M. (1988). The impact of audience information sources on media evolution. *Journal of Advertising Research, 28,* RC9–RC14.

Barnett, G. A., Chang, H., Fink, E. L., & Richards, W. D. (1991). Seasonality in television viewing: A mathematical model of cultural processes. *Communication Research, 18*(6), 755–772.

Baron, R. (1988). If it's on computer paper, it must be right. *Journal of Media Planning, 2,* 32–34.

Bart, P. (1999). *The gross: The hits, the flops—the summer that ate Hollywood.* New York: St. Martin's.

Barwise, T. P. (1986). Repeat-viewing of prime-time television series. *Journal of Advertising Research, 26,* 9–14.

Barwise, T. P., & Ehrenberg, A. S. C. (1984). The reach of TV channels. *International Journal of Research in Marketing, 1,* 34–49.

Barwise, T. P., & Ehrenberg, A. S. C. (1988). *Television and its audience.* London: Sage.

Barwise, T. P., Ehrenberg, A. S. C., & Goodhardt, G. J. (1979). Audience appreciation and audience size. *Journal of Market Research Society, 21,* 269–289.

Barwise, T. P., Ehrenberg, A. S. C., & Goodhart, G. J. (1982). Glued to the box? Patterns of TV repeat-viewing. *Journal of Communication, 32*(4), 22–29.

Batelle, J. (2005). *The search: How Google and its rivals rewrote the rules of business and transformed our culture.* New York: Portfolio.

Bechtel, R. K., Achelpohl, C., & Akers, R. (1972). Correlation between observed behavior and questionnaire responses on television viewing. In E. A. Rubinstein, G. A. Comstock, & J. P. Murray (Eds.), *Television and social behavior: Vol. 4. Television in day-to-day life: Patterns of use* (pp. 274–344). Washington, DC: U.S. Government Printing Office.

Becker, L. B., & Schoenback, K. (Eds.). (1989). *Audience responses to media diversification: Coping with plenty.* Hillsdale, NJ: Lawrence Erlbaum Associates.

Becknell, J. C. (1961). The influence of newspaper tune-in advertising on the size of a TV show's audience. *Journal of Advertising Research, 1,* 23–26.

Beebe, J. H. (1977). The institutional structure and program choices in television markets. *Quarterly Journal of Economics, 91,* 15–37.

Besen, S. M. (1976). The value of television time. *Southern Economic Journal, 42,* 435–441.

Besen, S. M., Krattenmaker, T. G., Metzger, A. R., & Woodbury, J. R. (1984). *Misregulating television: Network dominance and the FCC.* Chicago: University of Chicago Press.

Beville, H. M., Jr. (1988). *Audience ratings: Radio, television, cable* (Rev. ed.). Hillsdale, NJ: Lawrence Erlbaum Associates.

Blumler, J. G. (1979). The role of theory in uses and gratifications studies. *Communication Research, 6,* 9–36.

Blumler, J. G., Gurevitch, M., & Katz, E. (1985). Reaching out: A future for gratifications research. In K. Rosengren, L. Wenner, & P. Palmgreen (Eds.), *Media gratifications research: Current perspectives* (pp. 255–273). Beverly Hills, CA: Sage.

Boemer, M. L. (1987). Correlating lead-in show ratings with local television news ratings. *Journal of Broadcasting & Electronic Media, 31,* 89–94.

Bogart, L. (1972). *The age of television.* New York: Frederick Ungar.

Bogart, L. (1988). Research as an instrument of power. *Gannett Center Journal, 2*(3), 1–16.

Bogart, L. (1996). *Strategy in advertising: Matching media and messages to markets and motivations* (3rd ed.). Lincolnwood, IL: NTC Business Books.

Bower, R. T. (1973). *Television and the public.* New York: Holt, Rinehart & Winston.

Bower, R. T. (1985). *The changing television audience in America.* New York: Columbia University Press.

Bowman, G. W., & Farley, J. (1972). TV viewing: Application of a formal choice model. *Applied Economics, 4,* 245–259.

Bourdon, J., & Meadel, C. (2011). Inside television audience measurement: Deconstructing the ratings machine. *Media, Culture & Society, 33(5),* 791–800.

Brotman, S. N. (1988). *Broadcasters can negotiate anything.* Washington, DC: National Association of Broadcasters.

Bruno, A. V. (1973). The network factor in TV viewing. *Journal of Advertising Research, 13,* 33–39.

Bryant, J., & Zillmann, D. (1984). Using television to alleviate boredom and stress: Selective exposure as a function of induced excitational states. *Journal of Broadcasting, 28,* 1–20.

Bryant, J., & Zillmann, D. (Eds.). (2002). *Media effects: Advances in theory and research* (2nd ed.). Mahwah, NJ: Lawrence Erlbaum Associates.

Buzzard, K. (2012). *Tracking the audience: The ratings industry from analog to digital.* New York: Routledge.

Buzzard, K. S. (1990). *Chains of gold: Marketing the ratings and rating the markets.* Metuchen, NJ: Scarecrow Press.

Byrne, B. (1988). Barter syndicators. *Gannett Center Journal, 2(3),* 75–78.

Cabletelevision Advertising Bureau. (2004). *Cable TV facts.* New York: Author.

Cannon, H. M. (1983). Reach and frequency estimates for specialized target markets. *Journal of Advertising Research, 23,* 45–50.

Cannon, H., & Merz, G. R. (1980). A new role for psychographics in media selection. *Journal of Advertising, 9(2),* 33–36.

Cantril, H., & Allport, G.W. (1935). *The psychology of radio.* New York: Harper & Brothers.

Carroll, R. L., & Davis, D. M. (1993). *Electronic media programming: Strategies and decision making.* New York: McGraw-Hill.

CBS. (1937). *Radio in 1937.* New York: Author.

Chaffee, S. (1980). Mass media effects: New research perspectives. In D.C. Wilhoit & H. DeBock (Eds.), *Mass communication review yearbook* (pp. 77–108). Beverly Hills, CA: Sage.

Chandon, J. L. (1976). *A comparative study of media exposure models.* Unpublished doctoral dissertation, Northwestern University, Evanston, IL.

Chappell, M. N., & Hooper, C. E. (1944). *Radio audience measurement.* New York: Stephen Daye.

Cheong, Y., Leckenby, J. D., & Eakin, T. (2011). Evaluating the multivariate beta binomial distribution for estimating magazine and internet exposure frequency distributions. *Journal of Advertising, 40(1),* 7–24.

Christ, W., & Medoff, N. (1984). Affective state and selective exposure to and use of television. *Journal of Broadcasting, 28,* 51–63.

Christian, B. (2012, April 25). The A/B Test: Inside the technology that's changing the rules of business. *Wired.* Retrieved August, 6, 2012 at http://www.wired.com/business/2012/04/ff_abtesting/

Churchill, G. A., & Iachobucci, D. (2004). *Marketing research: Methodological foundations* (9th ed.). Belmont, CA: South-Western College Pub.

Cohen, E. E. (1989). *A model of radio listener choice.* Unpublished doctoral dissertation, Michigan State University, East Lansing.

Collins, J., Reagan, J., & Abel, J. (1983). Predicting cable subscribership: Local factors. *Journal of Broadcasting, 27,* 177–183.

Complaint for Equitable Relief and Civil Penalties. (March 21, 2012). Filed in the Superior Court of the State of California County of San Francisco.

Comstock, G. (1989). *The evolution of American television.* Newbury Park, CA: Sage.

Comstock, G., Chaffee, S., Katzman, N., McCombs, M., & Roberts, D. (1978). *Television and human behavior.* New York: Columbia University Press.

Comstock, G., & Scharrer, E. (1999). *Television: What's on, who's watching, and what it means.* San Diego: Academic Press.

Converse, T. (Speaker). (1974, May 2). *Magazine* [Television documentary]. New York: CBS, Inc.

Cook, F. (1988, January). Peoplemeters in the USA: An historical and methodological perspective. *Admap, 32–35.*

Cooper, R. (1993). An expanded, integrated model for determining audience exposure to television. *Journal of Broadcasting & Electronic Media, 37*(4), 401–418.

Cooper, R. (1996). The status and future of audience duplication research: An assessment of ratings-based theories of audience behavior. *Journal of Broadcasting & Electronic Media 40*(1), 96–111.

Cooper, R., & Tang, T. (2009). Predicting audience exposure to television in today's media environment: An empirical investigation of active-audience and structural theories. *Journal of Broadcasting & Electronic Media, 53*(3), 400–418.

Corporation for Public Broadcasting. (1980). *Proceedings of the 1980 technical conference on qualitative television ratings: Final report.* Washington, DC: Author.

CRE (2008). *Video consumer mapping study.* Council for Research Excellence. New York: Author.

Danaher, P. J., & Lawrie, J. M. (1998). Behavioral measures of television audience appreciation. *Journal of Advertising Research, 38,* 54–65.

Danaher, P. J., & Mawhinney, D. F. (2001). Optimizing television program schedules using choice modeling. *Journal of Marketing Research, 38*(3), 298–312.

Danaher, P. J., Dagger, T. S., & Smith, M. S. (2011). Forecasting television ratings. *International Journal of Forecasting, 27*(4), 1215–1240. doi:10.1016/j.ijforecast.2010.08.002Darmon, R. (1976). Determinants of TV viewing. *Journal of Advertising Research, 16,* 17–20.

Davis, D. M., & Walker, J. R. (1990). Countering the new media: The resurgence of share maintenance in primetime network television. *Journal of Broadcasting & Electronic Media, 34,* 487–493.

Dick, S. J., & McDowell, W. (2004). Estimating relative audience loyalty among radio stations using standard Arbitron ratings. *Journal of Radio Studies, 11,* 26–39.

Dimling, J. (1988). A. C. Nielsen: The "gold standard." *Gannett Center Journal, 2*(3), 63–69.

Dominick, J. R., & Fletcher, J. E. (1985). *Broadcasting research methods*. Boston: Allyn & Bacon.

Ducey, R., Krugman, D., & Eckrich, D. (1983). Predicting market segments in the cable industry: The basic and pay subscribers. *Journal of Broadcasting, 27,* 155–161.

Dumenco, S. (September 26, 2011). Will Fox's $50+ Million Gamble on 'Terra Nova' Pay Off?. Advertising Age. http://adage.com/article/media/fox-s-50-million-gamble-terra-nova-pay/230051/

Eastman, S. T. (1998). Programming theory under stress: The active industry and the active audience. In M. Roloff (Ed), *Communication Yearbook, 21,* 323–377.

Eastman, S. T., & Ferguson, D. A. (2013). *Media programming: Strategies and practices* (9th ed.). Boston, MA: Wadsworth.

Eastman, S. T., Newton, G. D., Riggs, K. E., & Neal-Lunsford, J. (1997). Accelerating the flow: A transition effect in programming theory? *Journal of Broadcasting & Electronic Media 41*(2), 265–283.

Ehrenberg, A. S. C. (1968). The factor analytic search for program types. *Journal of Advertising Research, 8,* 55–63.

Ehrenberg, A. S. C. (1982). *A primer in data reduction*. London & New York: Wiley.

Ehrenberg, A. S. C., & Wakshlag, J. (1987). Repeat-viewing with people meters. *Journal of Advertising Research, 27,* 9–13.

Elberse, A. (2008). Should you invest in the long tail? *Harvard Business Review, 86* (7/8), 88–96.

Ettema, J. S., & Whitney, C. D. (Eds.). (1982). *Individuals in mass media organizations: Creativity and constraint*. Beverly Hills, CA: Sage.

Ettema, J. S., & Whitney, C. D. (Eds.). (1994). *Audiencemaking: How the media create the audience*. Thousand Oaks, CA: Sage.

Everett, S. E. (1998, July). *The "UHF Penalty" demonstrated*. www.nab.org/research/webbriefs/uhfdis.html.

Federal Communications Commission. (1979). *Inquiry into the economic relationship between television broadcasting and cable television* (51 F.C.C. 2d 241). Washington, DC: U.S. Government Printing Office.

FICCI. (2011). *Hitting the high notes: FICCI/KPMG Indian media and entertainment industry report*. Federation of Indian Chamber of Commerce and Industry/KPMG International. Retrieved at http://www.kpmg.com/in/en/issuesandinsights/thoughtleadership/ficci-kpmg-report-2011.pdf

Fisher, F. M., McGowan, J. J., & Evans, D. S. (1980). The audience–revenue relationship for local television stations. *Bell Journal of Economics, 11,* 694–708.

Fletcher, A. D., & Bower, T. A. (1988). *Fundamentals of advertising research* (3rd ed.). Belmont, CA: Wadsworth.

Fletcher, J. E. (Ed.). (1981). *Handbook of radio and TV broadcasting: Research procedures in audience, program and revenues*. New York: Van Nostrand Reinhold.

Fletcher, J. E. (1985). *Squeezing profits out of ratings: A manual for radio managers, sales managers and programmers*. Washington, DC: National Association of Broadcasters.

Fletcher, J. E. (1987). *Music and program research*. Washington, DC: National Association of Broadcasters.

Fournier, G. M., & Martin, D. L. (1983). Does government-restricted entry produce market power? New evidence from the market for television advertising. *Bell Journal of Economics, 14,* 44–56.

Fowler, M. S., & Brenner, D. L. (1982). A marketplace approach to broadcast regulation. *Texas Law Review, 60,* 207–257.

Frank, R. E., Becknell, J., & Clokey, J. (1971). Television program types. *Journal of Marketing Research, 11,* 204–211.

Frank, R. E., & Greenberg, M. G. (1980). *The public's use of television.* Beverly Hills, CA: Sage.

Fratrik, M. R. (1989, April). *The television audience–revenue relationship revisited.* Paper presented at the meeting of the Broadcast Education Association, Las Vegas, NV.

Friedman, W. (June 8, 2012). Higher ratings should merit higher retrans fees. *Media-DailyNews.* http://www.mediapost.com/publications/article/176442/#ixzz203YbkZfv.

Furchtgott-Roth, H., Hahn, R. W., & Layne-Farrar, A. (2006). The law and economics of regulating ratings firms. *Journal of Competition Law and Economics, 3*(1), 49–96.

Gane, R. (1994). Television audience measurement systems in Europe. In R. Kent, (ed.). (1994). *Measuring media audiences* (pp. 22–41). London: Routledge.

Gantz, W., & Razazahoori, A. (1982). The impact of television schedule changes on audience viewing behaviors. *Journalism Quarterly, 59,* 265–272.

Gantz, W., & Eastman, S. T. (1983). Viewer uses of promotional media to find out about television programs. *Journal of Broadcasting, 27,* 269–277.

Gans, H. (1980). The audience for television and in television research. In S. B. Witney & R. P. Abeles (Eds.), *Television and social behavior: Beyond violence and children* (pp. 55–81). Hillsdale, NJ: Lawrence Erlbaum Associates.

Garrison, G. R.(1939). Current Radio Research in Universities: Wayne University. *Journal of Applied Psychology, 23*(1), 204–205.

Gensch, D. H. (1969, May). A computer simulation model for selecting advertising schedules. *Journal of Marketing Research, 6,* 203–214.

Gensch, D. H., & Ranganathan, B. (1974). Evaluation of television program content for the purpose of promotional segmentation. *Journal of Marketing Research, 11,* 390–398.

Gensch, D. H., & Shaman, P. (1980). Models of competitive ratings. *Journal of Marketing Research, 17,* 307–315.

Gerbner, G., Gross, L., Morgan, M., Signorielli, N., & Shanahan, J. (2002). Growing up with television: Cultivation processes. In J. Bryant & D. Zillmann (Eds.), *Media effects: Advances in theory and research* (2nd ed., pp. 43–67). Mahwah, NJ: Lawrence Erlbaum Associates.

Gertner, J. (2005, April 10). Our ratings ourselves. *New York Times Magazine.* Retrieved from http://www.nytimes.com/2005/04/10/magazine/10NIELSENS.html

Giddens, A. (1984). *The constitution of society: Outline of the theory of structuration.* Berkeley, CA: University of California Press.

Gitlin, T. (1983). *Inside prime time.* New York: Pantheon.

Glasser, G. J., & Metzger, G. D. (1989, December). *SRI/CONTAM review of the Nielsen people meter: The process and the results*. Paper presented at the eighth annual Advertising Research Foundation Electronic Media Workshop, New York.

Goodhardt, G. J. (1966). The constant in duplicated television viewing between and within channels. *Nature, 212,* 1616.

Goodhardt, G. J., & Ehrenberg, A. S. C. (1969). Duplication of viewing between and within channels. *Journal of Marketing Research, 6,* 169–178.

Goodhardt, G. J., Ehrenberg, A. S. C., & Collins, M. A. (1987). *The television audience: Patterns of viewing* (2nd ed). Westmead, UK: Gower.

Grant, A. E. (1989). *Exploring patterns of television viewing: A media system dependency perspective*. Unpublished doctoral dissertation, University of Southern California, Los Angeles.

Greenberg, E., & Barnett, H. J. (1971). TV program diversity—New evidence and old theories. *American Economic Review, 61,* 89–93.

Greenberg, B., Dervin, B., & Dominick, J. (1968). Do people watch "television" or "programs"?: A measurement problem. *Journal of Broadcasting, 12,* 367–376.

Gunter, B. (2000). *Media research methods: Measuring audiences, reactions and impact*. London: Sage.

Hall, R. W. (1988). *Media math: Basic techniques of media evaluation*. Lincoln, IL: NTC Business Books.

Hartmann, T. (Ed.). (2009). *Media choice: A theoretical and empirical overview*. New York: Taylor & Francis.

Hayes, D., & Bing, J. (2004). *Open wide: How Hollywood box office became a national obsession*. New York: Miramax Books Hyperion.

Headen, R., Klompmaker, J., & Rust, R. (1979). The duplication of viewing law and television media schedule evaluation. *Journal of Marketing Research, 16,* 333–340.

Headen, R. S., Klompmaker, J. E., & Teel, J. E. (1977). Predicting audience exposure to spot TV advertising schedules. *Journal of Marketing Research, 14,* 1–9.

Headen, R. S., Klompmaker, J. E., & Teel, J. E. (1979). Predicting network TV viewing patterns. *Journal of Advertising Research, 19,* 49–54.

Heeter, C., & Greenberg, B. (1985). Cable and program choice. In D. Zillmann & J. Bryant (Eds.), *Selective exposure to communication* (pp. 203–224). Hillsdale, NJ: Lawrence Erlbaum Associates.

Heeter, C., & Greenberg, B. S. (1985). Profiling the zappers. *Journal of Advertising Research, 25*(2), 15–19.

Heeter, C., & Greenberg, B. S. (1988). *Cable-viewing*. Norwood, NJ: Ablex.

Helberger, N. (2011). Diversity by Design. *Journal of Information Policy, 1*(0), 441–469.

Henriksen, F. (1985). A new model of the duplication of television viewing: A behaviorist approach. *Journal of Broadcasting & Electronic Media, 29,* 135–145.

Herzog (1944) Lazarsfeld, P. F., & Stanton, F. N. (Eds.). (1944). *Radio research 1942–1943 (pp 23–36)*. New York: Duell, Sloan & Pearce.

Hernandez, R., & Elliot, S. (2004, June 14). Advertising: The odd couple vs. Nielsen. *The New York Times*. Retrieved at http://www.nytimes.com/2004/06/14/business/media/14nielsen.html?pagewanted = all

Hiber, J. (1987). *Winning radio research: Turning research into ratings and revenues.* Washington, DC: National Association of Broadcasters.

Hill, D., & Dyer, J. (1981). Extent of diversion to newscasts from distant stations by cable viewers. *Journalism Quarterly, 58,* 552–555.

Hindman, M. (2009). *The myth of digital democracy.* Princeton, NJ: Princeton University Press.

Hindman, M. (2011). *Less of the same: The lack of local news on the Internet.* Federal Communications Commission.

Hirsch, P. (1980). An organizational perspective on television (aided and abetted by models from economics, marketing, and the humanities). In S. B. Withey & R. P Abeles (Eds.), *Television and social behavior* (pp. 83–102). Hillsdale, NJ: Lawrence Erlbaum Associates.

Horen, J. H. (1980). Scheduling of network television programs. *Management Science, 26,* 354–370.

Hotelling, H. (1929). Stability in competition. *Economic Journal, 34,* 41–57.

Hwang, H. (1998). *Audience and the TV networks rating games.* Unpublished manuscript.

IAB. (2009, February 23). Interactive advertising bureau audience reach measurement guidelines. New York: Author. Retrieved February 22, 2012 at http://www.iab.net/iab_products_and_industry_services/508676/guidelines/audiencemeasurement

IAB. (2011). *Making measurement make sense.* New York: Author. Retrieved March 14, 2012 at http://www.iab.net/insights_research/mmms/mmms_FAQ.

Israel, H., & Robinson, J. (1972). Demographic characteristics of viewers of television violence and news programs. In E. A. Rubinstein, G. A. Comstock, & J. P. Murray (Eds.), *Television and social behavior: Vol. 4. Television in day-to-day life: Patterns of use* (pp. 87–128). Washington, DC: U.S. Government Printing Office.

Jaffe, M. (1985, January 25). Towards better standards for post-analysis of spot television GRP delivery. *Television/Radio Age,* 23–25.

Jardine, B. B. (2012). *Retaining the primetime TV audience: Examining adjacent program audience duplication across markets.* Master of Business Thesis. Ehrenberg-Bass Institute for Marketing Science. University of Southern Australia.

Jeffres, L. W. (1997). *Mass media effects* (2nd ed.). Prospect Heights, IL: Waveland

Jhally, S., & Livant, B. (1986). Watching as working: The valorization of audience consciousness. *Journal of Communication, 36*(3), 124–143.

Just, N. (2009). Measuring media concentration and diversity: new approaches and instruments in Europe and the US. *Media, Culture & Society, 31*(1), 97–117. doi:10.1177/0163443708098248

Katz, E., & Lazarsfeld, P. F. (1955). *Personal influence: The part played by people in the flow of mass communications.* Glencoe, IL: Free Press.

Katz, H. E. (2010). *The media handbook: A complete guide to advertising media selection, planning, research and buying* (4th ed.). New York: Routledge.

Kaushik, A. (2010). *Web analytics 2.0: The art on online accountability & science of customer centricity.* Indianapolis, IN: Wiley.

Initiative Futures Worldwide. (2004, January). Spheres of influence 2004: Global advertising trends report.

Kaplan, S. J. (1978). The impact of cable television services on the use of competing media. *Journal of Broadcasting, 22*, 155–165.

Katz, E., Blumler, J. G., & Gurevitch, M. (1974). Utilization of mass communication by the individual. In J. G. Blumler & E. Katz (Eds.) *The uses of mass communications: Current perspectives on gratifications research* (pp. 19–32). Beverly Hills, CA: Sage.

Katz, E., Gurvitch, M., & Haas, H. (1973). On the use of mass media for important things. *American Sociological Review, 38*(2), 164–181.

Katz, E., Petters, J. D., Liebes, T., & Orloff, A. (2003). *Cononic texts in media research: Are there any? Should there be? How about these?* Cambridge: Polity Press.

Katz, H. E. (2003). *The media handbook: A complete guide to advertising media selection, planning, research and buying* (2nd ed.). Mahwah, NJ: Lawrence Erlbaum Associates.

Killion, K. C. (1987). Using peoplemeter information. *Journal of Media Planning, 2*(2), 47–52.

Kim, S. J., & Webster, J. G. (2012). The impact of a multichannel environment on television news viewing: A longitudinal study of news audience polarization in South Korea. *International Journal of Communication.*

Kirsch, A.D., & Banks, S. (1962). Program types defined by factor analysis. *Journal of Advertising Research, 2*, 29–31.

Klapper, J. (1960). *The effects of mass communication.* Glencoe, IL: The Free Press.

Klein, P. (1971, January). The men who run TV aren't stupid. . . . *New York,* pp. 20–29.

Krueger, R. A., & Casey, M. A. (2000). *Focus groups: A practical guide for applied research* (3rd ed.). Thousand Oaks, CA: Sage.

Krugman, D. M. (1985). Evaluating the audiences of the new media. *Journal of Advertising, 14*(4), 21–27.

Krugman, D. M., & Rust, R. T. (1993). The impact of cable and VCR penetration on network viewing: Assessing the decade. *Journal of Advertising Research, 33*(1), 67–73.

Krugman, D. M., Cameron, G. T., & White, C. M. (1995). Visual attention to programming and commercials: The use of in-home observations. *Journal of Advertising, 24*(1), 1–12.

Krugman, H. E. (1972). Why three exposures may be enough. *Journal of Advertising Research, 12*, 11–14.

Kubey, R., & Csikszentmihalyi, M. (1990). *Television and the quality of life: How viewing shapes everyday experience.* Hillsdale, NJ: Lawrence Erlbaum Associates.

Ksiazek, T. B. (2011). A network analytic approach to understanding cross-platform audience behavior. *Journal of Media Economics. 54*(4), 237–251.

Ksiazek, T. B., & Webster, J. G. (2008). Cultural proximity and audience behavior: The role of language in patterns of polarization and multicultural fluency. *Journal of Broadcasting & Electronic Media, 52*(3), 485–503.

Ksiazek, T. B., Malthouse, E. C., & Webster, J. G. (2010). News-seekers and avoiders: Exploring patterns of total news consumption across media and the relationship to civic participation. *Journal of Broadcasting & Electronic Media, 54*(4), 551–568.

LaCour, M. J. (2012). *A Balanced News Diet, Not Selective Exposure: Evidence from a Real World Measure of Media Exposure.* Paper presented at the Midwest Political Science Association, Chicago.

LaRose, R., & Atkin, D. (1988). Satisfaction, demographic, and media environment predictors of cable subscription. *Journal of Broadcasting & Electronic Media, 32,* 403–413.

Larson, E. (1992). *The naked consumer: How our private lives become public commodities.* New York: Henry Holt and Company.

Lavine, J. M., & Wackman, D. B. (1988). *Managing media organizations: Effective leadership of the media.* New York: Longman.

Leckenby, J. D., & Rice, M. D. (1985). A beta binomial network TV exposure model using limited data. *Journal of Advertising, 3,* 25–31.

LeDuc, D. R. (1987). *Beyond broadcasting: Patterns in policy and law.* New York: Longman.

Lehmann, D. R. (1971). Television show preference: Application of a choice model. *Journal of Marketing Research, 8,* 47–55.

Levin, H. G. (1980). *Fact and fancy in television regulation: An economic study of policy alternatives.* New York: Russell Sage.

Levy, M. R. (Ed.). (1989). *The VCR age: Home video and mass communication.* Newbury Park, CA: Sage.

Levy, M. R., & Fink, E. L. (1984). Home video recorders and the transience of television broadcasts. *Journal of Communication, 34*(2), 56–51.

Levy, M. R., & Windahl, S. (1984). Audience activity and gratifications: A conceptual clarification and exploration. *Communication Research, 11,* 51–78.

Lichty, L., & Topping, M. (Eds.). (1975). *American broadcasting: A sourcebook on the history of radio and television.* New York: Hastings House.

Lin, C. A. (1994). Audience fragmentation in a competitive video marketplace. *Journal of Advertising Research, 34,* 30–38.

Lin, C. A. (1995). Network prime-time programming strategies in the 1980's. *Journal of Broadcasting & Electronic Media, 39,* 482–495.

Lin, C. A., Atkin, D. J., & Abelman, R. (2002). The influence of network branding on audience affinity for network television. *Journal of Advertising Research, 42,* 19–32.

Lindlof, T. R. (Ed.). (1987). *Natural audiences: Qualitative research on media uses and effects.* Norwood, NJ: Ablex.

Lindlof, T. R., & Taylor, B. C. (2002). *Qualitative communication research methods* (2nd ed). Thousand Oaks, CA: Sage.

Litman, B. R., & Kohl, L. S. (1992). Network rerun viewing in the age on new programming services. *Journalism Quarterly, 69,* 383–391.

Little, J. D. C., & Lodish, L. M. (1969). A media planning calculus. *Operations Research, 1,* 1–35.

LoSciuto, L. A. (1972). A national inventory of television viewing behavior. In E. A. Rubinstein, G. A. Comstock, & J. P. Murray (Eds.), *Television and social behavior: Vol. 4. Television in day-to-day life: Patterns of use* (pp. 33–86). Washington, DC: U.S. Government Printing Office.

Lotz, A. (Ed.) (2009). *Beyond prime time: Television programming in the post-network era.* New York: Routledge.

Lowery, S., & DeFleur, M. L. (1994). *Milestones in mass communication research: Media effects* (3rd ed.). New York: Addison-Wesley.

Lull, J. (1980). The social uses of television. *Human Communication Research, 6,* 197–209.

Lull, J. (1982). How families select televisions programs: A mass observational study. *Journal of Broadcasting, 26*, 801–812.

Lull, J. (Ed.). (1988). *World families watch television*. Newbury Park, CA: Sage.

Lumley, F. H. (1934). *Measurement in radio*. Columbus, OH: The Ohio State University.

MacFarland, D. T. (1990). *Contemporary radio programming strategies*. Hillsdale, NJ: Lawrence Erlbaum Associates.

MacFarland, D. T. (1997). *Future radio programming strategies: Cultivating listenership in the digital age* (2nd ed.). Mahwah, NJ: Lawrence Erlbaum Associates.

Mandese, J. (2010, July 27). Clients weigh in on Nielsen plan to give less "weight" to internet households. *Media Post*. Retrieved at http://www.mediapost.com/publications/article/132707/clients-weigh-in-on-nielsen-plan-to-give-less-wei.html Ohio State University.

McCombs, M. E., & Shaw, D. L. (1972). The agenda-setting function of the mass media. *Public Opinion Quarterly, 36*, 176–187.

McDonald, D. G., & Reese, S. D. (1987). Television news and audience selectivity. *Journalism Quarterly, 64*, 763–768.

McDonald, D. G., & Schechter, R. (1988). Audience role in the evolution of fictional television content. *Journal of Broadcasting & Electronic Media, 32*, 61–51.

McDowell, W. S., & Dick, S. J. (2003). Has lead-in lost its punch? An analysis of prime time inheritance effects: Comparing 1992 and 2002. *International Journal of Media Management, 5*, 285–293.

McKnight, L. W., & Bailey, J. P. (Eds.). (1997). *Internet economics*. Boston: MIT Press.

McLeod, J. M., & McDonald, D. G. (1985). Beyond simple exposure: Media orientations and their impact on political processes. *Communication Research, 12*, 3–33.

McPhee, W. N. (1963). *Formal theories of mass behavior*. New York: The Free Press.

McQuail, D. (1994). *Mass communication theory: An introduction* (3rd ed.). Thousand Oaks, CA: Sage.

McQuail, D. (1997). *Audience analysis*. Thousand Oaks, CA: Sage.

McQuail, D., & Gurevitch, M. (1974). Explaining audience behavior: Three approaches considered. In J. G. Blumler & E. Katz (Eds.), *The uses of mass communications: Current perspectives on gratifications research* (pp. 287–302). Beverly Hills, CA: Sage.

Media Dynamics, Inc. (2004). *TV Dimensions 2004*. New York: Author.

Meehan, E. R. (1984). Ratings and the institutional approach: A third answer to the commodity question. *Critical Studies in Mass Communication, 1*, 216–225.

Metheringham, R. A. (1964). Measuring the net cumulative coverage of a print campaign. *Journal of Advertising Research, 4*, 23–28.

Miller, P. V. (1987, May). *Measuring TV viewing in studies of television effects*. Paper presented at the meeting of the International Communication Association, Montreal.

Miller, P. V. (1994). Made-to-order and standardized audiences: Forms of reality in audience measurement. In J. Ettema & C. Whitney (Eds.), *Audiencemaking: How the media create the audience*. Thousand Oaks, CA: Sage.

Moores, S. (1993). *Interpreting audiences: The ethnography of media consumption*. London: Sage.

Morley, D. (1986). *Family television: Cultural power and domestic leisure*. London: Comedia.

MRC. (2007, August 3). A guide to understanding internet measurement alternatives: A media research council staff point of view. Washington: MRC. Retrieved February 22, 2012 at http://mediaratingcouncil.org/MRC%20POV%20General%20Internet%20080307.pdf

Naples, M. J. (1979). *The effective frequency: The relationship between frequency and advertising effectiveness*. New York: Association of National Advertisers.

Napoli, P. M. (2001). *Foundations of communications policy: Principles and process in the regulation of electronic media*. Cresskill, NJ: Hampton Press.

Napoli, P. M. (2003). *Audience economics: Media institutions and the audience marketplace*. New York: Columbia University Press.

Napoli, P. M. (2011). *Audience evolution: New technologies and the transformation of media audiences*. New York: Columbia University Press.

Napoli, P. M. (2012, Summer). *Program value in the evolving television audience marketplace*. New York: Time Warner Cable Research Program on Digital Communication.

Neuendorf, K. A., Atkin, D. J., & Jeffres, L. W. (2001). Reconceptualizing channel repertoire in the urban cable environment. *Journal of Broadcasting & Electronic Media, 45*(3), 464–482.

Neuman, W. R. (1991). *The future of the mass audience*. Cambridge: Cambridge University Press.

Newcomb, H. M., & Alley, R. S. (1983). *The producer's medium*. New York: Oxford University Press.

Newcomb, H. M., & Hirsch, P. M. (1984). Television as a cultural forum: Implications for research. In W. Rowland & B. Watkins (Eds.), *Interpreting television* (pp. 58–73). Beverly Hills, CA: Sage.

Nielsen. (2005, November 14). *Research paper: Local people meter standard error of advertising schedules*. Retrieved August 10, 2012 athttp://www.nielsenmedia.com/forclients/LPMStandardError_11–05.pdf

Nielsen. (2009). *Introduction to Nielsen data fusion*. New York: Author. Retrieved at http://nielsen.com/content/dam/nielsen/en_us/documents/pdf/Fact%20Sheets/Nielsen%20Introduction%20to%20Data%20Fusion.pdf

Nielsen. (2011). *People first: A user-centric hybrid online audience measurement model*. New York: Author. Retrieved February 22, 2012 at http://www.nielsen.com/us/en/insights/reports-downloads/2011/user-centric-hybrid-online-audience-measurement-model.html

Nielsen. (2011). *State of the media: Consumer usage report 2011*. New York: Nielsen.

Nielsen. (2011). *The television audience 2010–2011*. New York: Nielsen.

Nielsen, A. C. (1988). Television ratings and the public interest. In J. Powell & W. Gair (Eds.), *Public interest and the business of broadcasting: The broadcast industry looks at itself* (pp. 61–63). New York: Quorum Books.

Nielsen Media Research. (1985–2004). *Television audience report*. New York: Author.

Nielsen Station Index (annually). *Your guide to reports & services*. New York: Nielsen Media Research.

Niven, H. (1960). Who in the family selects the TV program? *Journalism Quarterly, 37*, 110–111.

Noam, E. (Ed.). (1985). *Video media competition: Regulation, economics, and technology.* New York: Columbia University Press.

Noll, R. G., Peck, M. G., & McGowan, J. J. (1973). *Economic aspects of television regulation.* Washington, DC: Brookings Institution Press.

Noll, R. G., & Price, M. E. (Eds.). (1998). *A communications cornucopia: Markle Foundation essays on information policy.* Washington, DC: Brookings Institution Press.

Ofcom. (2012, June). Measuring media plurality: Ofcom's advice to the Secretary of State for Culture, Olympics, Media and Sport. Retrieved August 10, 2012 at http://stakeholders.ofcom.org.uk/binaries/consultations/measuring-plurality/statement/statement.pdf

Ogburn, W. F. (1933). The influence of invention and discovery. In W. F. Ogburn (Ed.), *Recent social trends* (pp. 153–156). New York: McGraw-Hill.

Owen, B. M. (1975). *Economics and freedom of expression: Media structure and the first amendment.* Cambridge, MA: Ballinger.

Owen, B. M., Beebe, J., & Manning, W. (1974). *Television economics.* Lexington, MA: D.C. Heath.

Owen, B. M., & Wildman, S. S. (1992). *Video economics.* Cambridge, MA: Harvard University Press.

Palmgreen, P., Wenner, L. A., & Rayburn, J. D. (1981). Gratification discrepancies and news program choice. *Communication Research, 8,* 451–478.

Park, R. E. (1970). *Potential impact of cable growth on television broadcasting* (R-587–FF). Santa Monica, CA: Rand Corporation.

Park, R. E. (1979). *Audience diversion due to cable television: Statistical analysis of new data.* R-2403-FCC. Santa Monica, CA: Rand Corporation.

Parkman, A. M. (1982). The effect of television station ownership on local news ratings. *Review of Economics and Statistics, 64,* 289–295.

Perse, E. M. (1986). Soap opera viewing patterns of college students and cultivation. *Journal of Broadcasting and Electronic Media, 30,* 175–193.

Peterson, R. (1972). Psychographics and media exposure. *Journal of Advertising Research, 12,* 17–20.

Phalen, P. F. (1996). *Information and markets and the market for information: An analysis of the market for television audiences.* Unpublished doctoral dissertation, Northwestern University, Evanston, IL.

Phalen, P. F. (1998). The market for information systems and personalized exchange: Business practices in the market for television audiences. *Journal of Media Economics, 11*(4), 17–34.

Phalen, P. F. (1999). *Buying Internet audiences: The more things change.* Paper presented at the Broadcast Education Association annual conference, Las Vegas, NV, April 16–19, 1999.

Phalen, P. F. (2003). Trading time and money for information in the television advertising market: Strategies and consequences. In A. Albarran & A. Arrese (Eds.), *Time and markets* (pp. 145–159). Mahwah, NJ: Lawrence Erlbaum Associates.

Phalen, P. F. (2005). Audience research and analysis. In Albarran, A., Chan-Olmsted, S., & Wirth, M. (Eds.), *Handbook of media management and economics*. Mahwah, NJ: Lawrence Erlbaum Associates.

Phalen & Ducey] Market Research: U.S. (2005). In Gomery, D., & Hockley, L. (Eds.). *The television industry book*. London: British Film Institute.

Philport, J. (1980). The psychology of viewer program evaluation. In *Proceedings of the 1980 technical conference on qualitative ratings*. Washington, DC: Corporation for Public Broadcasting.

Poltrack, D. (1983). *Television marketing: Network, local, and cable*. New York: McGraw-Hill.

Poltrack, D. (1988). The "big 3" networks. *Gannett Center Journal, 2*(3), 53–62.

Potter, W. J. (1996). *An analysis of thinking and research about qualitative methods*. Mahwah, NJ: Lawrence Erlbaum Associates.

Prior, M. (2009). The immensely inflated news audience: Assessing bias in self-reported news exposure. *Public Opinion Quarterly, 73*(1), 130–143. doi:10.1093/poq/nfp002

Prior, M. (2007). *Post-broadcast democracy: How media choice increases inequality in political involvement and polarizes elections*. New York: Cambridge University Press.

Proulx, M., & Shepatin, S. (2012). *Social TV: How marketers can reach and engage audiences by connecting television to the web, social media and mobile*. Hoboken, NJ: Wiley.

Rao, V. R. (1975). Taxonomy of television programs based on viewing behavior. *Journal of Marketing Research, 12*, 335–358.

Reagan, J. (1984). Effects of cable television on news use. *Journalism Quarterly, 61*, 317–324.

Robinson, J. P. (1977). *How Americans used their time in 1965*. New York: Praeger.

Robinson, J. P., & Levy, M. R. (1986). *The main source: Learning from television news*. Beverly Hills, CA: Sage.

Rogers, E. M. (1994). *A history of communication study: A biographical approach*. New York: The Free Press.

Rosengren, K. E., Wenner, L. A., & Palmgreen, P. (Eds.). (1985). *Media gratifications research: Current perspectives*. Beverly Hills, CA: Sage.

Rosenstein, A. W., & Grant, A. E. (1997). Reconceptualizing the role of habit: A new model of television audience activity. *Journal of Broadcasting & Electronic Media, 41*(3), 324–344.

Rothenberg, J. (1962). Consumer sovereignty and the economics of TV programming. *Studies in Public Communication, 4*, 23–36.

Rowland, W. (1983). *The politics of TV violence: Policy uses of communication research*. Beverly Hills, CA: Sage.

Rubens, W. S. (1978). A guide to TV ratings. *Journal of Advertising Research, 18*, 11–18.

Rubens, W. S. (1984). High-tech audience measurement for new-tech audiences. *Critical Studies in Mass Communication, 1*, 195–205.

Rubin, A. M. (1984). Ritualized and instrumental television viewing. *Journal of Communication, 34*(3), 67–77.

Rubin, A. M. (1993). Audience activity and media use. *Communication Monographs, 60*, 98–115.

Rubin, A. M., & Perse, E. M. (1987). Audience activity and soap opera involvement. *Human Communication Research, 14*, 246–268.

Rubin, A.M., & Perse, E. M. (1987). Audience activity and television news gratifications. *Communication Research, 14*, 58–84.

Rust, R. T. (1986). *Advertising media models: A practical guide.* Lexington, MA: Lexington Books.

Rust, R. T., & Alpert, M. I. (1984). An audience flow model of television viewing choice. *Marketing Science, 3*(2), 113–124.

Rust, R. T., & Donthu, N. (1988). A programming and positioning strategy for cable television networks. *Journal of Advertising, 17*, 6–13.

Rust, R. T., Kamakura, W. A., & Alpert, M. I. (1992). Viewer preference segmentation and viewing choice models of network television. *Journal of Advertising, 21*(1), 1–18.

Rust, R. T., & Klompmaker, J. E. (1981). Improving the estimation procedure for the beta binomial TV exposure model. *Journal of Marketing Research, 18*, 442–448.

Rust, R. T., Klompmaker, J. E., & Headen, R. S. (1981). A comparative study of television duplication models. *Journal of Advertising, 21*, 42–46.

Sabavala, D. J., & Morrison, D. G. (1977). A model of TV show loyalty. *Journal of Advertising Research, 17*, 35–43.

Sabavala, D. J., & Morrison, D. G. (1981). A nonstationary model of binary choice applied to media exposure. *Management Science, 27*, 637–657.

Salganik, M. J., & Levy, K. E. C. (2012, February 2). Wiki surveys: Open and quantifiable social data collection. Working paper retrieved February 22, 2012, at http://arxiv.org/pdf/1202.0500v1.pdf

Salomon, G., & Cohen, A. (1978). On the meaning and validity of television viewing. *Human Communication Research, 4*, 265–270.

Salvaggio, J. L., & Bryant, J. (Eds.). (1989). *Media use in the information age: Emerging patterns of adoption and consumer use.* Hillsdale, NJ: Lawrence Erlbaum Associates.

Schramm, W., Lyle, J., & Parker, E. B. (1961). *Television in the lives of our children.* Stanford, CA: Stanford University Press.

Schroder, K. (1987). Convergence of antagonistic traditions? The case of audience research. *European Journal of Communication, 2*, 7–31.

Schudson, M. (1984). *Advertising, the uneasy persuasion: Its dubious impact on American society.* New York: Basic Books.

Sears, D. O., & Freedman, J. L. (1972). Selective exposure to information: A critical review. In W. Schramm & D. Roberts (Eds.), *The process and effects of mass communication* (pp. 209–234). Urbana, IL: University of Illinois Press.

Sengupta, S., & Rusli, E. M. (2012, January 31). Personal data's value? Facebook is set to find out. *The New York Times.* Retrieved at http://www.nytimes.com/2012/02/01/technology/riding-personal-data-facebook-is-going-public.html

Shachar, R., & Emerson, J. W. (2000). Cast demographics, unobserved segments, and heterogeneous switching costs in a television viewing choice model. *Journal of Marketing Research, 37*, 173–186.

Sharp, B., Beal, V., & Collins, M. (2009, June). Television: Back to the future. *Journal of Advertising Research, 49*(2) 211–219. DOI: 10.2501/S002184990909031X

Sherman, B. L. (1995). *Telecommunications management: Broadcasting/cable and the new technologies* (2nd ed.). New York: McGraw-Hill.

Simon, H. (1997). *Administrative behavior: A study of decision-making processes in administrative organizations.* New York: The Free Press.

Sims, J. (1988). AGB: The ratings innovator. *Gannett Center Journal, 2*(3), 85–89.

Singer, J. L., Singer, D. G., & Rapaczynski, W. S. (1984). Family patterns and television viewing as predictors of children's belief's and aggression. *Journal of Communication, 34*(3), 73–89.

Sissors, J. Z., & Baron, R. B. (2002). *Advertising media planning* (6th ed.). Chicago: McGraw-Hill.

Sissors, J. Z., & Baron, R. B. (2010). *Advertising media planning (7th ed.).* New York: McGraw Hill.

Sizing up the Market. (2004, January 12). *Broadcast and Cable, 21.*

Smythe, D. (1981). *Dependency road: Communications, capitalism, consciousness, and Canada.* Norwood, NJ: Ablex.

Soong, R. (1988). The statistical reliability of people meter ratings. *Journal of Advertising Research, 28*, 50–56.

Sparkes, V. (1983). Public perception of and reaction to multi-channel cable television service. *Journal of Broadcasting, 27*, 163–175.

Spaulding, J. W. (1963). 1928: Radio becomes a mass advertising medium. *Journal of Broadcasting, 7*, 31–44.

Stanford, S. W. (1984). Predicting favorite TV program gratifications from general orientations. *Communication Research, 11*, 419–436.

Stanton, F. N. (1935). *Critique of present methods and a new plan for studying listening behavior.* Unpublished doctoral dissertation, The Ohio State University, Columbus, OH.

Statistical Research, Inc. (1975). *How good is the television diary technique?* (Report prepared for the National Association of Broadcasters). Washington, DC: Author.

Steiner, G. A. (1963). *The people look at television.* New York: Alfred A. Knopf.

Steiner, G. A. (1966). The people look at commercials: A study of audience behavior. *Journal of Business, 39*, 272–304.

Steiner, P. O. (1952). Program patterns and preferences, and the workability of competition in radio broadcasting. *Quarterly Journal of Economics, 66*, 194–223.

Stroud, N. J. (2011). *Niche news: The politics of news choice.* Oxford: Oxford University Press.

Sterling, C. H., & Kittross, J. M. (1990). *Stay tuned: A concise history of American broadcasting* (2nd ed.). Belmont, CA: Wadsworth.

Sterling, C. H., & Kittross, J. M. (2001). *Stay tuned: A History of American broadcasting* (3rd ed.). Mahwah, NJ: LEA.

Straubhaar, J. D. (2007). *World television: From global to local.* Los Angeles, CA: Sage Publications.

Sudman, S., & Bradburn, N. (1982). *Asking questions: A practical guide to questionnaire design.* San Francisco: Jossey-Bass.

Sunstein, C. (2001). *Republic.com.* Princeton, NJ: Princeton University Press.

Surmanek, J. (2003). *Advertising media A to Z.* New York: McGraw Hill.

Swanson, C. I. (1967). The frequency structure of television and magazines. *Journal of Advertising Research, 7,* 3–7.

Takada, H., & Henry, W. (1993, Fall). Analysis of network TV commercial time pricing for top-rated prime time programs. *Journal of Current Issues and Research in Advertising, 15*(2) 59–70.

Taneja, H., Webster, J. G., Malthouse, E. C., & Ksiazek, T. B. (2012). Media consumption across platforms: Identifying user-defined repertoires. *New Media & Society, 14*(6), 951–968.

Television Audience Assessment. (1983a). *The audience rates television.* Boston, MA: Author.

Television Audience Assessment. (1983b). *The multichannel environment.* Boston, MA: Author.

Terranova, J. (1998, October). Ratings wars. *American Demographics,* 31–35.

Tiedge, J. T., & Ksobiech, K. J. (1986). The "lead-in" strategy for prime-time: Does it increase the audience? *Journal of Communication, 36*(3), 64–76.

Tiedge, J. T., & Ksobiech, K. J. (1987). Counterprogramming primetime network television. *Journal of Broadcasting & Electronic Media, 31,* 41–55.

Turow, J. (1997). *Breaking up America: Advertisers and the new media world.* Chicago: University of Chicago Press.

Turow, J. (1997). *Media systems in society: Understanding industries, strategies and power* (2nd ed.). New York: Longman.

Turow, J., & Tsui, L. (Eds.). (2008). *The hyperlinked society: Questioning connections in the digital age.* Ann Arbor: University of Michigan Press.

Turow, J. (2006). *Niche envy: Marketing discrimination in the digital age.* Cambridge, Mass.: MIT Press.

Turow, J. (2012). *The daily you: How the new advertising industry is defining your identity and your worth.* New Haven: Yale University Press.

Urban, C. D. (1984). Factors influencing media consumption: A survey of the literature. In B. M. Compaine (Ed.), *Understanding new media: Trends and issues in electronic distribution of information* (pp. 213–282). Cambridge, MA: Ballinger.

Varian, H. R. (2006). Revealed preference. In M. Szenberg, L. Ramrattan & A. A. Gottesman (Eds.), *Samuelsonian economics and the twenty-first century.* Oxford; New York: Oxford University Press.

Veronis Suhler Stevenson. (2012). *Communications industry forecast & report* (26th ed.). New York: Author.

Vogel, H. L. (1986). *Entertainment industry economics: A guide for financial analysis*. Cambridge: Cambridge University Press.

Vogel, H. L. (2004). *Entertainment industry economics: A guide for financial analysis* (6th ed.). Cambridge: Cambridge University Press.

Vogel, H. L. (2011). *Entertainment industry economics: a guide for financial analysis (8th ed.)*. Cambridge, UK: Cambridge University Press.

Wakshlag, J., Agostino, D., Terry, H., Driscoll, P., & Ramsey, B. (1983). Television news viewing and network affiliation change. *Journal of Broadcasting, 27*, 53–68.

Wakshlag, J., Day, K., & Zillmann, D. (1981). Selective exposure to educational television programs as a function of differently paced humorous inserts. *Journal of Educational Psychology, 73*, 27–32.

Wakshlag, J., & Greenberg, B. (1979). Programming strategies and the popularity of television programs for children. *Human Communication Research, 6*, 58–68.

Wakshlag, J., Reitz, R., & Zillmann, D. (1982). Selective exposure to and acquisition of information from educational television programs as a function of appeal and tempo of background music. *Journal of Educational Psychology, 74*, 666–677.

Wakshlag, J., Vial, V. K., & Tamborini, R. (1983). Selecting crime drama and apprehension about crime. *Human Communication Research, 10*, 227–242.

Walejko, G. K. (2010). *Addressing the challenges of measuring self-reported media use: Using contingent feedback to increase data quality in web and face-to-face survey modes*. Doctoral dissertation. Northwestern University.

Walker, J. R. (1988). Inheritance effects in the new media environment. *Journal of Broadcasting & Electronic Media, 32*, 391–401.

Walker, J., & Ferguson, D. (1998). *The broadcast television industry*. Boston: Allyn and Bacon.

Wand, B. (1968). Television viewing and family choice differences. *Public Opinion Quarterly, 32*, 84–94.

Warner, C. (2003). *Selling media: Broadcast, cable, print and interactive* (3rd ed.). Ames, IA: Iowa State Press.

Waterman, D. (1986). The failure of cultural programming on cable TV: An economic interpretation. *Journal of Communication, 36*(3), 92–107.

Waterman, D. (1992). "Narrowcasting" and "broadcasting" on nonbroadcast media: A program choice model. *Communication Research, 19*(1), 3–28.

Watts, D. J. (2011). *Everything is obvious: Once you know the answer*. New York: Crown Books.

Weber, R. (2003). Methods to forecast television viewing patterns for target audiences. In A. Schorr, B. Campbell, & M. Schenk (Eds.), *Communication research in Europe and abroad: Challenges for the first decade* (pp. 271–285). Berlin: DeGruyter.

Webster, J. G. (1982). *The impact of cable and pay cable on local station audiences*. Washington, DC: National Association of Broadcasters.

Webster, J. G. (1983a). *Audience research*. Washington, DC: National Association of Broadcasters.

Webster, J. G. (1983b). The impact of cable and pay cable television on local station audiences. *Journal of Broadcasting, 27,* 119–126.

Webster, J. G. (1984a). Cable television's impact on audience for local news. *Journalism Quarterly, 61,* 419–422.

Webster, J. G. (1984b, April). Peoplemeters. In *Research & Planning: Information for management.* Washington, DC: National Association of Broadcasters.

Webster, J. G. (1985). Program audience duplication: A study of television inheritance effects. *Journal of Broadcasting & Electronic Media, 29,* 121–133.

Webster, J. G. (1986). Audience behavior in the new media environment. *Journal of Communication, 36(3),* 77–91.

Webster, J. G. (1989a). Assessing exposure to the new media. In J. Salvaggio & J. Bryant (Eds.), *Media use in the information age: Emerging patterns of adoption and consumer use* (pp. 3–19). Hillsdale, NJ: Lawrence Erlbaum Associates.

Webster, J. G. (1989b). Television audience behavior: Patterns of exposure in the new media environment. In J. Salvaggio & J. Bryant (Eds.), *Media use in the information age: Emerging patterns of adoption and consumer use* (pp. 197–216). Hillsdale, NJ: Lawrence Erlbaum Associates.

Webster, J. G. (1990). The role of audience ratings in communications policy. *Communications and the Law, 12(2),* 59–72.

Webster, J. G. (1998). The audience. *Journal of Broadcasting & Electronic Media, 42(2),* 190–207.

Webster, J. G. (2005). Beneath the veneer of fragmentation: Television audience polarization in a multi-channel world. *Journal of Communication, 55(2),* 366–382.

Webster, J. G. (2006). Audience flow past and present: Inheritance effects reconsidered. *Journal of Broadcasting & Electronic Media, 50(2),* 323–337.

Webster, J. G. (2010). User information regimes: How social media shape patterns of consumption. *Northwestern University Law Review, 104(2),* 593–612.

Webster. J. G. (2011). The duality of media: A structurational theory of public attention. *Communication Theory, 21,* 43–66.

Webster, J. G., & Coscarelli, W. (1979). The relative appeal to children of adult versus children's television programming. *Journal of Broadcasting, 23,* 437–451.

Webster, J. G., & Ksiasek, T. B. (2012). The dynamics of audience fragmentation: Public attention in an age of digital media. *Journal of Communication, 62,* 39–56.

Webster, J. G., & Lin, S. F. (2002). The Internet audience: Web use as mass behavior. *Journal of Broadcasting & Electronic Media, 46(1),* 1–12.

Webster, J. G., & Newton, G. D. (1988). Structural determinants of the television news audience. *Journal of Broadcasting & Electronic Media, 32,* 381–389.

Webster, J. G., & Phalen, P. F. (1997). *The mass audience: Rediscovering the dominant model.* Mahwah, NJ: Lawrence Erlbaum Associates.

Webster, J. G., & Wakshlag, J. (1982). The impact of group viewing on patterns of television program choice. *Journal of Broadcasting, 26,* 445–455.

Webster, J. G., & Wakshlag, J. (1983). A theory of television program choice. *Communication Research, 10,* 430–446.

Webster, J. G., & Wakshlag, J. (1985). Measuring exposure to television. In D. Zillmann & J. Bryant (Eds.), *Selective exposure to communication* (pp. 35–62). Hillsdale, NJ: Lawrence Erlbaum Associates.

Webster, J. G., & Wang, T. (1992). Structural determinants of exposure to television: The case of repeat viewing. *Journal of Broadcasting & Electronic Media, 36*(4), 125–136.

Weibull, L. (1985). Structural factors in gratifications research. In K. E. Rosengren, L. A. Wenner, & P. Palmgreen (Eds.), *Media gratifications research: Current perspectives* (pp. 123–148). Beverly Hills, CA: Sage.

Wells, W. D. (1969). The rise and fall of television program types. *Journal of Advertising Research, 9*, 21–27.

Wells, W. D. (1975). Psychographics: A critical review. *Journal of Marketing Research, 12*, 196–213.

WFA. (2008). The WFA/EACA Guide to organizing audience research. World Federation of Advertisers/European Association of Communications Agencies: Brussels. Retrieved at http://www.wfanet.org/pdf/med_documents/WFA_EACA_Organising_Audience_Research_2008.pdf

White, K. J. (1977). Television market shares, station characteristics and viewer choice. *Communication Research, 4*, 415–434.

White, B. C., & Satterthwaite, N. D. (1989). *But first these messages ... The selling of broadcast advertising.* Boston: Allyn and Bacon.

Why's and wherefores of syndex II. (1988, May 23). *Broadcasting, 58*–59.

Wildman, S. S., & Owen, B. M. (1985). Program competition, diversity, and multichannel bundling in the new video industry. In E. Noam (Ed.), *Video media competition: Regulation, economics, and technology* (pp. 244–273). New York: Columbia University Press.

Wildman, S. S., & Siwek, S. E. (1988). *International trade in films and television programs.* Cambridge: Ballinger.

Wimmer, R., & Dominick, J. (2002). *Mass media research: An introduction* (7th ed.) Belmont, CA: Wadsworth.

Winterberry (2012, January). *From information to audiences: The emerging marketing data use cases.* A Winterberry Group White Paper. Retrieved at http://www.iab.net/media/file/FromInformatonToAudiences-AWinterberryGroupWhitePaper-January2012.pdf

Wirth, M. O., & Bloch, H. (1985). The broadcasters: The future role of local stations and the three networks. In E. Noam (Ed.), *Video media competition: Regulation, economics, and technology* (pp. 121–137). New York: Columbia University Press.

Wirth, M. O., & Wollert, J. A. (1984). The effects of market structure on local television news pricing. *Journal of Broadcasting, 28*, 215–224.

Wise, B. (2011, Dec 6). Why the operational half of metrics is in trouble (and how to fix it). *Media Post.* Retrieved at http://www.mediapost.com/publications/article/163653/why-the-operational-half-of-metrics-is-in-trouble.html

Wober, J. M. (1988). *The use and abuse of television: A social psychological analysis of the changing screen.* Hillsdale, NJ: Lawrence Erlbaum Associates.

Wober, J. M., & Gunter, B. (1986). Television audience research at Britain's Independent Broadcasting Authority, 1974–1984. *Journal of Broadcasting and Electronic Media, 30,* 15–31.

Wonneberger, A., Schoenbach, K., & van Meurs, L. (2009). Dynamics of individual television viewing behavior: Models, empirical evidence, and a research program. *Communication Studies, 60* (3), 235–252.

Wulfemeyer, K. T. (1983). The interests and preferences of audiences for local television news. *Journalism Quarterly, 60,* 323–328.

Yuan, E. J. (2010). Audience loyalty and its determinants. *Asian Journal of Communication 20*(3), 354–366.

Yuan, E. J., & Ksiazek, T. (2011). The duality of structure in China's national television market: A network analysis of audience behavior. *Journal of Broadcasting & Electronic Media, 55*(2). 180–197.

Yuan, E., &, Webster, J. G. (2006). Channel repertoires: Using peoplemeter data in Beijing. *Journal of Broadcasting & Electronic Media, 50*(3), 524–536.

Zeigler, S. K., & Howard, H. (1991). *Broadcast advertising: A comprehensive working textbook* (3rd ed.). Ames, IA: Iowa State University Press.

Zenaty, J. (1988). The advertising agency. *Gannett Center Journal, 2*(3), 79–84.

ZenithOptimedia (2011). Market and MediaFact Report. Author.

Zillmann, D. (2000). Mood management in the context of selective exposure theory. *Communication Yearbook, 23,* 103–122.

Zillmann, D., & Bryant, J. (Eds.). (1985). *Selective exposure to communication.* Hillsdale, NJ: Lawrence Erlbaum Associates.

Zillmann, D., Hezel, R. T., & Medoff, N. J. (1980). The effect of affective states on selective exposure to televised entertainment fare. *Journal of Applied Social Psychology, 10,* 323–339.

Zillmann, D., & Vorderer, P. (2000). *Media entertainment: The psychology of its appeal.* Mahwah, NJ: Lawrence Erlbaum Associates.

Author Index

Page numbers in *italics* indicate figures or tables.

Subject Index

Page numbers in *italics* indicate figures or tables.